BRUNEI

T0295780

BUSINESS SUCCESS GUIDE
BASIC PRACTICAL INFORMATION AND CONTACTS

International Business Publications, USA
Washington DC, USA - Bandar Seri Begawan

BRUNEI
BUSINESS SUCCESS GUIDE
BASIC PRACTICAL INFORMATION AND CONTACTS

UPDATED ANNUALLY

We express our sincere appreciation to all government agencies and international organizations which provided information and other materials for this guide

Cover Design: International Business Publications, USA

2017 Edition Updated Reprint International Business Publications, USA
ISBN 978-1-5145-0265-5

For additional analytical, business and investment opportunities information,
please contact Global Investment & Business Center, USA
at (703) 370-8082. Fax: (703) 370-8083. E-mail: ibpusa3@gmail.com
Global Business and Investment Info Databank - www.ibpus.com

Printed in the USA

For additional analytical, business and investment opportunities information,
please contact Global Investment & Business Center, USA
at (703) 370-8082. Fax: (703) 370-8083. E-mail: ibpusa3@gmail.com
Global Business and Investment Info Databank - www.ibpus.com

BRUNEI

BUSINESS SUCCESS GUIDE

BASIC PRACTICAL INFORMATION AND CONTACTS

TABLE OF CONTENTS

For additional analytical, business and investment opportunities information,
please contact Global Investment & Business Center, USA
at (703) 370-8082. Fax: (703) 370-8083. E-mail: ibpusa3@gmail.com
Global Business and Investment Info Databank - www.ibpus.com

For additional analytical, business and investment opportunities information,
please contact Global Investment & Business Center, USA
at (703) 370-8082. Fax: (703) 370-8083. E-mail: ibpusa3@gmail.com
Global Business and Investment Info Databank - www.ibpus.com

For additional analytical, business and investment opportunities information, please contact Global Investment & Business Center, USA at (703) 370-8082. Fax: (703) 370-8083. E-mail: ibpusa3@gmail.com Global Business and Investment Info Databank - www.ibpus.com

- 6 -

For additional analytical, business and investment opportunities information,
please contact Global Investment & Business Center, USA
at (703) 370-8082. Fax: (703) 370-8083. E-mail: ibpusa3@gmail.com
Global Business and Investment Info Databank - www.ibpus.com

For additional analytical, business and investment opportunities information,
please contact Global Investment & Business Center, USA
at (703) 370-8082. Fax: (703) 370-8083. E-mail: ibpusa3@gmail.com
Global Business and Investment Info Databank - www.ibpus.com

For additional analytical, business and investment opportunities information,
please contact Global Investment & Business Center, USA
at (703) 370-8082. Fax: (703) 370-8083. E-mail: ibpusa3@gmail.com
Global Business and Investment Info Databank - www.ibpus.com

For additional analytical, business and investment opportunities information,
please contact Global Investment & Business Center, USA
at (703) 370-8082. Fax: (703) 370-8083. E-mail: ibpusa3@gmail.com
Global Business and Investment Info Databank - www.ibpus.com

STRATEGIC AND BUSINESS PROFILE

BRUNEI DARUSSALAM

Capital and largest city	Bandar Seri Begawan 4°53.417′N 114°56.533′E4.890283°N 114.942217°E
Official languages	Malay
Recognised	English
Other languages	• Brunei Malay • Tutong • Kedayan • Belait • Murut • Dusun • Bisaya • Melanau • Iban • Penan
Ethnic groups (2004)	• 66.3% Malays • 11.2% Chinese • 3.4% Indigenous • 19.1% other
Demonym	Bruneian
Government	Unitary Islamic absolute monarchy
- Sultan	Hassanal Bolkiah
- Crown Prince	Al-Muhtadee Billah
Legislature	Legislative Council
Formation	
- Sultanate	14th century
- British protectorate	1888
- Independence from the United Kingdom	1 January 1984
Area	
- Total	5,765 km² (172nd) 2,226 sq mi
- Water (%)	8.6
Population	
- Jul 2013 estimate	415,717 (175th)
- Density	67.3/km² (134th) 174.4/sq mi
GDP (PPP)	2012 estimate
- Total	$21.907 billion
- Per capita	$50,440
GDP (nominal)	2012 estimate
- Total	$17.092 billion
- Per capita	$39,355
HDI (2013)	▲0.855 very high · 30th
Currency	Brunei dollar (BND)
Time zone	BDT (UTC+8)
Drives on the	left

**For additional analytical, business and investment opportunities information,
please contact Global Investment & Business Center, USA
at (703) 370-8082. Fax: (703) 370-8083. E-mail: ibpusa3@gmail.com
Global Business and Investment Info Databank - www.ibpus.com**

Calling code	+673
ISO 3166 code	BN
Internet TLD	.bn

Brunei officially the **Nation of Brunei, the Abode of Peace** is a sovereign state located on the north coast of the island of Borneo in Southeast Asia. Apart from its coastline with the South China Sea, it is completely surrounded by the state of Sarawak, Malaysia; and it is separated into two parts by the Sarawak district of Limbang. It is the only sovereign state completely on the island of Borneo; the remainder of the island's territory is divided between the nations of Malaysia and Indonesia. Brunei's population was 408,786 in July 2012.

At the peak of Bruneian Empire, Sultan Bolkiah (reigned 1485–1528) is alleged to have had control over the northern regions of Borneo, including modern-day Sarawak and Sabah, as well as the Sulu archipelago off the northeast tip of Borneo, Seludong (modern-day Manila), and the islands off the northwest tip of Borneo. The maritime state was visited by Spain's Magellan Expedition in 1521 and fought against Spain in 1578's Castille War.

During the 19th century the Bruneian Empire began to decline. The Sultanate ceded Sarawak to James Brooke as a reward for his aid in putting down a rebellion and named him as rajah, and it ceded Sabah to the British North Borneo Chartered Company. In 1888 Brunei became a British protectorate and was assigned a British Resident as colonial manager in 1906. After the Japanese occupation during World War II, in 1959 a new constitution was written. In 1962 a small armed rebellion against the monarchy was ended with the help of the British.

Brunei regained its independence from the United Kingdom on 1 January 1984. Economic growth during the 1990s and 2000s, averaging 56% from 1999 to 2008, has transformed Brunei into a newly industrialised country. It has developed wealth from extensive petroleum and natural gas fields. Brunei has the second-highest Human Development Index among the South East Asia nations after Singapore, and is classified as a developed country. According to the International Monetary Fund (IMF), Brunei is ranked fifth in the world by gross domestic product per capita at purchasing power parity. The IMF estimated in 2011 that Brunei was one of two countries (the other being Libya) with a public debt at 0% of the national GDP. *Forbes* also ranks Brunei as the fifth-richest nation out of 182, based on its petroleum and natural gas fields

Brunei can trace its beginnings to the 7th century, when it was a subject state of the Srivijayan empire under the name Po-ni. It later became a vassal state of Majapahit before embracing Islam in the 15th century. At the peak of its empire, the sultanate had control that extended over the coastal regions of modern-day Sarawak and Sabah, the Sulu archipelago, and the islands off the northwest tip of Borneo. The thalassocracy was visited by Ferdinand Magellan in 1521 and fought the Castille War in 1578 against Spain. Its empire began to decline with the forced ceding of Sarawak to James Brooke and the ceding of Sabah to the British North Borneo Chartered Company. After the loss of Limbang, Brunei finally became a British protectorate in 1888, receiving a resident in 1906. In the post-occupation years, it formalised a constitution and fought an armed rebellion. Brunei regained its independence from the United Kingdom on 1 January 1984. Economic growth during the 1970s and 1990s, averaging 56% from 1999 to 2008, has transformed Brunei Darussalam into a newly industrialised country.

Brunei has the second highest Human Development Index among the South East Asia nations, after Singapore and is classified as a Developed Country. According to the International Monetary Fund (IMF), Brunei is ranked 4th in the world by gross domestic product per capita at purchasing power parity.

According to legend, Brunei was founded by Awang Alak Betatar. His move from Garang [location required] to the Brunei river estuary led to the discovery of Brunei. His first exclamation upon landing on the shore, as the legend goes, was "Baru nah!" (Which in English loosely-translates as "that's it!" or "there") and thus, the name "Brunei" was derived from his words.

It was renamed "Barunai" in the 14th Century, possibly influenced by the Sanskrit word varunai (वरुण), meaning "seafarers", later to become "Brunei". The word "Borneo" is of the same origin. In the country's full name "Negara Brunei Darussalam" "Darussalam" means "Abode of Peace" in Arabic, while "Negara" means "Country" in Malay. "Negara" derives from the Sanskrit Nagara , meaning "city".

Brunei Darussalam, the host of the 1995 BIMP-EAGA EXPO is a stable and prosperous country which offers not only a well-developed infrastructure but also a strategic location within the Asean region. The country is chugging full steam ahead to diversify its economy away from an over-dependence on oil and gas, and has put in place flexible and realistic policies to facilitate foreign and local investment. The cost of utilities are the lowest in the region, while political stability, extensive economic and natural resources and a business environment attuned to the requirements of foreign investors go towards making Brunei an excellent investment choice

At present the country's economy is dominated by the oil and liquefied natural gas industries and government expenditure patterns. Brunei exports crude oil, petroleum products and LNG mainly to Japan, the United States and the Asean countries. The second most important industry is construction, a direct result of the government's investment in development and infrastructure projects. Gearing up towards putting on the mantle of a developed country in January 1996, Brunei allocated in its 1991-95 Five Year Plan a hefty B$5 billion for national development, over a billion dollars more than in the previous budget. About B$510 million was allotted for 619 projects while B$550 million or 10 percent of the development budget went to industry and commerce. Some B$100 million alone was reserved for industrial promotion and development.

STABLE, CONDUCIVE ENVIRONMENT

The oil-rich country, lying on the north-western edge of the Borneo island, has never experienced typhoons, earthquakes or severe floods. Profitable investment can be had as the country levies no personal income tax, no sales tax, payroll, manufacturing or export tax.

Competitive investment incentives are available for investors throughout the business cycle marked by the start up, growth, maturity and expansion stages. The tax advantages at start up and the on-going incentives during growth and expansion are among the most competitive around. There is no difficulty in securing approval for foreign workers, from labourers to managers. With a small labour pool of 284,500 Brunei people and Bruneians showing a marked preference for the public sector as employer, the country has had to rely on foreign workers. These make up a third of its work force.

In line with moves to promote the private sector, it is encouraging to note the contribution from the non-oil and gas sector of the economy has risen, contributing about 25 percent to GDP compared to the oil and gas sector's 46 percent. In terms of infrastructure, Brunei is ready for vigorous economy activity. At its two main ports at Muara and Kuala Belait, goods can be shipped direct to Hong Kong, Singapore and other Asian destinations. Muara, a deep-water port 29 km away from the capital of Bandar Seri Begawan, has seen continual increase in container traffic over the past two decades.

The Brunei International Airport at Bandar offers expanded passenger and cargo facilities. Its new terminal can accommodate 1.5 million passengers and 50,000 tonnes of cargo a year, which is expected to suffice till the end of the decade. A 2,000-km road network serving the whole country undergoes continual expansion. A main highway runs the entire length of its coastline, linking Muara, the port entry point at one end, and Belait, the oil-production centre, at another end.

Telecommunications-wise, Brunei has one of the best systems in the region with plans for major upgrading. Telephone availability is about one to every three people.

Two earth satellite stations provide direct telephone, telex and facsimile links to most parts of the world. Operating systems include an analogue telephone exchange, fibreoptic cable links with Singapore and Manila, a packet switching exchange for access to high-speed computer bases overseas, cellular mobile telephone and paging systems. Direct phone links are also available in the more remote parts of the country via microwave and solar-powered telephones.

PIONEER INDUSTRY INCENTIVES

Companies granted pioneer status enjoy tax holidays of up to eight years. Brunei's regulations governing foreign participation in equity are the most flexible in the region, with 100 percent foreign ownership permitted. A pioneer company is also exempt from customs duty on items to be installed in the pioneer factory and from paying import duties on raw materials not available locally or produced in Brunei for the manufacture of pioneer products.

GEOGRAPHY

Location: Southeastern Asia, bordering the South China Sea and Malaysia
Geographic coordinates: 4 30 N, 114 40 E
Map references: Southeast Asia

Area:
total: 5,770 sq km
land: 5,270 sq km
water: 500 sq km

Area—comparative: slightly smaller than Delaware

Land boundaries:
total: 381 km
border countries: Malaysia 381 km

Coastline: 161 km
Land use:
arable land: 1%
other: 12%

permanent crops: 1%
permanent pastures: 1%
forests and woodland: 85%

Irrigated land: 10 sq km
Natural hazards: typhoons, earthquakes, and severe flooding are very rare
Environment—current issues: seasonal smoke/haze resulting from forest fires in Indonesia

For additional analytical, business and investment opportunities information,
please contact Global Investment & Business Center, USA
at (703) 370-8082. Fax: (703) 370-8083. E-mail: ibpusa3@gmail.com
Global Business and Investment Info Databank - www.ibpus.com

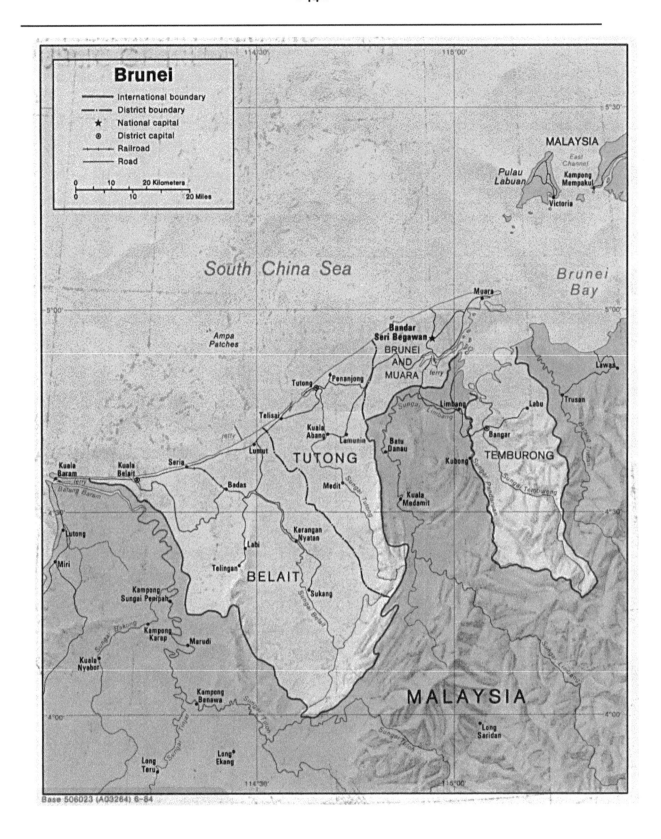

For additional analytical, business and investment opportunities information,
please contact Global Investment & Business Center, USA
at (703) 370-8082. Fax: (703) 370-8083. E-mail: ibpusa3@gmail.com
Global Business and Investment Info Databank - www.ibpus.com

Environment—international agreements:
party to: Endangered Species, Law of the Sea, Ozone Layer Protection, Ship Pollution
signed, but not ratified: none of the selected agreements

Geography—note: close to vital sea lanes through South China Sea linking Indian and Pacific Oceans; two parts physically separated by Malaysia; almost an enclave of Malaysia

PEOPLE

Population: 322,982

Age structure:
0-14 years: 33% (male 54,154; female 51,766)
15-64 years: 63% (male 106,492; female 95,921)
65 years and over: 4% (male 7,945; female 6,704)

Population growth rate: 2.38%
Birth rate: 24.69 births/1,000 population
Death rate: 5.21 deaths/1,000 population
Net migration rate: 4.35 migrant(s)/1,000 population

Sex ratio:
at birth: 1.06 male(s)/female
under 15 years: 1.05 male(s)/female
15-64 years: 1.11 male(s)/female
65 years and over: 1.19 male(s)/female
total population: 1.09 male(s)/female

Infant mortality rate: 22.83 deaths/1,000 live births

Life expectancy at birth:
total population: 71.84 years
male: 70.35 years
female: 73.42 years

Total fertility rate: 3.33 children born/woman

Nationality:
noun: Bruneian(s)
adjective: Bruneian

Ethnic groups: Malay 64%, Chinese 20%, other 16%
Religions: Muslim (official) 63%, Buddhism 14%, Christian 8%, indigenous beliefs and other 15% (1981)
Languages: Malay (official), English, Chinese

Literacy:
definition: age 15 and over can read and write
total population: 88.2%
male: 92.6% *female:* 83.4%

GOVERNMENT

Country name:
conventional long form: Negara Brunei Darussalam
conventional short form: Brunei

Data code: BX
Government type: constitutional sultanate
Capital: Bandar Seri Begawan

Administrative divisions: 4 districts (daerah-daerah, singular—daerah); Belait, Brunei and Muara, Temburong, Tutong

Independence: 1 January 1984 (from UK)
National holiday: National Day, 23 February (1984)

Constitution: 29 September 1959 (some provisions suspended under a State of Emergency since December 1962, others since independence on 1 January 1984)

Legal system: based on English common law; for Muslims, Islamic Shari'a law supersedes civil law in a number of areas

Suffrage: none

Executive branch:
Brunei

Sultan	HASSANAL Bolkiah, Sir
Prime Minister	HASSANAL Bolkiah, Sir
Min. of Communications	Awang ABU BAKAR bin Apong
Min. of Culture, Youth, & Sports	MOHAMMAD bin Daud, Gen. (Ret.)
Min. of Defense	HASSANAL Bolkiah, Sir
Min. of Development	ABDULLAH bin Begawan
Min. of Education	Abdul RAHMAN bin Mohamed Taib
Min. of Energy	YAHYA bin Begawan
Min. of Finance	HASSANAL Bolkiah, Sir
Min. of Finance II	ABDUL RAHMAN bin Ibrahim
Min. of Foreign Affairs	MOHAMED Bolkiah, Prince
Min. of Foreign Affairs II	LIM Jock Seng
Min. of Health	SUYOI bin Osman
Min. of Home Affairs	ADANAN bin Begawan
Min. of Industry & Primary Resources	AHMAD bin Jumat, Dr.
Min. of Religious Affairs	MOHD ZAIN bin Serudin, Dr.
Senior Min. in the Prime Minister's Office	Al Muhtadee BILLAH, Crown Prince
Ambassador to the US	PUTEH ibni Mohammad Alam
Permanent Representative to the UN, New York	SHOFRY bin Abdul Ghafor

Legislative branch: unicameral Legislative Council or Majlis Masyuarat Megeri (a privy council that serves only in a consultative capacity; NA seats; members appointed by the monarch)
elections: last held in March 1962
note: in 1970 the Council was changed to an appointive body by decree of the monarch; an

elected Legislative Council is being considered as part of constitutional reform, but elections are unlikely for several years

Judicial branch: Supreme Court, chief justice and judges are sworn in by the monarch for three-year terms

Political parties and leaders: Brunei Solidarity National Party or PPKB in Malay [Haji Mohd HATTA bin Haji Zainal Abidin, president]; the PPKB is the only legal political party in Brunei; it was registered in 1985, but became largely inactive after 1988; it has less than 200 registered party members; other parties include Brunei People's Party or PRB (banned in 1962) and Brunei National Democratic Party (registered in May 1985, deregistered by the Brunei Government in 1988)

International organization participation: APEC, ASEAN, C, CCC, ESCAP, G-77, IBRD, ICAO, ICRM, IDB, IFRCS, IMF, IMO, Inmarsat, Intelsat, Interpol, IOC, ISO (correspondent), ITU, NAM, OIC, OPCW, UN, UNCTAD, UPU, WHO, WIPO, WMO, WTrO

Diplomatic representation in the US:
chief of mission: Ambassador Pengiran Anak Dato Haji PUTEH Ibni Mohammad Alam
chancery: Watergate, Suite 300, 3rd floor, 2600 Virginia Avenue NW, Washington, DC 20037
telephone: (202) 342-0159
FAX: (202) 342-0158

Diplomatic representation from the US:
chief of mission: Ambassador Craig B. Allen
embassy: Third Floor, Teck Guan Plaza, Jalan Sultan, Bandar Seri Begawan
mailing address: PSC 470 (BSB), FPO AP 96534-0001
telephone: [673] (2) 229670 *FAX:* [673] (2) 225293

Flag description: yellow with two diagonal bands of white (top, almost double width) and black starting from the upper hoist side; the national emblem in red is superimposed at the center; the emblem includes a swallow-tailed flag on top of a winged column within an upturned crescent above a scroll and flanked by two upraised hands

ECONOMY

Brunei is an energy-rich sultanate on the northern coast of Borneo in Southeast Asia. Brunei boasts a well-educated, largely English-speaking population; excellent infrastructure; and a stable government intent on attracting foreign investment. Crude oil and natural gas production account for approximately 65% of GDP and 95% of exports, with Japan as the primary export market.

Per capita GDP is among the highest in the world, and substantial income from overseas investment supplements income from domestic hydrocarbon production. Bruneian citizens pay no personal income taxes, and the government provides free medical services and free education through the university level.

The Bruneian Government wants to diversify its economy away from hydrocarbon exports to other industries such as information and communications technology and halal manufacturing, permissible under Islamic law. Brunei's trade in 2016 was set to increase following its regional economic integration in the ASEAN Economic Community, and the expected ratification of the Trans-Pacific Partnership trade agreement.

GDP (purchasing power parity):

$32.76 billion (2016 est.)
$33.17 billion (2015 est.)
$32.95 billion (2014 est.)
note: data are in 2016 dollars
country comparison to the world: 127

GDP (official exchange rate):
$11.4 billion (2016 est.)

GDP - real growth rate:
-2.5% (2016 est.)
-0.4% (2015 est.)
-2.5% (2014 est.)
country comparison to the world: 209

GDP - per capita (PPP):
$77,500 (2016 est.)
$80,600 (2015 est.)
$81,900 (2014 est.)
note: data are in 2016 dollars
country comparison to the world: 10

Gross national saving:
43.5% of GDP (2016 est.)
51.3% of GDP (2015 est.)
58.1% of GDP (2014 est.)
country comparison to the world: 6

GDP - composition, by end use:
household consumption: 22.5%
government consumption: 26.6%
investment in fixed capital: 35.3%
investment in inventories: 0%
exports of goods and services: 52.1%
imports of goods and services: -36.5% (2016 est.)

GDP - composition, by sector of origin:
agriculture: 1.2%
industry: 56.5%
services: 42.4% (2016 est.)

Agriculture - products:
rice, vegetables, fruits; chickens, water buffalo, cattle, goats, eggs

Industries:
petroleum, petroleum refining, liquefied natural gas, construction, agriculture, transportation

Industrial production growth rate:
-2.9% (2016 est.)
country comparison to the world: 179

For additional analytical, business and investment opportunities information,
please contact Global Investment & Business Center, USA
at (703) 370-8082. Fax: (703) 370-8083. E-mail: ibpusa3@gmail.com
Global Business and Investment Info Databank - www.ibpus.com

Labor force:
203,600 (2014 est.)
country comparison to the world: 169

Labor force - by occupation:
agriculture: 4.2%
industry: 62.8%
services: 33% (2008 est.)

Unemployment rate:
6.9% (2016 est.)
9.3% (2011 est.)
country comparison to the world: 90

Budget:
revenues: $2.679 billion
expenditures: $4.561 billion (2016 est.)

Taxes and other revenues:
24% of GDP (2016 est.)
country comparison to the world: 123

Budget surplus (+) or deficit (-):
-16.8% of GDP (2016 est.)
country comparison to the world: 213

Public debt:
3.1% of GDP (2016 est.)
3% of GDP (2015 est.)
country comparison to the world: 203

Fiscal year:
1 April - 31 March

Inflation rate (consumer prices):
-0.7% (2016 est.)
-0.4% (2015 est.)
country comparison to the world: 24

Commercial bank prime lending rate:
5.5% (31 December 2016 est.)
5.5% (31 December 2015 est.)
country comparison to the world: 130

Stock of narrow money:
$3.232 billion (31 December 2016 est.)
$3.31 billion (31 December 2015 est.)
country comparison to the world: 115

Stock of broad money:
$10.08 billion (31 December 2016 est.)
$10.16 billion (31 December 2015 est.)
country comparison to the world: 105

For additional analytical, business and investment opportunities information,
please contact Global Investment & Business Center, USA
at (703) 370-8082. Fax: (703) 370-8083. E-mail: ibpusa3@gmail.com
Global Business and Investment Info Databank - www.ibpus.com

Stock of domestic credit:
$4.066 billion (31 December 2016 est.)
$5.323 billion (31 December 2015 est.)
country comparison to the world: 131

Current account balance:
$1.091 billion (2016 est.)
$2.071 billion (2015 est.)
country comparison to the world: 41

Exports:
$5.023 billion (2016 est.)
$6.126 billion (2015 est.)
country comparison to the world: 105

Exports - commodities:
mineral fuels, organic chemicals

Exports - partners:
Japan 36.5%, South Korea 16.8%, Thailand 10.6%, India 9.8%, Malaysia 6.6%, China 4.6% (2016)

Imports:
$3.119 billion (2016 est.)
$3.216 billion (2015 est.)
country comparison to the world: 140

Imports - commodities:
machinery and mechanical appliance parts, mineral fuels, motor vehicles, electric machinery

Imports - partners:
US 28.4%, Malaysia 24%, Singapore 7.1%, Indonesia 5.7%, Japan 5.3%, China 4.9%, Australia 4.3% (2016)

Debt - external:
$0 (2014)
$0 (2013)
note: public external debt only; private external debt unavailable
country comparison to the world: 207

Exchange rates:
Bruneian dollars (BND) per US dollar -
1.3814 (2016 est.)
1.3814 (2015 est.)
1.3749 (2014 est.)
1.267 (2013 est.)
1.25 (2012 est.)

ENERGY

Electricity - production:
3.723 billion kWh (est.)
country comparison to the world: 126

Electricity - consumption:
3.391 billion kWh (est.)
country comparison to the world: 127

Electricity - exports:
0 kWh (est.)
country comparison to the world: 111

Electricity - imports:
0 kWh (est.)
country comparison to the world: 123

Electricity - installed generating capacity:
759,000 kW (est.)
country comparison to the world: 129

Electricity - from fossil fuels:
100% of total installed capacity (est.)
country comparison to the world: 9

Electricity - from nuclear fuels:
0% of total installed capacity (est.)
country comparison to the world: 57

Electricity - from hydroelectric plants:
0% of total installed capacity (2010 est.)
country comparison to the world: 161

Electricity - from other renewable sources:
0% of total installed capacity (est.)
country comparison to the world: 162

Crude oil - production:
141,000 bbl/day (est.)
country comparison to the world: 45

Crude oil - exports:
147,900 bbl/day (est.)
country comparison to the world: 35

Crude oil - imports:
0 bbl/day (est.)
country comparison to the world: 166

Crude oil - proved reserves:
1.1 billion bbl (1 January 2013 est.)
country comparison to the world: 41

Refined petroleum products - production:
13,500 bbl/day (est.)

For additional analytical, business and investment opportunities information,
please contact Global Investment & Business Center, USA
at (703) 370-8082. Fax: (703) 370-8083. E-mail: ibpusa3@gmail.com
Global Business and Investment Info Databank - www.ibpus.com

country comparison to the world: 101

Refined petroleum products - consumption:
14,640 bbl/day (est.)
country comparison to the world: 144

Refined petroleum products - exports:
0 bbl/day (est.)
country comparison to the world: 159

Refined petroleum products - imports:
3,198 bbl/day (est.)
country comparison to the world: 169

Natural gas - production:
12.44 billion cu m (est.)
country comparison to the world: 38

Natural gas - consumption:
2.97 billion cu m (est.)
country comparison to the world: 73

Natural gas - exports:
9.42 billion cu m (est.)
country comparison to the world: 25

Natural gas - imports:
0 cu m (est.)
country comparison to the world: 167

Natural gas - proved reserves:
390.8 billion cu m (1 January 2013 est.)
country comparison to the world: 35

Carbon dioxide emissions from consumption of energy:
8.656 million Mt (2011 est.)

COMMUNCATION

Telephones - main lines in use:
70,933
country comparison to the world: 154

Telephones - mobile cellular:
469,700
country comparison to the world: 170

Telephone system:
general assessment: service throughout the country is good; international service is good to Southeast Asia, Middle East, Western Europe, and the US

For additional analytical, business and investment opportunities information,
please contact Global Investment & Business Center, USA
at (703) 370-8082. Fax: (703) 370-8083. E-mail: ibpusa3@gmail.com
Global Business and Investment Info Databank - www.ibpus.com

domestic: every service available
international: country code - 673; landing point for the SEA-ME-WE-3 optical telecommunications submarine cable that provides links to Asia, the Middle East, and Europe; the Asia-America Gateway submarine cable network provides new links to Asia and the US; satellite earth stations - 2 Intelsat (1 Indian Ocean and 1 Pacific Ocean)

Broadcast media:
state-controlled Radio Television Brunei (RTB) operates 5 channels; 3 Malaysian TV stations are available; foreign TV broadcasts are available via satellite and cable systems; RTB operates 5 radio networks and broadcasts on multiple frequencies; British Forces Broadcast Service (BFBS) provides radio broadcasts on 2 FM stations; some radio broadcast stations from Malaysia are available via repeaters (2009)

Internet country code:
.bn

Internet hosts:
49,457
country comparison to the world: 96

Internet users:
314,900
country comparison to the world: 128

TRANSPORTATION

Railways:
total: 13 km (private line)
narrow gauge: 13 km 0.610-m gauge

Highways:
total: 1,150 km *paved:* 399 km *unpaved:* 751 km

Waterways: 209 km; navigable by craft drawing less than 1.2 m
Pipelines: crude oil 135 km; petroleum products 418 km; natural gas 920 km
Ports and harbors: Bandar Seri Begawan, Kuala Belait, Muara, Seria, Tutong
Merchant marine:
total: 7 liquefied gas tankers (1,000 GRT or over) totaling 348,476 GRT/340,635 DWT

Airports: 2

Airports—with paved runways:
total: 1
over 3,047 m: 1
Airports—with unpaved runways:
total: 1 *914 to 1,523 m:* 1 **Heliports:** 3

MILITARY

Military branches: Land Forces, Navy, Air Force, Royal Brunei Police
Military manpower—military age: 18 years of age

Military manpower—availability:
males age 15-49: 88,628
Military manpower—fit for military service:
males age 15-49: 51,270
Military manpower—reaching military age annually:
males: 3,078
Military expenditures—dollar figure: $343 million
Military expenditures—percent of GDP: 6%

TRANSNATIONAL ISSUES

Disputes—international: possibly involved in a complex dispute over the Spratly Islands with China, Malaysia, Philippines, Taiwan, and Vietnam; in 1984, Brunei established an exclusive fishing zone that encompasses Louisa Reef in the southern Spratly Islands, but has not publicly claimed the island.

IMPORTANT INFORMATION FOR UNDERSTANDING BRUNEI

PROFILE
OFFICIAL NAME: Negara Brunei Darussalam

Geography
Area: 5,765 sq. km. (2,226 sq. mi.), slightly larger than Delaware.
Cities: *Capital*--Bandar Seri Begawan.
Terrain: East--flat coastal plain rises to mountains; west--hilly lowland with a few mountain ridges.
Climate: Equatorial; high temperatures, humidity, and rainfall.

People
Nationality: *Noun and adjective*--Bruneian(s).
Population : 383,000.
Annual growth rate: 3.5%.
Ethnic groups: Malay, Chinese, other indigenous groups.
Religion: Islam.
Languages: Malay, English, Chinese; Iban and other indigenous dialects.
Education: *Years compulsory*--9. *Literacy* (2006)--94.7%.
Health: *Life expectancy (years)*--74.4 (men), 77.4 (women) yrs. *Infant mortality rate* --12.25/1,000.

Government
Type: Malay Islamic Monarchy.
Independence: January 1, 1984.
Constitution: 1959.
Branches: *Executive*--Sultan is both head of state and Prime Minister, presiding over a fourteen-member cabinet. *Legislative*--a Legislative Council has been reactivated after a 20-year suspension to play an advisory role for the Sultan. *Judicial* (based on Indian penal code and English common law)--magistrate's courts, High Court, Court of Appeals, Judicial Committee of the Privy Council (sits in London).
Subdivisions: *Four districts*--Brunei-Muara, Belait, Tutong, and Temburong.

Economy
Natural resources: Oil and natural gas.
Trade: *Exports*--oil, liquefied natural gas, petroleum products, garments. Major markets--Japan, Korea, ASEAN, U.S. *Imports*--machinery and transport equipment, manufactured goods. *Major suppliers*--ASEAN, Japan, U.S., EU.

PEOPLE

Many cultural and linguistic differences make Brunei Malays distinct from the larger Malay populations in nearby Malaysia and Indonesia, even though they are ethnically related and share the Muslim religion.
Brunei has hereditary nobility, carrying the title Pengiran. The Sultan can award to commoners the title Pehin, the equivalent of a life peerage awarded in the United Kingdom. The Sultan also can award his subjects the Dato, the equivalent of a knighthood in the United Kingdom, and Datin, the equivalent of damehood.

Bruneians adhere to the practice of using complete full names with all titles, including the title Haji (for men) or Hajah (for women) for those who have made the Haj pilgrimage to Mecca. Many Brunei Malay women wear the tudong, a traditional head covering. Men wear the songkok, a traditional Malay cap. Men who have completed the Haj can wear a white songkok.
The requirements to attain Brunei citizenship include passing tests in Malay culture, customs, and language. Stateless permanent residents of Brunei are given International Certificates of Identity,

which allow them to travel overseas. The majority of Brunei's Chinese are permanent residents, and many are stateless. An amendment to the National Registration and Immigration Act of 2002 allowed female Bruneian citizens for the first time to transfer their nationality to their children.

Oil wealth allows the Brunei Government to provide the population with one of Asia's finest health care systems. Malaria has been eradicated, and cholera is virtually nonexistent. There are five general hospitals--in Bandar Seri Begawan, Tutong, Kuala Belait, Bangar, and Seria--and there are numerous health clinics throughout the country.

Education starts with preschool, followed by 6 years of primary education and up to 7 years of secondary education. Nine years of education are mandatory. Most of Brunei's college students attend universities and other institutions abroad, but approximately 3,674 study at the University of Brunei Darussalam. Opened in 1985, the university has a faculty of more than 300 instructors and is located on a sprawling campus overlooking the South China Sea.
The official language is Malay, but English is widely understood and used in business. Other languages spoken are several Chinese dialects, Iban, and a number of native dialects. Islam is the official religion, but religious freedom is guaranteed under the constitution.

HISTORY

Historians believe there was a forerunner to the present Brunei Sultanate, which the Chinese called Po-ni. Chinese and Arabic records indicate that this ancient trading kingdom existed at the mouth of the Brunei River as early as the seventh or eighth century A.D. This early kingdom was apparently conquered by the Sumatran Hindu Empire of Srivijaya in the early ninth century, which later controlled northern Borneo and the Philippines. It was subjugated briefly by the Java-based Majapahit Empire but soon regained its independence and once again rose to prominence.

The Brunei Empire had its golden age from the 15th to the 17th centuries, when its control extended over the entire island of Borneo and north into the Philippines. Brunei was particularly powerful under the fifth sultan, Bolkiah (1473-1521), who was famed for his sea exploits and even briefly captured Manila; and under the ninth sultan, Hassan (1605-19), who fully developed an elaborate Royal Court structure, elements of which remain today.

After Sultan Hassan, Brunei entered a period of decline due to internal battles over royal succession as well as the rising influences of European colonial powers in the region that, among other things, disrupted traditional trading patterns, destroying the economic base of Brunei and many other Southeast Asian sultanates. In 1839, the English adventurer James Brooke arrived in Borneo and helped the Sultan put down a rebellion. As a reward, he became governor and later "Rajah" of Sarawak in northwest Borneo and gradually expanded the territory under his control.

Meanwhile, the British North Borneo Company was expanding its control over territory in northeast Borneo. In 1888, Brunei became a protectorate of the British Government, retaining internal independence but with British control over external affairs. In 1906, Brunei accepted a further measure of British control when executive power was transferred to a British resident, who advised the ruler on all matters except those concerning local custom and religion.

In 1959, a new constitution was written declaring Brunei a self-governing state, while its foreign affairs, security, and defense remained the responsibility of the United Kingdom. An attempt in 1962 to introduce a partially elected legislative body with limited powers was abandoned after the opposition political party, Parti Rakyat Brunei, launched an armed uprising, which the government put down with the help of British forces. In the late 1950s and early 1960s, the government also resisted pressures to join neighboring Sabah and Sarawak in the newly formed Malaysia. The Sultan eventually decided that Brunei would remain an independent state.

In 1967, Sultan Omar abdicated in favor of his eldest son, Hassanal Bolkiah, who became the 29th ruler. The former Sultan remained as Defense Minister and assumed the royal title Seri Begawan. In 1970, the national capital, Brunei Town, was renamed Bandar Seri Begawan in his honor. The Seri Begawan died in 1986.

On January 4, 1979, Brunei and the United Kingdom signed a new treaty of friendship and cooperation. On January 1, 1984, Brunei Darussalam became a fully independent state.

GOVERNMENT AND POLITICAL CONDITIONS

Under Brunei's 1959 constitution, the Sultan is the head of state with full executive authority, including emergency powers since 1962. The Sultan is assisted and advised by five councils, which he appoints. A Council of Ministers, or cabinet, which currently consists of 14 members (including the Sultan himself), assists in the administration of the government. The Sultan presides over the cabinet as Prime Minister and also holds the positions of Minister of Defense and Minister of Finance. His son, the Crown Prince, serves as Senior Minister. One of the Sultan's brothers, Prince Mohamed, serves as Minister of Foreign Affairs.

Brunei's legal system is based on English common law, with an independent judiciary, a body of written common law judgments and statutes, and legislation enacted by the sultan. The local magistrates' courts try most cases. More serious cases go before the High Court, which sits for about 2 weeks every few months. Brunei has an arrangement with the United Kingdom whereby United Kingdom judges are appointed as the judges for Brunei's High Court and Court of Appeal. Final appeal can be made to the Judicial Committee of the Privy Council in London in civil but not criminal cases. Brunei also has a separate system of Islamic courts that apply Sharia law in family and other matters involving Muslims.
The Government of Brunei assures continuing public support for the current form of government by providing economic benefits such as subsidized food, fuel, and housing; free education and medical care; and low-interest loans for government employees.

The Sultan said in a 1989 interview that he intended to proceed, with prudence, to establish more liberal institutions in the country and that he would reintroduce elections and a legislature when he "[could] see evidence of a genuine interest in politics on the part of a responsible majority of Bruneians." In 1994, a constitutional review committee submitted its findings to the Sultan, but these have not been made public. In 2004 the Sultan re-introduced an appointed Legislative Council with minimal powers. Five of the 31 seats on the Council are indirectly elected by village leaders.

Brunei's economy is almost totally supported by exports of crude oil and natural gas. The government uses its earnings in part to build up its foreign reserves, which at one time reportedly reached more than $30 billion. The country's wealth, coupled with its membership in the United Nations, Association of Southeast Asian Nations (ASEAN), the Asia Pacific Economic Cooperation (APEC) forum, and the Organization of the Islamic Conference give it an influence in the world disproportionate to its size.

Principal Government Officials
Sultan and Yang di-Pertuan, Prime Minister, Minister of Defense, and Minister of Finance--His Majesty Sultan Hassanal Bolkiah
Senior Minister--His Royal Highness Crown Prince Billah
Minister of Foreign Affairs--His Royal Highness Prince Mohamed Bolkiah
Ambassador to the United States--Pengiran Anak Dato Haji Puteh
Ambassador to the United Nations--Dr. Haji Emran bin Bahar
Brunei Darussalam maintains an embassy in the United States at 3520 International Court, NW, Washington, DC 20008; tel. 202-237-1838.

ECONOMY

Currency	Brunei dollar BND
Fixed exchange rates	1 Brunei dollar = 1 Singapore dollar
Fiscal year	1 April – 31 March (from April 2009)
Trade organisations	APEC, ASEAN, WTO. BIMP-EAGA
Statistics	
GDP	$20.38 billion PPP Rank: 123rd
GDP growth	2.8% Q1
GDP per capita	$51,600
GDP by sector	agriculture (0.7%), industry (73.3%), services (26%)
Inflation (CPI)	1.2%
Population below poverty line	1000 person
Labour force	188,800
Labour force by occupation	agriculture 4.5%, industry 63.1%, services 32.4%
Unemployment	3.7%
Main industries	petroleum, petroleum refining, liquefied natural gas, construction
Ease-of-doing-business rank	83rd
External	
Exports	$10.67 billion
Main export partners	Japan 46.5% South Korea 15.5% Australia 9.3% India 7.0% New Zealand 6.7% (est.)
Imports	$12.055 billion c.i.f.
Main import partners	Singapore 26.3% China 21.3% United Kingdom 21.3% Malaysia 11.8%
Public finances	
Public debt	$0
Revenues	$10.49 billion
Expenses	$5.427 billion
Credit rating	Not rated

Main data source: CIA World Fact Book *All values, unless otherwise stated, are in US dollars.*

Brunei is a country with a small, wealthy economy that is a mixture of foreign and domestic entrepreneurship, government regulation and welfare measures, and village tradition. It is almost totally supported by exports of crude oil and natural gas, with revenues from the petroleum sector accounting for over half of GDP. Per capita GDP is high, and substantial income from overseas investment supplements income from domestic production. The government provides for all medical services and subsidizes food and housing. The government has shown progress in its basic policy of diversifying the economy away from oil and gas. Brunei's leaders are concerned that steadily increased integration in the world economy will undermine internal social cohesion although it has taken steps to become a more prominent player by serving as chairman for the 2000 APEC (Asian Pacific Economic Cooperation) forum. Growth in 1999 was estimated at 2.5% due to higher oil prices in the second half.

For additional analytical, business and investment opportunities information, please contact Global Investment & Business Center, USA at (703) 370-8082. Fax: (703) 370-8083. E-mail: ibpusa3@gmail.com Global Business and Investment Info Databank - www.ibpus.com

Brunei is the third-largest oil producer in Southeast Asia, averaging about 180,000 barrels per day (29,000 m^3/d). It also is the fourth-largest producer of liquefied natural gas in the world.

Brunei is the fourth-largest oil producer in Southeast Asia, averaging about 219,000 barrels a day in 2006. It also is the ninth-largest exporter of liquefied natural gas in the world. Like many oil producing countries, Brunei's economy has followed the swings of the world oil market. Economic growth has averaged around 2.8% in the 2000s, heavily dependent on oil and gas production. Oil production has averaged around 200,000 barrels a day during the 2000s, while liquefied natural gas output has been slightly under or over 1,000 trillion btu/day over the same period. Brunei is estimated to have oil reserves expected to last 25 years, and enough natural gas reserves to last 40 years.

Brunei Shell Petroleum (BSP), a joint venture owned in equal shares by the Brunei Government and the Royal Dutch/Shell group of companies, is the chief oil and gas production company in Brunei. It also operates the country's only refinery. BSP and four sister companies--including the liquefied natural gas producing firm BLNG--constitute the largest employer in Brunei after the government. BSP's small refinery has a distillation capacity of 10,000 barrels per day. This satisfies domestic demand for most petroleum products.

The French oil company Total (then known as ELF Aquitaine) became active in petroleum exploration in Brunei in the 1980s. The joint venture Total E&P Borneo BV currently produces approximately 35,000 barrels per day and 13% of Brunei's natural gas.

In 2003, Malaysia disputed Brunei-awarded oil exploration concessions for offshore blocks J and K (Total and Shell respectively), which led to the Brunei licensees ceasing exploration activities. Negotiations between the two countries are continuing in order to resolve the conflict. In 2006, Brunei awarded two on-shore blocks--one to a Canadian-led and the other to a Chinese-led consortium. Australia, Indonesia, and Korea were the largest customers for Brunei's oil exports, taking over 67% of Brunei's total crude exports. Traditional customers Japan, the U.S., and China each took around 5% of total crude exports.
Almost all of Brunei's natural gas is liquefied at Brunei Shell's Liquefied Natural Gas (LNG) plant, which opened in 1972 and is one of the largest LNG plants in the world. Some 90% of Brunei's LNG produced is sold to Japan under a long-term agreement renewed in 1993.

The agreement calls for Brunei to provide over 5 million tons of LNG per year to three Japanese utilities, namely to TEPCo, Tokyo Electric Power Co. (J.TER or 5001), Tokyo Gas Co. (J.TYG or 9531) and Osaka Gas Co. (J.OSG or 9532). The Japanese company, Mitsubishi, is a joint venture partner with Shell and the Brunei Government in Brunei LNG, Brunei Coldgas, and Brunei Shell Tankers, which together produce the LNG and supply it to Japan. Since 1995, Brunei has supplied more than 700,000 tons of LNG to the Korea Gas Corporation (KOGAS) as well. In 1999, Brunei's natural gas production reached 90 cargoes per day. A small amount of natural gas is used for domestic power generation. Since 2001, Japan remains the dominant export market for natural gas. Brunei is the fourth-largest exporter of LNG in the Asia-Pacific region behind Indonesia, Malaysia, and Australia.

The government sought in the past decade to diversify the economy with limited success. Oil and gas and government spending still account for most of Brunei's economic activity. Brunei's non-petroleum industries include agriculture, forestry, fishing, aquaculture, and banking. The garment-for-export industry has been shrinking since the U.S. eliminated its garment quota system at the end of 2004. The Brunei Economic Development Board announced plans in 2003 to use proven gas reserves to establish downstream industrial projects. The government plans to build a power plant in the Sungai Liang region to power a proposed aluminum smelting plant that will depend on foreign investors. A second major project depending on foreign investment is in the planning stage: a giant container hub at the Muara Port facilities.

The government regulates the immigration of foreign labor out of concern it might disrupt Brunei's society. Work permits for foreigners are issued only for short periods and must be continually renewed. Despite these restrictions, the estimated 100,000 foreign temporary residents of Brunei make up a significant portion of the work force. The government reported a total work force of 180,400 in 2006, with a derived unemployment rate of 4.0%.

Oil and natural gas account for almost all exports. Since only a few products other than petroleum are produced locally, a wide variety of items must be imported. Nonetheless, Brunei has had a significant trade surplus in the 2000s. Official statistics show Singapore, Malaysia, Japan, the U.S., and the U.K. as the leading importers in 2005. The United States was the third-largest supplier of imports to Brunei in 2005.

Brunei's substantial foreign reserves are managed by the Brunei Investment Agency (BIA), an arm of the Ministry of Finance. BIA's guiding principle is to increase the real value of Brunei's foreign reserves while pursuing a diverse investment strategy, with holdings in the United States, Japan, Western Europe, and the Association of Southeast Asian Nations (ASEAN) countries.

The Brunei Government encourages more foreign investment. New enterprises that meet certain criteria can receive pioneer status, exempting profits from income tax for up to 5 years, depending on the amount of capital invested. The normal corporate income tax rate is 30%. There is no personal income tax or capital gains tax.

One of the government's priorities is to encourage the development of Brunei Malays as leaders of industry and commerce. There are no specific restrictions of foreign equity ownership, but local participation, both shared capital and management, is encouraged. Such participation helps when tendering for contracts with the government or Brunei Shell Petroleum.

Companies in Brunei must either be incorporated locally or registered as a branch of a foreign company and must be registered with the Registrar of Companies. Public companies must have a minimum of seven shareholders. Private companies must have a minimum of two but not more than 50 shareholders. At least half of the directors in a company must be residents of Brunei.

The government owns a cattle farm in Australia through which the country's beef supplies are processed. At 2,262 square miles, this ranch is larger than Brunei itself. Eggs and chickens are largely produced locally, but most of Brunei's other food needs must be imported. Agriculture, aquaculture, and fisheries are among the industrial sectors that the government has selected for highest priority in its efforts to diversify the economy.

Recently the government has announced plans for Brunei to become an international offshore financial center as well as a center for Islamic banking. Brunei is keen on the development of small and medium enterprises and also is investigating the possibility of establishing a "cyber park" to develop an information technology industry. Brunei has also promoted ecotourism to take advantage of the over 70% of Brunei's territory that remains primal tropical rainforest.

DEFENSE

The Sultan is both Minister of Defense and Supreme Commander of the Armed Forces (RBAF). All infantry, navy, and air combat units are made up of volunteers. There are two infantry battalions equipped with armored reconnaissance vehicles and armored personnel carriers and supported by Rapier air defense missiles and a flotilla of coastal patrol vessels armed with surface-to-surface missiles. Brunei has ordered, but not yet taken possession of, three offshore patrol vessels from the U.K.
Brunei has a defense agreement with the United Kingdom, under which a British Armed Forces Ghurka battalion (1,500 men) is permanently stationed in Seria, near the center of Brunei's oil

For additional analytical, business and investment opportunities information,
please contact Global Investment & Business Center, USA
at (703) 370-8082. Fax: (703) 370-8083. E-mail: ibpusa3@gmail.com
Global Business and Investment Info Databank - www.ibpus.com

industry. The RBAF has joint exercises, training programs, and other military cooperation with the United Kingdom and many other countries, including the United States. The U.S. and Brunei signed a memorandum of understanding (MOU) on defense cooperation in November 1994. The two countries conduct an annual military exercise called CARAT.

FOREIGN RELATIONS

Brunei joined ASEAN on January 7, 1984--one week after resuming full independence--and gives its ASEAN membership the highest priority in its foreign relations. Brunei joined the UN in September 1984. It also is a member of the Organization of the Islamic Conference (OIC) and of the Asia-Pacific Economic Cooperation (APEC) forum. Brunei hosted the APEC Economic Leaders' Meeting in November 2000 and the ASEAN Regional Forum (ARF) in July 2002.

U.S.-BRUNEI RELATIONS

Relations between the United States and Brunei date from the 1800s. On April 6, 1845, the U.S.S. Constitution visited Brunei. The two countries concluded a Treaty of Peace, Friendship, Commerce and Navigation in 1850, which remains in force today. The United States maintained a consulate in Brunei from 1865 to 1867.

The U.S. welcomed Brunei Darussalam's full independence from the United Kingdom on January 1, 1984, and opened an Embassy in Bandar Seri Begawan on that date. Brunei opened its embassy in Washington in March 1984. Brunei's armed forces engage in joint exercises, training programs, and other military cooperation with the U.S. A memorandum of understanding on defense cooperation was signed on November 29, 1994. The Sultan visited Washington in December 2002.

Principal U.S. Embassy Officials
Ambassador-- Craig Allen

Ambassador Craig Allen was sworn in as the United States ambassador to Brunei Darussalam on December 19, 2014.
Deputy Chief of Mission--John McIntyre
Management Officer--Michael Lampel

The U.S. Embassy in Bandar Seri Begawan is located on the third & fifth floors of the Teck Guan Plaza, at the corner of Jalan Sultan and Jalan MacArthur; tel: 673-2229670; fax: 673-2225293; e-mail: usembassy_bsb@state.gov

TRAVEL AND BUSINESS INFORMATION

The U.S. Department of State's Consular Information Program advises Americans traveling and residing abroad through Consular Information Sheets, Public Announcements, and Travel Warnings. **Consular Information Sheets** exist for all countries and include information on entry and exit requirements, currency regulations, health conditions, safety and security, crime, political disturbances, and the addresses of the U.S. embassies and consulates abroad. **Public Announcements** are issued to disseminate information quickly about terrorist threats and other relatively short-term conditions overseas that pose significant risks to the security of American travelers. **Travel Warnings** are issued when the State Department recommends that Americans avoid travel to a certain country because the situation is dangerous or unstable.

For the latest security information, Americans living and traveling abroad should regularly monitor the Department's Bureau of Consular Affairs Internet web site at http://www.travel.state.gov, where the current Worldwide Caution, Public Announcements, and Travel Warnings can be found. Consular Affairs Publications, which contain information on obtaining passports and planning a safe trip abroad, are also available at http://www.travel.state.gov. For additional

information on international travel, see
http://www.usa.gov/Citizen/Topics/Travel/International.shtml.

The Department of State encourages all U.S citizens traveling or residing abroad to register via the State Department's travel registration website or at the nearest U.S. embassy or consulate abroad. Registration will make your presence and whereabouts known in case it is necessary to contact you in an emergency and will enable you to receive up-to-date information on security conditions.

Emergency information concerning Americans traveling abroad may be obtained by calling 1-888-407-4747 toll free in the U.S. and Canada or the regular toll line 1-202-501-4444 for callers outside the U.S. and Canada.

The National Passport Information Center (NPIC) is the U.S. Department of State's single, centralized public contact center for U.S. passport information. Telephone: 1-877-4USA-PPT (1-877-487-2778). Customer service representatives and operators for TDD/TTY are available Monday-Friday, 7:00 a.m. to 12:00 midnight, Eastern Time, excluding federal holidays.

Travelers can check the latest health information with the U.S. Centers for Disease Control and Prevention in Atlanta, Georgia. A hotline at 877-FYI-TRIP (877-394-8747) and a web site at http://www.cdc.gov/travel/index.htm give the most recent health advisories, immunization recommendations or requirements, and advice on food and drinking water safety for regions and countries. A booklet entitled "Health Information for International Travel" (HHS publication number CDC-95-8280) is available from the U.S. Government Printing Office, Washington, DC 20402, tel. (202) 512-1800.

EU-BRUNEI RELATIONS

Official Name	Negara Brunei Darussalam
Population	0.38 million
Area	6000 km²
Gross Domestic Product	5 bn euros
GDP Per Capita	14.173 €
Real GDP (% growth)	3.0 %
Exports GDP %	0.85
Imports GDP %	0.27
Rate of inflation %	1.0
Exports to Brunei from EU (mn €, 2001)	108 EU imports from Brunei (mn €)
Imports to EU from Brunei (mn €, 2001)	72
Human Development Index (rank of 175°)	33
Head of State	HM Paduka Seri Baginda Sultan Haji Hassanal Bolkiah Mu'izzadddin Waddaulah (Sultan, prime minister, minister of finance and defence)

FRAMEWORK

The framework for co-operation dialogue with Brunei is the EC-ASEAN Agreement of 1980. There is no bilateral cooperation agreement.

POLITICAL CONTEXT

Brunei Darussalam became independent from the United Kingdom on 1 January 1984, and a week later joined the Association of South-East Asian Nations (ASEAN). Brunei is a constitutional monarchy with the Sultan Yang Di-Pertuan – Hassanal Bolkiah as the Head of State, Prime Minister, Defence Minister, as well as Minister for Finance. The Sultan presides over a 10-member cabinet which he appoints himself. Five councils advise the Sultan on policy matters: the Religious Council, the Privy Council, the Council of Succession, the Legislative Council and the Council of Ministers (the cabinet). Since 1962 the Sultan has ruled by decree. Thus, the system of government revolves around the Sultan as the source of executive power.

On 25 September 2004, the Legislative Council met for the first time in 20 years, with 21 members appointed by the Sultan. It passed constitutional amendments, calling for a 45-seat council with 15 elected members. In a move towards political reform an appointed parliament was revived in 2004. The constitution provides for an expanded house with up to 15 elected MPs. However, no date has been set for elections.

Brunei is a Muslim country, with a Ministry of Religious Affairs established to foster and promote Islam. Brunei continues to play a peacekeeping role in the Philippines, and is taking part in efforts to monitor peace in the Indonesian region of Aceh.

EUROPEAN COMMUNITY ASSISTANCE

By virtue of its advanced level of economic development Brunei does not benefit from bilateral development or economic projects.

EC co-operation with Brunei has for the greater part been limited to joint EC- ASEAN projects.

The EC has given financial support to the ASEAN-EC Management Centre (AEMC), located in Brunei, the contract for which has come to an end.

TRADE AND ECONOMIC

Since 1929, when oil was discovered in Brunei, the country has flourished. During 1998 and as a consequence of the Asia crisis, however, both exports and imports decreased in comparison with previous years.

> · **Key role of oil and gas**: Brunei suffered little directly from the Asian financial crisis of 1997. But, in 1998, the Sultanate was hit by the sharp fall in oil sales and the bankruptcy of a locally-owned oil and gas company, resulting in a contraction in GDP of 4%. Subsequently, economic activity recovered in step with the resumption of oil and gas extraction and, in recent years, the sharp rise in the oil price. The latest available data for GDP shows real annual growth around 3%. Oil reserves are officially estimated at 25 years, but, great hopes are placed in two new drilling concessions.

Economic structure: Almost everything the country needs is imported. Even the industrial labour force comes from abroad, mainly from India, the Philippines, Indonesia and Bangladesh as most of Brunei's citizens are employed as civil servants (60% of the population) and prefer the status related to that occupation. This also explains the apparent contradiction between the necessity to employ foreign manpower and the rising unemployment rate (officially at 4.7% but estimated at 9%).

> · At the beginning of 2000, the government of the Sultanate announced an ambitious programme of **economic reforms** in order to reduce the dependence on oil and gas.

Two initiatives have been taken up till know– to develop tourism and to support the creation of an off-shore financial centre in developing Islamic banking business.

· The tourism industry is, however, handicapped by the shortage of quality infrastructure, and the geographical insulation of the Sultanate.

Brunei's trade surplus fell by an estimated 74% in US dollar terms in 1999 as the price of oil and gas collapsed. A strengthening oil price and long-term contracts for natural gas, paid in US dollars, should, however, ensure that Brunei's trade position remains healthy.

At present Brunei produces oil and gas almost to the exclusion of other products. The government is trying hard, however, to develop manufactured exports, in particular cement and roofing (tiles) which are both protected sectors. The garment industry is struggling after the abolition of global quotas on the textile trade. The Sultan has announced financial reforms.

Brunei has signed a free-trade pact with New Zealand, Singapore and Chile. A Brunei Tourism Board has been set up

The domestic economy: Brunei's economic growth remains fairly sluggish, at 2.6% year on year but a recovery is likely to have taken place in the second quarter of 2005. The non-oil and gas sector is expanding more rapidly than the energy sector. High global oil prices have lifted transport prices, but overall inflation remains low.

Foreign trade and payments: High oil prices lay behind an increase in the merchandises-trade surplus in the first quarter of 2005.The oil and gas sector continues to account for the bulk of exports; garments exports were much lower than in the year-earlier period.

The investment policy in Brunei is largely open to foreign investors, as indicated by a favourable legal environment and a policy allowing full foreign ownership in a majority of economic sectors. Foreign investments have been more particularly in the last years as they are considered by the government as a key element to contribute to the targeted diversification of the country's economy.

As part of this strategy to attract foreign investments, an Economic Development Board (EDB) was created in 2001. The main sectors and projects promoted by the EDB and susceptible to attract foreign investments include port infrastructure, industry, communication (aviation hub), eco-tourism, and financial services. In parallel with the creation of the EDB, major policy changes have been made in the last years to promote foreign investments. August 2000 saw the introduction of an offshore legislation in Brunei. New laws were drafted covering international banking, insurance, offshore companies, trusts, limited partnerships and registered agents.

Changes in the legislation are too recent analyze its effects. The volume of FDI has doubled between 2001 and 2002, while the figures available until mid 2003 include that the trend is positive and that investments do not only target natural resources but also services.

STRATEGIC INFORMATION FOR BUSINESS

Brunei Darussalam is still very much dependent on revenues from crude oil and natural gas to finance its development programs. Aside from this, Brunei Darussalam also receives income from rents, royalties, corporate tax and dividends. Due to the non-renewable nature of oil and gas, economic diversification has been in Brunei Darussalam's national development agenda. In the current Seventh national Development Plan, 1996-2000, the government has allocated more than $7.2 billion for the implementation of various projects and programs.

Brunei Darussalam is the third largest oil producer in Southeast Asia and it produced 163,000 barrels per day. It is also the fourth largest producer of liquefied natural gas in the world.

Brunei Darussalam is the third largest oil producer in Southeast Asia and it produced 163,000 barrels per day. It is also the fourth largest producer of liquefied natural gas in the world. National Development Plan

Brunei welcomes foreign investment. Foreign investors are invited to actively participate in the current economic diversification programme of the country. The programme hinges on the development of the private sector. The Ministry of Industry and Primary Resources was formed in 1989 with the responsibility of promoting and facilitating industrial development in Brunei Darussalam. Brunei Darussalam offers all investors security, stability, continuity, confidence and competitiveness.

Competitive investment incentives are ready and available for investors throughout the business cycle of start up, growth, maturity and expansion. The Investment Incentive Act which was enacted in 1975 provides tax advantages at start up and ongoing incentives throughout growth and expansion that are comparable if not better than those offered by other countries in the region.

The Investment Incentives Act makes provision for encouraging the establishment and development of industrial and other economic enterprises, for economic expansion and incidental purposes.

Investment incentive benefits vary from one program to other. Amongst the benefits are:

- Exemption from income tax;
- Exemption from taxes on imported duties on machinery, equipment, component parts, accessories or building structures;
- Exemption from taxes on imported raw material not available or produced in Brunei Darussalam intended for the production of the pioneer products;
- Carry forward of losses and allowances.

This Act provides tax relief for a company which is granted pioneer status.

- Companies awarded pioneer status are exempted from corporate tax, tax import of raw materials and capital goods for a period ranging from 2 to 5 years, depending on fixed capital expenditure with possible extension at the discretion of the relevant authorities.
- Enterprises which are given expansion certificates are given tax relief for a period between 3 to 5 years.

- Approved foreign loans can be exempted from paying the 20% withholding tax for interest paid to non-resident lenders.

Brunei Darussalam is flexible towards foreign equity requirements. 100% foreign equity can be considered for export-oriented industries with the exception of industries based on local resources, industries related to national food security and car dealership whereby some level of local participation is required.
Industrial activities are classified into four categories:

- Industries related to national food security
- Industries for local market
- Industries based on local resources
- Industries for export market

Industrial policies including manpower, ownership, government support and facilities remain open and flexible for all categories of industrial activities. Brunei Darussalam maintains a realistic approach where a variety of arrangements are feasible. Policies relating to ownership allow for full foreign ownership, majority foreign ownership and minority foreign ownership, as per the type of industry and situation.
Only activities relating to national food security and those based on local resources require some level of local participation. Industries for the local market not related to national food security and industries for total export can be totally foreign owned. Overall, in Brunei Darussalam, any industrial enterprise will be considered.
The Investment Incentives Order 2001 expanded the tax holidays avaiable to investors. Examples include:

- Corporate tax relief of up to 5 years for companies that invest B$500,000 to B$2.5 million in approved ventures
- 8-years tax relief for investing more than B$2.5 million
- An 11-year tax break if the venture is located in a high-tech industrial park.

Brunei Darussalam is still very much dependent on revenues from crude oil and natural gas to finance its development programs. Aside from this, Brunei Darussalam also receives income from rents, royalties, corporate tax and dividends. Due to the non-renewable nature of oil and gas, economic diversification has been in Brunei Darussalam's national development agenda. In the current Seventh national Development Plan, 1996-2004, the government has allocated more than $7.2 billion for the implementation of various projects and programs.

Brunei Darussalam is the third largest oil producer in Southeast Asia and it produced 163,000 barrels per day. It is also the fourth largest producer of liquefied natural gas in the world.

Brunei Darussalam is the third largest oil producer in Southeast Asia and it produced 163,000 barrels per day. It is also the fourth largest producer of liquefied natural gas in the world.
National Development Plan 1996 – 2004

INVESTMENT AND BUSINESS CLIMATE[1]

Brunei Darussalam has enormous business potential that is yet to be exploited. The country has the advantage of peace and political stability, which is favourable for business activities. Foreign investments are always welcome in Brunei and foreign investors are invited to actively engage in the current economic diversification programme.

The Ministry of Industry and Primary Resources, which was established in 1989, is the main government agency that promotes and facilitates investment, business and trade activities in the country.
Competitive investment incentives are ready and available for investors throughout the business cycle of start up, growth, maturity and expansion.
The Investment Incentive Act enacted in 1975 provides tax advantages at start up and ongoing incentives throughout growth and expansion that are comparable if not better than those offered by other countries in the region.

WHY INVEST IN BRUNEI DARUSSALAM?
¨ Brunei Darussalam is a stable and prosperous country that offers not only excellent infrastructure but also a strategic location within the Asean group of countries.
¨ No personal income tax is imposed in Brunei. Businesses are also not imposed sales tax, payroll, manufacturing and export tax. Approved foreign investors can enjoy a company tax holiday of up to eight years.

¨ The regulations relating to foreign participation in equity are flexible. In many instances there can be 100% foreign ownership.

¨ Approval for foreign workers, ranging from labourers to managers, can be secured.
¨ The cost of utilities is among the lowest in the region.
¨ The local market, while relatively small, is lucrative and most overseas investors will encounter little or no competition.

¨ The living conditions in Brunei Darussalam are among the best and most secure in the region
¨ On top of all, His Majesty's Government genuinely welcomes foreign investment in almost any enterprise and will ensure that you receive speedy, efficient and practical assistance on all your inquiries.

SUPPORTIVE ENVIRONMENT

Brunei Darussalam offers vast land and a variety of facilities throughout all four districts in the country. The majority of the 12 industrial sites presently developed are ready and available for occupation. Large expanses for agroforestry and aquaculture are also available. Rental terms and tenancy agreements are competitive and the sites offer a range of facilities, infrastructure and resources. Brunei Darussalam gives priority to ensuring the stability of the natural environment. As such, all sites are free from pollution and are ecologically well balanced. The government's philosophy is sustainable development. Therefore, all polluting industries are banned and one of the continuing criteria for engaging any industry's participation is the impact on the environment.

INFRASTRUCTURE

---

[1] US Department of Commerce

For additional analytical, business and investment opportunities information, please contact Global Investment & Business Center, USA at (703) 370-8082. Fax: (703) 370-8083. E-mail: ibpusa3@gmail.com Global Business and Investment Info Databank - www.ibpus.com

The country's infrastructure is well developed and ready to cater for the needs of the new and vigorous economic activities under the current economic diversification programme. The country's two main ports, at Muara and Kuala Belait, offer direct shipping to Hong Kong, Singapore and several other Asian destinations. Muara, the deep-water port situated 29 kilometres from the capital was opened in 1973 and has since been considerably developed. It has 12,542 sq. metres of transit sheds. Container yards have been increased in size and a container freight station handles unstuffing operations. Meanwhile, Pulau Muara Besar is being developed as a centre for dockyard, ship salvaging and for other related industries. The recently expanded Brunei International Airport in Bandar Seri Begawan can now handle 1.5 million passengers and 50,000 tonnes of cargo a year. The 2,000 kilometre road network serving the entire country is being expanded and modernised. A main highway runs the entire length of the country's coastline. It conveniently links Muara, the port of entry at one end, to Belait, the oil producing district at the western end of the state.

ECONOMY

The economy of the country is dominated by the oil and gas and liquefied natural gas industries and Government expenditure patterns. The country's exports consist of three major commodities namely crude oil, petroleum products and liquefied natural gas. Exports are destined mainly for Japan, the United States and Asean countries. The second most important industry is the construction industry. This is directly the result of increased investment by the Government in development and infrastructure projects within the five-year National Development Plans. Brunei Darussalam has entered a new phase of development in its drive towards economic diversification from dependence on the oil and liquefied natural gas-based economy. Official statistics showed that exports during the 1996 to 2004 period increased from B$3,682.1 million in 1996 to B$6,733.5 million in 2004, while imports declined from B$3,513.6 million to B$1,907.8 million. This trend has increased the balance of trade from B$168.9 million in 1996 to B$3289.0 million in 2004. In the current 8th National Development Plan, which is the last phase of Brunei's 20-year National Development Programme, the government is allocating a total of B$1.1 billion for commerce and industry. The Brunei International Financial Centre (BIFC) set up in 2004, is another effort undertaken by the government to diversify the country's economy. Brunei Darussalam has the potential to become an international financial centre and has the capability to provide similar facilities as those available in other successful financial centres. Brunei has political stability, modern infrastructure and up-to-date international communications system. Seven bills have been passed to govern the establishment and supervision of BIFC. These include the International Business Companies Order 2004, International Limited Partnership Order 2004, International Banking order 2004, International Trust Order 2004, Registered Agents and Trust Licensing order 2004, Money Laundering Order 2004 and Criminal Conduct (Recovery of Proceed) Order 2004. The BIFC also plans to establish international Islamic banks in Brunei whose legal framework has been provided under the International Banking Order 2004. The establishment of the international Islamic banks is in line with the national aspirations of encouraging the development of Islamic finance and also of making the Sultanate as a regional and international Islamic financial centre.

INDUSTRIES

Industrial activities are classified into four categories:

1. Industries related to national food security
2. Industries for local market
3. Industries based on local resources
4. Industries for export market

For additional analytical, business and investment opportunities information,
please contact Global Investment & Business Center, USA
at (703) 370-8082. Fax: (703) 370-8083. E-mail: ibpusa3@gmail.com
Global Business and Investment Info Databank - www.ibpus.com

FLEXIBLE POLICIES

Industrial policies including manpower, ownership, government support and facilities remain open and flexible for all categories of industrial activities. Brunei Darussalam maintains a realistic approach where a variety of arrangements are feasible. Policies relating to ownership allow for full foreign ownership, majority foreign ownership and minority foreign ownership, as per type of industry and situation. Only activities relating to national food security and industries for total export can be totally foreign owned. Overall, in Brunei Darussalam, any industrial enterprise will be considered.

FINANCE, BANK AND INSURANCE

Brunei Darussalam has no central bank, but the Ministry of Finance through the Treasury, the Currency Board and the Brunei Investment Agency exercises most of the functions of a central bank. Brunei Darussalam has not established a single monetary authority. All works related to finance are being carried out by three institutions.

· The Brunei Currency Board (BCB) is responsible for the circulation and management of currencies in the country.

· The Financial Institution Division (FID) is tasked with the issuing of licenses and regulations to financial institutions including the enforcement of minimum cash balance in accordance to specified rates for the interest of investors

· The Banks Association of Brunei determines the daily interest rates. However, there is also an indication that a single monetary authority may be established in the future to undertake these functions.

In 2004, it was recorded that there were 85 financial institutions including banks, financial companies, security companies, conventional insurance companies, Takaful companies, remittance companies and moneychangers. The existing nine commercial banks have established many branches from 29 in 1995 to 61 in 2004. The number of finance companies has also increased from three in 1996 to five in 2004. Security companies remain at two and the number of conventional insurance companies decreased from 22 in 1996 to 19 in 2004. This is the result of the merging of the branch and parent companies. The number of Takaful companies have risen from two in 1996 to three in 2004. In 1996 and 1997 there were 20 moneychangers operating in the country. The number increased to 33 in 1998 but has reduced to 24 in 2004. Remittance companies have also experienced the same trend as they increased from 16 in 1996 to 30 in 1998 but have reduced to 23 in 2004. The Brunei dollar is pegged to the Singapore dollar. The Ministry of Finance believes that the Monetary Authority of Singapore exercises sufficient caution and such a link will not have detrimental effects on the economies of either country.

CURRENCY

Currency matters are under the jurisdiction of the Brunei Currency Board (BCB) which manages and distributes currency notes and coins in the country with the main mission of ensuring the integrity of the currency issued to safeguard public interest. In September 2004, the money supply comprising currency in circulation and demand deposits amounted to B$2,295 million compared to B$3,366 million, B$2,430 million, B$2,493 million and B$2,727 million in 1996, 1997, 1998 and 1999 respectively.

FOREIGN EXCHANGE

There is no restriction in foreign exchange. Banks permit non-resident accounts to be maintained and there is no restriction on borrowing by non-residents.

TAXATION

Brunei Darussalam has no personal income tax. Sole proprietorship and partnership businesses are not subject to income tax. Only companies are subject to income tax and it is one of the lowest in the region. Moreover tax advantages at start-up and ongoing incentives throughout growth and expansion offer investors profitable conditions that are comparable if not better than those offered by other countries in the region.

COMPANY TAXATION

Companies are subject to tax on the following types of income: -
¨ Gains of profits from any trade, business or vocation,
¨ Dividends received from companies not previously assessed for tax in Brunei Darussalam
¨ Interest and discounts
¨ Rent, royalties, premiums and any other profits arising from properties.

There is no capital gains tax. However, where the Collector of Income Tax can establish that the gains form part of the normal trading activities, they become taxable as revenue gains.

a. Scope of Income Tax
A resident company in Brunei Darussalam is liable to income tax on its income derived from or accrued in Brunei Darussalam or received from overseas. A non-resident company is only taxed on its income arising in Brunei Darussalam.

b. Concept of Residence
A company, whether incorporated locally or overseas, is considered as resident in Brunei Darussalam for tax purposes if the control and management of its business is exercised in Brunei Darussalam. The control and management of a company is normally regarded as resident in Brunei Darussalam if, among other things, its directors' meetings are held in Brunei Darussalam. The profits of a company are subject to tax at the rate of 30%. Tax concession may be available. The profit or loss of a company as per its account is adjusted for income tax purposes to take into account certain allowable expenses, certain expenses prohibited from deduction, wear and tear allowances and any losses brought forward from previous years, in order to arrive at taxable profits.

TREATMENT OF DIVIDENDS

Dividends accruing in, derived from, or received in Brunei Darussalam by a corporation are included in taxable income, apart from dividends received from a corporation taxable in Brunei Darussalam which are excluded.No tax is deducted at source on dividends paid by a Brunei Darussalam corporation. Dividends received in Brunei Darussalam from United Kingdom or Commonwealth countries are grossed up in the tax computation and credit is claimed against the Brunei Darussalam tax liability for tax suffered either under the double tax treaty with the United Kingdom or the provision Commonwealth tax relief.
Any other dividends are included net in the tax computation and no foreign tax is available. Brunei Darussalam does not impose any withholding tax on dividends.

ALLOWABLE DEDUCTIONS

All expenses wholly or exclusively incurred in the production of taxable income are allowable as deduction for tax purposes.
These deductions include:
¨ Interest on borrowed money used in acquiring income
¨ Rent on land and buildings used in the trade or business
¨ Costs of repair of premises, plant and machinery
¨ Bad debts and specific doubtful debts, with any subsequent recovery being treated as income when received, and
¨ Employer's contribution to approved pensions or provident funds

DISALLOWABLE DEDUCTIONS

Expenses not allowed as deductions for tax purposes include:
¨ Expenses not wholly or exclusively incurred in acquiring income
¨ Domestic private expenses
¨ Any capital withdrawal or any sum used as capital
¨ Any capital used in improvement apart from replanting of plantation
¨ Any sum recoverable under an insurance or indemnity contract
¨ Rent or repair expenses not incurred in the earning of income
¨ Any income tax paid in Brunei Darussalam or in other countries and
¨ Payments to any unapproved pension or provident funds

Donations are not allowable but claimable if they are made to approved institutions.

ALLOWANCES FOR CAPITAL EXPENDITURE

Depreciation is not an allowable expense and is replaced by capital allowances for qualifying expenditure. The taxpayer is entitled to claim wear and tear allowances calculated as follows:

a. Industrial Buildings
An initial allowance of 10% is given in the year of expenditure, and an annual allowance of 2% of the qualifying expenditure is provided on a straight-line basis until the total expenditure is written off.

b. Machinery and Plant
An initial allowance of 20% of the cost is given in the year of expenditure together with annual allowances calculated on the reducing value of the assets. The rates prescribed by the Collector of Income Tax range from 3% to 25%, depending on the nature of the assets. Balancing allowances or charges are made on disposal of the industrial building machinery or plant. These adjustments cover the shortfall or excess of the tax written down value as compared to the sale proceeds. Any balancing charge is limited to tax allowances previously granted, and any surplus is considered a capital gain and therefore does not become part of chargeable income. Unabsorbed capital allowances can be carried forward indefinitely but must be set off against income from the same trade.

LOSS CARRYOVERS
Losses incurred by a company can be carried forward for six years for setoff against future income and can be carried back one year. There is no requirement regarding continuity of ownership of the company and also the loss set-off is not restricted to the same trade.

FOREIGN TAX RELIEF

A double taxation agreement exists with the United Kingdom and provides proportionate relief from Brunei Darussalam income tax upon any part of the income which has been or is liable to be charged with United Kingdom income tax.

Tax credits are only available for resident companies. Unilateral relief may be obtained on income arising from Commonwealth countries that provide reciprocal relief. However, the maximum relief cannot exceed half the Brunei Darussalam rate. This relief applies to both resident and non-resident companies.

STAMP DUTY

Stamp duties are levied on a variety of documents. Certain types of documents attract an ad valorem duty, whereas with other documents the duty varies with the nature of the documents.

PETROLEUM TAXES

Special legislation exists in respect of income tax from petroleum operations, which is taxable under the Income Tax (Petroleum) Act 1963 as amended.

WITHHOLDING TAXES

Interest paid to non-resident companies under a charge, debenture or in the respect of a loan, is subject to withholding tax of 20%. There are no other withholding taxes.

ESTATE DUTY

Estate duty is levied on an estate of over $2 million at 3% flat rate for a person who has died on or after 15th December 1988.

IMPORT DUTY

In general, basic foodstuffs and goods for industrial use are exempted from import duties. Electrical equipment and appliances, timber products, photographic materials and equipment, furniture, motor vehicles and spare parts are levied minimum duties, while cosmetics and perfumes are subject to 30% duty. Cigarettes are dutiable items, but the rates are low compared with neighbouring countries.

BUSINESSES AND COMPANIES

Registration and Guidelines
In Brunei Darussalam a business may be set up under any of the following forms:
¨ Sole proprietorship
¨ Partnership
¨ Company (Private or Public Company)
¨ Branch of foreign company

All businesses must be registered with the Registrar of Companies and Business Names.
The proposed name of business or companies must first of all be approved by the Registrar of Companies and Business Names. For each name proposed, a fee of $5.00 is imposed.

Sole Proprietorship
¨ Upon arrival, a business name certificate is issued and a fee of $30.00 is imposed
¨ At the moment, it is not subject to corporate tax
¨ Foreigners are not eligible to register

Partnership
¨ May consist of individuals, local companies and/or branches of foreign companies

¨ The maximum permitted number of partners is 20
¨ Upon approval, a business name certificate is issued and a fee of $30.00 is imposed
¨ Application by foreign individuals are subject to prior clearance by the Immigration Department, Economic Planning and Development Unit and the Labour Department before they are registered
¨ At the moment, it is not subject to corporate tax

Private Company

¨ May be limited by shares, guarantee or both by shares and guarantee or unlimited
¨ Must have at least two and not more than 50 shareholders
¨ Shareholders need not be Brunei citizens or residents.
¨ Restrict the right of members to transfer shares and prohibit any invitations to the public to subscribe for shares and debentures
¨ A subsidiary company may hold shares in its parent company
¨ Memorandum and Articles of Association must be filed with the Registrar of Companies and Business Names with other incorporation documents in the prescribed form
¨ Upon arrival, a Certificate of Incorporation will be issued and a fee of $25 is imposed
¨ The registration fees are based on a graduated scale on the authorised share capital of the company
¨ No minimum share capital is required
¨ Private Companies are required to do the following:
1. Appoint auditors who are registered in Brunei Darussalam
2. Prepare a profit and loss account and balance sheet, accompanied by the Director's Report annually
3. Submit accounting data annually to the Economic Development and Planning Department of the Ministry of Finance
4. File annual returns, containing information on directors and shareholders
5. Keep the following records:
a. Minute Book of Members' Meetings
b. Minute Book of Director's Meetings
c. Minute Book of Manager's Meetings
d. Register of Members
e. Register of Directors and Managers
f. Register of Charges
¨ Subject to corporate tax of 30% of the gross yearly profit

PUBLIC COMPANY

¨ May be limited or unlimited
¨ May issue freely transferable shares to the public
¨ Must have at least seven shareholders
¨ Shareholders need not be Brunei citizens or residents
¨ Subsidiary company may hold shares in its parent companies
¨ Half the directors in the company must be either Brunei Citizens or ordinary residents in Brunei Darussalam.
¨ Memorandum and Articles of Association must be registered with other incorporation documents in the prescribed forms
¨ Upon approval, Registration of Companies Certificate will be issued and a fee of $25.00 is imposed
¨ The registration fees are based on a graduated scale on the authorised share capital of the company.
¨ No minimum share capital is required
¨ Public Companies are required to do the following:
1. Appoint auditors who are registered in Brunei Darussalam
2. Prepare each year's profit and loss account and balance sheet, accompanied by the Director's Report annually.

**For additional analytical, business and investment opportunities information,
please contact Global Investment & Business Center, USA
at (703) 370-8082. Fax: (703) 370-8083. E-mail: ibpusa3@gmail.com
Global Business and Investment Info Databank - www.ibpus.com**

3. Submit accounting data annually to the Economic Development and Planning Department of the Ministry of Finance
4. File annual returns, containing information on directors and shareholders
5. Keep the following records:
a. Minute Book of Members' Meetings
b. Minute Book of Director's Meetings
c. Minute Book of Manager's Meetings
d. Register of Members
e. Register of Directors and Managers
f. Register of Charges
¨ Subject to corporate tax of 30% of the gross yearly profit.

BRANCH OF FOREIGN COMPANY
The following documents must be filed with the Registrar of Companies and Business Names.
a. A certified copy of the charter, statutes or Memorandum and Articles of Association or other instruments defining the constitution of the foreign company duly authenticated and, when necessary, with English translation.
b. A list of directors together with their particulars and the names and addresses of one or more persons residing in Brunei Darussalam authorised to accept notices on the company's behalf.

¨ Upon approval, a Certificate of Incorporation will be issued and a fee of $25 is imposed
¨ The registration fees are based on a graduated scale on the authorised share capital of the company.
¨ No minimum share capital is required
¨ Branch of foreign company is required to do the following:
1. Appoint auditors who are registered in Brunei Darussalam
2. Prepare each year's profit and loss account and balance sheet, accompanied by the Director's Report annually.
3. Submit accounting data annually to the Economic Development and Planning Department of the Ministry of Finance
4. File annual returns, containing information on directors and shareholders
5. Keep the following records:
a. Minute Book of Members' Meetings
b. Minute Book of Director's Meetings
c. Minute Book of Manager's Meetings
d. Register of Members
e. Register of Directors and Managers
f. Register of Charges
¨ Subject to corporate tax of 30% of the gross yearly profit.

REGISTRATION OF TRADEMARKS AND PATENTS
Trademarks are registrable provided the requirements laid down in the Trademarks Act (Cap 98) are satisfied. Once registered, they are viable for an initial period of seven years and renewable for a further period of 14 years.
Any person who obtains a grant of a patent in the UK or Malaysia or Singapore may apply to the Ministry of Law within three years of the date of issue of such grant to have the grant registered in Brunei Darussalam under the Invention Act (Cap 72). There is no specific legislation for copyright protection, but UK legislation would apply where necessary.

EMPLOYMENT REGULATIONS
All non-Brunei Darussalam citizens require a work permit which are valid for two years. Application must first be made to the Labour Department for a labour license. On the recommendation of the Labour Department, the Immigration Department will give permission for the workers to enter Brunei Darussalam. The Labour Department requires either a cash deposit

or a banker's guarantee to cover the cost of a one-way airfare to the home country of an immigrant worker. An approved labour licence cannot be altered for at least six months after issue. Applications will not be accepted until the formation of a local company or branch of a foreign company has been officially approved and registered.

INDUSTRIAL RELATIONS

The Trade Disputes Act (Cap 129) accords to trade unions the customary immunities and protections in respect of facts done in furtherance of trade disputes. It prescribes procedures for conciliation and subject to the consent of the parties, arbitration in disputes where machinery within the industry concerned does not exist or has failed to achieve settlement. Trade unionism of either the employers or workers is extensively practiced in Brunei Darussalam. As has been already observed, the industrial structure consists almost entirely of small scale enterprises. This state of affairs and nature and cultural characteristics of the population are conductive to accommodation and a 'give and take attitude' rather than a confrontational attitude. Except in the oil industry, the system of collective bargaining has not emerged. Relations between employers and employees are generally good. Existing labour laws have adequate provisions such as for termination of employment, medical care, maternity leave and compensation for disablement. Labour disputes are very rare. The Government has recently implemented the Workers' Provident Fund Enactment to cover workers both in the public and private sectors.

INTERNATIONAL RELATION AND TRADE DEVELOPMENT

In the perspectives of economic co-operation with foreign countries at the bilateral and multilateral levels, Brunei Darussalam seeks relevant agencies that can contribute to development and networking.
The areas of concern are:
¨ To facilitate investment into Brunei Darussalam
¨ To facilitate the development of trade
¨ To enhance human resources development and technology transfer, and
¨ To enhance bilateral, regional and multilateral economic cooperation
In pursuing these areas, mechanism for consultations and cooperation have been established through bilateral, regional and multilateral forum such as Association of Southeast Asian Nations (ASEAN), Asia Pacific Economic Cooperation (APEC), Organisation of Islamic Countries (OIC), European Union (EU), the Commonwealth, United Nation (UN) and the Non-Aligned Movement (NAM).

INVESTMENT PROMOTION

In the area of investment, Brunei Darussalam is currently engaged in a programme to improve its investment climate to create and enhance investment opportunities in Brunei Darussalam, both for local and foreign investors. The programme involves the establishment of bilateral trade investment treaties with foreign Government and Memorandums of Understanding (MoUs) between Brunei Darussalam's private sector and private sectors of other countries.

TRADE DEVELOPMENT

In the area of trade development, Brunei Darussalam is facilitating market opportunities to increase market access in the region as well as globally. Brunei Darussalam practices open multilateral trading system which are being pursued through regional and multilateral trading arrangements such as the ASEAN Free Trade Area (AFTA) and General Agreement of Trade and Tariffs (GATT). This open trade policy is consistent with Brunei Darussalam's efforts in pursuing outward looking economic policies that will assist the country in expanding its industrial and primary resource-based industries.

HUMAN RESOURCE DEVELOPMENT AND TECHNOLOGY TRANSFER

In the area of human resource development and technology transfer, there is a need to improve the technological capabilities of existing local industries, which are mainly small and medium scale enterprises. This is in view of the existing shortage of local manpower and thus the need to import foreign workers. The programmes are targeted towards the development of the mid-band occupational structure in which Brunei Darussalam has the advantage in view of cost factors such as the non-existence of income tax. Within the context of general economic cooperation, Brunei Darussalam will continue to enhance economic linkages with other countries in the region as well as outside the region.

THE INVESTMENT & TRADING ARM OF THE GOVERNMENT

Semaun Holdings Sdn Bhd

Semaun Holdings Sendirian Berhad, incorporated on 8th December 1994, is a private limited company that serves as an investment/trading arm of the Government with the purpose of accelerating industrial development in Brunei Darussalam through direct investment. Semaun Holdings is wholly owned by His Majesty's Government and plays an important role in supporting the economic diversification programmes in the country. The Chairman is the Honourable Minister of Industry and Primary Resources, Pehin Orang Kaya Setia Pahlawan Dato Seri Setia Haji Awang Abdul Rahman bin Dato Setia Haji Mohammad Taib, who is also the Chairman to the Industrial and Trade Development Council, a body entrusted with facilitating the industrialisation programme of Brunei Darussalam. The mission of Semaun Holdings is to spearhead industrial and commercial development through direct investment in key industrial sectors. Its primary objectives are:

¨ To accelerate and commercial development in Brunei Darussalam
¨ To generate industrial and commercial opportunities for active participation of citizens

Investment Philosophy

a. Local investment
First priority shall be given to investment in the country. Investment shall be in areas of strategic importance and NOT in direct competition with local companies
b. Overseas Capital
The Holdings may invest overseas in activities which reinforce the position of its local investment, preferably through strategic partnering with suitable local companies

Authorised Capital

BND 500 million (Five hundred million dollars)

Type of Investment

The Holdings shall invest through its
¨ Wholly owned operations
¨ Joint Venture Companies
¨ Equity Participation

Scope of Operation

The Holdings shall invest in business, trading and commercial enterprises including agriculture, fishery, forestry, industry and mining activities in Brunei Darussalam. Participation in investment related activities outside the country are also considered.
For more information please contact:
Semaun Holdings Sdn Bhd,
Office Unit No. 02, Block D,

Complex Yayasan Sultan Haji Hassanal Bolkiah,
Bandar Seri Begawan 2085,
Brunei Darussalam
Telephone no: (673) 223-2957 Fax : (673) 223-2956

BRUNEY INDUSTRIAL ACHIEVEMENTS

Today, twelve years since its formation, BINA has managed to achieve a considerable measure of success in what it originally set out to do. In putting these achievements in perspective, one has to bear in mine circumstances Brunei has to contend with, the most critical of which is the local market which is approximately about 300,000 people compared to our regional neighbours.

DIVERSIFICATION OF INDUSTRIAL ACTIVITIES

Allocated at BINA's industrial sites in all the four districts, 213 projects have been approved to date which is a combination of new and relocation/expansion projects. The following list is a selection of those approved projects which should give some perspective of BINA's achievement so far.

- Clinker grinding plant (cement manufacture)
- Production of construction materials (e.g. paint aluminium doors & windows, roofing products, PVC pipes, concrete blocks, stainless steel products, etc)
- Bottling of artesian water
- Assembly of electrical appliances
- Electrical equipment (switchboard, control panels & feeder pillars)
- Production of electrical cables & wires
- Manufacturing of garments for export
- Food & beverages (e.g. ice cream, soft drinks, bakery, spices, etc)
- Production of solar panels for export
- Aluminium sulphate & sodium carbonate for use in water treatment
- Food repackaging
- Warehousing
- Manufacture of furniture
- Manufacture of cans
- Canning of tuna

Not just limited to the capability of setting up factories, some manufacturers have actually managed to get accreditation for their products ftorn reputable foreign establishments such as SIRIM & SISIR while others have successfully implemented the internationally recognised management standard ISO 9002.

INVESTMENT

The total investment value of those projects based on approved projects is B$619,608,331 in which foreign investments accounts for approximately one-quarter of the pie (B$126,071,802). Local investments stands at B$493,536,529.

EMPLOYMENT CREATION

Those investments have also helped to create 14,753 new job opportunities for both the skilled and unskilled categories. This positive development goes a long way in helping reduce the Government's burden of unemployment which is often accompanied by social problems.

EXPORT ACTIVITIES

Other developments are the creation of export industries, which at the moment is still limited to garment. Apart from enhancing the credibility of local companies, exports help to offset imports in the national balance of trade figures and is also the way forward if a company wants to grow sitinificantly because of the competitive nature and large size of the international market. The local garment industry export value still has a long way to go to offset the nations huge demand for imported products and services but has taken the right step forward to establish itself especially with trade liberalisation agreements, that Brunei is party to, coming into effect at the beginning of the next century. Below is a table of the industry's export figures:

Year	Value (US$)	Quantity (Dozen)
1989	5,377,741	179,936
1990	9,685,408	261,805
1991	18,942,925	406,764
1992	19,214,188	464,926
1993	24,309,781	569,238
1994	28,809,553	789,605
1995	41,514,308	969,472
1996	46,753,607	1,022,917
1997	57,528,747	1,230,730
Total	252,136,258	5,895,393

IMPORT SUBSTITUTION

It is admittedly difficult for local producers to replace the products that consumers import because the oil and gas industry aside, Brunei is a net importer. But in any case, Brunei has managed to produce certain products locally such as construction materials, processed food, furniture, electrical products, etc which is a good start in replacing simple products which are within the technological and financial capacity of local manufacturers/producers.

VALUE-ADDING

As mentioned earlier, some of the projects approved at BINA's sites are relocations with the aim of expansion. Some examples of these are the car dealership, warehousing, timber, and furniture industry where bigger land area, proper and better physical infrastructure provided at the industrial sites has given the industries the impetus to offer better and more varied products and services.

COOPERATIVE DEVELOPMENT

For additional analytical, business and investment opportunities information, please contact Global Investment & Business Center, USA at (703) 370-8082. Fax: (703) 370-8083. E-mail: ibpusa3@gmail.com
Global Business and Investment Info Databank - www.ibpus.com

Formed on Ist August 1974, Cooperative Development Department's function is to enhance community's unity and the social and economic status of the people. With its subsequent merger with Industrial Unit, Ministry of Industry and Primary Resources to become BINA, the primary function continues as it was but with more emphasis to promote and develop cooperatives to be more competitive and dynamic.

Over the twenty-four years of its establishment, 164 cooperatives have been registered with 14,314 members (as of September 1998). Recent data shows that there are only limited lines of business ventures these cooperatives are involved in, such as transportation, fishery, agriculture, consumer, school and multi-purpose with a net profit gained of about $2 millions Brunei (1998). Having gone through these developments, BINA have restructured its cooperative development section and taken few steps and some of these steps are being undertaken towards enhancing awareness and level of cooperative's expertise and professionalism. Future direction and strategies of cooperatives would be formulated following the national level seminar to be held at the end of this year. This would enable BINA in developing a cooperative development plan; analysing the existing Cooperative Act for any changes, deemed necessary; improve existing administrative assistance; encourage interaction and cooperation's with private sector; and for cooperatives to venture into other potential business sectors for example manufacturing, marketing, insurance, wholesales, etc.

BOOSTING THE ECONOMY THROUGH PRIVATISATION

Brunei Darussalam continued with efforts to diversify its economy from the oil and gas sector through encouraging industrial development and commerce.

Under the Sixth Five-Year Development Plan, the industry and commerce sector is allocated $550.9 million, which makes up 10 percent of the total budget for development.

Of this, $100 million has been specifically budgeted for industrial promotion and development. The government has consistently aimed its policies at maximising the economic utilisation of its national resources, develop new industries and encourage and nurture the development of Bumiputera leaders in industry and commerce.

In its endeavour to boost economic growth, the authorities are also introducing the concept of privatisation. Besides being a stimulus for economic growth, privatisation is also being seen as a way to remove spending while improving efficiency in public services. Crucial in the successful implementation of the privatisation programmes are the awareness and understanding of the people in the government, the private sector as well as the public.

Through privatisation, the government could optimize spending in providing services to the public, the Minister of Development Pengiran Dato Haji Ismail said. When opening a two-day seminar on privatisation in June.

It is also required in the expansion of the nation's economic base and in promoting the construction and service sectors, he added.

It would be better to implement the project on a small scale initially so that we can understand better the concept of privatisation, the minister said.

Plan to hold more seminars on privatisation
The two-day seminar was attended by more than 200 people from various ministries, departments and private companies.

In fact, more seminars are planned on privatisation aimed at preparing the business sector ready for the new business situation. The seminars would be organised on a smaller scale involving smaller groups of people. This would ensure that such sessions are more effective in achieving understanding and imparting knowledge to participants about privatisation.

The effort by the Ministry of Development in organising the seminar was seen by some participants as a signal that the ministry in particular is gearing up to privatise some of its service.

The Development Ministry is one of the largest in the government and includes the Public Works Department, the Electrical Services Department, Town and Country Planning, the Survey Department, the Housing Development Department and the Land Department.

The government in its Sixth Five-Year Development Plan due to end this year, has allocated more than $5 billion for national development, more than a billion dollars more than it had spent in the Fifth FDP.

Some 50.9 million dollars for the Sixth Plan was allocated to developing 619 projects starting from 1991 to 1995.

29.3 percent or $1614.6 million of the total budget is for social services that include national housing, education, medical and health, religious affairs and public facilities.

ECONOMIC INDICATORS

GDP at current prices (Million B$) : 8.051.0 (1997 estm.)
Average annual inflation rate: 2.7 percent
Unemployment rate: 4.9 percent

Although Brunei Darussalam is no giant when it comes to landmass, it has been blessed with rich natural resources and a strategic location within the region. The majority of the country is covered in tropical rainforests teeming with exotic flora and fauna. Anxious to promote the conservation of its lush surroundings, eco-tourism has gained importance in the country's economic activities.

Human resources are central to the successful transformation of Brunei Darussalam into a diversified industrial economy. As in most developing nations, there is a shortage of skilled workforce in the country. Therefore, greater emphasis is placed upon education. The main areas of interest in human resources development are managerial and industrial skills, with particular emphasis on entrepreneurial skills as well as vocational and technical training.

Brunei Darussalam's main exports consist of three major commodities - crude oil, petroleum products and liquefied natural gas - sold largely to Japan, the United States and ASEAN countries. The Government's move to promote non-oil and gas activities has been largely successful with figures showing 64% of GDP in 1996 compared to only 24.3% in 1991.

AGRICULTURE

Agriculture plays a major role in the security of food supply. To ensure a continuity of supply of food in the country, the Department of Agriculture promotes domestic agricultural activities and at the same time facilitate import of foods to meet national requirements. The Department has

For additional analytical, business and investment opportunities information,
please contact Global Investment & Business Center, USA
at (703) 370-8082. Fax: (703) 370-8083. E-mail: ibpusa3@gmail.com
Global Business and Investment Info Databank - www.ibpus.com

established a new framework to encourage greater efficiency in farm production, revitalise rural communities, foster agro-industrial development and encourage sustainable agriculture to conserve the natural resources. The aim is to accelerate food production in the country to promise a meaningful degree of food security.

Over the past few years, special efforts have been made to encourage greater private participation in food production. Incentives and agricultural services have been provided to attract investment. These facilities have stimulated greater private sector involvement in agriculture.

The cooperation from the farming communities has been overwhelming. We are now completely self-sufficient in table eggs (99.6%), produce 76.1 percent of the poultry meat requirement, satisfy 70 percent of the demand for vegetables, meet 7.7 percent (and increasing) of the tropical fruits requirement, and have expanded food processing and packaging activities. The symbiotic relationship between Department of Agriculture and the farmers has sustained growth in food production.

Today, Department of Agriculture through its dedicated staff and within the operational machinery have, and will continue to provide, the supportive services to develop agriculture and increase local food production. The Department is conscious of the need to protect the environment and conserve the country's natural resources and biodiversity for the benefit of future generations. To meet the changing needs of the producers and consumers, the Department has implemented a coordinated approach in administration, regulation, research and extension.

Future challenges and opportunities are enormous. The Department of Agriculture is constantly adjusting and consolidating to increase efficiency in order to meet the needs of the farming communities and consumers. The goals are to strengthen and direct efforts towards a stable relationship between the Department of Agriculture, importers, farmers and consumers in shaping a strong and efficient agricultural sector. Collectively, these efforts will guarantee the country's security of food supply.

The agro-economy makes up just one per cent of GDP and Brunei has to import 80 per cent of its food needs. Efforts are being made to diversify the economy, away from a heavy dependence on oil and gas towards a more independent agricultural sector. While land, finance and irrigation facilities are available, what is needed is manpower resources.

The first of the Government's four major objectives is to enhance domestic production of padi, vegetables, poultry and livestock. Secondly, to develop the agro-industry as a whole, and thirdly, to produce high value-added products using advanced technological farming methods. Last but not least, Brunei aims to conserve and protect the existing bio-diversity.

Since 1994, Brunei egg farms have successfully supplied the 20 eggs a month that each person in Brunei consumes. The figures for rice, a staple for the Asian country's 283,500 people, however show that the country is able to meet just 2 percent of the 27,500-tonne demand a year.

Almost all of its beef are imported. Brunei brings in live cattle, mostly from Australia, where the Sultanate has a 579,000-hectare ranch in Willeroo, and substantially from Malaysia and New Zealand. Frozen and chilled beef are imported from all over the world.

Local production of chicken, a favorite meat as much for its taste as for its reputation as a healthier, lower-cholesterol white meat, has made great strides. About 28 percent of the chicken sold in Brunei markets is local produce. To supplement the 17,400 tones of chicken meat the country consumes annually, a proportion of Brunei hens are grown from imported day-old chicks.

The growing concern for a healthier way of life also tends towards including more vegetables in the Bruneian diet. Brunei has done well to encourage this trend by ensuring that more than half of the vegetables prepared in kitchens here are locally grown, with the other 46 percent imported mostly from Sabah and Sarawak, particularly from Limbang, Miri and Lawas.

In Brunei, you get a good variety of both tropical and temperate climate fruits, though only a small proportion of what you eat here are locally grown. A hefty 93 percent of it is bought from neigboring countries, mostly from Thailand.

Efforts are being made to collect specimens of local fruit trees and to develop small plantations as well as to produce seedlings which will subsequently support the development of large-scale, less labor-intensive mechanized fruit farms. Areas in the Tutong district have been singled as ideal for planting orchards.

The government is trying to stimulate greater interest in the agriculture industry through the establishment of model farms, providing training, advice and support.

Existing infrastructure and facilities are being upgraded in rural areas. As the high rainfall, temperature and humidity conditions are not conducive to manual labor, localized farming may be encouraged with sophisticated machinery and equipment,

With agriculture playing a major role in the security of food supply, the Department of Agriculture has actively been promoting domestic agricultural activities while facilitating import of various foods to meet national requirements.

Over the past few years, special efforts have been made to encourage greater private sector participation in the production of food. Incentives and agricultural services have been provided to attract investment. These efforts have successfully stimulated an increase in private sector involvement in agriculture.

AGRICULTURE & LIVESTOCK

The cooperation from the farming communities has been overwhelming. The Department is now completely self-sufficient in table eggs (99.6%). They produce 76.1% of the poultry meat requirement, satisfy 70% of the demand for vegetables, meet 7.7% (and increasing) of the tropical fruits requirement, and has expanded food processing and packaging activities. The symbiotic relationship between the Department of Agriculture and farmers has sustained growth in food production.

RICE

Various efforts have been made by the government to encourage rice production during the last decade and the yield per acre has increased due to the introduction of better agricultural methods.

Approximately 290 tonnes or 1% of the nation's rice needs are produced locally from 613 hectares of rice fields scattered around the country.

As a first step towards the attainment of self-sufficiency in rice, the Government launched an experimental large scale mechanised rice planting project at Kampong Wasan in 1978. Covering

For additional analytical, business and investment opportunities information,
please contact Global Investment & Business Center, USA
at (703) 370-8082. Fax: (703) 370-8083. E-mail: ibpusa3@gmail.com
Global Business and Investment Info Databank - www.ibpus.com

an area of 400 hectares, the project was a joint undertaking between the Agriculture Department and the Public Works Department.

The responsibility of the Public Works Department was to provide the required infrastructure, clear the land and give other basic provisions. The responsibility of the Agriculture Department was to plant, maintain, harvest and process. The aim was to plant paddy twice a year, from April to September and from October to March.

VEGETABLES
Locally grown vegetables constitute about 6,700 tonnes or just over 65% of the country's needs. With more people taking up vegetable farming, the amount is increasing gradually.

Vegetable production in Brunei Darussalam has progressed well with the entry of commercial operators. Much of the tropical leafy vegetables are now produced locally.

The Department of Agriculture is encouraging the development of high technology protected cultivation to produce quality pesticide-free vegetative crops of high market value to complement the production from conventional farms.

Brunei Darussalam is still dependent on imports to satisfy demand for temperate vegetables, fruit vegetables, roots and tubers. Most of these vegetables can be produced locally.

The local consumption for tropical and temperate vegetables recorded during the year 2001 was 17,131.1 metric tonnes. According to the statistics, 52.1% was produced locally.

FRUITS
Fruit farming is largely performed on a small scale. There is a vast range of locally produced tropical fruits that meet about 11% of the domestic requirement of more than 14,000 tonnes.

In 1975, the Agriculture Department initiated a fruit-farming scheme to encourage fruit cultivation in the country. In an effort to increase the production of local fruits, the Government through the agricultural stations in Batang Mitus, Tanah Jambu and Lumapas, planted seedlings of various fruit trees.

Orchards and backyard gardens produce a wide range of seasonal and non-seasonal tropical fruits. Traditional production systems produce non-seasonal fruits such as bananas, papayas, pineapples, watermelons, and seasonal fruits namely, durian, chempedak, tarap, rambutan, langsat, belunu, asam aur aur, and membangan to meet the domestic demand for fruits.

Many other types of indigenous fruits, some of which are not commonly found in other parts of Southeast Asia, are also supplied by these traditional production systems.

Production is insufficient to meet local demand and large quantities of both tropical and temperate fruits are imported annually. The total consumption for tropical and temperate fruits in the year 2001 was estimated at 23,083.2 metric tonnes. Only 17.9% were produced locally, according to the provided statistics.

LIVESTOCK

The country produces about 1,000 heads of cattle and buffaloes for the market annually, making up about 6% of its own beef consumption. The Government assists local stock farmers with calves, machinery, feed, seedlings, fertilisers and veterinary care.

The country requires 3,000 to 5,000 tonnes of meat annually, with per capita consumption of between nine and 17 kg. To meet this demand, the government imports an average of between 4,000 and 7,000 heads of live cattle from its Willeroo Ranch in Northern Australia.

Another importer of slaughter cattle (of various breeds, including Angus and Brahman Cross) from Australia is PDS Abattoir. PDS Abattoir is a local company that owns an international standard abattoir in Tutong, specialising in the production of chilled and frozen western cuts. Meanwhile, local fresh milk production contributes about 199 thousand litres annually.

Research has been carried out to ascertain the best possible way to increase buffalo population. Towards this end, the Agriculture Department has launched a research project covering 4,000 hectares in the Batang Mitus area in the Tutong District. So far, over 200 hectares have already been initiated. The farm's main aim will be to assess local and imported stock towards producing highbred buffaloes for commercial purposes.

Local beef, which is mainly from cattle and buffaloes, is capable of supplying 4% (5,206.75 metric tonnes) of the total beef requirement in the year 2001. 92.1% of the total beef requirement comes from the importation of live animals (18,742 heads or an equivalent to 4,796.31 metric tonnes) and frozen and chilled beef amounting to 203.39 metric tonnes.

Meanwhile, a total of 2,449 heads of goats have been slaughtered and this is equivalent to 42.75 metric tonnes of mutton. Out of the total number of slaughtered goats, 8.7 per cent (331 heads or 3.72 metric tonnes) are locally produced while the rest are imported from Australia.

Goats are popularly consumed only by the ethnic groups and races such as Indians, Nepalese, Gurkhas, Malays and occasionally Chinese. The demand for goats tends to be higher during the Islamic festive months of Aidil-Fitri, Aidil-Adha and Ramadhan.

FISHERIES

Fisheries has been identified as one of the sectors that can contribute towards economic diversification.

The Fisheries Industry comprises three sectors: capture industry, aquaculture industry and processing industry. The estimate is that together, they will contribute at least B$200 million per year to the Gross Domestic Product (GDP) by 2003. The capture industry is estimated to contribute at least B$112 million, aquaculture B$71 million and processing at least B$17 million to the GDP.

Along with traditional fishing, marine fish is the principal source of protein for the people of Brunei Darussalam. The per capita fish consumption is one of the highest in the region at around 45 kilogrammes per year.

CAPTURE INDUSTRY
With an estimated population of about 344,500, the total annual consumption of fish is estimated to be around 15,500 metric tonnes. However, with only about 925 full-time fishermen, Brunei Darussalam still has to import about 50% of its fish requirement to supplement the local production.

The industry, however, is developing especially after the declaration of the 200 nautical miles Brunei Fishery Limits. There has also been a change in policy that allows joint ventures.

For additional analytical, business and investment opportunities information, please contact Global Investment & Business Center, USA at (703) 370-8082. Fax: (703) 370-8083. E-mail: ibpusa3@gmail.com Global Business and Investment Info Databank - www.ibpus.com

The Government, wanting to obtain maximum economic gains while ensuring the sustainability of the resources, is only allowing exploitation of up to the "maximum economic yield" (MEY), which is taken to be 20% below the usually used "maximum sustainable yield" (MSY) level. In this regard, the surveyed fishing areas of Brunei Darussalam have about 21,300 metric tonnes of fish at MEY: Demersal resources - 12,500 metric tonnes and Pelagic resources - 8,800 metric tonnes.

In addition, Brunei Darussalam is also found to be in the migration path of tuna resources. Their volume will be surveyed in the near future.

At the same time, there are large resources associated with the numerous offshore oil-rigs, purposely-sunk tyres, man-made concrete reefs and old oil-rigs that act as artificial reefs. With appropriate gear and technology, these resources can be exploited.

AQUACULTURE
The aquaculture industry in Brunei Darussalam, although in its infancy compared to other countries in the region, is developing quite fast. The high demand for aquaculture products and conducive physical conditions such as unpolluted waterways, the absence of typhoons and floods have made aquaculture a very promising industry.

The major activities in the aquaculture industry are the cage culture of marine fish and the pond culture of marine shrimp. Development of technology on seed production and culture of other species that are of high commercial value are one of the priorities of the Department of Fisheries.

It is anticipated that the steady increase of population will increase existing demand. With the current liberalisation of trade, opportunities for export are there, even though as it is, the local demand and market price in itself have already made the fisheries industry attractive.

The Government, through the Fisheries Department, has therefore been actively promoting suitable foreign involvement, either in the form of joint partnership or other forms of strategic alliances, aimed at developing the fisheries sector towards a competitive, efficient and commercially lucrative venture.

FORESTRY

Forests, Brunei's most permanent asset, cover about 81 percent of the total land area of 5,765 sq km. They grow in a diverse mix of mangrove, peat, swamp, heath, dipterocarp and montane. Primary forest makes up 58 percent of the land. The Department of Forestry, in line with the country's policy of continuous conservation, has marked out plans to sustain the forests as well as programs for environmental and industrial forestry.

The former covers the management of protected forests, conservation, recreational and national parks, while the latter involves guidelines for the development and management of forest products as well as their processing and consumption.

Logging is strictly controlled in a bid to nurture a stable environment, unlike countries which have severely depleted their forests. Brunei has escaped this fate in some measure because the availability of revenue from its hydrocarbon deposits allows it to exercise the freedom of refraining from exploiting the land for timber and other commercial uses.

Restricted timber production, destined only for local consumption, has been reduced to around 100,000 cubic meters per annum from the former 200,000 cubic meters limit. Timber extraction for export is strictly prohibited.

Within the framework of the Forest Conservation Policy, efforts to reforest earmarked areas were drawn up and a sum of $26 million was allocated in the sixth Plan. Up to the date of publication, 700 of the 30,000 hectares earmarked over the next 30 years have been cultivated. In time, about 1,000 hectares will be reforested every year.

There are 11 forest reserves managed by the department. Forestry projects include the building of biodiversity conservation centers, establishing facilities and sites for nurseries, fields for forest trees and commercial rattan and bamboo.

In the Ex-Situ Forest Conservation center in Sungai Lumut, efforts focus on enriching the plants in the Andulau Forest Reserve, which has seen almost 50 years of logging.

TRADITIONAL FOREST PRODUCTS

Aside from timber, the forests have also been the source of traditional products. In the early days, latex from jelutong trees was extracted and exported. It was used in the manufacture of chewing gum. Cutch used to be harvested from the bark of bakau trees in the mangroves; this was used primarily for leather tanning. Firewood and charcoal are to this day still derived from the mangroves. And even at the present time, wild animals, rattan, bamboo, leaves, fibers, bark, fruits, and a host of other materials are gathered from the forest. These are utilised for food, medicine, building houses, and related domestic and commercial applications.

For food, the shoots of bamboo (rabong), rattan (ombut), fern (paku and lamiding), and the fruit of petai (Parkia javanica) are widely popular as vegetable. The fruits of terap (Artocarpus odoratissimus), kembayau (Dacryodes spp.), durian (Durio spp.), etc. are also local favourites. Moreover, assorted materials collected from the forests are fashioned into furniture, handicraft, boats, and other traditional goods.

Another major commodity gathered from the forest are medicinal plants and related materials. These are of great importance in the lives of the local people, particularly those in rural areas. Traditional herbal medicine and native healing methods have of late, gained growing interest in global scene. Biotechnology and bioengineering have given rise to entirely new industries based on tropical biodiversity. Thus, in this context, the natural forests of the country play increasingly valuable conservation and socio-economic roles in national development.

COMMERCIAL TIMBER

There are at least 48 timber or species groups in the country which are of known commercial value. These are classified in accordance with conventions adopted by most Southeast Asian countries. Only one softwood species, tolong or bindang (Agathis borneensis), is represented and it occurs in higher elevations as well as on sand terraces in lowland peat swamps. It is a highly regarded decorative and fancy wood, particularly when used as paneling and interior finishing.

The hardwoods, on the other hand, are categorized into three groups, based on wood density and natural strength and durability. The first group consists of the heavy hardwoods, which have air-dry densities of over 880 kg. per cubic meter, and which are inherently durable. Examples are the selangan batu (heavy Shorea species) and resak (Cotylelobium spp.), which are used for key structural purposes. Shingles of belian (Eusideroxylon zwageri) had been traditionally used for house roofing, and it was not uncommon for the wood to last 50 or 60 years.

Second category is composed of the medium heavy hardwoods, with densities of 650-880 kg. per cubic meter, strong but which are not naturally durable. These include the kapur (Dryobalanops spp.), keruing (Dipterocarpus spp.), and kempas (Koompassia malaccensis). For places in h wood deterioration is not a problem these timbers can be used as structural material. Otherwise, their durability may be significantly lengthened preservative treatment.

The light hardwoods constitute the third group. These have densities of less 650 kg. per cubic meter, and are used mainly for general purposes. Among the species in this group are the red meranti (Shorea spp.), nyatoh (Sapotaceae species), ramin (Gonystylus spp.), medang (Lauraceae species), and others.

OIL AND GAS

The oil and gas industry remains the fundamental sector in Brunei's economy and it continues to play a dominant role even as the nation strives to diversify into non-oil industrialization.

The government's policy, initiated in 1988, is to conserve this natural resource by reducing production of crude oil to around 150,000 barrels per day (b/d).

At the same time, the search for new reserves and for alternative sources of energy is being intensified.

Brunei Shell Petroleum Sendirian Berhad (BSP) announced a major gas discovery in July 1995 at Selangkir-1 well, which is about 12 kilometers west of the Champion Field.

BSP has seven offshore oil fields, including Champion. The others are Southwest Ampa, Fairley, Fairley-Baram (which is shared with Malaysia), Magpie, Gannet and Iron Duke -BSP's newest field which came on stream in 1992. Two more fields are situated onshore.

The Brunei Government is an equal partner with the Royal Dutch Shell Company. Besides Shell, another active concession holder is Jasra-Elf.

Based in Brunei Darussalam since 1986, the Jasra-Elf Joint Venture has been actively exploring for hydrocarbons offshore and has made some discoveries, in particular in the Maharaja Lela Field (Block B).

Having confirmed technically that there is a significant amount of oil and gas reserves in this field, the Joint Venture is presently concentrating its efforts towards the development and production of these reserves in the most efficient and optimized way.

The country's production of oil reached a peak of 250,000 b/d 1979 but in the Eighties, a ceiling of about 150,000 b/d was introduced. In 1991, production went up to 162,000 b/d, rising to 180,000 b/d in 1992 and falling slightly to 174,000 b/d in 1993.

At the current rate of extraction, it is estimated that the country's oil reserve would run out in about 27 years' time.

Some 40 per cent of the country's reserves are found in the Champion Field, which is situated in 30 meters of water about 70 km north-east of Seria. This field produces more than 50,000 b/d.

The oldest field is Southwest Ampa, 13 kilometers off Kuala Belait. It holds more than half of Brunei's total gas reserves and the gas production accounts for 60 per cent of the country's total output.

The onshore oilfield in Seria, which is the country's first oil well drilled in 1929, still produces around 10,000 b/d used mainly for domestic consumption. On the domestic market, unleaded petrol was introduced in 1992.

The main foreign markets for Brunei's crude oil are Thailand, Singapore, the Philippines, Australia, China, Japan, South Korea, Taiwan and the United States of America.

The contribution of crude oil to the country's Gross Domestic Product has seen a decline from 88 per cent in 1974 to 58 per cent in 1990. In terms of employment, the oil and gas sector's share of the total labor force was only 5 per cent in 1990.

This means it has the highest value-added ratio per worker and labor productivity remains highest among all sectors while its workers are among the highest paid in the country.

Brunei is the world's fourth largest producer of liquefied natural gas (LNG). The current gas production is approximately 27 million cubic meters per day, and 90 per cent of it is exported to Japan, namely the Tokyo Electric, Tokyo Gas and Osaka Gas Companies.

The Japanese companies and Brunei Coldgas of Brunei LNG signed a further 20-year contract in 1993. The new contract is believed to have raised the quantity and price of gas.

The Brunei Liquefied Natural Gas plant in Lumut, one of the largest in the world, was upgraded and expanded at a cost of around B$100 million in 1993.

The LNG from the plant is transported to Japan by a fleet of seven specially-designed 100,000-tonne tankers with a capacity of 73,000 cubic meters of LNG each. The sale of LNG has grown to be as important a revenue earner as oil exports.

The domestic market takes up only 2 per cent of the LNG produced.

At the current rate of production, the proven reserves of natural gas is estimated to last another 40 years.

However, the discoveries of new gas fields and the possibility of more finds will enable Brunei to benefit from the growing demand for LNG in Asia, which is needed primarily for power generation.

Despite the uncertainty that surrounds the global oil market, the hydrocarbon industry looks set to continue to be the beacon of Brunei's economy. The Brunei Petrochemical Industry Master Plan, completed in May 2001, has identified a number of potential petrochemical industries - both upstream and downstream - for development over the next decades.

Brunei has been described as "the next epicenter of deepwater activity in Asia." Deepwater exploration for oil and gas is going on strong in Brunei, with a number of offshore acreages awarded to major prospectors in the industry.
In 1982, Brunei made legal claims to its EEZ, allowing the Sultanate to take measures to tap the wealth potential of its offshore areas. But Brunei has been prospecting offshore for oil since the 1960s. The first offshore discovery was made in 1963, at the South West Ampa Offshore Field.

DEEPWATER DRILLING

Deepwater drilling allows:

1. for the full realisation of the country's potential oil and gas reserves
2. for the tapping of mature fields to their full potential, with the advent of new technologies
3. for the rejuvenation of existing fields and infrastructures

Deepwater prospecting in Brunei takes place in blocks located some 200 kilometres off the country's coastline, but still within its EEZ. Drilling would be conducted into waters between 1.5 to 2.5 kilometres deep.

Brunei is fortunate in that the waters of the South China Sea where the prospecting takes place is rather calm, posing very little or no threat at all to the safety of drilling rigs. Ultra deepwater drilling is, however, relatively new to Brunei. Thus far, only two ultra deepwater blocks - of 10,000 square kilometers each - had been awarded to drilling consortia, consisting of major players in the global oil and gas industry.

TotalFinaElf owns 60% of the consortium that operates in Block J, followed by BHP Billiton with 25% and Amerada Hess with 15%. The Block K group, meanwhile, consists of Shell (50%), Conoco (25%) and Mitsubishi (25%).

An average of 50 producer and injection wells are anticipated for each drilling field, which should result in a massive drilling activity in the next 10 to15 years, involving a very high demand for specialised technology and engineering services.

It is hoped that deepwater-drilling endeavours in Brunei would also result in a transfer of new technology and skills to benefit locals. These activities are also expected to stimulate business activities in support services and create new job opportunities, as well as increase the number of local and international joint venture opportunities.

THE FUTURE OF OIL

Economic and social development in Asia over the next decades will fuel the need for power supply, vis-a-vis oil and gas, to drive generators. Worldwide demand for oil is expected to increase some 60% in the next 25 years, with an "economically buoyant" Asia to lead the rise, said industry experts during the OSEA 2002 oil and gas conference in Singapore in October 2002.

"Energy consumption continues to grow especially in the Asia-Pacific region," an industry captain said. "This growing trend shows a greater increasing demand for gas to be used for power generation and this will continue to fuel the development of offshore oil fields."

Rising demand for oil and gas will drive the sector in the medium and long term, especially in the "increasingly popular" field of deep-sea exploration for natural gas deposits, experts said.

By 2020, Asia will be the largest net importer of oil, "surpassing Europe and North America," said Singapore's Minister of State for Foreign Affairs and Trade, Raymond Lim at the conference. The demand for gas is projected to exceed the demand for oil as well by 2020.

All these bode well for the Brunei hydrocarbons industry, as it endeavours to tap its vast offshore oil and gas potential. The move to explore the deep waters of Brunei presents both risks and opportunities, wrote the Managing Director of TotalFinaElf John Perry in the magazine 'Asia Inc'.

For additional analytical, business and investment opportunities information,
please contact Global Investment & Business Center, USA
at (703) 370-8082. Fax: (703) 370-8083. E-mail: ibpusa3@gmail.com
Global Business and Investment Info Databank - www.ibpus.com

"In their location and required technology, the deep water permits are literally at the frontier of exploration and production activities," he added. "Developing oil and gas fields in 2,000 metres of water is no easy business. It carries significant risk and huge costs, perhaps US$3-4 billion to develop a commercial discovery.

"Yet, the potential is there to succeed."

Success, he said, will take not just the form of a revenue stream for His Majesty's Government, but will also provide a "stable economic base, founded on a global commodity, to enable Brunei's economy to diversify beyond the oil and gas sector."

But the country is not going just upstream with its deepwater ventures. The afore-mentioned Petrochemical Industry Master Plan also has a number of downstream industries that could be developed to complement the new drilling activities in Brunei. For instance, the Plan mentioned methane-based industries like the production of ammonia, urea and methanol from hydrocarbon derivatives; olefins and aromatic derivatives from naphtha crackers, "with the possible integration with a refinery" and energy-intensive activities like aluminium smelting.

DOWNSTREAM ACTIVITIES

Indeed, the Government has set aside two sites for use of such downstream industries. The 1,000sq km Pulau Muara Besar, located just across the Muara deepwater port, will be used for the development of integrated petrochemical projects in the mid-term. In addition, the 230 hectare Sungai Liang site is "readily available for development", complete with existing gas pipelines to the nearby Lumut BLNG plant, as well as the TFE onshore gas processing plant.

The Sungai Liang site is given "priority" for immediate development, especially for stand-alone projects.

The Government agency that oversees the oil and gas industry in Brunei is PetroleumBRUNEI. It was formed in 2001 to:
1. strengthen and to push, and to jointly spearhead the development of the local petroleum industry
2. play a more active role in the exploration and development of the petroleum industry
3. accelerate economic development based on the domestic petroleum industry

Still, "gas is the energy of the future," Perry wrote. The GASEX gathering in May 2002 - a "quality event" which attracted "quality delegates" - was an indication of the high regard Brunei is held in the gas industry.

The Minister of Industry and Primary Resources, Pehin Dato Hj Abd Rahman, in his capacity as chairman of the Brunei Oil and Gas Authority (BOGA), in 2001 said: "The Government of His Majesty continues to place a great importance on the long-term sale of LNG in generating revenue, while at the same time strengthening efforts in diversifying its economy from non-renewable resources.

"Having said that, the government has also ensured that sufficient gas will be made available to fulfil the nation's energy requirements well into the next millennium."

INDUSTRY

The industry sector plays a crucial role in the creation of employment as well as contributing to the country's GDP. Thus, there is a pressing need to expand this sector. Aside from strengthening the oil and gas industry, the economic diversification policy to accelerate the development of the non-oil sector will continue to be implemented in the Eighth National Development Plan (NDP).

The main focus of industrial development is to widen the industrial base through small and medium enterprises. To make this possible, a conducive business environment and attractive investment incentives have been made available.

The development of the Industry sector focuses on activities that could create ample employment opportunities for locals, as well as on areas where the country has a competitive advantage. This includes high technology industries, tourism, and financial services, value-added and export-oriented industries that have the potential to expedite industrial development.

Brunei has drawn up an Industrial Development Plan to help the country diversify its oil-based economy. The plan lists four sectors, which are being actively promoted to attract foreign investors. They are; Manufacturing, Primary Resources, Services and Human Resources.

THE MANUFACTURING SECTOR
The growth rate for the manufacturing/quarrying sector decreased from 4.1% in 1996 to 3.5% in 2004, while its contribution to the GDP increased from 3.2% to 3.5% during the corresponding period.

Statistics for the Manufacturing/Quarrying Sector

Year	% Contributin	% Growth
1999	3.6	2.3
2004	3.5	3.1
2001*	3.8	3.2
2002*	3.9	4.0

Note: * Provisional

THE GARMENT INDUSTRY

The Garment Industry has expanded rapidly with the whole production geared for export. Ready-made garments provide the country's second largest exports after oil and gas. In 1999, the value of exports of ready-made garments was $211.6 million, which increased by 43.7% to $304.0 million in 2004. In 2001, the value of exports was around $396 million.
The increase in export was due to the setting up of new factories and the expansion of existing ones. In 2004, there were nine garment factories in operation. 99% of the ready-made garments have been exported to the United States of America, Canada and the European Union.

Statistics for Garment Export in Brunei Darussalam

Destination	1999	2004	2001
ASEAN	77,435,423	115,723,745	152,517,081

For additional analytical, business and investment opportunities information, please contact Global Investment & Business Center, USA at (703) 370-8082. Fax: (703) 370-8083. E-mail: ibpusa3@gmail.com
Global Business and Investment Info Databank - www.ibpus.com

EU 322,920 981,990 1,556,660

Rest of the world 133,845,493 193,257,199 131,769,643

TOTAL 211,604,836 309,962,934 285,843,384

OTHER EXPORT-ORIENTED PRODUCTS

Apart from producing ready-made garments for export, other products produced locally include construction materials such as roofing and cement, mineral water, electrical products, electrical cables and wire, furniture, food and beverages.

To attract more foreign investments into the country, Brunei Darussalam's attractions will be improved through the provision of sites equipped with all the basic facilities, plus provision of incentive packages and other related packages that are transparent, fast and effective.

The primary resources sector includes agriculture (poultry, fruits and vegetables, and floriculture), fishery (which includes capture fishing and aquaculture), forestry (which includes the fields of eco-tourism and biotechnology) and integrated production like poultry, farming and product processing.

The primary sectors comprising agriculture, fisheries and forestry grew by 2.3% in 2001, up from 1.8% in 2004. The agriculture and fisheries sectors provided the main impetus for growth where the agriculture sector grew by 2.9% from 1.7%, while the fisheries sector fell by 2.5% from 2.6% in the previous year.

THE TOURISM INDUSTRY
Besides export-oriented activities, tourism is also one of the industries that is being promoted as part of the overall diversification programme. In 2001, the restaurants and hotels sector grew at 2.5% which indicated an improvement from the 1.8% growth in 2004. The growth is largely due to Visit 'Brunei Year 2001'.

To further strengthen the development of the tourism industry, a tourism master plan has been commissioned and implemented. The master plan outlines strategies for promoting the industry that includes the provision of facilities, places of interests and development of human resources in spearheading the industry.

HIGH TECHNOLOGY INDUSTRY
For the high technology industry, the targeted areas to be developed are the telecommunications, computer software, biotechnology and value-added industries such as food processing, multimedia industry and information technology. These industries are suitable in view of the small but educated and skilful local workforce.

INDUSTRIAL DEVELOPMENT

To support industrial development, a total area of 705 hectares was allocated for industrial sites in all the four districts, with 289 hectares in the Brunei-Muara district, 371 hectares in the Belait district, 40 hectares in the Tutong district and 5 hectares in the Temburong district.

All these industrial sites are managed by BINA except for the 283 hectares (of the 371 hectares) in the Belait district, which is managed by the Petroleum Unit. By the end of 2004, a total of 277 hectares (66%) out of the 422 hectares under BINA's management had been developed and allocated to the various industries.

HUMAN RESOURCE DEVELOPMENT

Total employment grew by 1.9% in 2001 to 144,000 as a result of a favourable economic growth performance of 1.5%. Close to 3,000 new jobs were created. The overall labour force participation rate in 2004 was 65.1% with an increase in the participation rate of women from 55.1% in 2004 to 55.5% in 2001. During the same period, the participation rate of men also showed an increase from 73.8% in 2004 to 74.2% in 2001. However, from 2004 to 2001, the unemployment rate remained at 4.7%.

The human resource development strategies under the Eighth NDP will focus on meeting the needs of the new knowledge based economy and skills in the field of technology. It will also focus on increasing productivity, enhancing labour mobility through training and retraining and upgrading the quality of education. Steps will be taken to accelerate local manpower supply at professional, management, technical and skill levels particularly in selected industrial activities.

ECONOMIC DIVERSIFICATION

To realise the Government's objective of economic diversification through the development of the non-oil sector, the continuous proactive involvement of the private sector needs to be sustained and widened.

Thus, the Government through the various relevant agencies will continue its efforts to create a more advantageous investment climate through the existing rules and regulations and creating new ones, if necessary.

Facilities for private sector development such as industrial sites, financial assistance schemes and attractive incentives will be expanded. Such measures are expected to accelerate further industrial development programmes and attract more foreign direct investments into the country.

At the same time, the Government through the Ministry of Industry and Primary resources has established a Resource Centre and Standards to assist small and medium enterprises.

SMALL BUSINESS

The Government recognises the strategic role that SMEs play in the overall economic growth and diversification of the country. Data obtained from the Department of Economic Planning and Development reveals that in 1994, SMEs in Brunei accounted for approximately 98% of all active business enterprises.

SMEs contribute 92% of employment in the private sector and a little over 66% of the country's GDP in the non-oil sector of the economy. The Government expects SMEs to continue to play a pivotal role in the country's economic development in this new millennium.

SMEs, in the context of Brunei, are businesses with between one to 100 employees. However, statistics reveal that a majority of businesses in Brunei are micro-enterprises (between one to five employees) and small enterprises (between six to 50). Micro-enterprises account for 43% of SMEs, while small enterprises account for 53% and lastly medium enterprises account for 4% of them.

HISTORICAL DEVELOPMENT

The present policies on SMEs are those enunciated in the Industrial Development Plan Report of 1995. This report identifies Enterprise and Entrepreneurship Development Programmes as a means to expand economic growth and diversification and proposes the establishment of an Entrepreneurship Development Centre to lead the Government's programme on SME development.

The significant role of SMEs in economic growth & diversification was further recognised and highlighted in the Seventh National Development Plan (1996-2004). The Plan pinpointed the need to establish a Resource Centre (now called Resource and Standard Centre).

The Centre, located at Sinaut Agricultural Training Centre, focuses on the development of SMEs and on product standards monitoring. It also provides services such as counselling, training, incubation scheme, seminars, workshops and short courses particularly on finance, management and technical areas.

The Government plan acknowledges that Brunei's SMEs are the engine of the country's economic growth and development in the next millennium. On May 2, 1996, His Majesty The Sultan and Yang Di-Pertuan of Brunei Darussalam consented to the establishment of the Resource Centre in the Ministry of Industry and Primary Resources.

On January 5, 1997 the Honourable Minister of Industry and Primary Resources made a formal public announcement of the establishment of the Resource Centre. The Centre has been established to act as a nucleus for the growth and development of small and medium enterprises (SMEs) in Brunei Darussalam. To achieve its vision and mission to promote entrepreneurship and SME development, it has been given 10 functions.

BDEC

In 1998, the Brunei Darussalam Economic Council (BDEC) was organised. BDEC is the highest economic policy making body of the Government.

This was formed in response to the Asian financial crisis in 1997 and is tasked with implementing various programmes that would lead to the economic recovery and sustainable long-term development of the economy.

According to the strategies as mapped out in the Eighth National Development Plan 2001-2005, the Government - through the Resource and Standards Centre - is taking several measures, such as designing the business facility scheme focusing on agriculture, fisheries, manufacturing and tourism sectors for the development of SMEs.

The scheme provides loans to local entrepreneurs at a reducing rate of 4% per annum with a loan limit of B$1.5 million per company. BDEC has also recommended to the Government to provide a special allocation of B$200 million to assist SMEs. This allocation is to be used to create the financial credit fund scheme implemented by the eight appointed locally established banks.

ENTREPRENEURIAL DEVELOPMENT UNIT
The entrepreneurial development unit was set up at Universiti Brunei Darussalam (UBD) in March 2004, in view of the importance of human resource development to the growth of industry and commerce.

For additional analytical, business and investment opportunities information,
please contact Global Investment & Business Center, USA
at (703) 370-8082. Fax: (703) 370-8083. E-mail: ibpusa3@gmail.com
Global Business and Investment Info Databank - www.ibpus.com

The unit does not only provide academic course but also practical ones such as small business management, entrepreneurial and business development, financial strategy, planning and information technology (IT).

It also undertakes a strategic plan study for the development of local Malays in the industrial sector.

SME POLICY MEASURES

For sustained economic growth, BDEC in its report recommends a 10-policy measure that would impact on SME development.
1. Streamline Government expenditures
2. Expand and stabilise Government revenues
3. Launch privatisation plan
4. Launch investment promotion drive
5. Create wider participation in Brunei Darussalam's economy
6. Expand and improve competitiveness of the oil and gas industry
7. Enhance the capabilities of local SMEs
8. Strengthen and modernise institutions
9. Launch national productivity drive
10. Enhance human resources development and deployment

ACTION ITEMS FOR IMPLEMENTATION

To enhance the capabilities of local SMEs for sustained economic growth, the BDEC report has listed six specific action items for implementation. These areas are shown below:

1. Expand existing financial assistance programmes for SMEs
2. Strengthen the role and capabilities of the Resource and Standards Centre in providing support for SMEs
3. Establish a fund to assist SMEs in securing professional support in upgrading their management capabilities
4. Improve the structure of Government contracts and tenders by packaging them to facilitate SME participation
5. Expand the efforts of Brunei Shell and others in helping to develop local technical and managerial capabilities
6. Strengthen the capacity and professionalism of the Chambers of Commerce in representing and providing marketing support to businesses operating in Brunei Darussalam

PROGRAMMES FOR SMEs
SMEs in Brunei have several avenues for support services, both from Government and non-government bodies.

The specific programmes for SMEs by the Ministry of Industry and Primary Resources are implemented primarily through the Resource and Standards Centre. Other divisions and departments within the Ministry such as the Departments of Agriculture, Fisheries, Forestry and BINA (Brunei Industrial Development Authority) have sector-specific programmes.

Other Government agencies such as the Ministries of Education and Development, University of Brunei Darussalam (UBD), and regional organisations (ASEAN-EC Management Centre, SEAMEO-Voctech), private companies (Brunei Shell Petroleum Company Sdn Bhd (BSP) and the non-Government organisation, Young Entrepreneurs Association of Brunei Darussalam (YEAB) have programmes that support entrepreneurship development.

THE LIST OF MAJOR PROGRAMMES FOR SMES

· Entrepreneurship Development Programme
· Enterprise Development Programme
· Financial Assistance Schemes
· Information Support Programme
· Standards Programme
· Research and Development Programme
· Technology Development Programme
· Linkage Programme

E-COMMERCE

SMEs in Brunei are encouraged to take advantage of Information Technology by engaging their business through e-commerce as it would help to expand their business locally and abroad.

PREFERRED INDUSTRIES FOR SMES TO VENTURE

1. Agriculture - vegetables, fruits, landscape plants, herbs and spices etc
2. Fisheries - Fish (off or onshore), aquaculture (fish and crustaceans) and expanding stock
3. Forestry - Tree plantation, non-timber products, reforestation
4. Manufacturing of food products - dairy and beverage products
5. Manufacturing of machineries and electronic and electrical appliances
6. Printing industry - Printed material, signages and advertisements
7. Manufacturing of garment products
8. Manufacturing of chemical tree: colouring materials, paint, varnish, fertiliser and soap.

TARGETTED SECTORS FOR GROWTH

The targeted sectors for growth as projected in the Eighth National Development Plan for the years 2001-2005 are the export-oriented industries and export specialised services such as engineering, Islamic banking, economy, laws, accounting, architecture, estate management and others.

Other sectors targeted for growth include the services and trade sectors (construction, transport and communications, finance and banking, insurance, wholesale and retail), tourism services, high technology (telecommunications, computer software, biotechnology, value added industries like food processing, multimedia industries etc) and manufacturing.

The Government will continue its efforts in developing the growth of SMEs in Brunei through several programmes. These programmes include an industry and business incubator scheme, adoption of international standards by SMEs, IT programmes and technical and management training programmes for entrepreneurs.

Financially, apart from the ongoing financial assistance provided by the selected local banks, other forms of financial assistance in the form of micro credit will also be created to encourage and support new players to run their business.

HOME IMPROVEMENT

When initiating improvements to the home, it is still a matter of personal interest whether one chooses contemporary or vintage designs or just adds to existing furnishings.

For additional analytical, business and investment opportunities information,
please contact Global Investment & Business Center, USA
at (703) 370-8082. Fax: (703) 370-8083. E-mail: ibpusa3@gmail.com
Global Business and Investment Info Databank - www.ibpus.com

In Brunei Darussalam, the market for teak furniture has grown over the years. Teak, renowned for its longevity, is said to require low maintenance and is extremely durable. Requiring little or no care, it will maintain its lustre and beauty for decades.

Teak is also ideal for use as outdoor furniture due to the immense stability of the timber, which has high oil content and 'built in' natural water repellent. These qualities make it rot-resistant.

In Brunei, retailers of teak furniture usually own a factory in Indonesia where teak trees are grown for the sole purpose of construction and furniture production. The Dutch first grew teak trees in plantations in Indonesia in 1816. Today it is still controlled by the Indonesian Government.

Teak is the common name for Tectona Grandis from the family Verbenaceae, a native of India, Myanmar (Burma), and Thailand. The Tectona Grandis tree matures to a height of 46-m (150 ft) with a straight trunk. Leaves are similar to that of tobacco leaves and grow to approximately 30cm (1ft) in length by approximately 30cm (1ft) in width. The tree also produces many small white flowers. The bark of the tree is grey and the trunk has white sapwood. The "heartwood" or timber of the teak tree is a yellow brown color.

Teakwood gained its fame from the early times as a valuable resource due to its long life, reliability, weather resistant characteristics and workable qualities. The wood is probably most well known for its use in boat building, wharves and bridges as well as fine furniture, Venetian blinds and veneers. The name 'Teak' also refers specifically to the wood and its characteristic color, which ranges from olive to yellowish grey or moderate brown.

The history of teak furniture dates back to the 19th century when the Chinese exported it to Europe. The Victorian era incorporated the use of the wood to the mechanical era of the 1840's with the invention of the presses, veneer cutters and so on. These tools and machines enabled artisans to create decorative, elegant high-class furniture. With fine craftsmanship and hand sanding, combined with the latest technology, teak furniture can bring a quality and finish that is astounding. The only maintenance necessary is periodic cleaning which can be done with a solution of four parts laundry detergent or dishwashing soap and one part bleach.

Most of the teak furniture shops in Brunei cater to the needs of its people who fancy distinctive designs and styles. Their extensive selection of teak furniture may include something for every room in the house to decorations in the garden.

Bruneian customers may place orders at shops for their teak furniture to be handcrafted according to their own taste or style. Such is the role played by teak in beautifying the home.

Apart from teakwood, rattan is also a popular and exotic choice. Casual yet elegant, it distinctive style improves one's home.

Rattan is a palm that grows like a vine with long, barbed leaves. It has a bark-covered stalk that can reach up to 200 metres, while measuring only half to four centimetres in diameter. Both the bark and the stalk are used in furniture production, so nothing is wasted.

The bark, cut into long strips, is used for the seats and backs of chairs. The bamboo-like stalk is used for the main structure of the furniture. Furthermore, it can be cut into strips to create various designs to accent the furniture.

Rattan is extremely pliable when steamed or heated with a blowtorch. It can then be shaped to create a variety of unique designs without cracking or splintering.

Rattan or rattan combined with leather, wrought iron, glass and fabric are among the many designs available in furniture shops in Brunei. This, combined with a variety of choice lighting and elegant fixtures and fittings, make a typical house in Brunei, a distinguished and very individualised home.

AUTOMOBILES

According to the official statistics of the Land Transport Department, car sales in Brunei in the first half of 2002 (January to June) exceeded the overall sales in 2001. The number of vehicles registered from January to June 2002 reached 5,372 compared to only 2,436 vehicles registered during the same period in 2001, exceeding the total sales figure of 2001 (from January to December) which amounted to 5,222 vehicles.

RISING CAR SALES
The statistics also revealed that private cars and multi-purpose vehicles (MPV) were the two most popular items with a total sale of 3,111 and 1,905 vehicles respectively in the first half of this year.

From January to December 2001, the total sales figure of private cars and MPV's were 3,207 and 1,493 cars. The statistics also showed that a record number of 810 vehicles were registered in December 2001 alone, possibly a result of the import duty slash which took effect in November 2001.

Since then, the automobile industry has seen dramatic results. In November 2001 when Brunei was hosting the Asean Summit, His Majesty The Sultan and Yang Di-Pertuan of Brunei Darussalam made an announcement that the car import duty, which was at a sky high 200% in previous years, was to be cut to a flat rate of 20% and 15% for heavy duty vehicles.

THE DUTY IN PREVIOUS YEARS
The import duty for cars once ranged from 40, 60, 80, 100 and 200 per cent depending on engine capacities. Statistics revealed that because of these duties, the car to population ratio in Brunei had decreased from one car for every 3.15 people in 1996 to one car for every 2.94 people in 2001.

It was in 1995 that drastic duties were suddenly imposed on cars, resulting in heavier payments for car buyers in the country. Many preferred the cheaper alternative such as reconditioned cars and used cars. With this imposition, old vehicles were a common sight on Brunei streets.

Today, dealers, distributors and customers are reveling in the good news. Ever since the tax reduction, dealers have been expressing their delight. One even said, "now I can see the light over the horizon."

BENEFITS REAPED

Other benefits from the car sales include more employment opportunities for the locals in the automobile industry and a reduction of second hand and older cars on the road.

With the new ruling, many new car models were launched in the Brunei market in 2002, among which were popular models such as multi-purpose vehicles (MPVs), sports utility vehicle (SUVs) and 4-Wheel Drive off-road vehicles. The large cars are the more popular variety due in part to the large size of Bruneian families and also to the frequency of over-the-border weekend trips to Kota Kinabalu, Limbang and Miri.

For additional analytical, business and investment opportunities information, please contact Global Investment & Business Center, USA at (703) 370-8082. Fax: (703) 370-8083. E-mail: ibpusa3@gmail.com Global Business and Investment Info Databank - www.ibpus.com

But while the country was rejoicing in the resurgence of its car industry, some unscrupulous dealers took advantage of the loopholes.

RULES CONTRAVENED
To counter this, the Licensing Authority of the Land Transport Department urged all car dealers to provide a place for their showroom and a place to store their vehicles while showing clearly, the price list of all their vehicles. This is to allow the public to scrutinise the cars and to make an informed decision before buying, or risk action that may result in their licenses being revoked or cancelled as stated under the 1978 Chapter 2 of the Miscellaneous Licenses Act.

The Economic Planning Unit has also fixed the price of vehicles as part of the Government's efforts to re-establish the local car industry and to protect consumers rights.

It is now compulsory for dealers to get new vehicle price certificates approved by the Economic Planning Unit, which must be displayed clearly at the showroom. Other than displaying the showroom price and the on-the-road-price, the certificate must also contain the date the on-the-road-price of the vehicle was approved. Buyers are urged to see the certificates and verify the expiry date of the offer.

Another new rule was also put in place to used car agents. The Land Transport Department has urged used car agents to provide after sales service and to operate with a proper workshop.

BANKING AND FINANCE

The Borneo Bulletin reported on September 23, 2002 that through the Brunei International Financial Centre (BIFC), Brunei hopes to "become a more relaxed Singapore, with a touch of Bahrain."

In that same report, the head of supervision at the BIFC, Robert Miller, was quoted to say that Brunei "draws hope" from Bermuda - the second largest reinsurance market after London - as it endeavours to develop itself as a major global financial centre.

The Dow Jones newswires was quoted as saying that Brunei is shaping itself to "compete for a share of ... Islamic funds as part of its strategy to diversify away from its reliance on the oil and gas industries." It was estimated that investment funds from Islamic countries reach US$1 trillion.

A large part of these funds need to be invested along Islamic principles, the report went on, "which means they cannot be parked in interest-bearing debt instruments or companies involved in unIslamic activities like producing and marketing alcohol, or in gaming or gambling activities."

The US$129 million tanker financing facility, led-managed by HSBC out of Brunei and involving some banks from the Middle East, was cited by Miller as "another step in the development of Brunei Darussalam as a financial centre."

ISLAMIC BANKING

Islamic investments do not allow:
· Al-riba (usury)
· Al-maisir (gambling). Al-maisir arises as a result of al-gharar, as for example, guaranteeing dividends after a certain period of time, without due regard to the business outcome
· Al-gharar (unknown or uncertain factors in the operation of a contract). According to an Islamic

scholar, al-gharar occurs when one party takes what is due to him, but the other party does not receive his entitlement. It also pertains to such uncertainties like, whether the insured person gets the promised compensation; how much benefit would the insured person get; and when would the compensation be paid?

Although Muslims are encouraged to do business, including financial endeavours, they must do so by mutual consent and not make money through unfair and unlawful means. Islam seeks to ensure justice, equity and fair play in all business dealings.

Takaful (Islamic insurance) in business transactions actually refers to "joint guarantees." It is an act whereby a group of people reciprocally guarantees each other against losses or damages caused by acts of calamities in which the needy would need to be given financial compensation.

Takaful contracts are based on al-mudharabah, which means "the sharing of profits in business." If, for example, there were to be a nett surplus in an operator's takaful fund - after the deduction of expenses, claims and other expenses - the profit would then be shared between the operator and its clients, according to the principle of al-mudharabah upon the expiry of the respective policies, at a ratio stipulated beforehand.

Dow Jones, meanwhile, reported that Brunei is "actively encouraging financial firms to set up operations while developing mechanisms to help entrepreneurs tap the large pool of Islamic money available for investments."

CHALKING MILESTONES
The Sultanate's first securities exchange, the International Brunei Exchange (IBX) was launched in the second half of 2002. Its establishment was described as "another building block in the creation of Brunei's e-finance network," the report said.

Brunei's moves can best be summarised by the country's Foreign Affairs Minister, HRH Prince Mohamed Bolkiah, in his address during an official dinner in London, in late September 2002 who said, "As far as we are concerned, we are hoping to find a special niche for Brunei Darussalam in the regional and even the global economy."

The IBX has been described by the business magazine 'Asia Inc' as a pan-Asian virtual market place where dealers from around the region's capital markets can trade international share futures, derivatives and Islamic instruments, while offering all the services investors would expect of a stock exchange - including the opportunity to buy shares in listed local and international companies.

A Developing Enterprises Equity Market (DEEM) would also be created "to help companies raise equity from investors prior to an IPO."

The setting up of a regional office in Bandar Seri Begawan by the Bahrain-based Emerging Markets Partnership marked yet another milestone as Brunei inches its way to becoming a major financial player. EMP is a "leading global adviser" to private infrastructure funds, and manager to the $1.5 billion Islamic Development Bank Infrastructure Fund.

Brunei offers financial investors four types of banking license, namely:
1. full international banking
2. international investment banking
3. international Islamic banking
4. a restricted banking license

To counter the possibility of money laundering, the Sultanate has incorporated laws to protect investors, so much so that "If you're a criminal, Brunei is not for you, " as BIFC head of supervision Miller says of these laws.

BRUNEI'S STRONG BUYING POWER

Bruneians have strong buying-power. The country's 340,000 residents have a GDP per capita of US$13,500. Furthermore, the Government-run Brunei Investment Agency (BIA), as it seeks to invest country's wealth, has plenty at its disposal - from the country's oil and gas revenue, the workers' provident fund (TAP) and numerous other sources of income.

All these make "an attractive bait for fund managers considering setting up in Brunei" said a local entrepreneur. It is probably for these reasons that the Royal Bank of Canada (RBC) opened a branch here in Brunei in July 2002 - the first institution to win the BIFC's foreign bank license.

Matthew Yong, the deputy regional head of sales says, "With the investment in modern communications and business infrastructure and with so many direct links to important financial centres like Singapore, Hong Kong and London, Brunei has much to offer to the international financial services community."

Brunei also has the added advantage of having a very stable political scene; a sound and independent legal structure based on the British common law; a proper regulatory infrastructure; and widespread use of English among its well-educated populace, complemented by a wealth of lawyers and accountants.

The Brunei branch of RBC - Canada's largest bank by both assets and market capitalisation, and one of the world's top 50 financial institutions - forms a part of its global private banking division, and offers wealth management as well as private banking services to "high nett worth private individuals throughout Asia and the Middle East." (Movie buffs will remember RBC as the financier for many of Hollywood's top movies and TV shows).

THE BANKING SECTOR

The Ministry of Finance - through the Currency Board, the Financial Institutional Unit and the Brunei Investment Agency - performs the functions of a central bank in the country.

The Currency Board issues the local currency, and is responsible for maintaining monetary stability. The Financial Institutional Unit, meanwhile, acts as the principal licensing and monitoring agency for the country's banks and financial companies. The Brunei Association of Banks sets the Prime Lending Rate.

The Sultanate currently has nine commercial banks operating branches throughout Brunei, including three locally incorporated financial institutions. However, the number is expected to increase as investors in the banking industry become aware of the plethora of opportunities offered by the country.

Strong competition among banks has resulted in a variety of banking facilities designed to benefit customers while enticing more patronage. Common among these facilities is what could be best described as "wealth management," to use a term by the Standard Chartered Bank (SCB).

INVESTMENT SERVICES

Practically all banks in Brunei provide investment services. And with connections to major financial institutions overseas, customers are assured of the best possible "opportunities," to quote the Hongkong and Shanghai Banking Corp (HSBC).

One of the bigger investment services providers is the Perbadanan Tabung Amanah Islam Brunei (TAIB). The Brunei government had invested B$10 million as a grant for TAIB's establishment in 1991, although the number of locals specialising in Islamic financial management was at that time very minimal.

In the first quarter of 2002 alone, TAIB held 10% of the assets and 8% of the deposits of the whole market share of all Islamic financial institutions in Brunei.

Today, TAIB has a workforce of 210 and has four branches, in Kuala Belait, Sengkurong and Kiulap and the newly opened Lambak branch.

Meanwhile, Both the Asian and Global Equity Funds by the Islamic Bank of Brunei (IBB), seek "to maximise capital growth through investing primarily in equities of companies" while achieving "long-term capital growth and preservation through investing worldwide in all major markets."

The SCB's Total Money Management Solutions (TMMS) is about "proactively ensuring that (the customers') money works hard through all eventualities. It is about helping (the customers) make the most of what (they) have today through the process of financial planning."

The Islamic Development Bank of Brunei (IDBB) "provides financing to corporate and small-and-medium-sized enterprises (SMEs)."It is also a commercial bank, operating as a "fully-corporatised Government-owned financial institution."

SME SCHEMES
The aim of the service is "to encourage and assist local enterprises to upgrade, modernise and expand their operation" while offering "new opportunities to support the growth of SMEs, and to expand employment opportunity" in the country.

The SMEs financing scheme comes under:
a. The Enterprise Facilitation Scheme - for ventures in agriculture, fisheries, manufacturing and tourism;
b. The Working Capital Credit Fund - which is targeted at entrepreneurs with projects in low-cost housing, tourism services, information technology et al;
c. The Microcredit Financing Scheme - to support the growth of small/micro socio-economy, and open up employment opportunities in Brunei, via financial assistance to SMEs.

The positive outlook of Brunei's economic future - helped by the introduction of the ASEAN Free Trade Agreement (AFTA); proximity to the large markets of China and Northeast Asia, as well as of India and the Asian sub-continent; and bright prospects for strong economic growth within the region - makes the country a potential gold mine for financial investors.

The local banks, through their financial facilities, participate actively to promote domestic economic activity. Coupled with "continuous support" from the Government to realise local enterprise, the prospects for economic development in Brunei are expected to improve in the years to come.

As part of efforts to revive the local economy, the Brunei Darussalam Economic Council (BDEC) has organised several stimulus packages under its Short Term Economic Recovery Plan. The Working Capital Credit Fund launched on January 17, 2004 was such a measure.

The Fund, with its $20 million provision pledged by local banks, "provides Small and Medium Enterprises (with) access to low-interest Government-backed loans to improve their liquidity and capability to participate in economic recovery projects as well as undertake productive economic activity."

The opening of the Development Bank of Brunei this year brings to nine the number of banks operating in Brunei Darussalam.

The locally incorporated banks are the Islamic Bank of Brunei Berhad, Baiduri Bank Bhd and Development Bank of Brunei while the rest are branches of foreign banks.

Significant banks in terms of operations are Hongkong and Shanghai Banking Corporation, the Standard Chartered Bank and Citibank, among others.

Banks have been encouraged to support local businessmen in their endeavour to engage in industrial activities. His Majesty the Sultan Yang Di-Pertuan Negara Brunei Darussalam, when launching the Islamic Bank of Brunei Berhad (IBB) in 1993, said the establishment of IBB was one of ways of applying Islamic practices into the financial administration and management of the country.

Prior to its establishment, it functioned as the International Bank of Brunei under the same acronym IBB.The government, under the Banking Act and the Finance Companies Act, regulates the banking industry.

The Ministry of Finance closely regulates all banking activities to assure a stable and fiscally sound business environment.

There is no central bank in Brunei. However, its functions are undertaken by the Department of Financial Services (Treasury), the Brunei Currency Board and the Brunei Investment Agency. All come under the jurisdiction of the Ministry of Finance.

The Brunei dollar is at par with the Singapore dollar, and both are freely traded in their respective countries. There are no exchange controls in Brunei, except in the case of capital or profits to be repatriated to a country outside the "Scheduled Territories" of the Sterling area, for which permission must be obtained from the Currency Board.

The first banking facility started more than 50 years ago when the government set up the Post Office Savings Bank (POSB) in 1935. The POSB was destroyed during the Japanese occupation and all records were lost. It reopened in 1946 but was finally shut down in 1978 when it was felt that numerous other banks were offering comparable services.

BANKS OPERATING IN BRUNEI:

Citibank NA
12-15 Bang Darussalam
Bandar Seri Begawan
Tel: 02-243983 Fax: 02-225704

Hongkong and Shanghai Bank Corp
Main Office:
Jalan Sultan/Jalan Pemancha
General Office: Tel: 02-242305/10, 02-242204 Fax: 02-241316

Baiduri Bank Bhd
145 Jalan Permancha

PO Box 220, Bandar Seri Begawan 1922
Tel: 02-233233 Fax: 02-237575

Islamic Bank of Brunei Bhd
Head Office:
Bangunan IBB Lot 155, Jalan Roberts
PO Box 2725, Bandar Seri Begawan 1927
Tel: 02-220686, 221692, 220676
Fax: 02-221470

Development Bank of Brunei Bhd
1st Floor RBA Plaza, Jalan Sutlan BSB 2085
PO Box 3080 , Bandar Seri Begawan 1930
Tel: 02-233430
Fax: 233429

Malayan Banking Berhad
148 Jalan Permancha
Bandar Seri Begawan 2085
Tel: 02-242494 Telex: BU 2316

Overseas Union Bank Ltd
Unit G5 RBA Plaza, Bandar Seri Begawan
Tel: 02-225477 Fax: 02-240792

Standard Chartered Bank
Main Office:
51-55 Jalan Sultan
General Office: Tel 02-242386 Fax: 02-242390

United Malayan Banking Corporation Berhad
141 Jalan Permancha
Bandar Seri Begawan
Tel: 02-222516 Fax: 02-237487

INSURANCE

Every member of the community in his day to day life is invariably exposed to the possibility of encountering incidents which give rise to misfortunes and tragedies such as injury, death, fire, motor accidents and so on.

A Muslim believes any catastrophe that befalls him as 'Qadha' and 'Qadar' from Allah, and he must face these events of ill luck with strength of faith and patience.

Nevertheless, it is also the duty of every Muslim to find ways and means to legitimately avoid such incidents of misfortunate wherever possible, and to lighten his or her family's burden should such events occur.

A takaful policy is an Islamic form of cover that a Muslim can avail himself of as a means of protection against consequences of catastrophe. Brunei Darussalam now has three takaful operators, namely:

For additional analytical, business and investment opportunities information,
please contact Global Investment & Business Center, USA
at (703) 370-8082. Fax: (703) 370-8083. E-mail: ibpusa3@gmail.com
Global Business and Investment Info Databank - www.ibpus.com

1. Insurans Islam TAIB Sdn Bhd
2. Takaful IBB Berhad and
3. Takaful IDBB Sdn Bhd

INSURANS ISLAM TAIB
Insurans Islam TAIB Sdn Bhd (IITSB) is a wholly owned subsidiary company of Perbadanan Tabung Amanah Islam Brunei (TAIB) and it provides Islamic insurance products in Brunei Darussalam. This company was established on 3rd March 1993 when it was first known as Takaful TAIB Sdn Bhd. On 11th June 1997, Takaful TAIB Sdn Bhd changed its name to Insurans Islam TAIB Sdn Bhd (IITSB).

TAKAFUL IBB SDN BHD
Takaful IBB Berhad, established on 5 May 1993, is one of the Islamic insurance companies in Brunei. It is limited by shares incorporated under the Companies Act, 1957 with an authorised capital of B$20 million and a paid up capital of B$10.2 million. At present, there are already nine branches in service in all districts with Kiarong as its main office.

TAKAFUL IDBB SDN BHD
Takaful IDBB Sdn Bhd is a new subsidiary company of the Islamic Development Bank of Brunei Berhad. It was launched on 1st March 2001 and is intended to further complement the takaful and insurance industry in Brunei with the belief in educating individuals and the community about its services and its ltimate protection plans. Its main branch is situated at the Setia Kenangan Complex in Kiulap.

TYPES OF POLICIES
Essentially these Takaful operators offer two types of policies:
- Savings plan which cover losses against untimely death under family takaful and
- General takaful which covers disasters against fire, theft, etc.

Each takaful operator offers a variety of schemes and plans for individuals, groups and companies. The contributions (premiums) are price-value leaders for the services provided and this has made takaful operators the benchmark in the insurance industry orders.

The participation by Muslims in these takaful policies offered by the takaful operators is in full compliance with the Islamic syariah law where the main concern in takaful is to avoid these three elements:
- AL RIBA - the practice of Al-Riba (or interest) and other related practices in investment activities, which contravene the rules of the syariah
- AL MAISIR - the element of Al-Maisir (or gambling) which arises as a consequence of the presence of Al-Gharar (uncertain factor). An example is a promised profit at a certain period of time
- AL GHARAR - the element of Al-Gharar (unknown or uncertain factor in the operation of a contract) in contracts. According to Ibn Taymiyyah, 'gharar' occurs when one party takes what is due to him but the other does not receive his entitlement. Gharar also pertains to 'deliverability' of the subject matter, that is uncertainty as to:
1. Whether the insured will get the compensation promised
2. How much the insured will get?
3. When the compensation will be paid?

WHY GHARAR IS PROHIBITED
The reason why the Holy Prophet prohibited 'gharar' in any business contract is obviously to ensure that one party does not have unfair advantage over the other. There are numerous verses

in the Quran and examples from the sunnah of the Holy prophet to support the fact that Islam seeks to ensure justice, equity and fair play in all business dealings.

Although Muslims are encouraged to do business, they must do so by mutual consent and not to make money by unfair and unlawful means.

WHAT IS THE FUNCTION OF TAKAFUL?
It is one of the many ways to manage risk and is an effective risk transfer/homogenisation mechanism. It functions as a social device where the fortunate may compensate the unfortunate few with a financial solution to a financial problem.

HOW DOES TAKAFUL CONTRIBUTE TO THE SOCIETY?
In view of the necessity to provide cover against misfortunes to Muslims, Muslim jurists conducted a detailed study with a view of designing an alternative form of cover, which strictly conforms to the rules of the syariah. On the basis of this study, the Muslims jurists unanimously agreed that a cover which fits the requirements of the syariah be based on the Islamic concepts of takaful.

Takaful in this context means 'joint guarantee'. It is an act where groups of people reciprocally guarantee each other against losses or damages caused by any catastrophe or disaster whereby the needy will be given financial compensation.

Under this concept, a takaful company will provide takaful plans and schemes for both Family takaful and General takaful for the benefit of any member of the community who wishes to participate in the takaful programme. The contract of takaful is based on the principle of Al-Mudharabah, which is the sharing of profit in business.

HOW IS THE FUND MANAGED IN TAKAFUL?
Al-Mudharabah is derived in an altruistic and benevolent manner with the takaful operators fund managing in the following ways:

The contributions from the participants of General takaful scheme will be pooled into the General takaful Fund. This fund will be invested in any investment approved in accordance to syariah guidelines.

The profits received from the investments will be ploughed back into the fund where it is used to cover all the operational and administrative costs of General takaful , for example claims, retakaful costs and any cost related to it.

If there is a surplus from this fund, the surplus will then be shared between participants and the takaful operators. The ratio of surplus shared (depending on the ratio stipulated by takaful operators) is at the rate of 50:50; i.e. the participants will receive 50% from the surplus and 50% to takaful operators.

MANAGEMENT OF FAMILY TAKAFUL FUND
All installments contributed by the participants participating in the Family takaful Plan will be pooled into the Family takaful Fund. The fund will be divided into two accounts, namely the Participant's Account (PA) and Participant's Special Account (PSA).

This fund will also be invested through investment instruments or Islamic counters approved by syariah principles. The takaful operator and its participants will share profits earned from the investments according to the principles of Al-Mudharabah with the ratio as per agreed. The Al-

For additional analytical, business and investment opportunities information,
please contact Global Investment & Business Center, USA
at (703) 370-8082. Fax: (703) 370-8083. E-mail: ibpusa3@gmail.com
Global Business and Investment Info Databank - www.ibpus.com

Mudharabah ratio shaped (depending on the ratio stated by takaful operators) is 30% to the takaful operator and 70% to participants.

CONTRIBUTIONS OF TAKAFUL TO ECONOMY
In many developed countries, the Takaful or insurance industries together with pension fund institutions are major players in the development of the domestic capital market.

The takaful and insurance industry in the ASEAN region was urged to prepare itself to be a major player and be an engine for creating an efficient and liquid capital market.

Above all, aside from contributing to the economy of Brunei Darussalam, it is also the duty of takaful operators to educate the public on the beauty and the importance of takaful in our every day lives.

OTHER INSURANCE IN BRUNEI
In general, insurance policies in Brunei can be broken down into Motor and Non-Motor Insurance. Motor Insurance covers can be provided for Private Vehicles, Commercial Vehicles and Motorcycles and can be covered by a Third party or Comprehensive Insurance Coverage.

The most common form of Non-Motor Insurance is coverage for fire related damage to property and content followed by Workman Compensation, Public Liability, Personal Accident, Group Personal Accident (for corporate clients), Contractors, Marine Cargo, Marine Hull (boat operators) and Guarantees.

THE GENERAL INSURANCE ASSOCIATION OF BRUNEI
The General Insurance Association of Brunei (GIAB) was formally registered and approved on 23rd of August 1986 with the full endorsement and support from the Ministry of Finance, in particular its Insurance section.

The principal activity of GIAB is to act as a representative body of the general insurance industry in Brunei Darussalam and to promote and protect the interests of all members in connection with the general insurance industry in the Sultanate.

The members of the Association are:-
· AXA Insurance (B) Sdn Bhd
· Borneo Insurance Sdn Bhd
· Cosmic Insurance Corporation Sdn Bhd
· CGU Insurance Bhd
· Liberty Citystate Insurance Pte Ltd
· MBA Insurance Company Sdn Bhd
· Malaysia National Insurance Bhd
· Motor and General Insurance Sdn Bhd
· National Insurance Company Bhd
· Royal & Sun Alliance Insurance (Global) Ltd
· South East Asia Insurance (B) Sdn Bhd
· Standard Insurance Sdn Bhd
· The Asia Insurance Company Ltd
· Winterthur Insurance (Far East) Pte Ltd

CHAMBERS OF COMMERCE

The four chambers of commerce in Brunei play a very important role in the development of SMEs (small medium enterprises) in the country and were set up to promote the interests of the different business groups.

FUNCTIONS

The Brunei Darussalam International Chamber of Commerce and Industry is active in creating dialogue opportunities between its members and Government officials, diplomatic representatives and groups from the private sector.

The Chamber also receives numerous contacts from overseas for business opportunities and distributes contact information to all its members. The chamber also serves as a bridge between local and international businesses, fostering friendly co-existence.

The National Chamber of Commerce and Industry of Brunei Darussalam, Brunei Malay Chamber of Commerce and Industry and the Chinese Chamber of Commerce have more or less the same functions as the Brunei Darussalam International Chamber of Commerce and Industry.

The chambers of commerce in Brunei Darussalam often meet and exchange information and views on matters of common interest. Some of the chambers of commerce organise trade fairs to promote products and business.

HOW TO CONTACT THEM

· The Brunei Darussalam International Chamber of Commerce and Industry
(Dewan Perniagaan dan Perindustrian Antarabangsa Negara Brunei Darussalam)
Address:
Unit 402-403A, 4th Floor, Wisma Jaya
Jalan Pemancha Bandar Seri Begawan 8811
Postal Address: PO Box 2988
BS 8675
Tel: 222-8382, 223-6888
Fax: 222-8389

· Brunei Malay Chamber of Commerce and Industry
(Dewan Perniagaan dan Perusahaan Melayu Brunei)
Address: Unit B1, 2nd Floor
P.O Box B1-3, Lot 44252,
Kg. Kiulap, BE1518
Tel: 223-7113
Fax: 223-7112

· Chinese Chamber of Commerce
(Dewan Perniagaan Tionghua)
Address: 2nd/3rd/4th Floor Chinese Chamber of Commerce Building
72 Jalan Roberts, Bandar Seri Begawan

Postal address: PO Box 281 Bandar Seri Begawan
Tel: 223-5494/5/6
Fax: 222-35492/3

For additional analytical, business and investment opportunities information,
please contact Global Investment & Business Center, USA
at (703) 370-8082. Fax: (703) 370-8083. E-mail: ibpusa3@gmail.com
Global Business and Investment Info Databank - www.ibpus.com

· National Chamber of Commerce and Industry
(Dewan Perniagaan dan Perusahaan Kebangsaan Brunei Darussalam)
Address: Unit 10-14, First Floor
Bangunan Halimatul Saadiah, Jalan Gadong
BE 3519, Bandar Seri Begawan

Postal Address: PO Box 1099 Bandar Seri Begawan BS 8672
Tel: 222-7297
Fax: 222-7298

BRUNEI INTERNATIONAL FINANCIAL CENTRE (BIFC)

In an effort to establish itself in a world capital market, Brunei is slowly but surely catching the eyes of global financial players as one of the emerging bright stars of the world money market.

Since the inception of its International Offshore Financial Centre in June 2004, some 150 international business companies have checked in and set up their operations here. Many more are coming to join the growing community of international financiers, advisors, consultants and other players already in the country.

Brunei, as a new player, has comparatively many advantages that are conducive for a healthy growth of international financial business. Indeed this worries some International Offshore Financial Centres like Hong Kong.

While there are many other, more established, international offshore financial centres in the world such as those in Africa, Asia, Europe, the Western Hemisphere and the United States, Brunei as a newcomer, has sowed good seeds for the growth of international business companies that deal in the world capital market.

THE FIRST INTERNATIONAL SECURITY EXCHANGE IN BRUNEI
The decision by the Royal Bank of Canada to open its branch in the Sultanate last year was a testimony to this. Soon after that, Brunei saw its first international security exchange come into being. The Brunei International Exchange or IBX became the first securities exchange of international stature to win a license to operate in the country.

The establishment of the two entities was indeed historic in the development of the Brunei's fledgling financial services sector.

REASON TO INVEST

There are many factors that attract international companies to Brunei. For example the law of the country is based on the British Legal System with an independent judiciary that has the right of final appeal to the Privy Council.

In addition, there is the zero tax for individual income and the country's political stability. The high ratio of its educated population, its excellent infrastructure with direct connection to most major cities in Asia and Europe and wealth in resources are the additional plus points to investors.

In addition, Brunei's matured banking sector, with foreign banks such as HSBC, and its initiative to adopt the latest sets of offshore laws and regulation that include the provision on money laundering (MLO 2004) are some of the good elements that have lured them to Brunei.

For additional analytical, business and investment opportunities information,
please contact Global Investment & Business Center, USA
at (703) 370-8082. Fax: (703) 370-8083. E-mail: ibpusa3@gmail.com
Global Business and Investment Info Databank - www.ibpus.com

Investors looking for a good halal place to invest are also encouraged by the open door policy adopted by Brunei to develop Islamic services and products. There are 1.3 billion Muslims in the world. The amount of Arab funds looking for syariah-compliant products has been estimated at US$670 billion in 1998 and US$950 billion in 2001.

NEW FRONTIERS

With the establishment of its first securities exchange, Brunei is now in a position to tackle the money markets in Asia, the Middle East and Europe as well as the United States.

His Majesty The Sultan and Yang Di-Pertuan of Brunei in his recent birthday titah highlighted his hope of seeing Brunei play an important role in the global financial market. The setting up of the IBX is one of the vehicles to realise this goal.

With IBX, Brunei will be the virtual hub of the pan-Asian securities market place that will allow trade in a range of financial instruments in multiple markets. Using Brunei as a base, IBX would use Internet and communication technologies to develop a global financial platform to connect to the world's major capital markets called CitiDEXes.

GOALS OF THE IFC

Brunei's motives in establishing the International Offshore Financial Centre are more subtle and socio-economic in inclination than simply generating an income-stream to supplement tourism. These goals include developing the capacity to:
· Diversify, expand into and grow the value added financial service sector of the economy of Brunei and the Asia Pacific Region (APR)
· Provide a secure, cost-effective, sensibly regulated IFC facility which will offer a safe harbour for the conduct of significant regional and international business for corporate and private clients
· Attract overseas professionals to assist in running the IFC to the highest standards, encourage expatriate professionals to become involved in the training and development of rewarding opportunities for professionally qualified and trained Bruneians in the International Business Sector
· Increase returns for the hospitality, transport and amenity industries, including eco-tourism, culminating in a holistic result for the country's economy
· Position Brunei as an equal partner in the globalisation of financial and commercial activity, thereby generating greater communication with and between other nations

In its efforts to realise this goal, Brunei has deployed its sovereignty, wealth and human resources in a conservative but assertive manner to establish a jurisdictional environment which will be tax-free, and free from over-regulation or "business pollution".

Brunei IFC now offers a range of international legislation carefully crafted to permit flexible, cost effective capabilities which are up-to-date. Such capabilities include the full range of facilities necessary for the efficient conduct of global business.

As a sovereign nation of high repute (capable, for example, of hosting Apec Summit), Brunei is serving notice at the outset that criminal abuses of its financial systems will not be tolerated.

The country is taking these steps voluntarily, rather than under pressure. This reflects responsible economic and social attitudes.

The first tranche of legislation enacted for the IFC regime therefore includes Money-Laundering and Proceeds of (serious) Crime measures implemented to international standards. As for Severe Drug Trafficking, that legislation has been in place for some time along with enforceable regulations on the Trust, Company Administration, Insurance and Banking industries.

For additional analytical, business and investment opportunities information,
please contact Global Investment & Business Center, USA
at (703) 370-8082. Fax: (703) 370-8083. E-mail: ibpusa3@gmail.com
Global Business and Investment Info Databank - www.ibpus.com

The initial legislation consists of anti-crime measures already mentioned and the following:
· International Banking Order, 2004 ('IBO')
· International Business Companies Order, 2004 (IBCO')
· Registered Agents and Trustees Licensing Order, 2004 ('RATLO')
· International Trusts Order, 2004 ('ITO')
· International Limited Partnerships Order, 2004 ('ILPO')
· Insurance, Securities and Mutual fund legislation.

BRUNEI'S NATIONAL VISION AND OPPORTUNITIES

The following is Brunei Darussalam's National Vision or Wawasan as authorised by His Majesty Sultan Haji Hassanal Bolkiah, Sultan and Yang Di-Pertuan of Brunei Darussalam, launched in January 2008.

WAWASAN BRUNEI 2035

By 2035 we wish to see Brunei Darussalam recognised everywhere for:

- the accomplishments of its well-educated and highly skilled people
- the quality of life

- the dynamic, sustainable economy

As we work towards these aims, we will be united in:

- our loyalty to our Sultan and our Country
- our belief in the values of Islam
- our traditional tolerance and social harmony

TOWARDS 2035: CONTINUITY AND CHANGE

Brunei Darussalam today enjoys one of the highest standards of living in Asia.

Its per capita income is one of the highest in Asia and it has already achieved almost all the target of the Millennium Development Goals.

Its standards of education and health are among the highest in the developing world.

This has been largely the result of political stability created by His Majesty's Government's investment of oil and gas revenues in infrastructure and in the development of far-reaching programme of social welfare.

Current prosperity, however, cannot be taken for granted. If the people are to continue to enjoy their high standard of living, planning must take account of a number of emerging social and economic facts.

- Although oil and gas resources have contributed much to the nation's prosperity, economic growth has, on the whole, not kept pace with population growth.
- The public sector that is the main employer of the majority of the citizens and residents can no longer adequately absorb the growing numbers of young people wishing to enter the work force each year.

- There is a widening gap between the expectations and capabilities of the nation's youth and the employment opportunities currently being created.
- The oil and gas sector that makes up about half of the economy and over 90% of export earnings employs less than 3% of the work force.
- The local business community continues to be weak and is unable to create the employment opportunities now required.

In order to offer its people a bright and prosperous future, Brunei Darussalam must, therefore, adapt to change and all that this entails by way of ambition, innovation and bold planning.

The challenge facing the nation lies in finding ways to do this successfully whilst, at the same time, upholding the values upon which the nation has developed and progressed.

OUR VISION FOR 2035

To meet this challenge successfully by 2035 we aspire to excel in the following key areas:

An educated, highly skilled and accomplished people

We will seek to build a first class education system that provides opportunities for every citizen and resident to meet the requirements of our changing economy and encourages life-long learning as well as achievements in sport and the arts.

Our success will be measured by the highest international standards.

Our quality of life

Our people deserve the best home we can give them. We will seek to provide our people with high standards of living and political stability while ensuring proper care of our environment and the vital support needed by all members of our society.

We will measure our quality of life by reference to the United Nations Human Development Index and aim to be among the top 10 nations in the world.

Our dynamic and sustainable economy

A continued high standard of living requires our economic growth to keep pace with our population growth. We will seek to build an economy that provides our people with quality employment in both public and private sectors and also offers great economic opportunities.

We will measure our economy by reference to its capacity to support continuously rising living standards. Our aim is for Brunei Darussalam's per capita income to be within that of the top 10 countries of the world.

ENDURING VALUES

While recognising the need to change, we will continue to uphold vigorously the values that have been the foundation of our political stability, social harmony and prosperity.

In our work we shall be guided at all times by our commitment to the Brunei monarchy and nation, our faith in the values of Islam, based on the *Ahli Sunnah Wal-Jemaah, Mazhaf Shafie* and our tradition of tolerance, compassion and social harmony.

For additional analytical, business and investment opportunities information,
please contact Global Investment & Business Center, USA
at (703) 370-8082. Fax: (703) 370-8083. E-mail: ibpusa3@gmail.com
Global Business and Investment Info Databank - www.ibpus.com

We believe that our ability to adapt and manage change is greatly enhanced by the MIB concept which is inspired by these core values.

ACHIEVING BRUNEI 2035

We will need to develop and implement an integrated and well-coordinated national strategy comprising the following key elements:

- **An education strategy** that will prepare our youth for employment and achievement in a world that is increasingly competitive and knowledge-based.
- **An economic strategy** that will create new employment for our people and expand business opportunities within Brunei Darussalam through the promotion of investment, foreign and domestic, both in downstream industries as well as in economic clusters beyond the oil and gas industry.
- **A security strategy** that will safeguard our political stability and our sovereignty as a nation and that links our defense and diplomatic capabilities and our capacity to respond to threats from disease and natural catastrophe.
- **An institutional development strategy** that will enhance good governance in both the public and private sectors, high quality public services, modern and pragmatic legal and regulatory frameworks and efficient government procedures that entail a minimum of bureaucratic "red tape".
- **A local business development strategy** that will enhance opportunities for local small and medium sized enterprises (SMEs) as well as enable Brunei Malays to achieve leadership in business and industry by developing greater competitive strength.
- **An infrastructure development strategy** that will ensure continued investment by government and through public-private sector partnerships in developing and maintaining world-class infrastructure with special emphasis placed on education, health and industry.
- **A social security strategy** that ensures that, as the nation prospers, all citizens are properly cared for.
- **An environmental strategy** that ensures the proper conservation of our natural environment and cultural habitat. It will provide health and safety in line with the highest international practices.

To realise our Vision of Brunei 2035, the strategies listed above will need to be developed by both government and private bodies and implemented as a well-coordinated national strategy.

NATIONAL DEVELOPMENT PLAN

th NATIONAL DEVELOPMENT PLAN (2007 - 2012) Total Allocation (B$)	9.5 bil	100%
ALLOCATION BY SECTOR	B$	%
Industry and Commerce	1,024,965,460	10.8
Agriculture	101,771,500	1.1
Forestry	65,368,000	0.7
Fishery	115,839,960	1.2
Industrial Development	404,334,000	4.3
Commerce & Entrepreneurial Development	38,514,000	0.4
Pulau Muara Besar	299,138,000	3.1
Transport and Communication	1,067,038,300	11.2
Roads	568,535,000	6

Civil Aviation	114,527,000	1.2
Marine and Ports	26,753,000	0.3
Telecommunications	116,517,000	1.2
Radio and Television	118,241,300	2.4
Postal Services	12,465,000	0.1
Social Services 'A'	1,294,267,900	13.6
Education	822,468,500	8.7
Medical and Health	149,152,000	1.6
Religious Affairs	27,180,600	0.3
Human Resource Development	295,466,800	3.1
Social Services 'B'	1,761,451,800	18.5
Government Housing	23,281,000	0.2
Public Facilities and Environment	182,500,800	1.9
National Housing	1,555,670,000	16.4
Public Utilities	1,492,717,900	15.7
Electricity	587,904,000	6.2
Sanitation	178,013,000	1.9
Water Supply	524,573,900	5.5
Drainage	202,227,000	2.1
Public Buildings	672,958,800	7.1
Science, Technology and R & D	165,178,400	1.7
ICT	1,145,687,800	12.1
Security	596,789,000	6.3
Royal Brunei Armed Forces	421,286,000	4.4
Police	175,503,000	1.8
Miscellaneous	278,944,640	2.9
Contingency Reserves	244,944,640	2.6
Site Development	15,000,000	0.2
Consultant Fee	15,000,000	0.2
Liabilities for Completed Project	4,000,000	0

COMMUNICATIONS

Airport

The present day Brunei International Airport, located at Berakas about fifteen minutes drive from Bandar Seri Begawan operates 24 hours a day, providing facilities for both regional and international air traffic. It has a 4000-metre runway that can accommodate any type of aircraft currently in service, including the 'Jumbo' 747s. Its passenger and cargo handling facilities can handle 1.5 million passengers and 50,000 tones of cargo a year. Equipped with the latest state-of the-art technology in surveillance and tracking, the airport boasts radar, flight and auxiliary data processing, 2,000-line, high-resolution color raster displays, simulation facilities, voice switching system, voice and data recording and VHF/UHF air-ground transmitters. The national air carrier is Royal Brunei Airlines founded in November 18, 1974.

Another airport, at Anduki near Seria, is used by the Brunei Shell Petroleum Company for its helicopter services.

Ports

The main Port is Muara, which is about 28 kilometers from Bandar Seri Begawan. The port can accommodate ships over 196 meters L.O.A. and take up to 7 or 8 vessels averaging 8,000 Gross Registered Tonnage {GRT} or a single ship of up to 30,000 {GRT} with a draught of not more than 9.5 meters.

Since 1973, the port has undergone extensive improvements. These include extensions to the wharf bringing the total length to 948 meters including 250 meters dedicated container wharf and 87 meters aggregate wharf. The overall storage space in the form of covered storage is 16,950 square meters, long storage warehouses 16,630 square meters and open storage space 5 hectares. Facilities for the dedicated container wharf covers an area of 92,034 square meters including 8,034 square meters covered areas.

Besides Muara Port, there are two smaller ports located one at Bandar Seri Begawan and one at Kuala Belait. The port at Bandar Seri Begawan is utilized by vessels under 93 meters LOA drawing less than 5 meters draught carrying conventional cargoes for direct deliveries and passenger launches plying between Bandar Seri Begawan, Limbang and Temburong. The wharf also accommodates various small government crafts. The port at Kuala Belait can accommodate vessels with draught of 4 meters which carries mainly general cargo for Kuala Belait and the Brunei Petroleum Shell Company.

Road

The road network in Brunei Darussalam is the primary means of movement for people, goods and services on land. It plays a vital role in the overall growth and development of the State. The network has been designed to integrate housing, commercial and industrial development. The Sultanate has constructed a good road network with various types of road throughout the country that includes highways, link roads, flyovers and round-abouts. A major road, which was completed in 1983, is a 28-kilometre highway linking Muara through Berakas and Jerudong to a point in Tutong, where it connects with the existing Bandar Seri Begawan-Tutong-Seria trunk road thus providing an alternative routes to these places.

An 11-km road between Sungai Teraban and Sungai Tujoh, makes the journey from Brunei Darussalam to Sarawak's Fourth Division such as Miri and other parts of Sarawak much easier.

The State had 2,525 kilometers (km) of roads, of which 2,328 km were covered with asphalt, 187 with pebbles, and 10 km with concrete. Of the total 1,514 km were in Brunei/Muara, 481 km in Belait, 400 km in Tutong and 130 km in Temburong district.

For additional analytical, business and investment opportunities information,
please contact Global Investment & Business Center, USA
at (703) 370-8082. Fax: (703) 370-8083. E-mail: ibpusa3@gmail.com
Global Business and Investment Info Databank - www.ibpus.com

BRUNEY INDUSTRIAL ACHIEVEMENTS

Today, twelve years since its formation, BINA has managed to achieve a considerable measure of success in what it originally set out to do. In putting these achievements in perspective, one has to bear in mine circumstances Brunei has to contend with, the most critical of which is the local market which is approximately about 300,000 people compared to our regional neighbours.

DIVERSIFICATION OF INDUSTRIAL ACTIVITIES

Allocated at BINA's industrial sites in all the four districts, 213 projects have been approved to date which is a combination of new and relocation/expansion projects. The following list is a selection of those approved projects which should give some perspective of BINA's achievement so far.

- Clinker grinding plant (cement manufacture)
- Production of construction materials (e.g. paint aluminium doors & windows, roofing products, PVC pipes, concrete blocks, stainless steel products, etc)
- Bottling of artesian water
- Assembly of electrical appliances
- Electrical equipment (switchboard, control panels & feeder pillars)
- Production of electrical cables & wires
- Manufacturing of garments for export
- Food & beverages (e.g. ice cream, soft drinks, bakery, spices, etc)
- Production of solar panels for export
- Aluminium sulphate & sodium carbonate for use in water treatment
- Food repackaging
- Warehousing
- Manufacture of furniture
- Manufacture of cans
- Canning of tuna

Not just limited to the capability of setting up factories, some manufacturers have actually managed to get accreditation for their products ftorn reputable foreign establishments such as SIRIM & SISIR while others have successfully implemented the internationally recognised management standard ISO 9002.

INVESTMENT

The total investment value of those projects based on approved projects is B$619,608,331 in which foreign investments accounts for approximately one-quarter of the pie (B$126,071,802). Local investments stands at B$493,536,529.

EMPLOYMENT CREATION

Those investments have also helped to create 14,753 new job opportunities for both the skilled and unskilled categories. This positive development goes a long way in helping reduce the Government's burden of unemployment which is often accompanied by social problems.

EXPORT ACTIVITIES

Other developments are the creation of export industries, which at the moment is still limited to garment. Apart from enhancing the credibility of

local companies, exports help to offset imports in the national balance of trade figures and is also the way forward if a company wants to grow

sitinificantly because of the competitive nature and large size of the international market. The local garment industry export value still has a long way to go to offset the nations huge demand for imported products and

services but has taken the right step forward to establish itself especially with trade liberalisation agreements, that Brunei is party to, coming into effect at the beginning of the next century. Below is a table of the industry's export figures:

IMPORT SUBSTITUTION

It is admittedly difficult for local producers to replace the products that consumers import because the oil and gas industry aside, Brunei is a net importer. But in any case, Brunei has managed to produce certain products locally such as construction materials, processed food, furniture, electrical products, etc which is a good start in replacing simple products which are within the technological and financial capacity of local manufacturers/producers.

VALUE-ADDING

As mentioned earlier, some of the projects approved at BINA's sites are relocations with the aim of expansion. Some examples of these are the car dealership, warehousing, timber, and furniture industry where bigger land area, proper and better physical infrastructure provided at the industrial sites has given the industries the impetus to offer better and more varied products and services.

COOPERATIVE DEVELOPMENT

Formed on Ist August 1974, Cooperative Development Department's function is to enhance community's unity and the social and economic status of the people. With its subsequent merger with Industrial Unit, Ministry of Industry and Primary Resources to become BINA, the primary function continues as it was but with more emphasis to promote and develop cooperatives to be more competitive and dynamic.

Over the twenty-four years of its establishment, 164 cooperatives have been registered with 14,314 members (as of September 1998). Recent data shows that there are only limited lines of business ventures these cooperatives are involved in, such as transportation, fishery, agriculture, consumer, school and multi-purpose with a net profit gained of about $2 millions Brunei (1998). Having gone through these developments, BINA have restructured its cooperative development section and taken few steps and some of these steps are being undertaken towards enhancing awareness and level of cooperative's expertise and professionalism. Future direction and strategies of cooperatives would be formulated following the national level seminar to be held at the end of this year. This would enable BINA in developing a cooperative development plan; analysing the existing Cooperative Act for any changes, deemed necessary; improve existing administrative assistance; encourage interaction and cooperation's with private sector; and for cooperatives to venture into other potential business sectors for example manufacturing, marketing, insurance, wholesales, etc.

For additional analytical, business and investment opportunities information,
please contact Global Investment & Business Center, USA
at (703) 370-8082. Fax: (703) 370-8083. E-mail: ibpusa3@gmail.com
Global Business and Investment Info Databank - www.ibpus.com

BOOSTING THE ECONOMY THROUGH PRIVATISATION

Brunei Darussalam continued with efforts to diversify its economy from the oil and gas sector through encouraging industrial development and commerce.

Under the Sixth Five-Year Development Plan, the industry and commerce sector is allocated $550.9 million, which makes up 10 percent of the total budget for development.

Of this, $100 million has been specifically budgeted for industrial promotion and development. The government has consistently aimed its policies at maximising the economic utilisation of its national resources, develop new industries and encourage and nurture the development of Bumiputera leaders in industry and commerce.

In its endeavour to boost economic growth, the authorities are also introducing the concept of privatisation. Besides being a stimulus for economic growth, privatisation is also being seen as a way to remove spending while improving efficiency in public services.

Crucial in the successful implementation of the privatisation programmes are the awareness and understanding of the people in the government, the private sector as well as the public.

Through privatisation, the government could optimize spending in providing services to the public, the Minister of Development Pengiran Dato Haji Ismail said. When opening a two-day seminar on privatisation in June.

It is also required in the expansion of the nation's economic base and in promoting the construction and service sectors, he added.

It would be better to implement the project on a small scale initially so that we can understand better the concept of privatisation, the minister said.

Plan to hold more seminars on privatisation
The two-day seminar was attended by more than 200 people from various ministries, departments and private companies.

In fact, more seminars are planned on privatisation aimed at preparing the business sector ready for the new business situation. The seminars would be organised on a smaller scale involving smaller groups of people. This would ensure that such sessions are more effective in achieving understanding and imparting knowledge to participants about privatisation.

The effort by the Ministry of Development in organising the seminar was seen by some participants as a signal that the ministry in particular is gearing up to privatise some of its service.

The Development Ministry is one of the largest in the government and includes the Public Works Department, the Electrical Services Department, Town and Country Planning, the Survey Department, the Housing Development Department and the Land Department.

The government in its Sixth Five-Year Development Plan due to end this year, has allocated more than $5 billion for national development, more than a billion dollars more than it had spent in the Fifth FDP.

Some 50.9 million dollars for the Sixth Plan was allocated to developing 619 projects starting from 1991 to 1995.

29.3 percent or $1614.6 million of the total budget is for social services that include national housing, education, medical and health, religious affairs and public facilities.

ECONOMIC INDICATORS

GDP at current prices (Million B$) : 8.051.0 (1997 estm.)
Average annual inflation rate: 2.7 percent
Unemployment rate: 4.9 percent

Although Brunei Darussalam is no giant when it comes to landmass, it has been blessed with rich natural resources and a strategic location within the region. The majority of the country is covered in tropical rainforests teeming with exotic flora and fauna. Anxious to promote the conservation of its lush surroundings, eco-tourism has gained importance in the country's economic activities.

Human resources are central to the successful transformation of Brunei Darussalam into a diversified industrial economy. As in most developing nations, there is a shortage of skilled workforce in the country. Therefore, greater emphasis is placed upon education. The main areas of interest in human resources development are managerial and industrial skills, with particular emphasis on entrepreneurial skills as well as vocational and technical training.

Brunei Darussalam's main exports consist of three major commodities - crude oil, petroleum products and liquefied natural gas - sold largely to Japan, the United States and ASEAN countries. The Government's move to promote non-oil and gas activities has been largely successful with figures showing 64% of GDP in 1996 compared to only 24.3% in 1991.

AGRICULTURE

Agriculture plays a major role in the security of food supply. To ensure a continuity of supply of food in the country, the Department of Agriculture promotes domestic agricultural activities and at the same time facilitate import of foods to meet national requirements. The Department has established a new framework to encourage greater efficiency in farm production, revitalise rural communities, foster agro-industrial development and encourage sustainable agriculture to conserve the natural resources. The aim is to accelerate food production in the country to promise a meaningful degree of food security.

Over the past few years, special efforts have been made to encourage greater private participation in food production. Incentives and agricultural services have been provided to attract investment. These facilities have stimulated greater private sector involvement in agriculture.

The cooperation from the farming communities has been overwhelming. We are now completely self-sufficient in table eggs (99.6%), produce 76.1 percent of the poultry meat requirement, satisfy 70 percent of the demand for vegetables, meet 7.7 percent (and increasing) of the tropical fruits requirement, and have expanded food processing and packaging activities. The symbiotic relationship between Department of Agriculture and the farmers has sustained growth in food production.

**For additional analytical, business and investment opportunities information,
please contact Global Investment & Business Center, USA
at (703) 370-8082. Fax: (703) 370-8083. E-mail: ibpusa3@gmail.com
Global Business and Investment Info Databank - www.ibpus.com**

Today, Department of Agriculture through its dedicated staff and within the operational machinery have, and will continue to provide, the supportive services to develop agriculture and increase local food production. The Department is conscious of the need to protect the environment and conserve the country's natural resources and biodiversity for the benefit of future generations. To meet the changing needs of the producers and consumers, the Department has implemented a coordinated approach in administration, regulation, research and extension.

Future challenges and opportunities are enormous. The Department of Agriculture is constantly adjusting and consolidating to increase efficiency in order to meet the needs of the farming communities and consumers. The goals are to strengthen and direct efforts towards a stable relationship between the Department of Agriculture, importers, farmers and consumers in shaping a strong and efficient agricultural sector. Collectively, these efforts will guarantee the country's security of food supply.

The agro-economy makes up just one per cent of GDP and Brunei has to import 80 per cent of its food needs. Efforts are being made to diversify the economy, away from a heavy dependence on oil and gas towards a more independent agricultural sector. While land, finance and irrigation facilities are available, what is needed is manpower resources.

The first of the Government's four major objectives is to enhance domestic production of padi, vegetables, poultry and livestock. Secondly, to develop the agro-industry as a whole, and thirdly, to produce high value-added products using advanced technological farming methods. Last but not least, Brunei aims to conserve and protect the existing bio-diversity.

Since 1994, Brunei egg farms have successfully supplied the 20 eggs a month that each person in Brunei consumes. The figures for rice, a staple for the Asian country's 283,500 people, however show that the country is able to meet just 2 percent of the 27,500-tonne demand a year.

Almost all of its beef are imported. Brunei brings in live cattle, mostly from Australia, where the Sultanate has a 579,000-hectare ranch in Willeroo, and substantially from Malaysia and New Zealand. Frozen and chilled beef are imported from all over the world.

Local production of chicken, a favorite meat as much for its taste as for its reputation as a healthier, lower-cholesterol white meat, has made great strides. About 28 percent of the chicken sold in Brunei markets is local produce. To supplement the 17,400 tones of chicken meat the country consumes annually, a proportion of Brunei hens are grown from imported day-old chicks.

The growing concern for a healthier way of life also tends towards including more vegetables in the Bruneian diet. Brunei has done well to encourage this trend by ensuring that more than half of the vegetables prepared in kitchens here are locally grown, with the other 46 percent imported mostly from Sabah and Sarawak, particularly from Limbang, Miri and Lawas.

In Brunei, you get a good variety of both tropical and temperate climate fruits, though only a small proportion of what you eat here are locally grown. A hefty 93 percent of it is bought from neigboring countries, mostly from Thailand.

Efforts are being made to collect specimens of local fruit trees and to develop small plantations as well as to produce seedlings which will subsequently support the development of large-scale, less labor-intensive mechanized fruit farms. Areas in the Tutong district have been singled as ideal for planting orchards.

The government is trying to stimulate greater interest in the agriculture industry through the establishment of model farms, providing training, advice and support.

Existing infrastructure and facilities are being upgraded in rural areas. As the high rainfall, temperature and humidity conditions are not conducive to manual labor, localized farming may be encouraged with sophisticated machinery and equipment,

With agriculture playing a major role in the security of food supply, the Department of Agriculture has actively been promoting domestic agricultural activities while facilitating import of various foods to meet national requirements.

Over the past few years, special efforts have been made to encourage greater private sector participation in the production of food. Incentives and agricultural services have been provided to attract investment. These efforts have successfully stimulated an increase in private sector involvement in agriculture.

AGRICULTURE & LIVESTOCK

The cooperation from the farming communities has been overwhelming. The Department is now completely self-sufficient in table eggs (99.6%). They produce 76.1% of the poultry meat requirement, satisfy 70% of the demand for vegetables, meet 7.7% (and increasing) of the tropical fruits requirement, and has expanded food processing and packaging activities. The symbiotic relationship between the Department of Agriculture and farmers has sustained growth in food production.

RICE

Various efforts have been made by the government to encourage rice production during the last decade and the yield per acre has increased due to the introduction of better agricultural methods.

Approximately 290 tonnes or 1% of the nation's rice needs are produced locally from 613 hectares of rice fields scattered around the country.

As a first step towards the attainment of self-sufficiency in rice, the Government launched an experimental large scale mechanised rice planting project at Kampong Wasan in 1978. Covering an area of 400 hectares, the project was a joint undertaking between the Agriculture Department and the Public Works Department.

The responsibility of the Public Works Department was to provide the required infrastructure, clear the land and give other basic provisions. The responsibility of the Agriculture Department was to plant, maintain, harvest and process. The aim was to plant paddy twice a year, from April to September and from October to March.

VEGETABLES

Locally grown vegetables constitute about 6,700 tonnes or just over 65% of the country's needs. With more people taking up vegetable farming, the amount is increasing gradually.

Vegetable production in Brunei Darussalam has progressed well with the entry of commercial operators. Much of the tropical leafy vegetables are now produced locally.

The Department of Agriculture is encouraging the development of high technology protected cultivation to produce quality pesticide-free vegetative crops of high market value to complement the production from conventional farms.

For additional analytical, business and investment opportunities information,
please contact Global Investment & Business Center, USA
at (703) 370-8082. Fax: (703) 370-8083. E-mail: ibpusa3@gmail.com
Global Business and Investment Info Databank - www.ibpus.com

Brunei Darussalam is still dependent on imports to satisfy demand for temperate vegetables, fruit vegetables, roots and tubers. Most of these vegetables can be produced locally.

The local consumption for tropical and temperate vegetables recorded during the year 2001 was 17,131.1 metric tonnes. According to the statistics, 52.1% was produced locally.

FRUITS

Fruit farming is largely performed on a small scale. There is a vast range of locally produced tropical fruits that meet about 11% of the domestic requirement of more than 14,000 tonnes.

In 1975, the Agriculture Department initiated a fruit-farming scheme to encourage fruit cultivation in the country. In an effort to increase the production of local fruits, the Government through the agricultural stations in Batang Mitus, Tanah Jambu and Lumapas, planted seedlings of various fruit trees.

Orchards and backyard gardens produce a wide range of seasonal and non-seasonal tropical fruits. Traditional production systems produce non-seasonal fruits such as bananas, papayas, pineapples, watermelons, and seasonal fruits namely, durian, chempedak, tarap, rambutan, langsat, belunu, asam aur aur, and membangan to meet the domestic demand for fruits.

Many other types of indigenous fruits, some of which are not commonly found in other parts of Southeast Asia, are also supplied by these traditional production systems.

Production is insufficient to meet local demand and large quantities of both tropical and temperate fruits are imported annually. The total consumption for tropical and temperate fruits in the year 2001 was estimated at 23,083.2 metric tonnes. Only 17.9% were produced locally, according to the provided statistics.

LIVESTOCK

The country produces about 1,000 heads of cattle and buffaloes for the market annually, making up about 6% of its own beef consumption. The Government assists local stock farmers with calves, machinery, feed, seedlings, fertilisers and veterinary care.

The country requires 3,000 to 5,000 tonnes of meat annually, with per capita consumption of between nine and 17 kg. To meet this demand, the government imports an average of between 4,000 and 7,000 heads of live cattle from its Willeroo Ranch in Northern Australia.

Another importer of slaughter cattle (of various breeds, including Angus and Brahman Cross) from Australia is PDS Abattoir. PDS Abattoir is a local company that owns an international standard abattoir in Tutong, specialising in the production of chilled and frozen western cuts.

Meanwhile, local fresh milk production contributes about 199 thousand litres annually.

Research has been carried out to ascertain the best possible way to increase buffalo population. Towards this end, the Agriculture Department has launched a research project covering 4,000 hectares in the Batang Mitus area in the Tutong District. So far, over 200 hectares have already been initiated. The farm's main aim will be to assess local and imported stock towards producing highbred buffaloes for commercial purposes.

Local beef, which is mainly from cattle and buffaloes, is capable of supplying 4% (5,206.75 metric tonnes) of the total beef requirement in the year 2001. 92.1% of the total beef requirement comes

For additional analytical, business and investment opportunities information,
please contact Global Investment & Business Center, USA
at (703) 370-8082. Fax: (703) 370-8083. E-mail: ibpusa3@gmail.com
Global Business and Investment Info Databank - www.ibpus.com

from the importation of live animals (18,742 heads or an equivalent to 4,796.31 metric tonnes) and frozen and chilled beef amounting to 203.39 metric tonnes.

Meanwhile, a total of 2,449 heads of goats have been slaughtered and this is equivalent to 42.75 metric tonnes of mutton. Out of the total number of slaughtered goats, 8.7 per cent (331 heads or 3.72 metric tonnes) are locally produced while the rest are imported from Australia.

Goats are popularly consumed only by the ethnic groups and races such as Indians, Nepalese, Gurkhas, Malays and occasionally Chinese. The demand for goats tends to be higher during the Islamic festive months of Aidil-Fitri, Aidil-Adha and Ramadhan.

FISHERIES
Fisheries has been identified as one of the sectors that can contribute towards economic diversification.

The Fisheries Industry comprises three sectors: capture industry, aquaculture industry and processing industry. The estimate is that together, they will contribute at least B$200 million per year to the Gross Domestic Product (GDP) by 2003. The capture industry is estimated to contribute at least B$112 million, aquaculture B$71 million and processing at least B$17 million to the GDP.

Along with traditional fishing, marine fish is the principal source of protein for the people of Brunei Darussalam. The per capita fish consumption is one of the highest in the region at around 45 kilogrammes per year.

CAPTURE INDUSTRY
With an estimated population of about 344,500, the total annual consumption of fish is estimated to be around 15,500 metric tonnes. However, with only about 925 full-time fishermen, Brunei Darussalam still has to import about 50% of its fish requirement to supplement the local production.

The industry, however, is developing especially after the declaration of the 200 nautical miles Brunei Fishery Limits. There has also been a change in policy that allows joint ventures.

The Government, wanting to obtain maximum economic gains while ensuring the sustainability of the resources, is only allowing exploitation of up to the "maximum economic yield" (MEY), which is taken to be 20% below the usually used "maximum sustainable yield" (MSY) level. In this regard, the surveyed fishing areas of Brunei Darussalam have about 21,300 metric tonnes of fish at MEY: Demersal resources - 12,500 metric tonnes and Pelagic resources - 8,800 metric tonnes.

In addition, Brunei Darussalam is also found to be in the migration path of tuna resources. Their volume will be surveyed in the near future.

At the same time, there are large resources associated with the numerous offshore oil-rigs, purposely-sunk tyres, man-made concrete reefs and old oil-rigs that act as artificial reefs. With appropriate gear and technology, these resources can be exploited.

AQUACULTURE
The aquaculture industry in Brunei Darussalam, although in its infancy compared to other countries in the region, is developing quite fast. The high demand for aquaculture products and conducive physical conditions such as unpolluted waterways, the absence of typhoons and floods have made aquaculture a very promising industry.

The major activities in the aquaculture industry are the cage culture of marine fish and the pond culture of marine shrimp. Development of technology on seed production and culture of other species that are of high commercial value are one of the priorities of the Department of Fisheries.

It is anticipated that the steady increase of population will increase existing demand. With the current liberalisation of trade, opportunities for export are there, even though as it is, the local demand and market price in itself have already made the fisheries industry attractive.

The Government, through the Fisheries Department, has therefore been actively promoting suitable foreign involvement, either in the form of joint partnership or other forms of strategic alliances, aimed at developing the fisheries sector towards a competitive, efficient and commercially lucrative venture.

FORESTRY

Forests, Brunei's most permanent asset, cover about 81 percent of the total land area of 5,765 sq km. They grow in a diverse mix of mangrove, peat, swamp, heath, dipterocarp and montane. Primary forest makes up 58 percent of the land. The Department of Forestry, in line with the country's policy of continuous conservation, has marked out plans to sustain the forests as well as programs for environmental and industrial forestry.

The former covers the management of protected forests, conservation, recreational and national parks, while the latter involves guidelines for the development and management of forest products as well as their processing and consumption.

Logging is strictly controlled in a bid to nurture a stable environment, unlike countries which have severely depleted their forests. Brunei has escaped this fate in some measure because the availability of revenue from its hydrocarbon deposits allows it to exercise the freedom of refraining from exploiting the land for timber and other commercial uses.

Restricted timber production, destined only for local consumption, has been reduced to around 100,000 cubic meters per annum from the former 200,000 cubic meters limit. Timber extraction for export is strictly prohibited.

Within the framework of the Forest Conservation Policy, efforts to reforest earmarked areas were drawn up and a sum of $26 million was allocated in the sixth Plan. Up to the date of publication, 700 of the 30,000 hectares earmarked over the next 30 years have been cultivated. In time, about 1,000 hectares will be reforested every year.

There are 11 forest reserves managed by the department. Forestry projects include the building of biodiversity conservation centers, establishing facilities and sites for nurseries, fields for forest trees and commercial rattan and bamboo.

In the Ex-Situ Forest Conservation center in Sungai Lumut, efforts focus on enriching the plants in the Andulau Forest Reserve, which has seen almost 50 years of logging.

TRADITIONAL FOREST PRODUCTS

Aside from timber, the forests have also been the source of traditional products. In the early days, latex from jelutong trees was extracted and exported. It was used in the manufacture of chewing gum. Cutch used to be harvested from the bark of bakau trees in the mangroves; this was used primarily for leather tanning. Firewood and charcoal are to this day still derived from the mangroves. And even at the present time, wild animals, rattan, bamboo, leaves, fibers, bark, fruits, and a host of other materials are gathered from the forest. These are utilised for food, medicine, building houses, and related domestic and commercial applications.

For food, the shoots of bamboo (rabong), rattan (ombut), fern (paku and lamiding), and the fruit of petai (Parkia javanica) are widely popular as vegetable. The fruits of terap (Artocarpus odoratissimus), kembayau (Dacryodes spp.), durian (Durio spp.), etc. are also local favourites. Moreover, assorted materials collected from the forests are fashioned into furniture, handicraft, boats, and other traditional goods.

Another major commodity gathered from the forest are medicinal plants and related materials. These are of great importance in the lives of the local people, particularly those in rural areas. Traditional herbal medicine and native healing methods have of late, gained growing interest in global scene. Biotechnology and bioengineering have given rise to entirely new industries based on tropical biodiversity. Thus, in this context, the natural forests of the country play increasingly valuable conservation and socio-economic roles in national development.

COMMERCIAL TIMBER

There are at least 48 timber or species groups in the country which are of known commercial value. These are classified in accordance with conventions adopted by most Southeast Asian countries. Only one softwood species, tolong or bindang (Agathis borneensis), is represented and it occurs in higher elevations as well as on sand terraces in lowland peat swamps. It is a highly regarded decorative and fancy wood, particularly when used as paneling and interior finishing.

The hardwoods, on the other hand, are categorized into three groups, based on wood density and natural strength and durability. The first group consists of the heavy hardwoods, which have air-dry densities of over 880 kg. per cubic meter, and which are inherently durable. Examples are the selangan batu (heavy Shorea species) and resak (Cotylelobium spp.), which are used for key structural purposes. Shingles of belian (Eusideroxylon zwageri) had been traditionally used for house roofing, and it was not uncommon for the wood to last 50 or 60 years.

Second category is composed of the medium heavy hardwoods, with densities of 650-880 kg. per cubic meter, strong but which are not naturally durable. These include the kapur (Dryobalanops spp.), keruing (Dipterocarpus spp.), and kempas (Koompassia malaccensis). For places in h wood deterioration is not a problem these timbers can be used as structural material. Otherwise, their durability may be significantly lengthened preservative treatment.

The light hardwoods constitute the third group. These have densities of less 650 kg. per cubic meter, and are used mainly for general purposes. Among the species in this group are the red meranti (Shorea spp.), nyatoh (Sapotaceae species), ramin (Gonystylus spp.), medang (Lauraceae species), and others.

OIL & GAS

The oil and gas industry remains the fundamental sector in Brunei's economy and it continues to play a dominant role even as the nation strives to diversify into non-oil industrialization.

For additional analytical, business and investment opportunities information, please contact Global Investment & Business Center, USA at (703) 370-8082. Fax: (703) 370-8083. E-mail: ibpusa3@gmail.com Global Business and Investment Info Databank - www.ibpus.com

The government's policy, initiated in 1988, is to conserve this natural resource by reducing production of crude oil to around 150,000 barrels per day (b/d).

At the same time, the search for new reserves and for alternative sources of energy is being intensified.

Brunei Shell Petroleum Sendirian Berhad (BSP) announced a major gas discovery in July 1995 at Selangkir-1 well, which is about 12 kilometers west of the Champion Field.

BSP has seven offshore oil fields, including Champion. The others are Southwest Ampa, Fairley, Fairley-Baram (which is shared with Malaysia), Magpie, Gannet and Iron Duke -BSP's newest field which came on stream in 1992. Two more fields are situated onshore.

The Brunei Government is an equal partner with the Royal Dutch Shell Company. Besides Shell, another active concession holder is Jasra-Elf.

Based in Brunei Darussalam since 1986, the Jasra-Elf Joint Venture has been actively exploring for hydrocarbons offshore and has made some discoveries, in particular in the Maharaja Lela Field (Block B).

Having confirmed technically that there is a significant amount of oil and gas reserves in this field, the Joint Venture is presently concentrating its efforts towards the development and production of these reserves in the most efficient and optimized way.

The country's production of oil reached a peak of 250,000 b/d 1979 but in the Eighties, a ceiling of about 150,000 b/d was introduced. In 1991, production went up to 162,000 b/d, rising to 180,000 b/d in 1992 and falling slightly to 174,000 b/d in 1993.

At the current rate of extraction, it is estimated that the country's oil reserve would run out in about 27 years' time.

Some 40 per cent of the country's reserves are found in the Champion Field, which is situated in 30 meters of water about 70 km north-east of Seria. This field produces more than 50,000 b/d.

The oldest field is Southwest Ampa, 13 kilometers off Kuala Belait. It holds more than half of Brunei's total gas reserves and the gas production accounts for 60 per cent of the country's total output.

The onshore oilfield in Seria, which is the country's first oil well drilled in 1929, still produces around 10,000 b/d used mainly for domestic consumption. On the domestic market, unleaded petrol was introduced in 1992.

The main foreign markets for Brunei's crude oil are Thailand, Singapore, the Philippines, Australia, China, Japan, South Korea, Taiwan and the United States of America.

The contribution of crude oil to the country's Gross Domestic Product has seen a decline from 88 per cent in 1974 to 58 per cent in 1990. In terms of employment, the oil and gas sector's share of the total labor force was only 5 per cent in 1990.

This means it has the highest value-added ratio per worker and labor productivity remains highest among all sectors while its workers are among the highest paid in the country.

Brunei is the world's fourth largest producer of liquefied natural gas (LNG). The current gas production is approximately 27 million cubic meters per day, and 90 per cent of it is exported to Japan, namely the Tokyo Electric, Tokyo Gas and Osaka Gas Companies.

The Japanese companies and Brunei Coldgas of Brunei LNG signed a further 20-year contract in 1993. The new contract is believed to have raised the quantity and price of gas.

The Brunei Liquefied Natural Gas plant in Lumut, one of the largest in the world, was upgraded and expanded at a cost of around B$100 million in 1993.

The LNG from the plant is transported to Japan by a fleet of seven specially-designed 100,000-tonne tankers with a capacity of 73,000 cubic meters of LNG each. The sale of LNG has grown to be as important a revenue earner as oil exports.

The domestic market takes up only 2 per cent of the LNG produced.

At the current rate of production, the proven reserves of natural gas is estimated to last another 40 years.

However, the discoveries of new gas fields and the possibility of more finds will enable Brunei to benefit from the growing demand for LNG in Asia, which is needed primarily for power generation.

Despite the uncertainty that surrounds the global oil market, the hydrocarbon industry looks set to continue to be the beacon of Brunei's economy. The Brunei Petrochemical Industry Master Plan, completed in May 2001, has identified a number of potential petrochemical industries - both upstream and downstream - for development over the next decades.

Brunei has been described as "the next epicenter of deepwater activity in Asia." Deepwater exploration for oil and gas is going on strong in Brunei, with a number of offshore acreages awarded to major prospectors in the industry.
In 1982, Brunei made legal claims to its EEZ, allowing the Sultanate to take measures to tap the wealth potential of its offshore areas. But Brunei has been prospecting offshore for oil since the 1960s. The first offshore discovery was made in 1963, at the South West Ampa Offshore Field.

DEEPWATER DRILLING
Deepwater drilling allows:
1. for the full realisation of the country's potential oil and gas reserves
2. for the tapping of mature fields to their full potential, with the advent of new technologies
3. for the rejuvenation of existing fields and infrastructures
Deepwater prospecting in Brunei takes place in blocks located some 200 kilometres off the country's coastline, but still within its EEZ. Drilling would be conducted into waters between 1.5 to 2.5 kilometres deep.

Brunei is fortunate in that the waters of the South China Sea where the prospecting takes place is rather calm, posing very little or no threat at all to the safety of drilling rigs. Ultra deepwater drilling is, however, relatively new to Brunei. Thus far, only two ultra deepwater blocks - of 10,000 square kilometers each - had been awarded to drilling consortia, consisting of major players in the global oil and gas industry.

TotalFinaElf owns 60% of the consortium that operates in Block J, followed by BHP Billiton with 25% and Amerada Hess with 15%. The Block K group, meanwhile, consists of Shell (50%), Conoco (25%) and Mitsubishi (25%).

An average of 50 producer and injection wells are anticipated for each drilling field, which should result in a massive drilling activity in the next 10 to15 years, involving a very high demand for specialised technology and engineering services.

It is hoped that deepwater-drilling endeavours in Brunei would also result in a transfer of new technology and skills to benefit locals. These activities are also expected to stimulate business activities in support services and create new job opportunities, as well as increase the number of local and international joint venture opportunities.

THE FUTURE OF OIL

Economic and social development in Asia over the next decades will fuel the need for power supply, vis-a-vis oil and gas, to drive generators. Worldwide demand for oil is expected to increase some 60% in the next 25 years, with an "economically buoyant" Asia to lead the rise, said industry experts during the OSEA 2002 oil and gas conference in Singapore in October 2002.

"Energy consumption continues to grow especially in the Asia-Pacific region," an industry captain said. "This growing trend shows a greater increasing demand for gas to be used for power generation and this will continue to fuel the development of offshore oil fields."

Rising demand for oil and gas will drive the sector in the medium and long term, especially in the "increasingly popular" field of deep-sea exploration for natural gas deposits, experts said.

By 2020, Asia will be the largest net importer of oil, "surpassing Europe and North America," said Singapore's Minister of State for Foreign Affairs and Trade, Raymond Lim at the conference. The demand for gas is projected to exceed the demand for oil as well by 2020.

All these bode well for the Brunei hydrocarbons industry, as it endeavours to tap its vast offshore oil and gas potential. The move to explore the deep waters of Brunei presents both risks and opportunities, wrote the Managing Director of TotalFinaElf John Perry in the magazine 'Asia Inc'.

"In their location and required technology, the deep water permits are literally at the frontier of exploration and production activities," he added. "Developing oil and gas fields in 2,000 metres of water is no easy business. It carries significant risk and huge costs, perhaps US$3-4 billion to develop a commercial discovery.

"Yet, the potential is there to succeed."

Success, he said, will take not just the form of a revenue stream for His Majesty's Government, but will also provide a "stable economic base, founded on a global commodity, to enable Brunei's economy to diversify beyond the oil and gas sector."

But the country is not going just upstream with its deepwater ventures. The afore-mentioned Petrochemical Industry Master Plan also has a number of downstream industries that could be developed to complement the new drilling activities in Brunei. For instance, the Plan mentioned methane-based industries like the production of ammonia, urea and methanol from hydrocarbon

For additional analytical, business and investment opportunities information, please contact Global Investment & Business Center, USA at (703) 370-8082. Fax: (703) 370-8083. E-mail: ibpusa3@gmail.com
Global Business and Investment Info Databank - www.ibpus.com

derivatives; olefins and aromatic derivatives from naphtha crackers, "with the possible integration with a refinery" and energy-intensive activities like aluminium smelting.

DOWNSTREAM ACTIVITIES

Indeed, the Government has set aside two sites for use of such downstream industries. The 1,000sq km Pulau Muara Besar, located just across the Muara deepwater port, will be used for the development of integrated petrochemical projects in the mid-term. In addition, the 230 hectare Sungai Liang site is "readily available for development", complete with existing gas pipelines to the nearby Lumut BLNG plant, as well as the TFE onshore gas processing plant.

The Sungai Liang site is given "priority" for immediate development, especially for stand-alone projects.

The Government agency that oversees the oil and gas industry in Brunei is PetroleumBRUNEI. It was formed in 2001 to:
1. strengthen and to push, and to jointly spearhead the development of the local petroleum industry
2. play a more active role in the exploration and development of the petroleum industry
3. accelerate economic development based on the domestic petroleum industry

Still, "gas is the energy of the future," Perry wrote. The GASEX gathering in May 2002 - a "quality event" which attracted "quality delegates" - was an indication of the high regard Brunei is held in the gas industry.

The Minister of Industry and Primary Resources, Pehin Dato Hj Abd Rahman, in his capacity as chairman of the Brunei Oil and Gas Authority (BOGA), in 2001 said: "The Government of His Majesty continues to place a great importance on the long-term sale of LNG in generating revenue, while at the same time strengthening efforts in diversifying its economy from non-renewable resources.

"Having said that, the government has also ensured that sufficient gas will be made available to fulfil the nation's energy requirements well into the next millennium."

BRUNEI DARUSSALAM INTERNATIONAL FINANCIAL CENTRE

The Sultanate of Brunei Darussalam ('the Abode of Peace") is situated on the north-west coast of the island of Borneo, at 5 degrees North of the equator. The total area of 5,769 square kilometers borders Sarawak in Malaysia, and the South China Sea.

The Sultanate is the geographical hub of Asia and flying time to Hong Kong, Peoples Republic of China, Taiwan, Bangkok, Jakarta, Kuala Lumpur, Manila and Singapore is between 1 ½ and 3 hours. Royal Brunei Airlines, the modern and well-equipped national carrier has daily direct flights to many centers, including Singapore, China, the Gulf, the Middle East, Europe, Perth, Brisbane, and London. Malaysian Airlines, Garuda, Singapore Airlines and Royal Thai Airways operate regular routes. Brunei's Time zone of GMT +8 coincides with Asia and Southeast Asia, with large time-windows to Australasia.

CENTURIES-LONG POLITICAL STABILITY

For additional analytical, business and investment opportunities information,
please contact Global Investment & Business Center, USA
at (703) 370-8082. Fax: (703) 370-8083. E-mail: ibpusa3@gmail.com
Global Business and Investment Info Databank - www.ibpus.com

Brunei Darussalam has an enviable centuries-long history of political stability under its monarchial system of government. This is further strengthened under the able, strong and visionary leadership of His Majesty Sultan Haji Hassanal Bolkiah Mui'zaddien Waddaulah and his late father, Sultan Haji Omar Ali Saifuddien Saadul Khairi Waddien. Brunei Darussalam is member of the major international and regional organizations, notably the United Nations and ASEAN, providing added security to the country.

CONTINUOUS ECONOMIC PROSPERITIES

Political stability and the excellent vision of His Majesty the Sultan and Yang DiPertuan have made it possible for Brunei Darussalam to achieve sustainable economic prosperity and stability which has benefited the whole population. Brunei Darussalam continues to register reasonable growth despite the turmoil of oil price and financial crisis in Asia. Central to this economic achievement is the government's Five-Year National Development Plans, which provide strategic guidelines and direction for the economy. The country continues to pursue an economic diversification policy away from the traditional reliance on the oil and gas sector in order to enjoy rapid growth like that of its partners in the Asia-Pacific region.

INFRASTRUCTURE

The government is totally committed to maintaining a sophisticated telecommunication system. There are two earth satellite stations providing direct telephone, telex and facsimile links to all parts of the world. Several systems currently in operation include digital telephone exchange, fibre-optic cable links with Singapore and Manila, exchanges for access to high-speed computer bases overseas, cellular mobile telephone and paging systems.

Through its National Development Plans, Brunei Darussalam continues to upgrade other communication facilities. Brunei International Airport is currently undergoing major upgrading work to cater substantial increase in both passengers and cargo traffic. There are two seaports that offer direct shipping to numerous destinations. More than 2,000-kilometre of modern and extensive road networks serving the entire country. An excellent and wide range of motor vehicles is provided, whether for purchase or hire. The country enjoys one of the highest ratios of vehicles per head of population in the world. Fuels sell at very economic rates.

EDUCATED POPULATION

The population of Brunei Darussalam is around 350,000 English is widely spoken and is used in business. The University of Brunei Darussalam and other higher educational institutes in the country release hundreds of graduates every year. There is also a significant resource of Bruneians who have taken good tertiary qualifications in various aspects of international business (mostly in the U.K.), and the IFC will offer these professionals rewarding careers in what will be a high class and very busy jurisdiction. The work ethic and commercial standards of the community are refreshing, with an emphasis on the provision of good service at a fair price.

EXPATRIATES AND PROFESSIONALS IN BRUNEI

Brunei Darussalam hosts a large expatriate community involved in the oil and gas and professional services industries. Government's assistance in granting approvals for foreign workers up to and including executive level is experienced and considerable.

HIGH QUALITY HEALTH AND EDUCATION FACILITIES

Both the health and education sectors are established to an extremely high standard at all levels. Indeed the Brunei opportunities and standards n these areas compare more than favorably with the facilities in most Developed Nations.

Expatriate staff always find that excellent in these areas is achieved at very reasonable cost in a manner which takes full advantage of the combination of a healthy lifestyle, quality of teaching staff and facilities which surpass those available "back home". In broader terms, both the environment and the cost of living in Brunei, coupled with zero tax, combine to produce a most attractive lifestyle.

HEALTHY LIFE STYLES

Eco-tourism is growing and great care has been taken with the preservation of extensive rain forest resources. Superb and very convenient facilities enable even the short-term visitor to observe and experience the natural resources of fauna and flora which the country has carefully preserved in a natural state. Similarly, magnificent fishing, diving, sailing, golfing, tennis, riding and other recreational facilities abound.

Alcohol and drug abuse is almost totally absent, and a serene and secure social environment prevails. Brunei maintains tranquil and moderate Islamic traditions, which flow through into its unique capabilities for Islamic financial growth. Fair dealing and avoidance of usury produces a philosophy, which has much in common with English based equitable principles. Religious freedom is guaranteed under the Constitution, and the country's commitment to the rule of law is built on the strong foundations of the inherited systems of English Common Law and the independence of its judiciary.

The climate is tropical and average daytime temperatures range between 26 C and 35 C. Brunei Darussalam has never experienced typhoons, earthquakes or severe flood conditions.

There are hotels to suit all tastes and pockets. Traditional hospitability and quality services reflect the experienced gained by operators in this very busy area of activity. Room occupancy rates are healthy, booking is desirable.

BRUNEI IFC: INTRODUCTION

Brunei has for many years been a significant player in the ASEAN region. Its very strong ties with the United Kingdom, Singapore and regional countries have led to the build-up of considerable commercial activity. The economy has been dominated by the oil and liquefied natural gas industries and Government expenditure patterns. Brunei Darussalam's exports consist of three major commodities, namely: crude oil, petroleum products and liquefied natural gas. Exports are destined mainly for Japan, the United Stated and ASEAN countries. But the country has entered a new phase of development in its drive towards economic diversification and maturity.

Prior to formal establishment of the IFC, Brunei was already a busy commercial centre, as witness the existing active presences in the Banking sector of HSBC, Standard Chartered, Overseas Union Bank, Citibank, Maybank, Baiduri Bank, Tabung Amanah Islam Brunei and Islamic Bank of Brunei Berhad. All the major accounting firms have significant presences, and there are some fifteen law firms.

NATIONAL GOALS

For additional analytical, business and investment opportunities information,
please contact Global Investment & Business Center, USA
at (703) 370-8082. Fax: (703) 370-8083. E-mail: ibpusa3@gmail.com
Global Business and Investment Info Databank - www.ibpus.com

Unlike many IFCs, Brunei has the advantage of already being an affluent society based on the fossil-fuel economy. The country's motives in establishing an IFC regime are therefore more subtle and soci0-economic than simply to generate and income-stream to supplement tourism.

The goals motivating the establishment of the IFC include developing the capacity to –

- Diversify, expand into and grow the value added financial service sector of the economy of Brunei and the Asia Pacific Region (APR).
- Provide a secure, cost-effective, sensibly regulated IFC facility, which will offer a safe harbour for the conduct of significant regional and international business for corporate and private clients.
- Attract overseas professionals to assist in running the IFC to the highest standards.
- Encourage expatriate professionals to become involved in training and development of rewarding opportunities for professionally qualified and trained Bruenians in the International Business Sector.
- Increase returns for the hospitality, transport and amenity industries, including eco-tourism, culminating in an holistic result for the country's economy.
- Position Brunei as an equal partner in the globalisation of financial and commercial activity, and thereby, to generate greater communication with and between other nations.

THE MEANS TO ACHIEVE THESE GOALS

Brunei will deploy its sovereignty, wealth and human resources in a conservative but assertive manner to establish a jurisdictional environment which will be tax-free, and free form over-regulation or "business pollution". Brunei IFC offers a range of international legislation carefully crafted to permit flexible, cost effective capabilities which are right up-to-date. Such capabilities will include the full range of facilities necessary for the efficient conduct of global business. There will be regular liaison with regulatory bodies internationally.

EXCLUSION OF MONEY LAUNDERING A FIRST PRIORITY

As a sovereign nation of high repute (capable, for example of hosting the September 2000 APEC Summit), Brunei is serving notice at the outset that criminal abuses of its financial systems will not be tolerated. The country is taking these steps voluntarily, rather than under pressure. This reflects responsible economic and social attitudes.

The first tranche of legislation enacted for the IFC regime therefore includes Money-Laundering and Proceeds of (serious) Crime measures implemented to international standards. Severe Drug Trafficking legislation has been in place for some time. Moreover, meaningful and enforceable regulation of the Trust, Company Administration, Insurance and Banking industries has been legislated for before these activities commence. At the outset Brunei IFC will in this regard be well prepared.

The initial legislation consists of the anti-crime measures already mentioned and the following:

International Banking Order, 2000 ('IBO')

International Business Companies Order, 2000 (IBCO')

Registered Agents and Trustees Licensing Order, 2000 ('RATLO')

International Trusts Order, 2000 ('ITO')

For additional analytical, business and investment opportunities information,
please contact Global Investment & Business Center, USA
at (703) 370-8082. Fax: (703) 370-8083. E-mail: ibpusa3@gmail.com
Global Business and Investment Info Databank - www.ibpus.com

International Limited Partnerships Order, 2000 ('ILPO')

Insurance, Securities and Mutual fund legislation is expected to be enacted early in the second half of the year 2000.

GENERAL SCHEME – PARALLEL JURISDICTIONS

Accordingly, Brunei will be a "dual jurisdiction", whereby the international legislation offers "offshore" facilities, alongside the usual ranges of "domestic" legislation drawn form the at of England and Wales. The jurisdictional distinction is thus jurisprudential rather than physical.

The judicial system will be common to both domestic and international law. In this regard, Brunei is fortunate in His Majesty's choice of senior and highly respected judges drawn form Commonwealth countries. In a recent judgment, Dato Sir Denys Roberts, KCMG, SPMP, a former Chief Justice of Hong Kong who for some years has held that office in Brunei had occasion to observe. "There has never been any interference by the executive with the judiciary, which has remained staunchly independent..." All members of the (Brunei) Court of Appeal are distinguished Commonwealth Judges. The importance of such a strong and experienced "British/Commonwealth" judiciary in an Asian regional context cannot be overstated. Final civil appeals are to the Privy Council in London.

REGULATORY – THE AUTHORITY

Brunei Darussalam has no central bank and the Ministry of Finance exercises most of those functions. Monetary policy has been determined by linking the Brunei Darussalam's dollar to the Singapore Dollar and there is parity between the two. The Singapore link is seen as a stabilizing influence. Nor are there any exchange controls. Domestic companies are taxed, but there is no personal income tax in Brunei.

The "international" legislation is supervised by "the Authority", a segregated unit of the Ministry of Finance acting through the Financial Institutions Division and the head of supervision (IFC). The Authority comprises a multi-disciplinary unit with appropriate banking, insurance, corporate and trust supervisory skills. It is a one-step Authority in the true sense, with line command passing directly form the Minister of Finance, the Minister responsible for the international legislation.

International Business Companies Order, 2000 (IBCO)

IBCO makes provision for tax-free corporate facilities at highly competitive cost levels. As an affluent State, Brunei is more concerned with attracting a critical mass of good business than with struggling to achieve a fee-based income stream at a high cost to end users. Thus the total Government Fee for company incorporation and year one maintenance is US$500, while renewal fees from year 2 onwards are set at US$400. Again, the private sector is encouraged to match Government's approach charging on a cost-plus basis, and to look beyond establishment to subsequent corporate transactional activity involving Brunei and overseas professionals.

International Business Companies may be:-

- Limited by shares
- Limited by guarantee
- Limited by shares and guarantee
- Of limited duration

- Dedicated Cell companies (akin to the Guernsey/Mauritius and other models more commonly referred to as "Protected" cell companies).
- Created by conversion (akin to continuance), re-domiciled (or discontinued) in Brunei
- Foreign, or overseas companies may register branch operations as Foreign International Companies.

IBCs are incorporated by trust companies subscribing to Memorandum and Articles. A Certificate of Due Diligence must be filed with the constituent documents. This Certificate contains an undertaking by the trust company concerned that the IBC complies with applicable provisions of IBCO and that due diligence in respect of beneficial owners and the source of finding has been conducted, or will be conducted prior to commencement of business. A similar certificate is required at every annual renewal.

IBCO requires the "official" name of an IBC to be in Romanised form. Chinese and Japanese characters or Arabic or Cyrillic script, or other characters, alphabet or script may by arrangement with the Registrar of International Business Companies be adopted in addition. Such alternative names and all documents in a foreign language are required to be presented with a certified translation.

There are simple prospectus provisions relating to invitations to subscribe for share or loan issues. However, an invitation or offer addressed to a restricted circle of persons whereby the invitation is addressed to an identifiable category, group or body of persons to whom it is directly communicated or where such persons are the only persons who may accept the offer and are in possession of sufficient information to be able to make a reasonable evaluation of the invitation or offer are not "invitations to the public". The number of persons to whom the invitation or offer is communicated cannot exceed fifty. Since "person" includes a body corporate, this is seen as liberal.

POWERS OF IBCS

Subject to its Memorandum and Articles, an IBC has, irrespective of corporate benefit, power to perform all acts conducive to its business, and may include in its Memorandum a statement that is objects are to engage in any act not prohibited under the laws of Brunei. In which case such objects are by statute attributed to the company in those terms. Standard Memorandum and Articles for the three classes of limited company are Scheduled and may be adopted in full or as modified. Other than bearer shares, which are prohibited, an IBC may issue the usual wide range of shares and classes of shares, including Dedicated Cell shares, options, warrants or rights to acquire securities of an IBC, including convertible securities.

Powers to purchase, redeem or acquire a company's own shares are contained in IBCO, and provisions facilitating the acquisition and treatment of Treasury shares are made, subject to solvency and creditor-related requirements. Assistance to purchase the shares of an IBC may similarly be provided by it.

Powers to purchase, redeem or acquire a company's own shares are contained in IBCO, and provisions facilitating the acquisition and treatment of Treasury shares are made, subject to solvency and creditor-related requirements. Assistance to purchase the shares of an IBC may similarly be provided by it.

Share capital may be reduced by 75% resolution, subject to solvency and creditor concerns being appropriately addressed. There is a mechanism whereby the Register of International Business Companies may adjudicate on creditor concerns, with power to refer to the Court where necessary.

**For additional analytical, business and investment opportunities information,
please contact Global Investment & Business Center, USA
at (703) 370-8082. Fax: (703) 370-8083. E-mail: ibpusa3@gmail.com
Global Business and Investment Info Databank - www.ibpus.com**

Directors may be individual or corporate, as may secretaries. A Resident Secretary provided by a Trust Company is mandatory. Audits are optional (except as required under banking, trust company, insurance and dealing licensing provisions).

Filing of charges or a statement of particulars of charge is provided for and where such a filling is not made, the charge may, so far as creating a security against the assets of the company, be void as against a liquidator or creditor. Comprehensive Mergers and Consolidation provisions are prescribed. Including mergers or consolidations will overseas companies. The rights of dissenting members are protected.

Foreign International companies are registered under Part XI, on lodgment through a trust company of the specified constituent documents, certain other information and a certificate of compliance and due diligence. Changes in particulars must be notified in the usual way.

Conversion/continuance occurs where permitted by the former domicile, subject to certain requirements including solvency and registration of (IBCO-compatible) Memorandum and Articles. There is provision for the Court to strike form the Brunei register a company, which continues to exist in another jurisdiction following conversion.

Dedicated Cell Companies ("DCC") are established pursuant to Part XIIA of IBCO, and subject to the prior consent of the Authority, may be initially established or reconstituted as a DCC. A DCC is a single legal person and may establish one or more cells for the purpose of segregating and protecting dedicated assets. The assets are either dedicated assets or general assets, and separate records and protection of dedicated assets by way of segregation and identification must be maintained.

Creditors are restricted in their rights to the cell in respect of which they have made funds available or have a claim.

There is implied in every transaction entered into by a DCC the following terms:-

- That no party may seek to exert any claim against assets attributable to a cell in respect of a liability not attributable to that cell;
- That if any party succeeds to the contrary, he will be liable to the company to repay the value of the benefit;

Further, a person who willfully and without colour of right "attacks" a cell in respect of which he has no rights commits an offence.

A DCC may by a 75% resolution of the company or of the holders of dedicated shares in a cell of a DCC effect of a reduction of capital generally, and without the need for confirmation by the Court)-

(a) where the resolution is passed by the company, in respect of any of the company's cells; or

(b) where the resolution is passed by the holders of dedicated shares, in respect of the cell in which the dedicated shares are held;

Any such reduction of dedicated share capital must comply with the requirements relating to reduction of capital of IBCs generally.

Notice of a proposed resolution authorizing the reduction of dedicated share capital must be given to:-

(a) the DCC (except where the company is itself the applicant);

(b) the receiver liquidator or administrator (if any) of the cell, the Authority, all holders of dedicated shares of the cell, every creditor and such other persons as the Authority may direct.

The name of a DCC must include the expression "Dedicated cell" or "DCC" or a cognate expression approved by the Authority, the memorandum shall state that it is a DCC, and each cell of a DCC shall have its own distinct name or designation.

Disputes as to liability attributable to cells. The Court may make a declaration in respect of the matter in dispute.

A DCC must inform any person with whom it transact that it is a DCC; and identify the cell in respect of which that person is transacting, failing which the directors may incur personal liability. The Court may relieve a director of personal liability if such director satisfies the Court that he ought fairly to be so relieved.

WINDING-UP OF IBCS

Basically, the provisions of Parts V (Winding-up) and VI (Receivers and Managers) of the (domestic) Companies Act (Chapter 39) apply to the winding-up of an IBC as they apply to the winding-up of a domestic company.

Striking off for failure to pay prescribed fees

If an IBC fails to pay a prescribed renewal fee and the failure continues for over two months the Registrar shall initiate striking-off. If an IBC has been struck off the register, the former IBC or a creditor, member or liquidator of it may apply to the Court to have the IBC restored to the register.

Confidentiality

The records of an IBC may only be searched subject to the prior grant of certain consents, except where circumstances, such as criminal activity, are adjudged by the Registrar to have arisen. This applies both to the Registrar's records and those of the IBC held at its registered office.

INTERNATIONAL LIMITED PARTNERSHIPS

An International Limited Partnerships is a partnership which

- Consists of one or more general partners;
- Is formed for any lawful purpose to be carried out;
- Is undertaken in or from within Brunei Darussalam or elsewhere; and
- Is registered in accordance with ILPO;
- Does not carry on business with any person resident in Brunei Darussalam

In an ILP a general partner is personally liable for all the debts and obligations of the ILP but, except in so far as the partnership agreement or ILPO otherwise provides, a limited partner is not so liable. At the time of becoming a limited partner, a limited partner contributes, or undertakes to contribute, a stated amount (or property valued at a stated amount) to the capital of the partnership. Provision for confirmation of value exists.

At least one partner in an ILP shall be either an IBC, a trust corporation or a wholly owned subsidiary thereof or a partnership which is an ILP.

Subject to that, the partners in an ILP shall be resident domiciled, established, incorporated or registered in a country or territory outside Brunei Darussalam.

Every ILP must

- Have a name which includes the words "International Limited Partnership" or the letters "ILP";
- Maintain a registered office in Brunei at the registered office of a trust corporation and
- Keep at this registered office such accounts and records as are sufficient to show and explain the ILPs transactions and to disclose with treasonable accuracy, at any time, the financial position of the ILP at that time.

Except as permitted or required under ILPO, a limited partner shall not take part in the conduct of the business of an ILP, and all letters, contracts, deeds, instruments or documents whatsoever must be entered into by the general partner on behalf of the ILP. If a limited partner, other than a trust corporation acting in such capacity for the purposes of ILPO, takes part in the conduct of the business of the ILP in its dealings with persons who are not partners, then in the event of the insolvency of the ILP, the limited partner many be liable as though he or she were a general partner.

ILPs are registered through a trust corporation by the payment of a year one fee of US$500. The annual renewal fee thereafter is US$400. A statement must be filed by the trust company concerned setting out:

(a) the name of the ILP;

(b) the general nature of the business of the ILP;

(c) the address in Brunei Darussalam of the ILP;

(d) the term, if any, for which the ILP is entered into or, if it is for unlimited duration, the date of its commencement and that the ILP is without limit of time; and

(e) the full name and address of the general partner or, if there is more than one, of each general partner.

A certificate of due diligence and a certificate signed by the trust corporation certifying that the requirements of the Order in respect of registration have been compiled with must also be filed. Until the date indicated on the certificate of registration (issued by the Registrar) of an ILP no limited partner in the ILP to which the certificate relates has limited liability.

The ILP Registrar maintains a record of each ILP and on payment of the prescribed fee any partner, director however described or liquidator of the ILP, the Authority or the trust corporation for the time being of the ILP or any other person with the written permission of such director, partner or liquidator or who can demonstrate to the Authority or the ILP Registrar that he has a cogent reason for doing so.

If at any time any change is made in any of the matters previously specified and filed, an ILP must file, within sixty days of the change, a statement in the prescribed form including, where a new partner is to be admitted an appropriate re-affirmation of the certificate of due diligence, specifying the nature of the change,. A brief annual return is required to be filed each year. Registration of an ILP may be revoked by the ILP Registrar acting on the advice of the Authority on the grounds set out in ILPO. However, where the ILP Registrar intends to revoke the legislation of an ILP he must give notice of his intention to the registered office of the ILP and allow a reasonable opportunity to show cause why the registration of partnership should not be revoked.

THE INTERNATIONAL BANKING ORDER

The International Banking Order ("IBO") governs the provision of international banking services to non-residents. While encompassing the traditional definition of banking by reference to taking of deposits, the IBO recognizes that this is not the daily concern of a sophisticated International Bank. The IBO expands its horizons in line with the banking industry's modern development and trends.

Four classes of license are provided for:

- A full international license for the purpose of carrying on international banking business generally;
- An international investment banking license for the purpose of carrying on international Islamic banking business, granted in respect of full, investment or restricted activities.
- A restricted international banking license for the purpose of carrying on international banking business subject to the restriction that the licensee may not offer, conduct or provide such business except to or for persons name d or described in an undertaking embodied in the application for the license.

"International banking business" includes the taking of deposits from the (non-resident) public, the granting of credits, the issue of credit cards and money collections and transmissions. /nut the definition is expanded to embrace foreign exchange transactions, the issue of guarantees., trade finance, development finance and sectoral credits, consumer credit, investment banking, Islamic banking business., broking and risk management services whether conducted by conventional practices or using Internet or other electronic technology and includes electronic banking.

"International investment banking business" includes –

- providing consultancy and advisory services relating to corporate and investment matters, industrial strategy and related questions, and advice and services relating to mergers and restructuring and acquisitions, or making and managing investments on behalf of any person;
- providing credit facilities including guarantees and commitments;
- participation in stock, or share issues and the provision of services relating thereto: or
- the arrangement and underwriting of debt and equity issues.

"International Islamic banking business" is banking business whose aims and operations do not involve any element which is not approved by the Islamic Religion. Provision for Shari'ah Law to over-ride a conflicting provision in the IBO is made, subject to good banking practice, and there is

For additional analytical, business and investment opportunities information,
please contact Global Investment & Business Center, USA
at (703) 370-8082. Fax: (703) 370-8083. E-mail: ibpusa3@gmail.com
Global Business and Investment Info Databank - www.ibpus.com

a requirement of the appointment of a Shari'ah Council. The restriction to local ownership which applies under the domestic Islamic Banking Act does not apply to the international regime.

The IBO imposes strict standards of confidentiality on both the Authority and the banks and their officers. In line with what are becoming expected international standards, mutual assistance between designated supervisory authorities exercising similar powers to the Authority in other jurisdictions is permitted. This is, subject to continuing confidentiality and guarantees of reciprocal assistance.

In respect of banking supervisory actions, the Authority will require –

- To receive audited annual accounts,
- To conduct on-site inspection
- To be given notice of significant charges in ownership and key personnel (which respectively attract consent procedures for Brunei headquartered banks), and
- To investigate and take action in appropriate cases of criminal or unlawful acts and when the circumstances of the bank justify intervention.

And is empowered to apply to the High Court for such assistance as may be necessary in appropriate cases to avert criminal or solvency / liquidity matters which are beyond the mutually-exercised corrective measures available to the bank and the Authority acting in concert.

Those who conduct activities included in the services also offered by the banks will be exempted from the IBO provisions. But companies which conduct banking activities without any regulatory controls, consents or licenses will not be permitted to do so in Brunei, except by means of full disclosure and Ministerial exemption in exceptional cases, on specified terms.

Brunei expects and looks to attract the presence of good quality institutions whose credentials are based on quality and activity rather than size alone.

International banks will pay no tax, and neither will their staff, customers or products.

Annual Fees: U.S.$

Full license $50,000

Investment $35,000

Islamic (Full, Investment) $50,000

Restricted $25,000

INTERNATIONAL TRUSTS ORDER

The Order applies only to an international trust ("IT") as defined. An It must be in writing, (including declarations and wills), settled by a non-resident of Brunei, declared in its terms to be an international trusts (on creation or migration to Brunei), and at least one trustee must be a licensed under The Registered Agents and Trustees Licensing Order, 2000 (RATLO) or an authorized wholly-owned subsidiary of a licensee. Generally, only non-residents may be beneficiaries when an IT is first established. The retention of certain powers (specified in the ITO)

For additional analytical, business and investment opportunities information,
please contact Global Investment & Business Center, USA
at (703) 370-8082. Fax: (703) 370-8083. E-mail: ibpusa3@gmail.com
Global Business and Investment Info Databank - www.ibpus.com

by the settler will not invalidate an IT. Such powers are not, however, deemed to exist in the absence of specific provision in the trust instrument.

There are wide powers of investment, with an ability for trustees to seek "proper advice" as defined. Having done so, a trustee will not be liable for acts taken pursuant to such advice.

There are powers to appoint agents and to delegate. Trustees may charge, and similar provisions appear for enforcers and protectors. Powers of maintenance and advancement are wide, spendthrift and protective trusts are recognized.

Arrangements for appointment or change of trustees follow generally accepted lines. The Court is given wide powers to interpret, assist and amend. Hearings may be held in camera. Trustees may pay funds into Court for determination of matters arising in the course of administering the fund, and there is power to apply to the Court for an opinion, advice or a direction relating to trust assets.

Purpose trusts are provided for, whether charitable or non-charitable. Without prejudice to the generality, a trust for the purpose of holding securities or other assets is by statute deemed a purpose trust. The purposes must be reasonable, practicable, not immoral nor contrary to public policy. The trust instrument must state that the trust is to be an authorized purpose trust at creation or on migration to Brunei. Provision must be made for the disposal of surplus assets (although no perpetuity period applies), and an enforcer is required. On completion or impossibility of achieving purposes, further trusts may be activated.

SPECIAL TRUSTS

In Part IX of ITO a power is said to be held on trust if granted or reserved subject to any duty to exercise the power. A trust or power is subject to Part IX and is described as a special trust, if at the creation of the trust or when it first becomes subject to the law of Brunei Darussalam the settler is non-resident and the trust instrument provides that the trust is to be a special trust. The objects of a special trust or power may be persons or purposes or both, the person may be of any number, and the purposes may be of any number of kind, charitable or non-charitable.

The hallmark of a special trust is that a beneficiary does not as such have standing to enforce the trust or any enforceable right to the trust property. The only persons who have standing to enforce a special trust are such persons as are appointed to be its enforcers –

- By the trust instrument; or
- Under the provisions of the trust instrument; or
- By the Court

An enforcer of a special trust has a duty to act responsibly with a view to enforcing the proper execution of the trust, and to consider at appropriate intervals whether and how to exercise his powers and then to act accordingly. A trustee or another enforcer, or any person expressly authoresses by the trust instrument, has standing to being an action against an enforcer to compel him to perform his duties. An enforcer is entitled to necessary rights of access to documents and records. Generally a special trust is not void for uncertainty, and its terms may give to the trustee or any other person power to resolve any uncertainty as to its objects or mode of execution.

If such an uncertainty cannot be resolved as aforesaid, the Court may act to resolve the uncertainty, and insofar as the objects of the trust are uncertain and the general intent of the trust cannot be found form the admissible evidence as a manner of probability, any declare the trust void. If the execution of a special trust is or becomes in whole or in part – impossible or impracticable; or

(a) unlawful or contrary to publish policy; or

(b) obsolete in that, by reason of changed circumstances it fails to achieve the general intent of the special trust,

the trustee must, unless the trust is reformed pursuant to it own terms, apply to the Court to reform the trust cy-pres.

REGISTERED AGENTS AND TRUSTEES LICENSING ORDER, 2000

Brunei has opted for a regulated trust and corporate regime ab initio. The Registered Agents and Trustees Licensing Order ("RATLO") restricts the provision of "international business services" to companies licensed under that Order.

"International business services" includes international companies management business, international partnerships management business and international trust business.

"International companies management business" includes –

acting as registered agent for the incorporation or registration of IBCs and Foreign International Companies ("IFCs") under the International Business Companies Order, 2000 ("IBCO"), the conversion of overseas companies into IBCs, and the merger, consolidation, continuation, renewal, extension of the duration of, or migration of IBCs.

Providing registered offices, share transfer offices or administration offices of the receipt of post or other articles, IBCs and FICs.

Providing or appointing persons to perform the functions of directors, (mandatory) resident, secretary, nominees, preparing, keeping or fillng books, accounts, registers, records, minutes and returns for IBCs and FICs, and other matters relating to corporate administration, including the establishment of IBCs as Dedicated Cell Companies or Limited Life Companies.

All documents to be filed with the Registrar of International Business Companies (and Limited Partnerships) are filed by trusts companies.

Similarly, trust companies must be involved in all International Limited Partnerships (ILP) and "qualifying" trusts – i.e. International Trusts formed pursuant to the ITO and trusts which are established under the laws of other jurisdictions but administered in Brunei.

Trust companies and banks will also be involved in the forthcoming Mutual Fund Order regime, which will govern both domestic and international schemes.

Trusts licenses will be available by way of application to the Authority to institutions, professional groups and independent trusts groups. A comprehensive licensing, process and approval of senior personnel, is involved and ongoing supervision will include the filing of audited accounts of the trust companies (but not their clients) with the Authority. Notifications and approvals of appointments and changes of Key Personnel apply. Minimum capitalization of B$150,000 either

For additional analytical, business and investment opportunities information,
please contact Global Investment & Business Center, USA
at (703) 370-8082. Fax: (703) 370-8083. E-mail: ibpusa3@gmail.com
Global Business and Investment Info Databank - www.ibpus.com

paid-up in full or 50% paid-up with the other 50% guaranteed is required. Insurance requirements (but no bond) apply. The Authority's concern is continuing liquidity and sufficiency of working capital, and a 3 year business plan is required with tall applications for licenses under RATLO.

The application fee for a Trust and registered Agent's license is US$2,500 and an Annual License Fee of US$2,000 is imposed.

Trust licensees will, with the approval of the Authority, be permitted to establish wholly-owned subsidiaries (whose operations trust be fully guaranteed by the licensee). Such a subsidiary may be an IBC (as may the licensee itself) and may for the purpose of the licensee's business act as a trustee, nominee, secretary or director in respect of international business services. The aim is to permit accountable flexibility and segregating in, for example, Collective Investment Scheme, Private Trust Company and Special Purpose Vehicle situations, including the commercial deployment of special and purpose trusts.

Trust companies, (including overseas trust companies establishing a branch in Brunei) as well as the entities they administer, will be totally exempt from all tax in respect of Brunei operations. Again, nor will their officers, customers or products be taxed.

This attractive entry-level package for RATLO licensees is intended to encourage suitable local and overseas applicants to seek licenses and to achieve a critical mass of private and corporate "trust" activities in the broader sense. The relatively low cost of living and of a well-educated support staff pool adds to the appeal. Low fees, however, should not be taken as an indication that the supervisory regime will be any other than through and strictly enforced. It is hoped that participants will follow Government's lead in keeping the cost of their services reasonable. It is a false argument that high class jurisdictions must charge high fees to maintain their reputation and that high fees will discourage criminals. Good corporate vehicles at reasonable cost is the aim.

BUSINESS AND INVESTMENT CLIMATE

Investors will find that Brunei Darussalam offers a favourable and conducive environment for a profitable investment. Some of the key reasons are:-

* Brunei Darussalam is a stable and prosperous country which offers not only excellent infrastructure but also a strategic location within the ASEAN group of countries;

* Brunei Darussalam has no personal income tax, no sales tax, payroll, manufacturing or export tax. Approved foreign investors can also enjoy a company tax holiday of up to 8 years;

* The regulations relating to foreign participation in equity are flexible. In many instances there can be 100 percent foreign ownership;

* There are no difficulties in securing approval for foreign workers, ranging from labourers to managers;

* The costs of utilities are among the lowest in the region;

* The local market, while relatively small, is lucrative and most overseas investors will encounter little or no local competition;

* The living conditions in Brunei Darussalam are among the best and most secure in the region.

* Above all else, His Majesty's Government genuinely welcomes foreign investment in almost any enterprise and will ensure that you receive speedy, efficient and practical assistance with all your enquries.

INFRASTRUCTURE

The country's infrastructure is well developed and ready to cater for the needs of the new and vigorous economic activities under the current economic diversification programme.

The country's two main ports, at Muara and Kuala Belait, offer direct shipping to Hong Kong, Singapore and several other Asian destinations. Muara, the deep-water port, 29 kilometers from the capital, was opened in 1973 and has since been considerably developed. There is 12,542 sq. metres of warehouse space and 6.225 sq. meters in transit sheds. Container yards have been increased in size and a container freight station handles unstuffing operations.

The recently expanded Brunei International Airport at Bandar Seri Begawan included the expansion of both passenger and cargo facilities to meet an expected substantial increase in demand. The new terminal, designed to handle 1.5 million passengers and 50,000 tonnes of cargo a year, is expected to meet demand until the end of the decade.

The 2,000-kilometre road network serving the entire country is being expanded and modernised. A main highway runs the entire length of the country's coastline. It conveniently links Muara, the port entry point at one end, to Belait, the oil-production centre, at the western end of the state.

TELECOMMUNICATIONS

Brunei Darussalam has one of the best telecommunication systems in South-East Asia and has major plans for improving it further. With an estimated population of about 270,000, the rate of telephone availability is currently 1 telephone for every 3 persons. And this is being continually upgraded.

There are two earth satellite stations providing direct telephone, telex and facsimile links to most parts of the world. Several systems currently in operation serving the country include an analogue telephone exchange, fibre-optic cable links with Singapore and Manila, a packet switching exchange for access to high speed computer bases overseas, cellular mobile telephone and paging system. Direct telephone links are available to the remotest parts of the country through microwave and solar-powered telephones.

ECONOMY

Brunei Darussalam's economy is dominated by the oil and liquified natural gas industries and Government expenditure patterns. Brunei Darussalam's exports consist of three major commodities, namely: crude oil, petroleum products and liquified natural gas. Exports are destined mainly for Japan, the United States and ASEAN countries.

The second most important industry is the construction industry. This is directly the result of increased investment by the Government in development and infrastructure projects within the current series of five-year National Development Plans.

For additional analytical, business and investment opportunities information,
please contact Global Investment & Business Center, USA
at (703) 370-8082. Fax: (703) 370-8083. E-mail: ibpusa3@gmail.com
Global Business and Investment Info Databank - www.ibpus.com

Brunei Darussalam has entered a new phase of development in its drive towards economic diversification from dependence on the oil and liquified natural gas-based economy. It is encouraging to note that the contribution from the non-oil and gas-based sector of the economy, as reflected in the contribution to GDP (Statistical Year Report 1991), has continued to increase. The private sector (other than the oil and natural gas sector) contributes 24.31 percent compared to 46.43 percent of the oil and natural gas sector. Moreover the total number of establishments (registered) in the private sector has increased from 3,591 in 1986 to 4,749 in 1990, a significant increase of 32.2 percent.

This encouraging trend was initiated by the Government's moves to diversify the economy and to promote the development of the private sector as a means to attain this goal. This strategy was solidly backed-up by the implementation of the Investment Incentive Act in 1975 and the formation of the Ministry of Industry and Primary Resources in 1989.

The Government has very large foreign reserves and no foreign debt. Brunei Darussalam is, in fact, a significant international investor. The Brunei Investment Agency (BIA), formed in 1983, is entrusted with the management of the foreign reserves.

EMPLOYMENT

The Government sector is the largest employer, providing jobs for more than half the working population. The rest largely worked for Brunei Shell Petroleum Sdn. Bhd. and Royal Brunei Airlines. In 1992 the number of employees in the private sector has increased to 61,761 from 53,613 in 1990. Of the total, 47,125 (76.3%) are foreign workers.

The small size of the indigenous work-force and the locals preference for public sector employment is a major constraint to development. Foreign workers have helped to ease labour shortages and make up over a third of the workforce. Regulations and procedures on recruitment of foreign workers are straight-forward and Government's assistance are readily available in securing approval for foreign workers ranging from labourers to executive managers.

FINANCE - POLICIES AND REGULATIONS

Although Brunei Darussalam has no central bank, the Ministry of Finance through the Treasury, the Currency Board and the Brunei Investment Agency exercises most of the functions of a central bank. Brunei Darussalam's monetary policy has been determined by linking the Brunei Darussalam's dollar to the Singapore dollar and there is parity between the two. The Ministry of Finance feels that the Monetary Authority of Singapore exercises sufficient caution and such a link will not have detrimental effects on the economies of either country. At the same time, this agreement is not seen as inhibiting the management of the domestic economy.

CURRENCY

Currency matters are the responsibility of the Brunei Darussalam Currency Board. It is responsible for the issuing and redemption of State banknotes and coins and the supervision of the banks. The setting up of a Central Monetary Authority is under consideration.

Money supply growth is presently around 20 percent per annum. The ratio of external assets to demand liabilities is around 110 percent - considerably more than the 70 percent laid down by the Board's governing Act.

EXCHANGE CONTROLS

There is no foreign exchange control. Banks permit non-resident account to be maintained and there is no restriction on borrowing by non-residents.

BANKING AND INSURANCE

There are currently eight commercial banks providing full banking services in the country. Two of these are locally incorporated. International banks such as Citibank, Hongkong and Shanghai Bank and Standard Chartered Bank have been operating branches in the state for decades. The financial sector also includes a number of locally incorporated and international finance and insurance companies. Interest rates are set by the Association of Banks.The authorities have been preparing to implement a comprehensive financial regulatory system via the proposed new Banking Act. The establishment of a development bank is also under consideration.

ECONOMIC DEVELOPMENT BOARD

The Economic Development Board is responsible for directly assisting local businessmen by providing loans at favourable rates of interest for start-up and expansion of their business. The scheme provides loans for up to a maximum amount of B$1.5 million at 4 percent interest rate repayable up to a maximum period not exceeding 12 years.

ONE-STOP AGENCY

As the focal point for all industrial development, the Ministry of Industry and Primary Resources coordinates all industrial development activities. For investments in Brunei Darussalam, the Ministry is a One-Stop Agency.

It is remarkably easy to start an industry in Brunei Darussalam. A totally private development which does not require Government facilities needs only the approval to start. Those requiring Government facilities and assistance need only deal with the Ministry, which will liaise with other agencies and expedite applications.

The Ministry realizes the importance of time frames and clear decision making processes to your business. The entire procedure has only four stages:-

a) Approval of the concept

b) Approval of firm proposal

c) Approval of physical plans

d) Approval to operate

In all four stages, the Ministry of Industry and Primary Resources is your contact as a One-Stop Agency. In Brunei Darussalam, we make it easy and look forward to being Your Profitable Partner. We invite you to invest in Brunei Darussalam as a Partner in Success. Please contact the Ministry of Industry and Primary Resources directly - we are ready and available to help.

CORPORATE INVESTMENTS

Semaun Holding Sendirian Berhad was incorporated as a Private Limited Company under the Brunei Darussalam's Companies Act on 8 December 1994. It serves as an investment and trading arm of the Ministry in enhancing economic diversification programs of Brunei Darussalam.

Semaun Holdings Sendirian Berhad can be contacted at the following address:

Unit 2.02, Block D, 2nd Floor
Yayasan Sultan Haji Hassanal Bolkiah Complex
Jalan Pretty
Bandar Seri Begawan BS8711
Brunei Darussalam
E-mail address: semaun@brunet.bn
Web3.asia.com.sg/brunei/semaun.html

MINISTRY OF INDUSTRY MISSION

Semaun Holdings's mission is to spearhead industrial and commercial development through direct investment in key industrial sectors in the interest of Brunei Darussalam.

The purpose of setting up Semaun Holdings is to accelerate industrial and commercial development in Brunei Darussalam and as well as to generate opportunities for active participation of Brunei citizen.

OBJECTIVES

Semaun Holding's objectives were established by taking into consideration the need to set up projects, which have high productivity level contributing to the national Gross Domestic product (GDP). This will be done through the transfer of technologies and utilise this technologies to improve productivity which will then be resulted in continuous growth and competitiveness of the company.

The setting up of new industrial sectors will generate employment opportunities for locals and as well as increase the technological expertise of Bruneians.

Semaun Holdings will lead and provide management support and control to enterprises that are willing to venture into strategic sectors. If necessary, Semaun Holdings will form partnership or joint ventures.

Semaun Holdings play as leading role in enhancing competitiveness and as well as to secure market for industrial productions and to ensure the concern of Islam particularly in food sectors.

CORPORATE OBJECTIVES

Integrated poultry projects
Food manufacturing and processing
Computer software development
Design of electronic components
Development of Technology Park
Silica based manufacturing
Steel rolling mills

Warehousing / Regional Distribution Centre
Commercial mushroom production
Local product outlet

MINISTRY ROLE

In order to carry out these objectives, Semaun Holdings plays an important role in Brunei Darussalam's economic development through the:

- Creation and expansion of existing industrial commercial activities.
- Introduction of new technologies to Bruneian companies.
- Provision of Joint-Venture partnership with foreign investors and suitable (emerging) local and foreign companies.

Industrial and commercial strategic alliances with leading international companies.

SCOPE OF OPERATIONS

Semaun Holdings invests in business, trading and commercial enterprises including services, manufacturing, agriculture, fishery, forestry, industry and mining activities in Brunei Darussalam. Participation in related investment activities and opportunities outside the country is also a consideration.

BUSINESS SECTORS

Semaun Holdings currently targets a variety of business sectors with strong investment potential highlighting food, high-tech manufacturing and services.

FOOD SECTOR

Halal Food Processing and Manufacturing
Integrated Poultry Projects
Integrated Fisheries Projects
Local Product Outlet
Commercial Mushroom Production

HIGH- TECH MANUFACTURING

Biotechnology from Natural Resources
Silica Based Product Processing and Manufacturing
Semiconductor Related Business
Value-added Products Based On Oil and Gas Related Industries and Semiconductors Related Business
Manufacture of Computer Hardware and Software
Design of Electronic Components
Steel Rolling Mill
Industrial Estate Management

SERVICES

Tourism and Related Services
Distribution and Warehouse Facilities
Transshipments

PHILOSOPHY

Our investment philosophy highlights our first priority to invest within the country in areas of strategic importance and not in direct competition within the local private sector.
As a high profile company, the strategy employed by Semaun Holdings can be broadly grouped under three main categories:

i.   Direct investment in high-technology, high value-added industrial and commercial ventures.
ii. Investment in Research and Development leading to commercialization.
iii. Investment in overseas companies to facilitate expansion and growth of local ventures.

MECHANISM

- Wholly owned.
- New Joint-Venture companies.

  Equity investment in existing or emerging companies.

JOINT VENTURES

In 1996, Semaun Holdings through its subsidiary company, SemaunPrim Sendirian Berhad signed a joint-venture agreement with Eiwa Enterprises Company Limited, one of the producer of Peneaus Japonicus Prawn in Japan. Seiwa Corporation Sendirian Berhad was formed with present objectives summarised as follows:

- Ensure continuity supply of Tiger Shrimp and Seabass Fry for local requirement.
- Production of 0.8 million Seabass Fry (Day 60) meeting about 15 % of local requirement.
- Production of 15 million Shrimp Fry (PL 20) per annum.

In the same year, Semaun Seafood Sendirian Berhad was formed between SemaunPrim Sendirian Berhad, SinSinBun Pte Ltd (Singapore) and Koperasi Perikanan Brunei Berhad. The formation of Semaun Seafood is to carry out activities such as capture fishery and production of high commercial value and processed seafood products for domestic and export market and to utilise low value fish for production of Surimi, to process halal seafood and value added seafood product.

In 1997, another joint-venture agreement signed between SemaunPrim Sendirian Berhad and Baiduri Holdings Sendirian Berhad to carry out cage culture of groupers and other high commercial value fish and marine life. Under SeaGro Sendirian Berhad for domestic and export market.

Also in 1997, Semaun Holdings Sendirian Berhad together with Global Expertise SA, a British Photovoltaic technology resource corporation had formed a Joint-Venture company named Solar Tech Systems (B) Sendirian Berhad to be a Photovoltaic (solar electric) module manufacturer company based in Brunei Darussalam.

The main objective of the company is to produce Photovoltaic panels for local and export market. The company has a combined output capacity per year of one and a half megawatts of Solar Electric Power.

PRACTICAL INFORMATION FOR BUSINESS AND INVESTMENTS[2]

INVESTMENT AND BUSINESS CLIMATE - STRATEGIC INFORMATION AND CONTACTS FOR STARTING BUSINESS

Brunei Darussalam is an energy-rich Sultanate on the northern coast of Borneo in Southeast Asia. Brunei boasts a well-educated, largely English-speaking population, excellent infrastructure, and a government intent on attracting foreign investment and projects. In parallel with Brunei's efforts to attract foreign investment, the country has improved its protections for Intellectual Property Rights (IPR).

Despite repeated calls for diversification, Brunei's economy remains dependent on the income derived from sales of oil and gas. Substantial revenue from overseas investment supplements income from domestic hydrocarbon production. These two revenue streams provide a comfortable quality of life for Brunei's population. Citizens are not required to pay taxe, have access to free education through to the university level,free medical care and, frequently, subsidized housing.

Brunei has a stable political climate and is generally sheltered from natural disasters. Brunei's central location in Southeast Asia, with good telecommunications, numerous airline connections, business tax credits in specified sectors, and no income, sales or export taxes offers a welcoming climate for would-be investors. Brunei is a founding member of the Trans-Pacific Partnership (TPP) trade negotiations. Sectors offering U.S. business opportunities in Brunei include Aerospace & Defense, Agribusiness, Construction, Petrochemicals, Energy & Mining, Environmental Technologies, Food Processing & Packaging, Franchising, Health Technologies, Information & Communication, Islamic Finance, and Services. In 2014 Brunei released an Energy White Paper outlining its vision of leveraging its oil wealth to diversify its economy, create local employment, increase foreign direct investment (FDI), and sharply increase the use of renewable energy by 2035.

The Export-Import Bank of the United States (EXIM) and the Energy Department of Brunei's Prime Minister's Office signed a Memorandum of Understanding (MOU) that calls for expanded information sharing regarding trade and energy business opportunities in the Asia-Pacific region, as well as exploring options for utilizing up to USD 1 billion EXIM Bank loans to finance U.S. exports in support of selected projects in the region. The MOU creates significant new opportunities for U.S. energy companies in Brunei and the Asia-Pacific region while advancing the goals set out by the United States-Asia Pacific Comprehensive Energy Partnership (USACEP).

In 2014 Brunei began supplementing the existing common law-based penal system with a penal code based on Islamic law, which will carry Sharia punishments. The Islamic Penal Code is applicable across the board. The first phase became effective on May 1, 2014. It expands restrictions regarding the drinking of alcohol, eating in public during the fasting hours in the month of Ramadan, and indecent behavior. Two subsequent phases, the timing of which is not yet clear, are expected to introduce severe punishments such as; stoning to death for certain sex-related offenses and the amputating of limbs. Brunei officials say the most severe punishments will rarely if ever be implemented given the very high standard of proof required under the Sharia Penal Code. While the law does not specifically address business-related matters, potential investors should be aware that there is controversy surrounding the Sharia Penal Code issue.

---

[2] US Department of Comemrce Materials.

For additional analytical, business and investment opportunities information, please contact Global Investment & Business Center, USA at (703) 370-8082. Fax: (703) 370-8083. E-mail: ibpusa3@gmail.com Global Business and Investment Info Databank - www.ibpus.com

1. OPENNESS TO, AND RESTRICTIONS UPON, FOREIGN INVESTMENT

Attitude toward Foreign Direct Investment

Brunei has an open economy favorable to foreign trade and foreign direct investment (FDI) as it continues its economic diversification efforts away from its long reliance on oil and gas exports.

FDI is important to Brunei as it plays a key role in economic and technological development. Brunei encourages FDI in the domestic economy through various investment incentives offered by the Brunei Economic Development Board (BEDB) and the Ministry of Industry and Primary Resources (MIPR) and through activities by the Ministry of Foreign Affairs and Trade (MOFAT).

The 2015 World Bank and the International Finance Corporation report indicated that Brunei's ease of doing business ranking had dropped 3 spots to rank 101 out of 189 economies. The report attributed the drop less to any action by Brunei to make it harder to do business and more to inaction while other countries made positive changes. The one significant gain was a change in rank of 16 spots on dealing with construction permits, largely attributed to Brunei consolidating final inspections under a single agency. The Authority for Building and Construction Industry (ABCi) one-stop shop also issues all pre-construction approvals and building permits. The rankings for six of the ten indicators slipped, including: starting a business; registering property; getting credit; protecting minority investors; enforcing contracts; and resolving insolvency.

Responding to the report, Brunei's Minister of Industry and Primary Resources stated that the culture of business-as-usual was no longer relevant in the increasingly competitive world facing Brunei. Brunei also amended its laws to make it easier and quicker for entrepreneurs to establish businesses. The Miscellaneous License Act (Amendment) 2015 cuts down the wait time for new business registrants to start operations, with low-risk businesses like eateries and shops able to start operations immediately. Brunei fell from the number four country in the Association of Southeast Asian Nations (ASEAN) in terms of ease of doing business to number six.

Other Investment Policy Reviews

Not applicable.

Laws/Regulations of Foreign Direct Investment

The basic legislation on investment includes the Investment Incentive Order 2001 and Income Tax (As Amended) Order 2001. Brunei does not yet have a stock exchange, but the creation of a securities market is reportedly under development. Brunei's constitution does specifically provide for judicial independence, but in practice the court system operates without government interference. Brunei's legal system includes parallel systems; one based on Common Law and the other based on Islamic Law.

Brunei's national strategy, Wawasan (National Vision) 2035, emphasizes attracting FDI as an important driver of growth. The Brunei Economic Development Board (BEDB) seeks to diversify Brunei's economy and create employment opportunities for its people. The BEDB administers incentives and loans to encourage investment projects from abroad.

The Ministry of Industry and Primary Resources is the main coordinating agency for investment and industrial development in the primary sector, manufacturing, and tourism. The Ministry encourages and assists local and foreign investors to participate in ventures to produce goods and services for export and local markets and to satisfy national food security and employment needs.

Industrial Promotion

Through its Investment Incentives Order 2001, Brunei seeks to stimulate economic development by encouraging the establishment and expansion of specified industrial and economic enterprises. The authority to administer this legislation is currently vested in the Minister of Industry and Primary Resources, who is able to offer investment incentives in the form of tax relief for the following:

Pioneer Industries: Any limited company that has been granted a pioneer certificate will then be given pioneer incentives, including exemption from the 30 percent corporate tax for a period ranging from five years for a fixed capital expenditure of BND 500,000 to BND 2.5 million (USD 370,000 to USD 1,852,000); eight years for an expenditure over BND 2.5 million; and 11 years for a project located in a designated high-tech industrial park, with permitted extensions; exemption from taxes on imported duties on machinery, equipment, components parts, accessories or building structures; exemption from taxes on imported raw materials not available or produced in Brunei intended as feedstock for the production of Pioneer products; and carry forward losses and allowances.

Industries that have been declared as pioneer industries and pioneer products include: Agribusiness (fertilizers and pesticides); Agricultural, Construction, Building & Heavy Equipment (cement finishing mill, manufacture of electrical industrial machinery and apparatus, rolling mill plant, sheet metal-forming); Chemicals, Petrochemicals, Plastics & Composites (plastics and synthetic, manufacture of non-metallic mineral products, gas); Consumer Goods & Home Furnishings (furniture, ceramic and potteries, tissue paper, toys); Environmental Technologies (related waste industry); Food Processing & Packaging (slaughtering, preparing and preserving halal meat, canning, bottling and packaging); Health Technologies (pharmaceuticals); Information & Communication (manufacture of radio, television and communication equipment and apparatus); Industrial Equipment & Supplies (glass, wood base); Marine Technology (ship repair and maintenance, supporting services to water transport); Metal Manufacturing & Products (aluminum wall tile); Services (aircraft catering services); Textiles, Apparel & Sporting Goods (textiles). Additional details are available at**http://www.bedb.com.bn/doing_incentives_pioneer.html**

Pioneer Service Companies: Pioneer service companies may be eligible for tax relief, depending on the fixed capital expenditure, for a period of 8 years with given extension not exceeding 11 years in total.

Activities that have been declared as pioneer services include: Agribusiness (agriculture technology related services and activities); Architecture & Engineering (any engineering or technical services including laboratory, consultancy and research and development activities, development or production of any industrial design); Automotive & Ground Transportation (operation or management of any mass rapid transit system); Education (provision of education related services); Finance (business, management and professional consultancy services, financial services, venture capital fund activity); Health Technologies (medical services); Information & Communication (computer-based information and other computer related services, publishing services); Media & Entertainment (maintaining and operating a private museum, provision of leisure and recreation related services and activities); Services (services and activities related to warehousing facilities); Travel (services and activities relating to the organization or management of exhibitions and conferences). Additional details are available at **http://www.bedb.com.bn/doing_incentives_pioneerservice.html**.

Production For Export: The Minister of Industry and Primary Resources may approve a company proposing to engage in specified activities either wholly or partly for export as an export enterprise. Certified companies may be exempted from income tax; from import duties on machinery, equipment, component parts, accessories or building structures; and from import duties on raw materials for a period of six to 15 years depending on the company's fixed capital expenditure and pioneer status.

Qualified activities have included: Agribusiness (agriculture, forestry and fishery activities). Additional details are available at **http://www.bedb.com.bn/doing_incentives_production.html**.

Service For Export: Specified services may be eligible for exemption from income tax and deduction of allowance and losses. The tax relief period of an export service company shall begin on its day of commencement and shall not exceed 11 years. Any given extension shall not exceed 3 years at one time and not exceed 20 years in total.

Qualified services have included: Architecture & Engineering (technical services including construction, distribution, design and engineering services); Education (educational and training service); Industrial Equipment & Supplies (fabrication of machinery and equipment, and procurement of materials, components and equipment); Information & Communication (data processing, programming, computer software development, telecommunications and other related ICT services); Services (consultancy, management supervisory or advisory services relating to any technical matter or to any trade or business; professional services including accounting, legal, medical and architectural services.) Additional details are available at **http://www.bedb.com.bn/doing_incentives_service.html**

Foreign Loan for Product Equipment: There is a 20% withholding tax for interest paid to non-resident lenders. However the government may grant a tax exemption for any approved foreign loan if the loan is utilized for the purchase of production equipment. Additional information is available at **http://www.bedb.com.bn/doing_incentives_foreign.html**. Information on additional forms of business and investment incentives is available at **http://www.bedb.com.bn/doing_incentives.html**.

Limits on Foreign Control

There has been no restriction on total foreign ownership of companies incorporated in Brunei Darussalam. The Companies Act requires locally incorporated companies to have at least one of the two directors—or if more than two directors, at least two of them—to be ordinarily resident in Brunei Darussalam. The Companies Act allows the board to be totally non-resident; however, the company concerned would have to apply to the appropriate authorities for permission and show justifications for such decisions. Notwithstanding whether the company is locally or foreign owned and managed, the rate of corporate income tax is the same.

Privatization Program

Brunei's Ministry of Communication has made corporatization and privatization part of its Strategic Plans 2008-2017, which call for the Ministry to shift its role from a service provider to a regulatory body with policy-setting responsibility. In that role, the Ministry will develop specific policies through corporatization and privatization; establish a regulatory framework and business facilitation. Currently, the Ministry is studying initiatives to privatize and corporatize four state-owned agencies: the Ports Department, the Maritime and Port Authority of Brunei

Darussalam, the Postal Services Department, and Brunei International Airport management. These services are not yet completely privatized and there is no timeline for privatization, as the Ministry is still in the process of considering the initiative. Guidelines regarding the role of foreign investors and the bidding process are not yet available. The strategy can be found in www.mincom.gov.bn.

Screening of FDI

Post is informed that Brunei, through BEDB, has one or more processes to screen, review or approve foreign investments. The processes are kept confidential. Post has received no complaints from U.S. businesses about the screening process.

Competition Law

Brunei does not have any general competition legislation pertaining to the regulation of competition issues. Brunei formally started the process of drafting the Brunei Competition Order in May 2012, which reportedly emulates the legislation and best practices in the international jurisdiction including prohibitions against anti-competitive agreements, abuse of dominance, and anti-competitive mergers. It is not known when the law will be approved and implemented.

Investment Trends

Brunei is a founding member in the Trans-Pacific Partnership (TPP) negotiations, through which the United States and 10 other Asia-Pacific partners are seeking to establish a comprehensive, next-generation regional agreement to liberalize trade and investment. This agreement will advance U.S. economic and trade policies within fast-growing economies, and aid in the economic integration across the Asia-Pacific region. The TPP agreement will include commitments on goods, services, intellectual property rights, labor, and other traditional trade and investment issues. It will also address a range of emerging issues not covered by past agreements. In addition to the United States and Brunei, the TPP negotiating partners currently include Australia, Canada, Chile, Japan, Malaysia, Mexico, New Zealand, Peru, Singapore, and Vietnam. Brunei is also a negotiating party to the Regional Comprehensive Economic Partnership (RCEP).

According to the U.S. Trade Representative, Brunei's annual trade balance decreased by 16.8 per cent from BND 11,765.5 million (USD 9,488.31 million) in 2012 to BND 9,788.4 million (USD 7,830.72 million) in 2013. Meanwhile the total trade showed a decline of 8.9 per cent from BND 20,675.9 million (USD 16,672.11 million) in 2012 to BND 18,829.6 million (USD 15,063.68 million) in 2013. The U.S. goods trade surplus with Brunei was BND 676 million (USD 541 million) in 2013, a decrease of USD 470 million (BND 587 million) from 2012. U.S. goods exports in 2013 were USD 559 million (BND 699 million), up 254.4 percent from the previous year. Corresponding U.S. imports from Brunei were USD 17 million (BND 21 million), down 81 percent. Brunei is currently the 100th largest export market for U.S. goods. The stock of U.S. foreign direct investment (FDI) in Brunei was USD 116 million (BND 160 million) in 2012 (latest data available), up 17.2% from 2011.

Table 1

Measure	Year	Index or Rank	Website Address
TI Corruption Perceptions index	2014	N/A	transparency.org/cpi2014/results

World Bank's Doing Business Report "Ease of Doing Business"	2015	101 of 189	doingbusiness.org/rankings
Global Innovation Index	2014	88 of 143	globalinnovationindex.org/content.aspx?page=data-analysis
World Bank GNI per capita	2013	n/a	data.worldbank.org/indicator/NY.GNP.PCAP.CD

2. Conversion and Transfer Policies

Foreign Exchange

In June 2013 the Financial Action Task Force (FATF) announced that Brunei Darussalam is no longer subject to FATF's monitoring process under its on-going global Anti-Money Laundering/Countering the Financing of Terrorism (AML/CFT) compliance process. Brunei Darussalam will work with the Asia-Pacific Group (APG) as it continues to address the full range of AML/CFT issues identified in its Mutual Evaluation Report. The report cited Brunei's significant progress in improving its AML/CFT regime and noted that Brunei had established the legal and regulatory framework to meet its commitments in its Action Plan regarding the strategic deficiencies that the FATF had identified in June 2011.

Remittance Policies

Not applicable/information not available.

3. Expropriation and Compensation

There is no history of expropriation of foreign owned property in Brunei. There have been cases of domestically owned private property being expropriated for infrastructure development. Compensation was provided in such cases, and claimants were provided with due process regarding their disputes.

4. DISPUTE SETTLEMENT

Legal System, Specialized Courts, Judicial Independence, Judgments of Foreign Courts

Onshore companies are governed by the Companies Act while offshore companies are governed by the International Business Companies Order of 2000. There are no specialized commercial courts. Brunei's constitution does not provide for judicial independence but in practice the court system operates without government interference. Post has received no complaints from companies regarding the judicial system.

The use of Alternative Dispute Mechanisms (ADR) is not new to Brunei. Both mediation and conciliation as a means of settling disputes has been deep rooted in Brunei's traditions and were originally carried out community leaders and important social figures

Bankruptcy

Brunei's bankruptcy act is available at http://www.agc.gov.bn/agc1/images/LAWS/ACT_PDF/cap067.pdf. Recent amendments to the act increased the minimum threshold for declaring bankruptcy from BND 500 to BND 10,000 (USD 370 to USD 7,407) and enabled the trustee to direct the Controller of Immigration to impound and retain the bankrupt's passport, certificate of identity or travel document to prevent him from leaving Brunei Darussalam. The amendments also saw the imposition of a number of duties on the bankrupt to deliver all his property under his possession, books, paper etc. to the trustee.

Information not available.

ICSID Convention and New York Convention

Brunei is a member state to the convention on the International Centre for Settlement of Investment Disputes (ICSID Convention) and a signatory to the Recognition and Enforcement of Foreign Arbitral Awards (1958 New York Convention.

5. PERFORMANCE REQUIREMENTS AND INVESTMENT INCENTIVES

WTO/TRIMS

Brunei became a World Trade Organization (WTO) member in 1995 and a signtory to the General Agreement on Tariffs and Trade (GATT) in 1993.

Investment Incentives

Companies producing goods and services for export can apply for a renewable 10-year tax exemption. Corporate tax relief of up to 5 years is available for companies that invest between BND 500,000 to BND 2.5 million (USD 370,000 to USD 1.85million), and up to 8 years for amounts exceeding BND 2.5million (USD 1.85 million) in approved ventures. An 11-year tax break is offered if the venture is located in a high-tech industrial park. Businesses wishing to compete in domestic markets can qualify for tax breaks for up to eight years. Sole proprietorships and partnerships are not subject to tax. Individuals do not pay any capital gains tax and profits arising from the sale of capital assets are not taxable. Brunei has double-taxation agreements with Britain, Indonesia, China, Singapore, Vietnam, Bahrain, Oman, Japan, and Pakistan. Tax on petroleum operations is codified in the 1960 Income Tax enactment, which is similar to tax policies in other oil-producing nations.

Performance Requirements

The Brunei government is actively seeking to increase the number of Bruneians working in the private sector. Brunei's 2014 Energy White Paper calls for the number of persons employed in the energy sector to increase from 20,000 in 2010 to 50,000 in 2035, and for the number of locals employed in the sector to increase from 10,000 to 40,000 in the same period. To advance this goal, all companies competing for a tender in the oil and gas industry are required to have at least half of their employees Bruneians.

Expatriate employment is controlled by a Labor Quota system from the Labor Department and the issuance of employment passes, by the Immigration Department. Brunei allows for new companies to apply for "special approval" to expedite the recruitment of expatriate workers in select positions for essential jobs. According to the Ministry of Home Affairs, this approval is only available to new companies operating in the urban and suburban areas for six months, and covers businesses such as restaurants and shops. The "special approval" cuts the waiting time down from 21 days to 7.

For additional analytical, business and investment opportunities information,
please contact Global Investment & Business Center, USA
at (703) 370-8082. Fax: (703) 370-8083. E-mail: ibpusa3@gmail.com
Global Business and Investment Info Databank - www.ibpus.com

6. RIGHT TO PRIVATE OWNERSHIP AND ESTABLISHMENT

All businesses in Brunei must be registered with the Registrar of Companies within the Attorney General's Chambers. Except for sole proprietorships, foreign investors can fully own incorporated companies, foreign company branches or representative offices. Partnerships generally require the participation of citizens. Foreign direct investments by multi-national corporations may not require local partnership in setting up a subsidiary of their parent company in Brunei. However, at least one company director must be a Brunei citizen or permanent resident in Brunei Darussalam. A multinational company with an operating plant on an MIPR industrial park is required to have 30% of the companies' board represented by Brunei citizens and permanent residents.

7. PROTECTION OF PROPERTY RIGHTS

Real Property

Mortgages are recognized and enforced in Brunei, however only Bruneians can own land property in Brunei. Foreigners and permanent residents can only hold properties under strata tiles or long-term leasehold rights. Most banks have stopped granting housing loans to foreigners and permanent residents. The 2011 data from the International Monetary Fund (IMF) showed no foreign direct investment (FDI) for real estate, rentals and business activity. In 2009 and 2010, the sector saw BND 3 million in FDI per year while in 2007 and 2008 it logged BND 2 million of FDI value.

Amendments to the Land Code are in the works to ban past practices of proxy sale of land to foreigners and permanent residents using the power of attorney (PA) and Trust Deeds (TD). PA and TD are no longer recognized as viable mechanisms in land deals involving non-citizens. The move to ban the PA and TD was announced at the 8th Legislative Council meeting on March 12, 2012. The proposed laws will also have retroactive effect, converting all existing property owned through PA and TD into 60-year leases. The rationale for the restriction is to ensure sufficient land ownership by citizens. PA's are still in land development transactions allowing for only 5-year ownership for land developers and 25-year ownership for banks. The PA in these cases was allowed to be used as collateral.

Intellectual Property Rights

Brunei's IP protection and enforcement regime is still in development but is increasingly strong and effective. The country was removed from the Special 301 report in 2013, and stayed off the list in 2014 and 2015, in recognition of its improving IPR protections, increasing enforcement, and efforts to educate the public about the importance of IPR.

Brunei's long-gestating Copyright (Amendment) Order 2013 was finalized and adopted in December 2013, a development long requested by the U.S. government. The change further enhanced enforcement provisions for copyright infringement by increasing penalties for offences; adding new offenses; strengthening the enforcement powers of the Royal Brunei Police Force and the Ministry of Finance Customs and Excise Department; and allowing for sanctioned private prosecution. The amendments are designed to deter copyright infringements with fines of BND 10,000 (USD 7,400) to BND 20,000 (USD 14,800) per infringing copy, imprisonment for a term up to five years or both. The new penalty is up to four times more severe than the previously existing penalty. Enforcement agencies are authorized to enter premises and arrest without warrant, to stop, search and board vehicles and also to access computerized and digitized data. The amendments further allow for admissibility of evidence obtained covertly and protect the identity of informants. Statistics on seizures of counterfeit goods are unavailable.

Brunei transferred its Registry of Trademarks from the Attorney General's Chambers (AGC) to the BEDB effective June 2013. The transfer expanded the BEDB Patents Registry Office's (PRO) capabilities to accept applications for the registration of trademarks in addition to patents and industrial designs. The office's name officially changed the Brunei Intellectual Property Office (BruIPO). The change created a national IP office, making policy coordination easier. The World Intellectual Property Organization's Singapore office described the move as a very positive step in terms of strengthening the IP protection efforts, because it provides comprehensive management of IP. In 2014, BruIPO reported that local trademark applications more than doubled in comparison to 2013, rising from 41 to 101.

In September 2013, Brunei acceded to the Geneva (1999) Act of the Hague Agreement Concerning the International Registration of Industrial Designs to protect IP from industrial designs, making it the second ASEAN Member country, following Singapore, to accede. The accession emphasized Brunei's commitment under the ASEAN Intellectual Property Rights Action Plan 2011 – 2015. Brunei also plans and has publicly committed to acceding to other World Intellectual Property Organization's (WIPO) treaties including the Madrid Protocol for the International Registration of Marks, the WIPO Performances and Phonograms Treaty

(WPPT), and the UPOV Convention 1991 for the protection of New Varieties of Plants (PV). In addition, Brunei is actively negotiating the Trans-Pacific Partnership's IPR chapter with the United States and other TPP participants. The Recording Industry Association of Malaysia, which in the past had criticized Brunei for a lack of support for IPR protection, opened its own office in Brunei in 2013. For additional information about treaty obligations and points of contact at local IP offices, please see WIPO's country profiles at http://www.wipo.int/directory/en/.

Resources for Rights Holders

Contact at Mission:
Allison M. Carragher
Political/Economic/Consular Officer
+673 238-4616 ext. 2165
CarragherAM@state.gov

Country/Economy resources:

The United States Embassy in Bandar Seri Begawan maintains a list of local attorneys at**http://brunei.usembassy.gov/list-of-attorneys.html**

8. TRANSPARENCY OF THE REGULATORY SYSTEM

Brunei's foreign direct investment policies are not fully transparent, particularly with respect to limits on foreign equity participation, partnership requirements, and the identification of sectors in which foreign direct investment is restricted.

9. EFFICIENT CAPITAL MARKETS AND PORTFOLIO INVESTMENT

Brunei recently signed a Memorandum of Understanding (MOU) with the Securities

Commission Malaysia (SCM) to boost cooperation in the capital markets. The MOU was designed to strengthen collaboration in the development of fair and efficient capital markets in the two countries. It also provided a framework to facilitate greater cross-border capital market

For additional analytical, business and investment opportunities information,
please contact Global Investment & Business Center, USA
at (703) 370-8082. Fax: (703) 370-8083. E-mail: ibpusa3@gmail.com
Global Business and Investment Info Databank - www.ibpus.com

activities and cooperation in the areas of regulation as well as capacity building and human capital development, particularly in the area of Islamic capital markets.

10. COMPETITION FROM STATE-OWNED ENTERPRISES

Brunei's state-owned enterprises are involved in key sectors of the economy, such as oil and gas, telecommunications, transport, and energy generation and distribution. However, Brunei has not yet notified its state trading enterprises to the WTO Working Party on State Trading Enterprises. There is no published list of SOE's, but specific examples include:

Semaun Holdings, incorporated as a private limited company, is wholly owned by the Brunei Government. Its emphasis is on joint ventures with foreign investors, mainly in aquaculture, food processing, glass crystal, and hi-tech manufacturing industries which are currently not open for 100% foreign ownership.

Under the Telecommunications Order 2001, the Authority for Info-communications Technology Industry (AiTi) regulates the licensing of the telecommunications industry. The establishment, installation, maintenance, provision or operation of unlicensed telecommunication systems or services within Brunei is a punishable offence, resulting in imprisonment, and large fines. AiTi has not opened up the telecommunications industry for foreign participation. The telecommunications industry is dominated by Telekom Brunei (TelBru) and Data Stream Technologies (DST) Communications both privatized state companies. Telbru is the sole provider of fixed lines. Its subsidiary company, B-mobile, provides 3G mobile services together with DST. DST is also the sole provider of Global Systems for Mobile communication (GSM) mobile phone service and the sole pay-television service provider.

Royal Brunei Technical Services (RBTS), established in 1988 as a wholly-government owned corporation, is responsible for managing the acquisition of a wide range of systems and equipment and maintaining those acquired systems and equipment.

Brunei National Petroleum Sendirian Berhad (PB) is the national oil company. PB is wholly owned by the Brunei Government and was incorporated on January 14, 2001 as a private limited company. The company was granted all the mineral rights in eight prime onshore and offshore petroleum blocks comprised of the deepwater offshore Blocks CA1 & CA2, inboard offshore Blocks N, P, Q, & B and onshore Blocks L & M totaling 20,552 sq. km. Currently, the company manages the production sharing contractors exploring the onshore and deepwater offshore blocks. The company is also working with the Block B operator in the development of the Maharaja Lela/Jamalulam Field.

OECD Guidelines on Corporate Governance of SOEs

Brunei does not adhere to the OECD guidelines on corporate governance of SOE's.

Sovereign Wealth Funds

The Brunei Investment Agency (BIA) manages the Government of Brunei's General Reserve Fund, and their external assets. Established in 1983, its assets are reportedly worth USD 30 billion. It has holdings in corporations, real estate, and currencies. BIA's activities are not publicly disclosed. It is ranked the lowest in transparency ratings by The Sovereign Wealth Fund Institute.

11. Corporate Social Responsibility

Corporate social responsibility (CSR) is still a relatively new concept in Brunei, and there are no specific government programs encouraging foreign and local enterprises to follow generally accepted CSR principles. However there is a broad awareness of corporate social responsibility among both producers and consumers, and individual private and public sector organizations have formalized CSR programs and policies. There are no reporting requirements and no independent NGOs in Brunei that promote or monitor CSR.

OECD Guidelines for Multinational Enterprises

Brunei does not adhere to the OECD guidelines for multinational enterprises.

12. POLITICAL VIOLENCE

Brunei has no recent history of political violence. The country experienced an uprising in 1962, when it was a British protectorate, which ended through the intervention of British troops. The country has been ruled peacefully under emergency law ever since.

13. CORRUPTION

Since January 1, 1982, Brunei has enforced the Emergency (Prevention of Corruption) Act. In1984, the Act was renamed the Prevention of Corruption Act (Chapter 131). The Anti-Corruption Bureau (ACB) was established on February 1, 1982 for the purpose of enforcing the Act. The Prevention of Corruption Act provides specific powers to the ACB for the purpose of investigating accusations of corruption. The Act also provides power for ACB to investigate certain offences under the Penal Code and offences under other written laws, provided such offences were disclosed during the course of ACB investigation into offences under the Prevention of Corruption Act.

The ACB strives to ensure a corruption-free public service. Corrupt practices are punishable under the Prevention of Corruption Act. The Act also applies to Brunei citizens abroad. There are perceptions that corruption in the private sector is more prevalent than in the public sector. This has prompted the ACB to focus on the private sector, as the private sector plays a critical role in Brunei's economic diversification. Brunei is a member of the International Association of Anti-Corruption Authorities.

In Transparency International's Corruption Perception Index (CPI) 2014, Brunei is ranked 38 out of 175 countries.

No U.S. Company has identified corruption as an obstacle to conduct business in Brunei.

UN Anticorruption Convention, OECD Convention on Combatting Bribery

Brunei has signed and ratified the UN Anticorruption Convention.

Resources to Report Corruption

Government Point of Contact:
Name: Hj Md Juanda Hj A. Rashid
Title: Director
Organization: Anti-Corruption Bureau Brunei Darussalam
Address: Old Airport Berakas, BB 3510 Brunei Darussalam
Tel: +673 238-3575 / +673 238-3197

Fax: +673-2383193
Mobile: +673 8721002
Email: **info.bmr@acb.gov.bn**

There are no international, regional, local or nongovernmental organizations operating in the country/economy that monitor corruption.

14. BILATERAL INVESTMENT AGREEMENTS

Brunei is a member of the Association of Southeast Asian Nations (ASEAN), which has Free Trade Agreements (FTA) with Australia, New Zealand, China, India, and South Korea, and a Comprehensive Economic Partnership Agreement with Japan.

Brunei currently has Bilateral Investment Treaties with China, Germany, India, the Republic of Korea, Oman, and South Africa.

Brunei was the ASEAN Coordinator in negotiations for the ASEAN-Australia-New Zealand Free Trade Agreement (AANZFTA), which was signed in Thailand on 27 February 2009 and entered into force on 1 January 2010. Brunei is a negotiating party to the TPP and the Regional Comprehensive Economic Partnership (RCEP).

Brunei was one of the original members of the Trans-Pacific Strategic Economic Partnership Agreement (P4), a Free Trade Agreement between Brunei Darussalam, Chile, Singapore, and New Zealand signed on 18 July 2005. The P4 later evolved into the Trans-Pacific Partnership (TPP) with the addition of new members, namely the United States, Australia, Canada, Japan, Peru, Malaysia, Mexico, and Vietnam, The TPP negotiations are currently ongoing.

Bilateral Taxation Treaties

Brunei does not have a bilateral taxation treaty with the United States.

15. OPIC AND OTHER INVESTMENT INSURANCE PROGRAMS

Overseas Private Investment Corporation (OPIC) programs are not available in Brunei given the country's affluence.

16. LABOR

The 2011 labor force estimate was 185,900 persons with an unemployment rate of 1.7 percent, according to the Brunei Darussalam Statistical Yearbook 2011 (latest data available), though unofficial estimates place the unemployment figures higher.

Brunei relies heavily on foreign labor in lower-skill and lower-paying positions, with approximately 120,000 guest workers brought in to fulfill specific contracts. The largest percentage of those work in construction, followed by wholesale and retail trade and then professional, technical, administrative and support services. Most unskilled laborers in Brunei are immigrants from Indonesia, Malaysia and the Philippines on renewable two year contracts.

The skilled labor pool includes both immigrants on short term visas and Bruneian citizens and permanent residents, who often are well educated but who often prefer to work for the government, with its better benefits such as bonuses, education allowance, interest-free loans, housing allowance, and other benefits, rather than the private sector. Approximately 25% of the total Brunei citizen workforce is employed in the public sector.

Matters relating to labor conditions are covered under the Labor Act, Employment Order 2009 and Workmen's Compensation Act. Expatriate employment is controlled by a Labor Quota system from the Labor Department and the issuance of employment passes, by the Immigration Department. Brunei allows for new companies to apply for "special approval" to expedite the recruitment of expatriate workers in select positions for essential jobs. According to the Ministry of Home Affairs, this approval is only available to new companies operating in the urban and suburban areas for six months, and covers businesses such as restaurants and shops. The special approval cuts the waiting time down from 21 days to 7.

The Brunei government is actively seeking to increase the number of Bruneians working in the private sector. Brunei's 2014 Energy White Paper calls for the number of persons employed in the energy sector to increase from 20,000 in 2010 to 50,000 in 2035, and for the number of locals employed in the sector to increase from 10,000 to 40,000 in the same period. To advance this goal, all companies competing for a tender in the oil and gas industry are required to have at least half of their employees Bruneians.

The law, including related regulations and statutory instruments, protects the right of workers to form and join unions. Under the Trade Unions Act, unions must be registered with the government. All workers, including civil servants other than those serving in the military and those working as prison guards or police officers, may form and join trade unions of their choice without previous authorization or excessive requirements. The only union in the country, which was composed of Brunei Shell Petroleum workers, dissolved in 2014. There are no other active unions or worker organizations.

While the law permits the formation of trade union federations, it forbids affiliation with international labor organizations unless there is consent from the minister of home affairs and the Department of Labor. The government prohibits strikes, and the law makes no explicit provision for the right to collective bargaining. The law prohibits employers from discriminating against workers in connection with union activities, but it does not provide for reinstatement for dismissal related to union activity.

Various domestic laws prohibit the employment of children under age 16. Parental consent and approval by the Labor Commission are required for those under age 18. Female workers under age 18 may not work at night or on offshore oil platforms. The Department of Labor, which is part of the Ministry of Home Affairs, effectively enforced laws related to the employment of children. There were no reports of violations of child labor laws.

The law does not set a minimum wage, but most employed citizens commanded good salaries. The public sector pay scale covers all workers in government jobs. Wages for employed foreign residents were wide ranging. Some foreign embassies set minimum wage requirements for their nationals working in the country.

The standard workweek is Monday through Thursday and Saturday, with Friday and Sunday off, allowing for two rest periods of 24 hours each week. The law provides for paid annual holidays, overtime for work in excess of 48 hours per week, and double time for work performed on legal holidays. The law also stipulates that an employee may not work more than 72 hours of overtime a month. Laws regarding hours were frequently not observed in practice. Occupational health and safety standards were established by government regulations. The Labor Department inspected working conditions both on a routine basis and in response to complaints. There were approximately 40 labor inspectors in the Labor Department in 2014. The government usually moved quickly to investigate abuses, and abusive employers faced criminal and civil penalties. All employment agencies have to be endorsed by the government and have to undergo government vetting and training before operating. In 2014, there were three cases of Employment Agencies operating without a license. Two of the cases were forwarded to the Law and Prosecution Division of the Department of Labor, while one case is still under investigation. The Labor Department had the power to terminate the license of abusive employers and revoke their foreign labor quota. The majority of abuse cases were settled out of court through agreements where the employer paid financial compensation to the worker.

The government generally enforced labor, health, and safety regulations effectively, but enforcement in the unskilled labor sector was lax. This was true especially for foreign laborers at construction sites, where wage arrears and inadequate safety and living conditions were reported. The government may close a workplace where health, safety, or working conditions are unsatisfactory, but this did not happen during the year.

Government data from 2011, the most recent available, indicated approximately 85,000 foreigners lived in the country temporarily. The law protected the rights of foreign workers through inspections of facilities and a telephone hotline for worker complaints. Immigration law allows for prison sentences and caning for workers who overstay their work permits, for workers who fall into irregular status due to their employers' negligence, for irregular immigrants seeking work, as well as for foreign workers employed by companies other than their initial sponsor. The law also requires recruiting agencies to be registered.

Government mediation by the Labor Department continued to be the most common means used to resolve labor disputes. The commissioner responsible for labor had the additional authority to protect foreign worker rights. The government prosecuted employers who employed irregular immigrants or did not process workers' documents, rendering them irregular. When grievances could not be resolved, regulations require employers to pay for the repatriation of the foreign workers and all outstanding wages. By custom, particularly for low-skilled workers, some employers held employee passports and restricted employee activities during non-work hours. Foreign workers who filed grievances sometimes did not receive their back wages. Foreign migrant workers often signed contracts with employment agents or other sponsors in their home countries that reduced their promised salaries through payments to the agencies or sponsors. The government forbade wage deductions to agencies or sponsors and mandated that employees receive their full salaries; nevertheless, foreign workers continued to pay high fees to manpower agents to obtain work in the country.

There were cases reported of nonpayment of salaries. The majority of cases involved domestic and construction workers. In many cases courts levied judicial penalties including convictions and fines against employers found guilty of nonpayment of wages.

17. FOREIGN TRADE ZONES/FREE PORTS/TRADE FACILITATION

Muara Port is Brunei's main seaport with an established Free Trade Zone called the Muara Export Zone (MEZ), which was established to promote and develop Brunei Darussalam as a trade hub of the region. The establishment of the MEZ was an initial step towards developing other Free Trade Zones in the country.

18. Foreign Direct Investment and Foreign Portfolio Investment Statistics

Table 2: Key Macroeconomic Data, U.S. FDI in Host Country/Economy

Economic Data	Host Country Statistical source*		USG or international statistical source		USG or International Source of Data: BEA; IMF; Eurostat; UNCTAD, Other
	Year	Amount	Year	Amount	
Host Country Gross Domestic Product (GDP) ($M USD)	2012	16,950	2014	14,914	www.worldbank.org/en/country
Foreign Direct Investment	Host Country Statistical source*		USG or international statistical source		USG or international Source of data: BEA; IMF; Eurostat; UNCTAD, Other
U.S. FDI in partner country ($M USD, stock positions)	N/A	N/A	2013	132	BEA
Host country's FDI in the United States ($M USD, stock positions)	N/A	N/A	N/A	N/A	
Total inbound stock of FDI as % host GDP	N/A	N/A	2013	Less than 1%	

*Host country GDP data available from Brunei Economic Development Board (BEDB)

CONTACT FOR MORE INFORMATION

U.S. Embassy Bandar Seri Begawan
Simpang 336-52-16-9
Jalan Duta BC 4115
(+673) 238-4616
BSBCommercial@state.gov

LEGAL CONTACTS

FATHAN, RUDI LEE, ANNIE KON & ASSOCIATES
Advocates & Solicitors / Commissioners For Oaths
Unit A1-1 & A2-1, 1st Floor, Block A Shakirin Complex
Simpang 88, Kampung Kiulap, BSB BE1518
Tel: +673.223.5111
Fax: +673.223.4206
Email: *fralaw2@gmail.com*

Services Provided: *adoptions, commercial/business law, foreign investments, trademarks, civil law, criminal law, damages, narcotics, collections, commerical law, contracts, corporations, foreign claims, estates, labor relations, immigration, auto/accidents*

PENGIRAN IZAD & LEE
Advocates & Solicitors / Commissioners For Oaths
6th Floor, Bangunan Hj. Ahmad Laksamana Othman
38-39, Jalan Sultan, BSB BS8811
Tel: +673.223.2945/6/7/8
Fax: +673.223.2944
Email: *pial@brunet.bn*

Services Provided: *family law, insurance, banking/financial, commercial/business law, foreign investments, marketing agreements, patents/trademarks/copyrights, civil law, criminal law, damages, collections, commerical law, contracts, corporations, aeronautical/maritime, foreign claims, estates, taxes, government relations, labor relations, immigration, auto/accidents*

SANDHU & COMPANY
Advocates & Solicitors
Unit 3, 4 & 5, Block A, Simpang 150, Bangunan Habza
Kg. Kiarong, BSB BE1518
Tel: +673.222.0783
Fax: +673.224.1237
Email: *sandhuco@brunet.bn*

Services Provided: *insurance, commercial/business law, patents/trademarks/copyrights, civil law, damages, commerical law, contracts, foreign claims, auto/accidents*

STARTING BUSINESS IN BRUNEI

MARKET OVERVIEW

* Brunei Darussalam is a Southeast Asian oil-rich Sultanate on the northern coast of Borneo. A British protectorate until 1984, it boasts a well-educated and largely English-speaking population, excellent infrastructure, and a government intent on diversifying the economy and bringing foreign investment to Brunei.

* Despite repeated calls for diversification, Brunei's economy remains overwhelmingly dependent on the income derived from the sale of oil and gas, which represents 91.5% of Brunei's total exports and 67.7% of gross domestic product (2011). Additionally, substantial revenue from overseas investment supplements income from domestic production. These two revenue streams provide a comfortable quality of life for Brunei's population. Citizens pay no taxes and receive free education through to the university level, free medical care and subsidized housing.

* Brunei's central location in Southeast Asia, with good telecommunications and airline connections; no personal income, sales or export taxes; and its stable political situation offer a welcoming climate for would-be investors. Brunei has an investment incentive scheme where companies that are granted a "pioneer" certificate can enjoy corporate tax exemptions up to 5, 8 or 11 years, with possible extensions, depending on the nature of industry and amount of fixed capital through a program administered by the Ministry of Industry and Primary Resources.. Additionally, a low crime rate, good schools, housing and sports facilities as well as low utility

costs make Brunei an attractive location for short and long-term residence. Life in Brunei reflects the national philosophy of the Malay Islamic Monarchy (MIB in Malay).

* Brunei has no debt, domestic or foreign, and has not been the recipient of economic aid. Despite importing most consumer goods and food, Brunei's large oil exports keep its trade balance positive. The Brunei dollar is pegged to the Singapore dollar at a one-to-one ratio, and the Singapore dollar is legal tender in the Sultanate.

* The five largest destinations for Brunei exports (mostly mineral fuels) in 2013 were Japan (39.8%), Korea (16.3%), India (7.6%), Australia (7.3%) and Vietnam (5.3%). The five largest sources of imports to Brunei during 2013 were Malaysia (21.9%), Singapore (19.1%), China (11.2%), the United States (11.1%), and Japan (5.8%). The largest import sectors by market value were machinery and transport equipment, manufactured goods, and food.

* Brunei is currently the United States' 121st largest goods trading partner with $576 million in total (two way) trade during 2013. The U.S. trade surplus with Brunei was $541 million in 2013: exports totaled $559 million; imports totaled $17 million. Brunei is a negotiating partner in the Trans Pacific Partnership (TPP).

MARKET CHALLENGES

* With a population of 425,000 in 2014, Brunei's local market is relatively small. Foreign enterprises are allowed 100% ownership of Business scope, operation and investment. As such, it is not a requirement for foreign investors to find a local partner to enter the market. However, in certain cases, foreign companies may be required to find a local partner to enter the market in order to be qualified for certain government and Brunei Shell Petroleum projects. U.S. businesses/investors should expect delays - sometimes long ones - when dealing with the local government.

MARKET OPPORTUNITIES

* Formed in 2001, the Brunei Economic Development Board (BEDB) promotes Brunei as an investment destination to stimulate and develop the domestic economy away from dependence on oil and gas revenues. BEDB is mandated to work with foreign and domestic investors to develop new economic opportunities where Brunei has competitive advantages, focusing on four key growth areas: attracting investments, strengthening local businesses, increasing Research and Development (R&D) and innovation, and delivering infrastructure projects.

* BEDB has identified several industries as potential investment sectors in its efforts to diversify the economy, including aviation, green energy, data centers and halal food/pharmaceutical processing. BEDB has also launched several National Housing supply and infrastructure projects. Further information on BEDB's projects is available at BEDB's website: http://www.bedb.com.bn . U.S. firms are welcome to participate in BEDB's projects.

* BEDB has identified and dedicated several industrial parks for the purpose of accommodating foreign direct investments, including:

1. Sungai Liang Industrial Park (SPARK): Gas-based petrochemicals

2. Pulau Muara Besar (PMB): oil and gas downstream and supporting activities

3. Salambigar Industrial Park (SIP) (Formerly known as Lambak Kanan East (LKE) : Food, pharmaceutical, cosmetics and light industries

4. Rimba Digital Junction : High technology industries and data center services

5. Bukit Panggal Industrial Park : Energy intensive industries

6. Telisai Industrial Site: Aquaculture and mixed industries

7. Anggerek Desa Technology Park (ADTP) (iCentre; KHub; ADTP phase 3): ICT related industries

* The Government of Brunei has established several agencies to promote foreign investment. In addition to BEDB, the Brunei Industrial Development Authority (the Malay acronym is BINA) has developed several industrial parks near the Muara Port and in other parts of Brunei close to transportation infrastructure to facilitate and nurture small- and medium-sized enterprises. The government has also solicited bids from foreign companies for a number of recent major infrastructure projects for both civilian and military uses. Further information on BINA is available at BINA's website: http://www.bina.gov.bn/ .

* The Ministry of Industry and Primary Resources offers an investment incentive scheme where companies that are granted the pioneer certificate can enjoy corporate tax exemption of up to 5, 8 or 11 years, with a possible extension, depending on the nature of industry and amount of fixed capital. Sole proprietorships and partnerships are not subject to tax. Individuals do not pay any capital gains tax and profits arising from the sale of capital assets are not taxable. Brunei has double-taxation agreements with Britain, Indonesia, China, Singapore, Vietnam, Bahrain, Oman, Japan, and Pakistan, Malaysia, Hong Kong, Laos and Kuwait. Tax on petroleum operations is codified in the 1960 Income Tax enactment, which is similar to tax policies in other oil-producing nations.

* Investment opportunities in Brunei are driven both by government planning and consumer demand. The most attractive commercial sectors include:

o Oil and Gas, Upstream and Downstream

o Commercial Aviation

o Construction

o Defense Industry Equipment

o Franchising

o Renewable Energy and Clean Technology

o Information and Communication Technology

* In the agricultural sector, the following two investment opportunities may offer lucrative investment opportunities:

o Food Imports/Food Production

o Fishing Industry/Aquaculture

* Brunei has a biotechnology industry that seeks to benefit from international expertise. There are also opportunities in the healthcare technology and medical devices sector .

MARKET ENTRY STRATEGY

* Brunei's population—largely clustered around the capital Bandar Seri Begawan, with other population centers connected by a well-maintained highway system—provides a ready destination for U.S. exports with low transit costs once goods arrive in country. The relatively small population of Brunei is an asset in that exported products, once a foothold is gained, may gain national prominence relatively quickly.

* Market access and promotion strategies typically focused on cities, may be applied with modification to enter the Brunei market. Firms that are able to export goods and services that will serve to increase the capacity of Bruneian enterprise and increase Bruneian employment will be particularly welcomed.

* U.S. businesses should build personal relationships with local representatives and customers through regular visits or by establishing resident representation. U.S. companies can set up their subsidiary companies or branch offices in Brunei as private limited companies registered with the Registrar of Companies and Business Names.

* Please note that throughout this report, except where otherwise noted, the following Brunei dollar/U.S. dollar exchange rates were used:

2009 1.513

2010 1.418

2011 1.308

2012 1.300

2013 1.245

2014 1.250

The source of the rates above is:

http://www.irs.gov/Individuals/International-Taxpayers/Yearly-Average-Currency-Exchange-Rates

SELLING U.S. PRODUCTS AND SERVICES

USING AN AGENT OR DISTRIBUTOR

For additional analytical, business and investment opportunities information,
please contact Global Investment & Business Center, USA
at (703) 370-8082. Fax: (703) 370-8083. E-mail: ibpusa3@gmail.com
Global Business and Investment Info Databank - www.ibpus.com

Personal relationships are important in Brunei and U.S. businesses may find a reputable local agent/distributor worthwhile. The individual should be thoroughly familiar with local business customs and high-ranking government officials. The Commercial Section of the U.S. Embassy provides services that can help U.S. businesses locate an appropriate agent/distributor. The U.S. Department of Commerce provides detailed descriptions of the commercial services provided to U.S. businesses wanting to do business in Brunei on its website, http://brunei.usembassy.gov/doing_business_in_brunei.html .

ESTABLISHING AN OFFICE

Businesses may be established in Brunei as sole proprietorships, partnerships, or branches of a foreign company. Generally, U.S. companies operating in Brunei must either register as a branch of a foreign company or incorporate as a Brunei limited company with the Registrar of Companies within the Ministry of Finance. Foreigners are not eligible for sole proprietorship.

With the exception of sole proprietorships, foreign investors can fully own incorporated companies, foreign company branches or representative offices. Partnerships generally require the participation of Brunei citizens, although some dispensation for companies with 100% foreign equity may be made for high-tech or export-oriented firms.

American businesses can establish a private or public corporation (Sendirian Berhad,) or limited (by Guarantee) company. As a private corporation, the business must have at

least two Directors, one of which must be a resident of Brunei. A public corporation must have at least seven shareholders with no residency requirement. Branches of foreign companies can be established in Brunei without local incorporation. The branch office must have a registered office in Brunei and must appoint two local authorized persons. Currently the branches are subject to a 20% corporate tax rate of annual gross profit but it was announced in the 2014 legislative council session that the corporate tax will be reduced to 18.5% by 2015.

Foreign direct investments by multi-national corporations may not require local partnership in setting up a subsidiary of their parent company in Brunei. However, at least one company director must be a Brunei citizen or permanent resident.

A multinational company with an operating plant in a Ministry of Industry and Primary Resources (MIPR) industrial park is required to have 30% of its board represented by Brunei citizens or permanent residents.

While no central system exists to help locate foreign and domestic partners, MIPR and the Brunei Economic Development Board (BEDB) can informally announce a company's interest in finding an agent, distributor, or partner through their business channels.

The Authority for Info-Communications Technology Industry (AITI) offers assistance to local information and communications technology (ICT) small- and medium-sized enterprises (SMEs) to connect with potential ICT partners and customers. The AITI website provides additional information on these services: http://www.aiti.gov.bn/industrydevelopment/ebusiness-marketcreation/Pages/ebusiness-marketcreation.aspx .

Additional Resources:

* BEDB's guide to setting up a company in Brunei:

http://www.bedb.com.bn/doing_guides_setting_company.html

* Ministry of Foreign Affairs and Trade's guide to setting up businesses in Brunei:

http://www.mofat.gov.bn/index.php/investing-in-brunei-darussalam/setting-up-businesses

* Ministry of Foreign Affairs and Trade's 2012 Ease of Doing Business Report:

http://www.industry.gov.bn/index.php?option=com_content&view=article&id=401:brunei-darussalam-ease-of-doing-business-2012

* Registry of Companies, Ministry of Finance:

http://www.mof.gov.bn/index.php/divisions/registry-of-companies-and-business-names

* Export.gov Brunei:

http://export.gov/singapore/doingbusinessinbrunei/index.asp

AITI: http://www.aiti.gov.bn/industrydevelopment/ebusiness-marketcreation/Pages/ebusiness-marketcreation.aspx

FRANCHISING

Brunei has a relatively large number of franchises for its size, including food services and apparel. Franchises must be registered with the Ministry of Finance's Registrar of Companies pursuant to Chapter 39 of the Companies Act. The Ministry of Finance assumed responsibility for the registry in 2013. After receiving approval from the parent company, franchises follow the same procedures as those for registering a business (20 people or fewer) or a company (more than 20 people). The Ministry of Finance will provide tax rates for registering a business or companies after the entity has submitted its registration.

DIRECT MARKETING

The use of direct marketing has gained popularity for businesses in Brunei. Many companies in Brunei have taken advantage of advertising techniques such as cell phone text messaging, email, interactive consumer websites and social media sites, online display ads, database marketing, fliers, catalog distribution, promotional letters, targeted television commercials, response-generating newspaper/magazine advertisements, and outdoor advertising.

JOINT VENTURES/LICENSING

A joint venture may take the form of a corporation or partnership. Several factors, including the nature of the project, would determine which type of joint venture is appropriate. In a corporate joint venture, the owners have limited liability whereas in a partnership joint venture, the partners have unlimited liability. If the parties to a partnership joint venture are corporations, then liability is limited to that of the participating corporations.

Obtaining a business license depends on a number of factors and can be time-consuming. Information and guidelines regarding forming and registering businesses and companies are

For additional analytical, business and investment opportunities information,
please contact Global Investment & Business Center, USA
at (703) 370-8082. Fax: (703) 370-8083. E-mail: ibpusa3@gmail.com
Global Business and Investment Info Databank - www.ibpus.com

contained in the Government of Brunei publication the "Business and Investment Guide". A copy of this guide can be obtained by contacting MIPR:

Promotion and Facilitation Services

Ministry of Industry and Primary Resources, 3rd Floor

Jalan Menteri Besar

Bandar Seri Begawan BB3910

Brunei Darussalam

Tel: +673 238-0107/+673 238-0026

Fax: +673 238 2835

E-mail: normah.ibrahim@industry.gov.bn

Website: http://industry.gov.bn

The first step towards setting up a business in Brunei is registration:

Registries' Division

Ministry of Finance

Tel: +673 238-0505

Website: http://www.mof.gov.bn/index.php/divisions/registry-of-companies-and-business-names

Even without a physical presence in Brunei, companies generally need a license to do business in the country. Local sales people engaging in door-to-door product marketing, however, do not need a permit.

One does not need a Brunei citizen representative to do business commercially or when selling directly to the government.

SELLING TO THE GOVERNMENT

Opportunities exist for selling to the government of Brunei in several sectors, including defense, transportation, machinery, infrastructure development and ICT. Royal Brunei Technical Services (RBTS) is a government-owned company that performs contracting, acquisition management, and equipment lifecycle management services for the Government of Brunei. The point of contact is:

Chief Executive Officer

Royal Brunei Technical Services

5th Floor, Setia Kenangan Office Block

Setia Kenangan Complex, Kg. Kiulap

Bandar Seri Begawan BE1518

Tel: +673 224-2700

Fax: +673 224-6747

The Centre of Science and Technology Research and Development (CSTRAD) is responsible for research, assessment, selection, and overseeing aspects of the acquisition of science and technology solutions for Royal Brunei Armed Forces (RBAF).

CSTRAD oversees Brunei's defense modernization efforts, advises the Ministry of Defense on science and technology matters, and supervises the transparency and timeliness of the defense-related acquisition process.

Centre of Science & Technology Research and Development

Lieutenant Colonel (L) Haji Mohd Amirul Shannoel Haji Mohd Noeh

Director of Centre of Science & Technology Research and Development

Block A, 1st Floor

Ministry of Defence

Bolkiah Garrison

Tel : +673 238-6369

Fax : +673 238-6633

E-mail : cstrad@mindef.gov.bn

The military services and police may procure non-lethal equipment directly. RBTS maintains a website at: http://www.rbts.com.bn/ .

For non-security related products, U.S. businesses may deal directly with individual government departments or ministries. Note that some ministries may have their own tender requirements. The Ministry of Health requires a written introduction to the Director General of Health Services to promote the company's products and services. The letter of introduction would include the purpose of the letter, description product and services accompanied by the product brochures. The letter should also include the target department or personnel that would benefit from the product and service provided.

The Brunei Government advertises its tenders in the Pelita Brunei, a Malay-language newspaper. The website for Pelita Brunei is http://www.pelitabrunei.gov.bn/ . The Prime Minister's Office (PMO) also publishes tender notices, which can be accessed at: http://www.pmo.gov.bn/Theme/Home.aspx .

Most government tenders require the participation of local companies and may require hiring of local employees. Foreign companies are encouraged to partner with local companies. A Project Performance Bond is required at the tender approval stage to guarantee the delivery of a project in accordance with the project specifications. The bond is returned to the company involved at successful project completion.

DISTRIBUTION AND SALES CHANNELS

Over 98% of products entering Brunei in 2013 came through Muara Port with 2% brought in as air cargo. There are at least 15 freight forwarding companies operating in Brunei. These companies have the capability to transport imported products. The logistic companies have developed reliable network connections with established shipping and logistics partners worldwide, and have the capacity to provide effective and reliable shipping agencies, stevedoring, courier service, freight forwarding, transshipment, packing and removal, warehousing and distribution, transport, crane hire and project cargo forwarding.

SELLING FACTORS/TECHNIQUES

U.S. exporters to Brunei face strong competition from producers in China, Japan, Australia, New Zealand, and the United Kingdom, especially when marketing food and agricultural products. As a former British protectorate, Brunei has deep trade connections and familiarity with the UK and Commonwealth nations and their products. However the market is diversifying.

To differentiate themselves from local and third country competitors, U.S. firms should emphasize their strengths in quality, innovation, technology enhancements and customer service. Bruneian customers have come to expect higher quality products from U.S. companies. Customers may choose U.S. products and services on the basis of "value for money," not solely on cost factors.

Brunei's government is eager to increase foreign direct investment (FDI), as it seeks to diversify its economy away from petroleum. The Brunei Economic Development Board (BEDB) has identified several key industry clusters it plans to encourage within the export-oriented manufacturing and services sectors, including pharmaceuticals, food, petrochemicals, renewable energy, information and communications technology and higher education. Foreign firms are often encouraged to bid for projects and are often invited to attend pre-qualification briefings.

When marketing general consumer goods, U.S companies should keep in mind the cultural norms and standards of the Bruneian population. For example, a majority of the population is Muslim which means that food, pharmaceuticals and cosmetics must be certified *halal* (meaning lawful and permissible to use/consume under Islamic law) in order to appeal to a larger market. Brunei's definition of *halal* is, in some cases, distinct from other Muslim-majority countries. Information about Brunei's certification process can be found at:
http://www.industry.gov.bn/index.php?option=com_content&view=article&id=81&Itemid=102

It is advisable to conduct research on the possible implications of advertising or promotional activities before initiating them in Brunei. Bruneians are very active on social networks, including Facebook, WhatsApp and Instagram, and these can be important marketing tools as customers will often rely more on these social networks for information on businesses than they rely on traditional marketing sources.

Selling techniques vary according to the industry or the product involved, but they are comparable to the techniques used in any other sophisticated market. To gain a competitive advantage in the marketplace, U.S. firms should develop and maintain good customer relationships. In-person meetings with key contacts in the government and private sector can be helpful in developing and

For additional analytical, business and investment opportunities information,
please contact Global Investment & Business Center, USA
at (703) 370-8082. Fax: (703) 370-8083. E-mail: ibpusa3@gmail.com
Global Business and Investment Info Databank - www.ibpus.com

maintaining these relationships. Industry events, trade shows and product expos are also common and provide good

opportunities to reach customers and potential business partners. Brunei customers flock to coupons, VIP discount cards and special deals and are very price point conscious.

ELECTRONIC COMMERCE

In 2000, Brunei enacted a commercial code for electronic transactions. The Electronic Transactions Act (Chapter 196) is based on the United Nations Commission on International Trade Law (UNCITRAL) Model Law on Electronic Commerce and the Singapore Electronic Transactions Act. The Singapore Act draws heavily from the U.S. Uniform Electronic Transactions Act and aims to encourage business and consumer confidence in e-commerce and provide legal protection for both the buyer and seller.

As Bruneians have gained increased access to mobile and internet capabilities, e-commerce has grown in popularity. E-commerce, however, is still largely concentrated in the tourism sector. Royal Brunei Airlines, the national air carrier, provides an on-line reservation system. Numerous hotels also provide e-booking services, some of which are contracted through business-to-business e-payment services located outside of Brunei.

Among telecommunications and radiofrequency spectrum responsibilities, Brunei's Authority for Info-Communications Technology Industry (AITI) is responsible for promoting e-business opportunities. AITI's E-Business and Market Creation Unit has two primary aims:

1. To encourage research and development activities by local businesses and academic institutions;

2. To assist local information and communication technology (ICT) small and medium enterprises to obtain markets and users for the ICT products and services they have designed, developed and produced.

2000 Electric Transactions Order:

http://unpan1.un.org/intradoc/groups/public/documents/apcity/unpan006031.pdf

Authority for Info-Communications Technology E-Business and Market Creation Unit

http://www.aiti.gov.bn/industrydevelopment/ebusiness-marketcreation/Pages/ebusiness-marketcreation.aspx

TRADE PROMOTION AND ADVERTISING

Businesses can easily purchase advertising space in Brunei's newspapers. The two English-language local newspapers are the Borneo Bulletin and the Brunei Times. The only local newspaper in Malay is Media Permata. All three newspapers have extensive circulation. Daily newspapers in English, Malay and Chinese from the neighboring countries of Malaysia and Singapore are also widely read.

Local advertising companies and promotion service agencies are also available.

Borneo Bulletin

http://borneobulletin.com.bn/

Brunei Times

http://www.bt.com.bn/

Media Permata

http://mediapermata.com.bn/

Radio Television Brunei

www.rtb.gov.bn

BRIDEX Organizer

Sultan Haji Hassanal Bolkiah Institute of Defence and Strategic Studies (SHHBIDSS) Ministry of Defence Bolkiah Garisson BB3510 Brunei Darussalam Tel: +673 2386987/986 Fax: +673 2381424 Email: bridexconference2013@mindef.gov.bn

D'Sunlit Sdn Bhd

Lot 71, Beribi Light Industrial Estate,

Phase II, Gadong BE1118,

Bandar Seri Begawan,

Brunei Darussalam

P.O. Box 470

Gadong Post Office BE3978,

Bandar Seri Begawan,

Brunei Darussalam

Tel: +673-2453 666

+673-2452 576

+673-2452 577

+673-2452 596

Fax: +673-2453 777

Email: admin@dsunlit.com

U.S. Embassy Bandar Seri Begawan works closely with the Foreign Commercial Service, U.S. Embassy Singapore, to provide trade assistance to a U.S. company or its local representative in organizing a promotional event in Brunei which could include seminars, luncheons, cocktail receptions, etc. The service is tailored to the specific needs of the U.S. Company.

Department of Commerce website for Commercial Services:

http://www.trade.gov/cs/

PRICING

Bruneians enjoy a high per capita income, but that includes both very wealthy residents and families with significant personal debt who depend on government subsidies for fuel, housing and education. There is a robust niche market for higher-end products and services, but shoppers are also cost-conscious for everyday purchases, and products of other nations are priced competitively. Bruneians increasingly use social media to spot deals and specials at stores, restaurants and online shops. U.S. exporters should generate a price survey of competitor products and services from both domestic and international firms.

Brunei currently does not charge any sales tax, value-added tax or goods and services tax. Hotel and rest and recreation facilities may charge up to a 10% service fee . They may also charge gratuity.

Brunei instituted the Price Control Act (Cap 142) and administered by the Department of Economic Planning and Development, Prime Minister's Office (www.depd.gov.bn). Maximum prices for selected goods such as those that are categorized as basic necessities (motor vehicles, infant milk powder, and cigarettes) may be fixed by the Price controller for consumer protection purposes. The Act controls the market activity of the specified goods.

SALES SERVICE/CUSTOMER SUPPORT

Bruneian customers, both corporate and individual, expect high-quality sales service and after-sale customer support like many other customers in markets worldwide. Better support and after-sales-service have placed U.S. suppliers in a much better position, compared with their European competitors selling products of equal quality, or Asian competitors that provide lower priced products. Bruneian customers generally have greater confidence in U.S. suppliers' service and support, due to their well-trained service and support teams. An increasing number of Bruneian buyers would rather

invest in higher-quality, more expensive products, in order to save expensive maintenance or replacement costs following warranty expirations.

PROTECTING YOUR INTELLECTUAL PROPERTY

Brunei was removed from the United States Trade Representative's (USTR) Special 301 report in 2013, and stayed off the list in 2014, in recognition of its improving IPR protections, increasing enforcement, and efforts to educate the public about the importance of IPR.

Brunei's Intellectual Property Rights (IPR) law is consistent with the World Trade Organization (WTO) Agreement on Trade-Related Aspects of Intellectual Property Rights (TRIPS). The law is complaint-based. The rights holder must appeal / take action with the government, which then may begin enforcement actions. The Bruneian government has made concerted efforts to remove pirated music from stores and prosecuted a local business owner for infringing the Patents Order 2011.

Strategies for Protecting Your Intellectual Property in Brunei:

Several general principles are important for effective management of intellectual property ("IP") rights in Brunei. First, it is important to have an overall strategy to protect your IP. Second, IP is protected differently in Brunei than in the United States. Third, rights must be registered and enforced in Brunei, under local laws. Your U.S. trademark and patent registrations will not protect you in Brunei. There is no such thing as an "international copyright" that will automatically protect an author's writings throughout the entire world. Protection against unauthorized use in a particular country depends, basically, on the national laws of that country. However, most countries do offer copyright protection to foreign works under certain conditions, and these conditions have been greatly simplified by international copyright treaties and conventions.

Registration of patents and trademarks is on a first-in-time, first-in-right basis, so you should consider applying for trademark and patent protection even before selling your products or services in the Brunei market. It is vital that companies understand that intellectual property is primarily a private right and that the U.S. government generally cannot enforce rights for private individuals in Brunei. It is the responsibility of the rights' holders to register, protect, and enforce their rights where relevant, retaining their own counsel and advisors. Companies may wish to seek advice from local attorneys or IP consultants who are experts in Brunei law.

While the U.S. Government stands ready to assist, there is little that can be done if the rights holders have not taken the fundamental steps necessary to secure and enforce IP in a timely fashion. Moreover, in many countries, rights holders who delay enforcing their rights on a mistaken belief that the U.S. government can provide a political resolution to a legal problem may find that their rights have been eroded or abrogated

due to legal doctrines such as statutes of limitations, laches, estoppel, or unreasonable delay in prosecuting a law suit. In no instance should U.S. Government advice be seen as a substitute for the obligation of a rights holder to promptly pursue its case.

It is always advisable to conduct due diligence on potential partners. Negotiate from the position of your partner and give your partner clear incentives to honor the contract. A good partner is an important ally in protecting IP rights. Consider carefully, however, whether to permit your partner to register your IP rights on your behalf. Doing so may create a risk that your partner will list itself as the IP owner and fail to transfer the rights should the partnership end. Keep an eye on your cost structure and reduce the margins (and the incentive) of would-be bad actors. Projects and sales in Brunei require constant attention. Work with legal counsel familiar with Brunei laws to create a solid contract that includes non-compete clauses, and confidentiality/non-disclosure provisions.

It is also recommended that small- and medium-size companies understand the importance of working together with trade associations and organizations to support efforts to protect IP and stop counterfeiting. There are a number of these organizations, based in the United States or in the region. These include:

* The U.S. Chamber of Commerce

* National Association of Manufacturers (NAM)

* International Intellectual Property Alliance (IIPA)

* International Trademark Association (INTA)

* The Coalition Against Counterfeiting and Piracy

* International Anti-Counterfeiting Coalition (IACC)

* Pharmaceutical Research and Manufacturers of America (PhRMA)

* Biotechnology Industry Organization (BIO)

IP Resources

A wealth of information on protecting IP is freely available to U.S. rights holders. Some excellent resources for companies regarding intellectual property include the following:

* For information about patent, trademark, or copyright issues -- including enforcement issues in the US and other countries -- call the STOP! Hotline: **1-866-999-HALT** or register at www.StopFakes.gov .

* For more information about registering trademarks and patents (both in the U.S. as well as in foreign countries), contact the US Patent and Trademark Office (USPTO) at: **1-800-786-9199**.

* For more information about registering for copyright protection in the US, contact the US Copyright Office at: **1-202-707-5959**.

* For more information about how to evaluate, protect, and enforce intellectual property rights and how these rights may be important for businesses, a free online training program is available at www.stopfakes.gov .

* For US small and medium-size companies, the Department of Commerce offers a "SME IP Advisory Program" available through the American Bar Association that provides one hour of free IP legal advice for companies with concerns in Brazil, China, Egypt, India, Russia, and . For details and to register, visit: http://www.abanet.org/intlaw/intlproj/iprprogram_consultation.html

* For information on obtaining and enforcing intellectual property rights and market-specific IP Toolkits visit: www.StopFakes.gov This site is linked to the USPTO website for registering trademarks and patents (both in the U.S. as well as in foreign countries), the U.S. Customs & Border Protection website to record registered trademarks and copyrighted works (to assist customs in blocking imports of IP-infringing products) and allows you to register for Webinars on protecting IP.

* The U.S. Commerce Department has positioned IP attachés in key markets around the world. The IP attaché who covers Brunei can be contacted at: Peter.Fowler@USPTO.GOV

DUE DILIGENCE

The Ministry of Finance maintains registration of companies and ongoing projects in Brunei. Anyone considering doing business in Brunei is urged to conduct their own due diligence. Most law firms and accountancies offer due diligence services as well. A list of attorneys can be obtained at http://www.judicial.gov.bn and a list of the accountants can be found below.

The U.S. Commercial Service also offers the International Company Profile (ICP) service to U.S. companies interested in evaluating potential business partners overseas. Researched and prepared by the U.S. Embassy Bandar Seri Begawan Commercial Assistant, ICPs enable U.S. small- and medium-sized businesses to more effectively evaluate overseas companies. Companies can obtain detailed answers about the specific overseas companies of interest, competitors, credit rating, profit and loss numbers, key officers, and our opinion on the overall viability of the firm in its market.

Department of Commerce website for Commercial Services:

http://www.trade.gov/cs/

LOCAL PROFESSIONAL SERVICES

Legal Services: The legal sector is governed under the Legal Profession Act (CAP.132 of Laws of Brunei). Section 4 of the Act provides the Chief Justice with the authority to admit a qualified individual as an advocate and solicitor. An application by a qualified person for admission is made by letter addressed to the Chief Justice at the office of the Chief Registrar. The Chief Registrar issues the license and maintains the advocate and solicitor's name on the roll. Law firms do not need to obtain a separate license to practice. The Law empowers the Law Society of Brunei to make rules in relation to the regulation of practice and disciplinary rules.

The Attorney General The Law Building Bandar Seri Begawan BA 1910, Brunei Darussalam Telephone: (673) 223 1200 or (673) 224 4872. http://www.agc.gov.bn/

Accounting and Tax Services: There are a number of large accounting firms operating in Brunei, namely KPMG, Deloitte & Touche, Ernst & Young, and Price Waterhouse Coopers. Brunei, in 2011, instituted the Accountants Order and Accounting Standards Order 2010 which oversees the registered public accountants providing accounting services. The Accountant Order stipulates the qualification of public accountants, the registration of accounting firms and requires practitioners to participate in the practice monitoring program and the disciplinary proceedings.

Engineering and Architectural Services: Engineering Services are regulated by the Ministry of Development. Currently, construction related engineering services are regulated through administrative procedures but legislation to regulate the whole spectrum of this sector is being finalized. The main disciplines include Civil and Structural; Mechanical and Electrical; and Chemical and Petroleum. Consultants are required to register with the Ministry of Development to be able to practice in Brunei.

LIMITATIONS:

No limitations exist whereby only citizens or a sub-set of the population are allowed to own or sell within the manufacturing or service sectors.
However, Brunei government does not permit foreigners to own land. Foreign businesses and individuals are permitted long term leases on buildings for their operations and residences.

WEB RESOURCES

Ministry of Industry and Primary Resources: http://www.industry.gov.bn

Brunei Economic Development Board: http://www.bedb.com.bn

Attorney General's Chambers: http://www.agc.gov.bn

Ministry of Foreign Affairs and Trade: http://www.mofat.gov.bn

Ministry of Finance: http://www.mof.gov.bn

LEADING SECTORS FOR U.S. EXPORT AND INVESTMENT

While Brunei's market size is smaller than its more populous neighbors, Brunei offers a number of important investment opportunities for U.S. firms. The Government of Brunei has placed a strong emphasis on diversification away from oil and gas, which has the potential to create opportunities in a host of emerging sectors. Brunei's proximity to larger markets in Indonesia, Malaysia, Singapore and the Philippines makes it an attractive regional hub.

Brunei's largest sector—upstream and downstream oil and gas production—offers attractive investment prospects. Beyond petrochemicals, U.S. businesses may consider exploring aviation, construction, defense industry equipment, franchising, renewable energy technology, and information and communications technology. In the agricultural sector, food imports/food production and the fishing industry/aquaculture are sizable industries as Brunei imports more than 80% of its food.

U.S. firms may also consider opportunities in the modest but growing niche technology sectors, including clean technology, biotechnology, healthcare technology and medical devices.

OIL AND GAS EXTRACTION

Unit: USD thousands

	2012	2013	2014 (estimated)	2015 (estimated)
Total Market Size	(743,368)*	N/A	N/A	N/A
Total Local Production	10,872,692	N/A	N/A	N/A
Total Exports	11,946,799	11,447,200	N/A	N/A
Total Imports	330,739	271,280	N/A	N/A
Imports from the U.S.	546	N/A	N/A	N/A

Brunei's economy has been dominated by the oil and gas upstream and downstream industries for the past 80 years. These industries will continue to provide important commercial opportunities for U.S. firms. Brunei's oil and gas fields produce approximately 159,000 barrels of oil per day (bbl/day) and 1,230 MMscf/day of natural gas. Brunei hopes to increase production in coming years. New oil extraction technology and the current market price of oil have made extracting oil from mature fields economically viable. As a result, companies with experience in extracting oil from mature fields may find new opportunities in Brunei. Other discoveries in the region have generated optimism that there may be additional on-shore and off-shore reserves which may assist Brunei's interest in increasing production.

Brunei has set out a long-term vision for the country and the energy sector. The target is to grow production from 400,000 BOEPD in 2010 to about 430,000 BOEPD by 2017. Under the Brunei Vision (Wawasan) 2035, the industry is set to increase to B$45 billion (USD36.1 billion) per year

For additional analytical, business and investment opportunities information,
please contact Global Investment & Business Center, USA
at (703) 370-8082. Fax: (703) 370-8083. E-mail: ibpusa3@gmail.com
Global Business and Investment Info Databank - www.ibpus.com

and aims to increase production to 800,000 bbl/day and to more than 650,000 BOEPD by 2035. The Energy Department at the Prime Minister's Office recently published an Energy White Paper (2013) that established a framework for action to help realize the National Vision. The White Paper presented three strategic goals to drive the growth in the energy sector:

Strategic Goal 1 – Strengthen and Grow Oil and Gas Upstream and Downstream Activities

Strategic Goal 2 – Ensure Safe, Secure, Reliable and Efficient Supply and Use of Energy

Strategic Goal 3 – Maximize Economic Spin-off from Energy Industry - Boost Local Content and Secure High Participation of Local Workforce.

SUB-SECTOR BEST PROSPECTS

* Exploration,

* Geophysical surveying and mapping services,

* Drilling operating,

* Operating oil and gas field properties,

* Site preparation

OPPORTUNITIES

There are a number of upstream opportunities for U.S. companies. U.S. firms are well positioned to provide oil and gas equipment and services through local representatives to Brunei Shell Petroleum (BSP), the largest private company in Brunei. In accordance with Brunei's Local Business Development framework, BSP gives preference to indigenous companies in their contracting activities. Aside from highly specialized equipment and spare parts sales from the original equipment manufacturers, local and international firms compete for contracts. Equipment or services from abroad must be supplied through a local agent or distributor or in partnership or joint venture with local Brunei companies.

Beyond BSP, Brunei Liquefied Natural Gas (BLNG) is also a major player in the petrochemical industry that may seek equipment and services from U.S. companies.

BSP and BLNG practice stringent quality control and suppliers must pass a series of quality tests before they can be registered. Most BSP suppliers are registered representatives or distributors of products and services from various foreign countries. U.S. companies may enter the Brunei market through a joint venture, agency agreement or distributor relationship with local Brunei companies. Many established companies in the oil and gas industry are members of the Brunei Energy Association or the Institute of Engineering and Technology.

On the downstream side, BSP is working closely with the Brunei Government to support downstream projects, which it is hoped will become springboards for further economic diversification in the country.

WEB RESOURCES

Brunei Industry Contacts

Brunei Shell Petroleum Co Sdn Bhd
Jalan Utara, Panaga
Seria KB3534 Negara Brunei Darussalam
Phone: +673 337-3999
Website: https://www.bsp.com.bn
Brunei LNG Sendirian Berhad
Lumut KC2935
Brunei Darussalam
Phone: +673 323-6901/902
Fax: +673 323-6892
E-mail: BLNG-Resourcing@BruneiLNG.com ; Enquiry@BruneiLNG.com
Website: http://www.bruneilng.com

Brunei National Petroleum Company Sdn Bhd

2nd Floor, Block A,B,C,

Yayasan Sultan Haji Hassanal Bolkiah Complex, Jalan Pretty,

Bandar Seri Begawan BS8711, Brunei Darussalam

Tel: (673) 2230720 (0-5)
Fax: (673) 2230654 / 2230712
Email: pb@pb.com.bn
The Energy White Paper may be found at:
http://www.usasean.org/sites/default/files/uploads/Energy%20White%20Paper%202014.pdf

Brunei Government Contacts
Brunei Economic Development Board
Block 2D, Jalan Kumbang Pasang,
Bandar Seri Begawan, BA 1311,
Brunei Darussalam
Phone: +673 223-0111
Fax: +673 223-0063
Website: http://www.bedb.com.bn
Energy Department, Prime Minister's Office, Jalan Menteri Besar, BB3913

Bandar Seri Begawan, Brunei Darussalam.

Tel: (673) 2384488 / 2380222 / 2383033 / 2383035

Email: energy@jpm.gov.bn and info.ed@jpm.gov.bn
Website: http://www.energy.gov.bn/Pages/default.aspx

Brunei Civil Society and Academic Contacts
Institute of Engineering and Technology
IET Office, Block B9 Unit 1,
Simpang 32-66, Kampong Anggerek Desa,
Berakas
Brunei Darussalam
E-mail: hon.sec@theiet.org.bn
Website: http://theiet.org.bn

COMMERCIAL AVIATION

Unit: USD thousands

For additional analytical, business and investment opportunities information,
please contact Global Investment & Business Center, USA
at (703) 370-8082. Fax: (703) 370-8083. E-mail: ibpusa3@gmail.com
Global Business and Investment Info Databank - www.ibpus.com

	2012	2013	2014 (estimated)	2015 (estimated)
Total Imports	42,993	N/A	N/A	N/A
Imports from the U.S.	24,937	N/A	N/A	N/A

Brunei has a small but growing fleet of commercial aircraft. Royal Brunei Airlines' fleet is currently composed of six Airbus and four Boeing aircraft, although this number will soon grow with the arrival of seven Airbus aircraft.

Royal Brunei Aircraft
* Airbus 319 = 2
* Airbus 320 = 4
* Boeing 787 = 4
* Airbus – purchased = 7

SUB-SECTOR BEST PROSPECTS

* Air commuter carriers, scheduled
* Scheduled air passenger carriers
* Scheduled air cargo carriers

OPPORTUNITIES

U.S. aviation firms may consider building upon existing relationships in order to secure future contracts. In addition to new sales, aviation maintenance is a potential area for U.S. commercial activity. The Brunei Economic Development Board (BEDB) recently identified this sector as a potential industry to promote economic diversification efforts,

opening up opportunities for maintenance, repair and overhaul (MRO) companies as well as flight and maintenance training organizations.

Beyond the MRO opportunities, the BEDB hopes to establish a flight simulator center and a training facility for maintenance engineers. The BEDB is prepared to collaborate, facilitate and invest in infrastructure development and site allocation for hangar construction, and backshop and training facilities.

WEB RESOURCES

Brunei Contacts

Royal Brunei Airlines
P.O. Box 737
Bandar Seri Begawan BS 8671
Brunei Darussalam
Tel: +673 221-2222
Fax: +673 224-4737
Website: http://www.bruneiair.com

Ministry of Communication
Jalan Menteri Besar Bandar Seri Begawan BB3910Brunei Darussalam
Email: info.mincom@mincom.gov.bn
Tel: (673)-2380127 (Administration and Services)
(673)-2381646 (Transportation)
(673)-2380389 (Communications)

(673)-2380398 (Information Technology & Research and Development)
(673)-2383838 Ext 1102 (Policy & Planning)
Department of Civil Aviation, Ministry of Communication, Brunei International Airport, Bandar Seri
Begawan BB2513 Brunei Darussalam
Email: info.dca@civil-aviation.gov.bn
Tel: +673 2330142
Fax: +673 2331706
http://www.civil-aviation.gov.bn

CONSTRUCTION

Unit: USD thousands

	2012	2013
Total Market Size	527,045	N/A
Total Local Production	472,769	N/A
Total Exports	604	N/A
Total Imports	214,000	312,903
Imports from the U.S.	15,384.6	79,032

The construction industry, with about 1,500 registered enterprises in 2014, ranks third in the number of enterprises among Brunei's industrial sectors and employs some 24,000 workers (2010). The vast majority of these workers are non-local laborers. The Construction industry is the largest employer of non-local laborers. Small enterprises (one to nine employees) account for 43% of construction enterprises, medium enterprises (10 to 99 employees) account for 51% of construction enterprises, and large enterprises (100 or more employees) account for 6% of construction enterprises.

During the 2014 Legislative Council (LegCo) meeting, the Brunei Economic Development Board (BEDB) was allocated a total of BND$20 million (USD$16 million) for the continued development of the 1,500 homes for the national housing scheme in Tutong. A further BND $104 million (USD$83.3 million) is expected to be spent this year on countrywide national housing projects. In the transportation sector, BND$400 million (USD$320 million) has been provided to support business and trade which includes the construction of a bridge to connect the exclave of Temburong District to Brunei Muara District and another across the Brunei River to connect residential areas in then north of the country to the capital, cutting short what is currently a considerable commute. Money will also be allocated to the continued upgrade of the International Airport and the upgrading of highways in the south of the country to enhance connectivity with the Malaysian state of Sarawak. Additionally, under the 10th National Development Plan, there is a provision of $61.6 million (USD$49.3 million) for the development of an oil and

gas refinery at Pulau Muara Besar. The joint project between China's Hengyi Industries and the Brunei Economic Development Board (BEDB) represents one of the largest direct foreign investments in Brunei to date, with phase 1 of the investment amounting to USD$4 billion. Despite the expenditure on infrastructure, LegCo announced the project to build a series of flyovers on the main highway to ease congestion is still a long way from completion. The majority of the proposed sites are still at the tendering stage.

Large construction contracts come mainly from the Brunei government and Brunei Shell Petroleum Co. Brunei follows a policy of awarding construction contracts wherever possible to local firms, meaning that foreign firms may have to form joint ventures with, or subcontract to, a local firm in order to participate in infrastructure projects.

SUB-SECTOR BEST PROSPECTS

* Concrete product (e.g., structural precast, structural prestressed) installation
* Rebar contractors
* Erecting structural steel
* Reinforcing steel contractors
* Placing and tying reinforcing rod at a construction site
* Structural steel contractors
* Precast concrete panel, slab, or form installation

OPPORTUNITIES

The proposed government-funded 30 kilometer bridge linking the districts of Muara and Temburong, currently separated by Malaysia, is poised to provide excellent opportunities for U.S. firms to provide services to the project and to the newly accessible regions. The Brunei government is particularly encouraging foreign firms to partner with local firms on this project. Upon the bridge's completion, slated for early 2018, additional construction projects in the currently low-population density Temburong District will almost certainly become viable. The Brunei government seeks to increase development in the currently relatively isolated Temburong region which contains Borneo's most pristine forests and natural resources. Construction of the bridge will pass through environmentally sensitive mangrove areas.

Brunei is proud of its natural environment and will seek to minimize adverse impact upon natural areas along the bridge's proposed route, and also along the supply chain and in water ways along the bridge's path. U.S. firms that have expertise in sustainable and environmentally-conscious construction procedures and have a proven track-record of sound environmental stewardship have an advantage in obtaining contracts and should leverage this credential in their efforts. Partnerships between firms which are expert in advanced and environmentally-sound construction techniques and local firms will be welcome, particularly if U.S. firms can offer training opportunities for Bruneians.

U.S. firms entering the construction industry in Brunei will find that Brunei faces a shortage of skilled laborers. Building materials must be largely imported, increasing construction costs. Due to the tropical climate, construction materials and methods differ substantially from those of temperate climates. Set concrete construction with reinforcing steel (rebar) is the norm for housing, wood frame construction is not common. High annual rainfall and humidity mean that concrete setting takes longer than in temperate climates, often reducing the speed at which structures can be completed. Despite these challenges, there are a range of construction opportunities in Brunei both from government contracts and private firms.

WEB RESOURCES

Brunei Government Contacts
Ministry of Development – Public Works Department
Website: http://www.pwd.gov.bn/

Ministry of Industry and Primary Resources
Website: http://www.industry.gov.bn/

MILITARY ARMORED VEHICLE, TANK, AND TANK COMPONENT MANUFACTURING

U.S. defense industry firms have an established history of supplying the Royal Brunei Armed Forces (RBAF) with defense equipment, after-sales support services, and training packages. RBAF is an all-volunteer force of nearly 5,750 service members. Defense spending accounts for 3.3% of GDP. The RBAF relies primarily upon helicopters to deploy its forces for border security, to perform coastal surveillance missions, for disaster response missions, and for law enforcement support. The Air Force possesses one troop transport fixed-wing plane, flight training aircraft, and a number of rotary wing aircraft. In 2011, Sikorsky Aircraft Corporation signed a deal with Brunei for delivery of 12 Blackhawk S-70i helicopters and delivery will be completed in late 2014. Brunei's naval capabilities are focused on Exclusive Economic Zone security, domain awareness and offshore oil facility protection.

OPPORTUNITIES

The Brunei Government has approved a US $585 Million budget for the Ministry of Defence for 2014-2015 fiscal year. U.S. defense contractors may discover equipment, training and other defense-related opportunities with Brunei, particularly in support of Brunei's 2011 Defense White Paper goals and objectives. Border security and surveillance, air defense platforms, maritime and domain awareness, regional disaster response, and domestic emergency preparedness are among Brunei's priority efforts.

Brunei places emphasis on the importance of science and technology, and Command and Control abilities to leverage the effectiveness of its relatively small armed forces.

In addition to working with regional partners, as it did during the Association for Southeast Asian Nations (ASEAN) Humanitarian Assistance and Disaster Relief (HA/DR) exercises in 2013 and in other regional HADR responses, Brunei is also seeking to increase its border and maritime defense capacity through improved regional military coordination and cooperation with its neighbors during various bilateral and multilateral interoperability engagements.

To enable these capacities, Brunei has stated its intent to acquire new defense equipment, including surface/maritime surveillance radar, airspace surveillance platforms, maritime patrol aircraft, fixed wing transport aircraft, medium range air defense systems, and related assets. Military services may also be interested in non-lethal equipment which may be procured through vendors registered with the Ministry of Defense.

The Centre of Science and Technology Research and Development (CSTRAD) is responsible for the research and development, assessment, and selection of defense technology solutions for RBAF. CSTRAD oversees Brunei's defense modernization efforts, advises the Ministry of Defense on science and technology matters, and supervises the transparency and timeliness of the defense-related acquisition process.

WEB RESOURCES

Brunei Government Resources
Ministry of Defense
Bolkiah Garrison BB3510
Brunei Darussalam
Tel: +673 2386-000
Fax: +673 238-1501
Website: http://www.mindef.gov.bn

Royal Brunei Technical Services
5th Floor, Setia Kenangan Office Block
Setia Kenangan Complex,
Kg. Kiulap
Bandar Seri Begawan BE1518
Tel: +673 224-2700

For additional analytical, business and investment opportunities information,
please contact Global Investment & Business Center, USA
at (703) 370-8082. Fax: (703) 370-8083. E-mail: ibpusa3@gmail.com
Global Business and Investment Info Databank - www.ibpus.com

Fax: +673 224-3767
Centre of Science and Technology Research and Development (CSTRAD)
http://www.mindef.gov.bn/MOD2/index.php?option=com_content&view=article&id=811&Itemid=314

Tender List
http://www.mindef.gov.bn/tender2/index.php?option=com_content&view=article&id=26&Itemid=39

Brunei Defense White Paper 2011
http://www.mindef.gov.bn/MOD2/index.php?option=com_docman&task=doc_details&gid=42&Itemid=331

U.S. Government Resources
For more information on procurement opportunities, contact:
Office of Defense Cooperation
U.S. Embassy Singapore
Tel: +65 6476-9379
Fax: +65 6476-9483

FRANCHISING

Numerous U.S. franchises operate in Brunei. Burger King, Auntie Anne's Pretzels, McDonalds, KFC, Pizza Hut, and Dairy Queen are common sights in Brunei and are very popular. Starbucks and Burger King are new to the market in 2014. The franchise industry is also popular among investors because it is perceived to be an attractive and relatively safe form of investment.

OPPORTUNITIES

Brunei's consumers seek out U.S. food and apparel brands. New franchises that service the food and fashion industries would likely be well-received, particularly in the fast food industry.

Local franchise operations will need to prepare for regional integration and competitiveness in the single market due to the implementation of the ASEAN Economic Community (AEC), which will go into effect in 2015. The single market will not only benefit exporters, but will also provide enhanced opportunities for U.S. franchise companies to access the wider Southeast Asian market from a foothold in Brunei or other ASEAN nations.

WEB RESOURCES

Ministry of Finance Registrar of Companies Website:
http://www.mof.gov.bn/index.php/divisions/registry-of-companies-and-business-names

POWER, DISTRIBUTION, AND SPECIALTY TRANSFORMER MANUFACTURING

Unit: USD thousands

	2012
Total Market Size	N/A
Total Local Production	N/A
Total Exports	78.8

Total Imports	2,171
Imports from the U.S.	20.6

Brunei is interested in diversifying its energy mix beyond oil and gas, looking to renewable energy technology as a viable supplement.

Renewable energy technology acquisition is a priority for Brunei and is encouraged by the United States. The U.S.-Asia-Pacific Comprehensive Partnership for a Sustainable Energy Future was launched in 2012 by President Obama, Sultan Haji Hassanal Bolkiah of Brunei, and President Yudhoyono of Indonesia to support renewable energy technology development in Brunei and across the region.

Brunei's renewable energy sector was not ranked in the U.S. Department of Commerce Renewable Energy Top Markets for U.S. Exports 2014 – 2015 report. Brunei's renewable energy market is currently in its infancy. Several companies operate in the country, namely Berakas Power Management Corporation and Wira Energy Brunei. The only renewable facility is the 1.2-MW Tenaga Suria Brunei solar plant in Seria. The plant is being run as a pilot project for three years by Mitsubishi Corporation in partnership with the Energy Department of the Prime Minister's Office to evaluate the capacity and output of different photovoltaic cells in generating solar-generated electricity. Currently, the plant produces about 1,700 MWh of solar energy per year. The target is to increase the country's share of renewable energy in the total power generation mix by 2.7 percent, or 124,000 MWh, by 2017 and by 10 percent, or 954,000 MWh, by 2035.

Beyond renewable energy projects, there is interest in "greening" Brunei's existing infrastructure. Brunei's Green Building Council, founded in March 2013, is partnering with the Ministry of Development to establish green building practices for government projects.

SUB-SECTOR BEST PROSPECTS

Electric Bulk Power Transmission and Control

OPPORTUNITIES

Brunei is currently accepting bids for renewable energy projects across the country. Brunei is particularly focused on solar photovoltaic and waste-to-energy technology and is also looking to increase energy efficiency through energy-saving appliances and green building construction.

A Memorandum of Understanding between the Energy Department Prime Minister's Office and U.S. Ex-Im Bank signed in March 2014 calls for expanded information sharing regarding trade and energy business opportunities in the Asia-Pacific region as well as exploring options for utilizing up to US$1 billion in Ex-Im Bank credit to finance U.S. exports in support of selected projects in the region. This creates new opportunities for U.S. companies, subject matter experts, and consultants to engage with Brunei as it seeks a new, sustainable economic future closely integrated with the Asia-Pacific region.

As these projects progress, there will be numerous opportunities for private sector investment.

The Green Building Council supports legislation that would make green building practices mandatory, which would open-up new opportunities for U.S. firms specializing in green building construction and green building materials.

The U.S. Department of Commerce launched the Renewable Energy and Energy Efficiency Export Initiative (RE4I) with 11 other U.S. Government agencies to better position U.S. exporters of these technologies for success in international markets. Each U.S. Government agency involved in the RE4I can offer specific programs to support U.S. companies looking to sell products and services abroad. A guide to U.S. Government export promotion programs from across the RE4I agencies can be found at www.export.gov/reee/guide .

WEB RESOURCES

Brunei Government Contacts

Energy Department, Prime Minister's Office, Jalan Menteri Besar, BB3913 Bandar Seri Begawan, Brunei Darussalam.
Tel: (673) 2384488 / 2380222 / 2383033 / 2383035
Email: energy@jpm.gov.bn and info.ed@jpm.gov.bn

Brunei National Petroleum Company Sdn Bhd
2nd Floor, Block A,B,C,
Yayasan Sultan Haji Hassanal Bolkiah Complex, Jalan Pretty,
Bandar Seri Begawan BS8711, Brunei Darussalam
Tel: (673) 2230720 (0-5)
Fax: (673) 2230654 / 2230712
Email: pb@pb.com.bn

Brunei National Energy Research Institute (BNERI)

Science and Technology Research Building
UBD Tungku Link BE1410
Tel: +673 246-1336
E-mail: info@bneri.org.bn

Brunei Civil Society Contacts

Green Brunei
No. 14 Simpang 853
Kg Tasek Meradun
Jln Tutong, BF1520
Brunei Darussalam
Tel: +673 862-6588
E-mail: info@green-brunei.com
Website: http://www.green-brunei.com

U.S. Government Contacts and Resources
U.S.-Asia-Pacific Comprehensive Partnership for a Sustainable Energy Future
E-mail: energyinasia@state.gov
Information on the Partnership:
Website: http://www.state.gov/e/enr/c56576.htm
Pamphlet: http://www.ustda.gov/news/events/2013/SouthAsia/USACEPBrochure.pdf

Export-Import Bank

Website: http://www.exim.gov
Overseas Private Investment Corporation
Website: http://www.opic.gov

U.S. Trade and Development Agency
Website: http://www.ustda.gov
For updated information programs, opportunities, market research, and news from across the
U.S. Government, please visit the RE41 website at: www.export.gov/reee .

TELECOMMUNICATIONS

Unit: USD thousands

	2012	2013
Total Imports	34,738	N/A
Imports from the U.S.	73,321	N/A

Driven both by government intervention and consumer demand, Brunei's information and communications technology (ICT) industry continues to grow. Brunei's *Wawasan 2035*, or 2035 National Vision, calls for a shift to a knowledge-based economy. Further development of the ICT sector will play a major role in helping diversify the economy away from oil and gas. The government is also seeking to increase the ICT contribution to the gross domestic product (GDP) to 6% by 2015. This would be a marked increase from the current 1.9% ICT contribution to GDP. Brunei's high literacy rate and strong per-capita demand for consumer goods will help propel Brunei toward this goal.

With almost 50% of the population between the ages of 15 and 40 years, Brunei's relatively young population is widely information and technology-savvy. The 440,000 mobile telephones in Brunei outnumber the residents, and approximately 78.5% of the population uses the internet. As internet connectivity increases, Brunei is hoping to transform a paper-based procedural system into an electronic system across all information and communication technology centers.

In 2014 the Brunei government issued a National Broadband Blueprint, with a primary objective being to increase the ICT industry's contribution to GDP to 6% by 2015. Brunei's connectivity has improved but continues to suffer from insufficient broadband capacity and high costs. Brunei was ranked 45 out of 148 countries in the 2013 World Economic Forum Networked Readiness Index, which grades economies on their usage, acceptance and efficiency of ICT. Brunei received a rank of 63 of 134 in 2008, the first year it was included in the index. Telekom Brunei Berhad (TelBru) offers broadband

capacity with a maximum of five megabits per second (Mbps) but it can drop to less than one Mbps, a strength that does not meet the international broadband benchmark of two Mbps. Lack of competition and a small customer base has made broadband average cost an expensive B$65 (USD51.80) per month.

Brunei is an investor in the Southeast Asia-Japan Cable (SJC), that when finished will connect Japan, Hong Kong, the Philippines, Brunei, and Singapore. This cable will add to the two existing cables, which have recently been strained by age and low capacity.

SUB-SECTOR BEST PROSPECTS

* Broadband Internet service providers, wired (e.g. cable, DSL)
* Local telephone carriers, wired

For additional analytical, business and investment opportunities information,
please contact Global Investment & Business Center, USA
at (703) 370-8082. Fax: (703) 370-8083. E-mail: ibpusa3@gmail.com
Global Business and Investment Info Databank - www.ibpus.com

* Cable television distribution services
* Long-distance telephone carriers, wired
* Closed circuit television (CCTV) services
* VoIP service providers, using own operated wired telecommunications infrastructure
* Direct-to-home satellite system (DTH) services
* Telecommunications carriers, wired
* Satellite television distribution systems

OPPORTUNITIES

The Brunei Economic Development Board (BEDB), tasked with identifying potential areas of economic diversification, has identified the ICT sector as one of the key areas for diversification efforts. To support the development of ICT, BEDB has developed the iCentre, Brunei's first ICT incubator, as part of the first phase of the Business and Technology Park. At the iCentre, a number of young entrepreneurs are developing innovative ideas helping to bring Made-in-Brunei technology overseas. Current projects in development at the iCentre include mobile communications content and software, barcode and Radio-Frequency Identification (RFID) applications, software development and public portal development. In addition, BEDB has identified the following opportunities in the ICT sector:

* Data Centers and Disaster Recovery Centers

* Software development opportunities in partnership with iCentre incubatees

Best prospects within the ICT sector are government projects, including software development and data centers. Brunei's market is very dependent on imports and U.S. products are traditionally well received in Brunei as the United States is seen as the source for state-of-the-art technologies.

When complete, the Southeast Asia Japan Cable (SJC) will open up numerous opportunities to develop Brunei's first data center. Brunei has awarded a B$3.1million (USD2.47 million) consulting contract to South Korea-based KT Corporation and Malaysian consulting firm Alliance Geotechnical Services (AGS). As part of the contract KT is providing technology consulting services for the Brunei's National Data Centre project.

WEB RESOURCES

Brunei Government Contacts

iCentre
Website: http://www.icentre.biz/

Chief Information Officer, Prime Minister's Office
Website: http://www.pmo.gov.bn

Chief Information Officer, E-Government National Center
Website: http://www.egnc.gov.bn/Pages/default.aspx
Ministry of Communications
Website: http://www.mincom.gov.bn

Authority for Info-Communications Industry of Brunei Darussalam (AITI)
Website: http://www.aiti.gov.bn
Brunei Telecommunications Companies
Telekom Brunei Berhad (TelBru)

For additional analytical, business and investment opportunities information,
please contact Global Investment & Business Center, USA
at (703) 370-8082. Fax: (703) 370-8083. E-mail: ibpusa3@gmail.com
Global Business and Investment Info Databank - www.ibpus.com

Website: http://www.telbru.com.bn

DataStream Technology Sdn Bhd (DST)
Website: http://www.dst-group.com

B-mobile Communications Sdn Bhd
Website: http://www.bmobile.com.bn

Radio Television Brunei (RTB), Prime Minister's Office
Website: http://www.rtb.gov.bn

Global Rankings

World Economic Forum Global Connectivity in Brunei 2013

Info-Graphic:
http://www3.weforum.org/docs/WEF_GlobalInformationTechnology_Report_2014.pdf

FOOD MANUFACTURING

Unit: USD thousands

	2012	2013
Total Market Size	452,172	N/A
Total Local Production	72,692	N/A
Total Exports	2,255	N/A
Total Imports	381,735	73,000
Imports from the U.S.	8,751	8,871

While Brunei has recently encouraged the redevelopment of the local food industry, more than 80% of Brunei's food is still imported. In 2013 alone, Brunei imported approximately B$599.83 million (USD477.95 million) worth of food products, a figure that lagged just behind imported machinery and manufactured goods. Brunei exported a modest B$14.305 million (USD11.4 million) in food products in 2013.

OPPORTUNITIES

Because of Brunei's heavy reliance on imports, commercial activity in food imports and food production are important potential markets for U.S. exporters.

In addition to ready-to-eat food imports, Brunei has a strong interest in the *halal* food production industry. As Brunei works to add products to its Brunei *halal* brand, assistance from companies who are already operating in these markets will be welcomed. Brunei is hoping to attract research organizations, product development companies and businesses interested in penetrating the *halal* market. Because of this heavy reliance on imports, commercial activity in food imports and food production are important potential markets for American exporters. American producers with experience in the *halal* foods market may find additional opportunities in food product exports to Brunei. However, exporters must be aware that *halal* standards may differ

between the United States and Brunei, and between Brunei and other Muslim-majority countries.

For additional analytical, business and investment opportunities information,
please contact Global Investment & Business Center, USA
at (703) 370-8082. Fax: (703) 370-8083. E-mail: ibpusa3@gmail.com
Global Business and Investment Info Databank - www.ibpus.com

U.S. Government Contacts
Alice Kwek
Foreign Agricultural Service
U.S. Embassy Singapore
Tel: +65 6476-9294
Fax: +65 6476-9517
E-mail: Alice.Kwek@fas.usda.gov
Website: http://www.fas.usda.gov

FISHING INDUSTRY/AQUACULTURE

Unit: USD thousands

	2012	2013
Total Market Size	78,856	20,496.05
Total Local Production	40,538	18.252.10
Total Exports	2,339	1,935.5
Total Imports	40,657	21,693.5
Imports from the U.S.	222	N/A

With one of the highest per capita consumption rates of about 15,500 metric tons in the region, fish is a critical part of the Brunei diet. Bruneians consume approximately 100 pounds of fish per year, half of which is imported. The Brunei government has identified fishing as a sector that can enable economic diversification and as such, the government is offering incentives to develop commercial fisheries in Brunei's Exclusive Economic Zone (EEZ), which extends 200 nautical miles offshore.

In June 2013, Brunei became the first country in the world to ban all shark trade and announced a commitment to enforce an August 2012 ban on shark fishing in Brunei's Exclusive Economic Zone/Brunei Fisheries Limit. Enforcement of the ban began in 2014. This commitment has garnered accolades from environmental groups.

SUB-SECTOR BEST PROSPECTS

Farm raising finfish and shellfish, boat and fishing equipment supplier

OPPORTUNITIES

Brunei has recently allowed for joint fishing ventures, making the fishing industry an attractive sector for international investors. The Fisheries Department of the Ministry of Industry and Primary Resources has identified capture fishing, aquaculture, and seafood processing as the three main business opportunities in Brunei.

Capture Fishing: Fishing licenses are available for operating purse-seiners, and tuna long-liners in the Exclusive Economic Zone/Brunei Fisheries Limit.

Aquaculture: With an estimated commercial potential of B$71 million (USD$56.5 million) per year, and with a growth projection of B$112 million (USD$89.2 million) by 2015, Brunei has identified aquaculture as one of the fastest growing fishing industries in the country. While shrimp

For additional analytical, business and investment opportunities information,
please contact Global Investment & Business Center, USA
at (703) 370-8082. Fax: (703) 370-8083. E-mail: ibpusa3@gmail.com
Global Business and Investment Info Databank - www.ibpus.com

farming is the most significant aquaculture opportunity, fish off-shore cage culture, ornamental fish production, and freshwater culture are also emerging industries.

Seafood Processing: Brunei has identified seafood processing – including frozen fish, fish ball and cakes, crackers, fish nuggets, marinated fish and dried fish – as a B$17 million (USD$13.5 million), underdeveloped market that could offer important investment opportunities for international companies. There is a significant domestic market for these products, and Brunei's *halal* certification would allow export to regional markets as well. Pre-existing industrial sites with basic processing infrastructure may also be available, cutting down on start-up costs.

KEY CONTACTS AND WEB RESOURCES

Brunei Government Contacts
For more information on fisheries in Brunei, contact:
Fisheries Department
Ministry of Industry and Primary Resources
Jalan Mentiri Besar
Bandar Seri Begawan
Brunei Darussalam.
Tel: +673 238-0107, +673 238-0026
Fax: +673 238-2835
Website: http://www.fisheries.gov.bn/

Brunei Fisheries Limit, Ministry of Industry and Primary Resources
Website: http://www.fisheries.gov.bn/potentials/capture.htm#limits

Capture Fishing, Ministry of Industry and Primary Resources
Website: http://www.fisheries.gov.bn/potentials/capture.htm

Aquaculture, Ministry of Industry and Primary Resources
Website: http://www.fisheries.gov.bn/potentials/aquaculture.htm

Seafood Processing, Ministry of Industry and Primary Resources
Website: http://www.fisheries.gov.bn/potentials/processing.htm

AGRICULTURAL SECTORS

Brunei Government Contacts

Brunei *Halal*
Brunei Wafirah Holdings Sdn Bhd
Ghanim International Food Corporation Sdn Bhd
Unit 6, First Floor, Lim Kah Sik Building, Jerudong
Brunei Darussalam, BG3122
Tel: +673 238-4533
Fax: +673 238-4537
E-mail: information@brunei-halal.com
Website: http://www.brunei-halal.com
Ministry of Industry and Primary Resources
Website:
http://www.industry.gov.bn/index.php?option=com_content&view=article&id=81&Itemid=102

RESEARCH AND DEVELOPMENT IN BIOTECHNOLOGY

Unit: USD thousands

	2012	2013
Total Exports	0.716	N/A
Total Imports	1,589	N/A
Imports from the U.S.	111	N/A

While there is high-level government interest in biotechnology, Brunei's biotechnology field currently lacks the technical expertise to scale-up in research and development.

SUB-SECTOR BEST PROSPECTS

* Recombinant DNA research and experimental development laboratories

* DNA technologies (e.g., microarrays) research and experimental development laboratories

* Cloning research and experimental development laboratories

* Protein engineering research and experimental development laboratories

* Nucleic acid chemistry research and experimental development laboratories

* Nanobiotechnologies research and experimental development laboratories

OPPORTUNITIES

Brunei is seeking to develop its biotechnology industry, particularly through the agro-biotechnology research and development and ethno-botany for *halal* cosmetics and pharmaceuticals. The government also hopes to develop incubator facilities for specialized companies to partner with local small and medium enterprises. The development of the incubator has the potential to create business opportunities for U.S. companies specializing in agro-biotechnology research and development in the field of ethno-pharmaceutical, cosmetics and food production. This emerging field has captured the interest of the government, which is a positive sign for potential investors.

WEB RESOURCES

Universiti Brunei Darussalam Research: http://www.ubd.edu.bn/researchs/

Assistance Schemes for Business Startups and SMEs:
http://www.bedb.com.bn/documents/sme/BEDB.SME.Guide.Book(2012).pdf

MEDICAL EQUIPMENT AND SUPPLIES MANUFACTURING

Unit: USD thousands

	2012	2013
Total Imports	18,076.9	27,822.6
Imports from the U.S.	3,307	6,612.9

Brunei has a small but growing medical industry and provides highly subsidized medical care. Brunei's two major hospitals – Raja Isteri Pengiran Anak Saleha Hospital (RIPAS Hospital) and Jerudong Park Medical Center– are supplemented by two provincial hospitals, three district hospitals, and 16 smaller health posts. Today, Bruneians with the means to seek advanced medical services outside of the country will travel to Singapore and the Brunei medical system pays for services rendered in Singapore when it is unable to provide them to its citizens. As Brunei's young population ages and requires medical care, this will be an important longer-term growth sector for Brunei's economy.

SUB-SECTOR BEST PROSPECTS

* Manufacturing laboratory instruments, X-ray apparatus, electromedical apparatus (including electronic hearing aids), and thermometers (except medical)--are classified in Industry 33451, Navigational,

* Measuring, Electromedical, and Control Instruments Manufacturing;

* Manufacturing molded glass lens blanks--are classified in Industry 32721, Glass and Glass Product Manufacturing;

* Manufacturing molded plastics lens blanks--are classified in Industry 32619, Other Plastics Product Manufacturing;

* Retailing and grinding prescription eyeglasses--are classified in Industry 44613, Optical Goods Stores;

* Manufacturing sporting goods helmets and protective equipment--are classified in Industry 33992, Sporting and Athletic Goods Manufacturing;

* Manufacturing general purpose hospital, laboratory and/or dental furniture (e.g., stools, tables, benches)-- are classified in Industry 33712, Household and Institutional Furniture Manufacturing;

* Manufacturing laboratory scales and balances, laboratory furnaces and ovens, and/or laboratory centrifuges--are classified in Industry 33399, All Other General Purpose Machinery Manufacturing;

* Manufacturing laboratory distilling equipment--are classified in Industry 33324, Industrial Machinery Manufacturing; and

* Manufacturing laboratory freezers--are classified in Industry 33341, Ventilation, Heating, Air-Conditioning, and Commercial Refrigeration Equipment Manufacturing.

OPPORTUNITIES

A reported increase in patient demand for advanced medical devices and a willingness of medical facilities to upgrade existing technology has driven sales of new technology in recent years.

Slated for implementation in late 2014, the draft Association of Southeast Asian Nations (ASEAN) Medical Device Directive (AMDD) requires ASEAN countries to abide by standardized medical device classifications and institute monitoring systems to ensure the devices work effectively. The AMDD would also require international manufactures to establish a presence in Brunei if they

For additional analytical, business and investment opportunities information,
please contact Global Investment & Business Center, USA
at (703) 370-8082. Fax: (703) 370-8083. E-mail: ibpusa3@gmail.com
Global Business and Investment Info Databank - www.ibpus.com

wish to sell devices in the local market. Though not a binding directive, the AMDD required all ASEAN countries to adopt laws with the same provisions within their own constitutions.

KEY CONTACTS AND WEB RESOURCES

Brunei Government Contacts

Ministry of Health
Commonwealth Drive Bandar Seri Begawan BB3910
Brunei Darussalam
Tel: +673 238 1640
Fax: +673 238 1440
Website: http://www.moh.gov.bn/

U.S. Government Contacts

For more information on Association of Southeast Asian Nations Medical Device Directive, contact:
U.S. Mission to ASEAN Jl. Medan Merdeka Selatan 5 Jakarta 10110, Indonesia
Tel: +62 21 3435-9000

International Organization Contacts

World Health Organization Medical Devices Survey findings:
http://www.who.int/medical_devices/countries/brn.pdf

TRADE REGULATIONS, CUSTOMS AND STANDARDS

IMPORT TARIFFS

Brunei generally has very low tariffs. The Customs Import Duty Order 2012 and Excise Duty Order 2012 were created with the aim of facilitating trade and attracting foreign direct investment. Basic foodstuffs and goods for many industrial uses are exempted from import duties. Excise duties are levied on certain goods, including cars at 20%, and 15% for heavy vehicles. There is no tax on computers and peripherals. Other consumer products such as perfume, cosmetics, clothes, carpets, shoes, jewelry, office equipment, telephones, television sets, lamps, and cameras, are taxed at 5%. Import duties for electronically operated industrial machines are at 5%. Tariff and excise rates for Brunei are available at:

http://www.mofat.gov.bn/index.php/information-for-exporters-and-importers/import/custom-duties-and-preferential-tariff-rates

http://www.mof.gov.bn/index.php/departments/royal-custom-a-excise-department

http://hts.usitc.gov/

TRADE BARRIERS

The United States and Brunei enjoy a long history of trade, dating to an 1850 treaty whereby Brunei and the United States agreed to trade freely and without barriers, under Most Favored

Nation (MFN) status. Trade relations between the United States and Brunei are modest but growing. According to the Brunei Department of Economic

Planning and Development, annual bilateral trade exceeded B$539.92 (USD435.41) million in 2013. Following the successful conclusion of the negotiations, the proposed Trans-Pacific Partnership (TPP) will provide enhanced opportunity for US exporters to access the ASEAN region, serving to make Brunei and the wider Southeast Asian region an increasingly attractive destination for U.S. exports.

Today U.S. companies and businesses doing business in Brunei or wishing to export products to Brunei may do so freely, with the exception of food products, an area in which Brunei takes particular interest. Brunei is emphasizing its *halal* food industry as one of the key pillars of an effort to diversify its economy. Brunei is promoting its own *halal* food certification regime, one entirely distinct from other *halal* certification organizations, which would require Bruneian inspectors to travel to production facilities in the home country of the food exporter, at the exporter's expense, to inspect the food production process. This requirement places constraints on the ability of U.S. exporters of food products to enter the Brunei market without complying with requirements that may not be necessary in other markets.

IMPORT REQUIREMENTS AND DOCUMENTATION

The import of all goods into Brunei is monitored by The Royal Customs and Excise Department. Importers must register with the port of entry. Determination of duty classification is based on the Excise Duty Orders 2012 and 2007. Import permits are required for some products. Licenses for import are available from the relevant government agencies. Nonprohibited goods can be imported under open general license.

Completed Customs Declaration Forms must be submitted together with supporting documentation such as invoices, freight and insurance slips, airway bills and packing lists.

Additional documentation that may be required includes certificate of origin and analysis, Approval Permit (A.P.), import licenses and other documentation as deemed necessary by the Customs and Excise Department.

Further information can be obtained from:

Royal Customs & Excise Department

Ministry of Finance

Tel: +673 238-2333

Fax: +673 238-2666

Website: http://www.mof.gov.bn/index.php/departments/royal-custom-a-excise-department

The Department of Health Services under the Ministry of Health ensures food imported and distributed in Brunei is safe for human consumption. Food importers are required to comply with the Public Health (Food) Act (Chapter 182), and Public Health (Food) Regulations 2000. Food importers are required to comply with the provisions of the food legislation and import requirements. Importers are required to submit customs declaration forms along with the relevant export health certificates from the countries of origin.

Other requirements include provision of Hazard Analysis Critical Control Point (HACCP) certificates, samples of all items to be imported to Brunei, lists of all ingredients and additives used and other valid documentation or certification as determined by the Ministry of Health. Imported food products are mainly *halal*, for the consumption of the majority Muslim population. *Halal* food cannot contain alcohol or derivatives from non-*halal* animals.

Processed food imports must be registered and must identify additives' origin under Regulation 9, Public Health (Food) Regulation, 2000.

Further information can be obtained from:

Food Safety and Quality Control Division

Department of Health Services

Environmental Health Service

Ministry of Health

Tel: +673 233-1100

Fax: +673 233-1107

Website: http://www.moh.gov.bn

U.S. EXPORT CONTROLS

Companies wishing to export controlled items to Brunei must apply for licenses from the appropriate government agencies in the United States. The Bureau of Industry and Security (BIS) is responsible for implementing and enforcing the Export Administration Regulations (EAR). Certain specialized exports are regulated by other U.S. government agencies. A list of agencies involved in export controls can be found at http://www.bis.doc.gov

TEMPORARY ENTRY

Brunei has not adopted the *Admission Temporaire*/Temporary Admission (ATA) Carnet Convention but allows temporary entry of commodities for demonstration, exhibition and trade samples for a duration of three months. Instructions are available at the Royal Customs and Excise website:

http://www.mof.gov.bn/index.php/departments/royal-custom-a-excise-department

LABELING AND MARKING REQUIREMENTS

Under the Public Health (Food) Act (Chapter 182), Public Health (Food) Regulations 2000, all food imported into the country must bear a label containing information including a list of ingredients, expiration date and details of the local importer, distributor or agent. Printed expiry dates must not be less than three millimeters in height. Information on food labels is required to be labeled in a prominent and conspicuous position on the package.

Importation of food products that require date markings include food supplements are subject to "set requirements" as outlined by the Public Health (Food) Regulation 2000. They are required to be registered with the Food Quality and Safety Control Division, Environmental Health Services, and Department of Health Services. Health supplements that contain ingredients which can be used therapeutically or contain any medical claims are required to be referred to the Department of Pharmaceutical Services, Ministry of Health for clearance.

The labeling requirement shall include:
* Name of food
* List of ingredients and their sources (including additives)
* Net weight/volume
* Date marking
* Storage instruction
* Name of country of origin
* Name and address of the local importer for imported food/name and address of the manufacturer/packager in the case of a food of local origin

Detailed information on the food labeling requirements can be obtained from:

Food Safety and Quality Control Division

Department of Health Services

Environmental Health Service

Ministry of Health

Tel: +673 233-1100

Fax: +673 233-1107

Website: http://www.moh.gov.bn

PROHIBITED AND RESTRICTED IMPORTS

Brunei imposes restrictions/prohibitions on the import of certain goods under the Customs Order 2006 (Section 31). Imports and manufacture of alcohol and alcohol products are restricted for religious reasons under the Customs (Prohibition and

Restriction of Imports and Exports) Amended Order 1990. Details of restricted/prohibited goods are available from:

Royal Customs & Excise Department

Ministry of Finance

Tel: +673 238-2333

Fax: +673 238-2666

Website: http://www.mof.gov.bn/index.php/departments/royal-custom-a-excise-department

Importers of *halal* meat and food products need prior approval from the Ministry of Religious Affairs. Prior to approval, inspection of the foreign plant facilities will be carried out by two officers from the Religious Affairs Department. Importers have to pay for the trip. Currently only selected approved plants in Australia, Malaysia and India are accredited to supply *halal* beef.

Brunei imports live cattle from a Brunei-owned cattle ranch located in Northern Australia for slaughter locally. Brunei claims to be 90% self-sufficient for poultry production. *Halal* certification for poultry is issued on strict compliance with slaughter methods set by the Ministry of Religious Affairs.

Importation of alcoholic beverages has been prohibited with minor exceptions for personal, private consumption by non-Muslims since 1991. Pork is consumed only by non-Muslims. There is no pork production in Brunei. Brunei imports fresh and frozen pork from the neighboring Malaysian state of Sarawak.

The *Halal* Certificate and *Halal* Label Order 2005 cover the issuance of *Halal* Certificate and *Halal* Labels on processed food, separation of food storage and business premises such as restaurants and others.

Halal Certification Contact:

The Secretary

Board for Issuing *Halal* Import Permits

Ministry of Religious Affairs

Jalan Elizabeth II

Bandar Seri Begawan BS8510

Brunei Darussalam

Tel: +673 224-2565 / 6

Fax: +673 222-3106

Website: http://www.religious-affairs.gov.bn/index.php?ch=bm_service &pg=bm_service_halhar (Malay only)

CUSTOMS REGULATIONS AND CONTACT INFORMATION

Brunei's Customs legislation was amended to harmonize its tariff nomenclature, make custom-related information more readily available to traders and the public, align its laws with the WTO agreements and intellectual property protection, and improve the appeal procedures. All imports into Brunei must be accompanied by:

* A bill of lading/delivery order or airway bill

* Packing list;

* Commercial invoice;

* Three copies of the customs declaration form, which include the number of individual packages;

* Detailed description of the goods being imported; gross and net weights or quantities of packages;

* Value (f.o.b. and c/i.f.);

* Place of shipment and destination; and

* Country of origin.

The invoice must be signed by the exporter or seller. The importer can request an exemption of duty determination to be issued by the Brunei Economic Development Board and a certificate of origin may be requested.

Detailed information on Customs regulation can be found from:

Royal Customs & Excise Department

Ministry of Finance

Jalan Menteri Besar

Bandar Seri Begawan BB3910

Tel: +673 238-2333

Fax: +673 238-2666

Website: http://www.mof.gov.bn/English/RCE/Pages/default.aspx

TRADE STANDARDS

Brunei adheres to a range of international standards, including the International Organization for Standardization (ISO) and the International Electrotechnical Commission (IEC) regimes. Brunei also recognizes certifications from bodies that have been accredited by the members of the Pacific Accreditation Cooperation. Conformance certificates and laboratory accreditations are also accepted from Asia Pacific Laboratory Accreditation Cooperation (APLAC) Mutual Recognition Arrangement members.

The National Standards Council was established in December 2009 and operates under the auspices of the Ministry of Industry and Primary Resources.

Telecommunications standards are regulated by the Authority for Info-Communication and Technology (AITI) under Section 9 of Telecommunications Order, 2001. AITI regulates the use of telecommunication equipment in Brunei, requiring that services meet national standards.

STANDARDS ORGANIZATIONS

For additional analytical, business and investment opportunities information,
please contact Global Investment & Business Center, USA
at (703) 370-8082. Fax: (703) 370-8083. E-mail: ibpusa3@gmail.com
Global Business and Investment Info Databank - www.ibpus.com

In April 2010, the National Standards Council created and endorsed the National Standards Center as the accreditation body of Brunei. As of 2014, the National Standards Act is currently being developed. When complete, it will standardize local products and service quality and will provide a legislative framework to guide the enforcement activities in the implementation and management of the standards.

The National Standard Centre (NSC) consists of five units:

1. Conformity Assessment

2. Certification

3. Legal and Standards Development

4. International Relations

5. Standard Promotion and Information

The National Standards Centre provides a range of services to small- and medium-sized enterprises, including:

* Certification Service

* Standards and Quality Product Training Service

* Quality and Promotion Development Service

* Standard and Information Service

* Consultation Service

* Factory Visit Service

* Testing and Metrology Collaboration Lab Service

Under section nine of Telecommunications Order, 2001, companies importing equipment to be used for connection to any telecommunications system or equipment belonging to

a telecommunication licensee must have prior approval from AITI before use. Any equipment that is not approved must be returned to the country of origin by the importer.

CONFORMITY ASSESSMENT

Brunei's Conformity Assessment Procedure is available:
http://www.mod.gov.bn/en/Theme/Home.aspx
Ministry of Development
Old Airport Complex
Berakas BB3510
Brunei Darussalam
Tel: +673 238-3222
Fax: +673 238-0298

E-mail: info@mod.gov.bn

PRODUCT CERTIFICATION

Restaurants and food manufacturing operators catering to the Muslim community are required to have a *halal* certificate and permit as well as *halal* branding in accordance with the *Halal* Certificate and Label Order 2005. Under the order, the manufacturer or restaurant is only permitted to produce and prepare *halal* products using raw ingredients from *halal* suppliers. Multinational companies or medium-sized enterprises are required to form an Internal *Halal* Audit Committee to handle and ensure the company is in compliance with all *halal* requirements. A *halal* certificate and permit cost B$90 (USD72) for a term of three years, and B$50 (USD40) per product for food manufacturers.

Hazard Analysis and Critical Control Points (HACCP) recognition is a requirement for local food manufacturers in order to export products outside of Brunei.

Food traders must comply with the Public Health (Food) Act (Chapter 182). A registration letter is issued within five to seven working days from date of application.

ACCREDITATION

Halal permits and certificates are issued by Ministry of Religious Affairs.

Bureau Veritas, a local certification body, issues HACCP certificates to local food manufacturers.

Under the Telecommunications Order 2001 Section 5, the Authority for the Info-Communications Industry (AITI) grants licenses for the operation of telecommunication systems and services.

PUBLICATION OF TECHNICAL REGULATIONS

Brunei's laws, acts, and orders are published in the Brunei Government Gazette. The Gazette is published by the Government of Brunei Printing Department. Copies can be purchased from the Printing Department of the Prime Minister's Office.

Printing Department: http://www.printing.gov.bn/

NIST Notify U.S. Service

Member countries of the World Trade Organization (WTO) are required under the Agreement on Technical Barriers to Trade (TBT Agreement) to report to the WTO all proposed technical regulations that could affect trade with other Member countries. **Notify U.S.** is a free, web-based e-mail subscription service that offers an opportunity to review and comment on proposed foreign technical regulations that can affect your access to international markets. Register online at Internet URL: http://www.nist.gov/notifyus/

CONTACTS

Contact at Embassy:
Matthew B. Stannard
Political/Economic/Consular Officer
+673 238-4616
stannardmb@state.gov

Head, Food Safety and Quality Control Division
Department of Health Services
Ministry of Health
Brunei Darussalam
Tel: +673 233-1100
Fax: +673 233-1107
E-mail: fsqc@moh.gov.bn
Website: www.moh.gov.bn

Authority for Info-Communications Technology Industry of Brunei Darussalam (AITI)
Block B14, Simpang 32-5
Kampung Anggerek Desa
Jalan Berakas BB3713
Brunei Darussalam.
Tel : +673 232-3232
Fax : +673 238-2447
E-mail: info@aiti.gov.bn

TRADE AGREEMENTS

Brunei is a member of Association of Southeast Asian Nations (ASEAN); Asia-Pacific Economic Cooperation (APEC); World Trade Organization (WTO); Brunei, Indonesia, Malaysia & the Philippines-East ASEAN Growth Area (BIMP-EAGA); and the Multilateral Agreement on the Liberalization of International Air Transportation (MALIAT). In addition to trade liberalization regimes under ASEAN, Brunei is a party to the Trans-Pacific Partnership (TPP) negotiations. Brunei is also party to the Regional Comprehensive Economic Partnership (RCEP) negotiations, an ASEAN + 6 (Australia, the People's Republic of China, India, Japan, the Republic of Korea and New Zealand) trade agreement. ASEAN hopes to conclude RCEP negotiations by 2015.

WEB RESOURCES

Ministry of Development:
Website: http://www.mod.gov.bn
Royal Customs and Excise Department:
Website: http://www.mof.gov.bn/
Authority of Info-Communication and Technology
Website: http://www.aiti.gov.bn/Pages/Home.aspx
Ministry of Industry and Primary Resources
Website: http://www.industry.gov.bn

TRADE AND PROJECT FINANCING

(METHODS OF PAYMENT

Brunei's banking system offers a full range of export finance instruments, including letters of credit and drafts.

BANKING SYSTEM

Although small, Brunei's banking system is reliable and well monitored. The Ministry of Finance oversees the Department of Financial Services (Treasury) and the Brunei Investment Agency. The Brunei Monetary Authority (Monetari Autoriti Brunei Darussalam - AMBD) acts as the central bank of Brunei and handles the formulation and implementation of monetary policies, supervision of financial institutions and currency management.

FOREIGN-EXCHANGE CONTROLS

There is no restriction on foreign exchange. Banks permit non-resident accounts and there is no restriction on borrowing by non-residents.

U.S. BANKS AND LOCAL CORRESPONDENT BANKS

There are five foreign commercial banks operating in Brunei:

* Hong Kong and Shanghai Banking Corporation (HSBC)

* Standard Chartered Bank

* Malayan Banking Berhad

* United Overseas Bank Ltd

* RHB Bank Berhad

These banks all provide full banking services and have branches throughout the country.

The locally incorporated banks include the following:

* Bank Islam Brunei Darussalam Berhad (BIBD)

* Baiduri Bank Berhad (a partnership of BNP Paribas)

Tabung Amanah Islam Brunei (TAIB) is a locally incorporated trust fund offering Islamic banking services. Four foreign banks are registered as offshore financial institutions. State Street is a U.S. banking institution offering non-commercial services.

PROJECT FINANCING

Government contractors are required to collateralize their future contract proceeds and seek project financing from local banks until the project is completed. Authoriti Monetari Brunei Darussalam (AMBD) imposes a single-borrower limit for large projects. In order to finance mega projects, banks tend to pool their efforts in a "club-deal" arrangement similar to a syndicate loan which may also involve the participation of foreign banks. The foreign banks bolster the capacity that the local banks lack in supporting these projects.

WEB RESOURCES

Brunei Government Resources

Ministry of Finance
Website: http://www.mof.gov.bn/

Brunei Monetary Authority
Website: http://www.ambd.gov.bn/

U.S. Government Resources

Export-Import Bank of the United States
Website: http://www.exim.gov

Country Limitation Schedule
Website: http://www.exim.gov/tools/countrylimitationschedule/index.cfml

OPIC
Website: http://www.opic.gov

Trade and Development Agency
Website: http://www.ustda.gov

SBA's Office of International Trade
Website: http://www.sba.gov/oit/

USDA Commodity Credit Corporation:
http://www.fsa.usda.gov/FSA/webapp?area=about&subject=landing&topic=sao-cc
U.S. Agency for International Development
Website: http://www.usaid.gov

Regional Resources

Asian Development Bank
Website: http://www.adb.org

BUSINESS TRAVEL

BUSINESS CUSTOMS

Brunei is a predominately Muslim country and a hereditary Sultanate. Visitors are expected to show respect for both Islam and the Royal Family. The national language is Malay although English, Hokkien, and Mandarin are widely spoken.

Introductions and connections are important and necessary in Brunei. Relationship-building precedes business negotiations and brokering deals can sometimes require several visits.

Visitors should avoid passing in front of a seated person or pointing with the index finger; Bruneians point with their thumb and clenched hand. Yellow is the royal color and should not be worn in the presence of royalty. When invited for a meal, the host will likely be offended if the guest offers to pay the bill. Guests should remove shoes before entering a private home. Handshakes are common among male businessmen. Female business visitors should not reach to shake a man's hand unless he extends it, but can touch a hand to the chest as a sign of respect instead.

The visitor to Brunei will find restaurants to fit all budgets and tastes. Malaysian, Indian, Chinese, and Western food are all ubiquitous. Tipping is not customary in Brunei. Large hotels and restaurants may add a 10% service charge to the bill. Alcohol is not available for purchase in Brunei and restaurants do not serve alcohol. The consumption of alcohol in any public place is prohibited and should be avoided. Offering alcohol to a Muslim is a crime in Brunei. Public

For additional analytical, business and investment opportunities information,
please contact Global Investment & Business Center, USA
at (703) 370-8082. Fax: (703) 370-8083. E-mail: ibpusa3@gmail.com
Global Business and Investment Info Databank - www.ibpus.com

consumption of food or drink during Ramadan is illegal in Brunei; takeout can be purchased in restaurants and should be eaten in a private location.

TRAVEL ADVISORY

Brunei has a warm, humid climate year-round but most places of business are well air-conditioned. The Department of State advises travelers to view its travel advisory site at http://travel.state.gov for the latest updates. Brunei's official website offers tourism, government, business, and other information, and can be accessed at http://www.jpm.gov.bn/ . Within Brunei, the information centers at the airport and downtown can provide maps and tourist services. Travel agencies are located throughout the capital.

VISA REQUIREMENTS

Business visitors and tourists from the United States do not need visas for visits of up to 90 days. Renewals and residency permits are routine and simple.

Brunei citizens are eligible to participate in the U.S. Visa Waiver Program allowing travel to the U.S. without a visa for short business and pleasure trips.

U.S. companies that require travel of foreign businesspersons to the United States should be advised that security evaluations are handled via an interagency process. Visa applicants should go to the following links.

State Department Visa Website: http://travel.state.gov/visa/

Embassy website: http://brunei.usembassy.gov/visas.html

TELECOMMUNICATIONS/ELECTRIC

Brunei has a good telecommunication system and is in the midst of a major fiber-to-home improvement project which will increase bandwidth access. There are three operators providing telecommunications services in Brunei: Syarikat Telekom Brunei Berhad (TelBru), DST Communications (DSTCom) and B-mobile Communications Sdn Bhd. Most hotels have wifi and wifi is also available at many cafes and restaurants.

Brunei Voltage: The voltage in Brunei is 240 V.

Brunei Electrical Frequency: The electrical frequency in Brunei is 50 Hz.

Brunei Plug/Socket Type(s): Brunei uses the G plug. Universal travel adapters can be bought from hardware and electrical stores.

Brunei GSM Freqencies: Brunei uses the GSM 900 frequency. When travelling, mobile phones used in Brunei must support the GSM frequency.

The Authority for Info-Communications Technology Industry of Brunei Darussalam (AITI) administers the regulatory function and development of the Info-Communications industry in Brunei. Brunei aims to establish itself as the cyber hub of the region, and under the Ninth National Development Plan (NDP), the government plans to continue enhancing telecommunications infrastructure as well as the integration of ICT/on-line services. As with past NDPs, ongoing training will be provided in the government's efforts to enhance human and institutional capital.

Brunei is connected with the rest of the world through the SEA-ME-WE3 Submarine Cable System at Tungku Submarine Cable Station. The SEA ME WE3 has a total capacity of 2,634,214 minimum investment unit kilometers (Miu*km) with at least 80% of this capacity open for further utilization. This link is diversified and backed up through a land-based transmission system, the Trans-Borneo Optical Fiber System. The Intelsat Satellite Network and new teleport at Telesai Earth Station sustain highly reliable international services via satellite while simultaneously providing back up and alternative telecommunication services via submarine cable system.

To date, the main licensed operators are:

* TelBru – sole fixed-line operator, and provides fixed and wireless internet services. Website: http://www.telbru.com.bn/

* B-mobile – 3.5G cellular operator utilizing WCDMA technology. B-mobile is a joint venture between TelBru and QAF-Conserve. Website: http://www.bmobile.com.bn/index.php

* DST Com – First cellular operator in country, growing from GSM to 3.5G HSDPA (High Speed Downlink Packet Access). DST Com provides a range of mobile services. Kristal-Astro, a subsidiary company partners with Astro Malaysia to bring cable TV to Brunei homes. Website: http://www.dst-group.com

In June 2009, state-owned broadcaster, Radio Television Brunei (RTB) unveiled its plans to introduce a new High Definition (HD) channel to give local audiences access to digital quality viewing and to provide full digital broadcasting by 2017. HD trials are currently being carried out using a 100 Watt transmitter located at the Subok earth station near Bandar Seri Begawan.

TRANSPORTATION

The international airport is a fifteen-minute drive from downtown Bandar Seri Begawan, the capital, and should cost approximately B$25-30 (USD 19.90-23.90). Taxis and buses serve the capital and the outskirts although hours of operation are limited. Buses also travel to the oil towns of Seria and Kuala Belait. Rental cars and drivers are the most reliable form of transportation and can be hired with ease at competitive rates.

LANGUAGE

Brunei's official language is Malay, with English, Hokkien, and Mandarin also widely spoken. English is normally the language of business. Menus and signs in English are

common. The Chinese community that makes up 12% of the total population generally speaks Mandarin and Hokkien.

When in doubt, Sir, Mr., Mrs. and Ms. can be used without fear of insult. Should U.S. businesses wish to follow local custom, Bruneian males can be called Awang, and women, Dayang. These titles roughly correspond to Mr. and Ms.

Additionally, Pehin and Dato are the two principal titles bestowed by the Sultan. Pehin is a conferred honorary title generally associated with an official position within the royal court. Dato is a state honorary medal conferred by the Sultan, and may be bestowed on anyone the Sultan wishes to honor, regardless of nationality. The female equivalent to Dato is Datin, as is the wife of a Dato. Dato is roughly equivalent to Sir in Britain.

Pengiran refers to a Bruneian of royal descent. Children of Pengirans are referred to as Dayangku (daughter) and Awangku (son), and assume the title of Pengiran upon marriage. At the highest end of the scale is the title Pengiran Anak, denoting Bruneians closely related to the Sultan's family.

HEALTH

Brunei offers all its citizens free and modern health care at state run hospitals and clinics. Most doctors speak English, and many have studied in the United Kingdom, United States and Europe.

There is adequate care for basic medical conditions in Brunei; however, for certain elective surgery or complicated care, the Brunei medical system will send patients to Singapore. Brunei has a number of public hospitals and clinics. The biggest ones are RIPAS Hospital in Bandar Seri Begawan and Tutong Hospital in the district of the same name. The largest private hospital is Jerudong Park Medical Center about 20 minutes by car outside of Bandar Seri Begawan.

Brunei also hosts a number of private clinics, many of which are staffed by expatriates. More information can be found at the U.S. Embassy Website: http://brunei.usembassy.gov/ .

Medication and prescriptions for common conditions are generally available, although finding specific medications, such as decongestants, may be challenging. Local pharmacies may not carry the same brands as U.S. pharmacies. Visitors are advised to bring sufficient quantities of medicines that they know they will need prior to arriving in Brunei. It is important to be aware however of Brunei's strict laws on the import of controlled substances. To avoid complications, a prescription note should accompany any prescribed medicine brought to Brunei.

There has been a surge in cases of dengue fever in Southeast Asia, including Brunei. As there is no vaccine for dengue fever, visitors are advised to avoid mosquito bites by wearing skin-covering clothing and using insect repellent containing DEET.

The Center for Disease control maintains information on vaccinations and other health precautions: http://wwwnc.cdc.gov/travel/destinations/traveler/none/brunei . For information about outbreaks of infectious diseases abroad, consult the World Health Organization (WHO) website at http://www.who.org . The WHO website also contains additional health information for travelers, including detailed country-specific health information at http://www.who.int/countries/brn/en/ .

LOCAL TIME, BUSINESS HOURS, AND HOLIDAYS

Government offices are open for business from 7:45 am to 12:00 pm and from 1:30 pm to 4:30 pm, Monday through Thursday and Saturday, and are closed on Fridays and Sundays. The Ministry of Defense is the only ministry open on Fridays and closed on Saturdays. By law, everything in Brunei is closed on Fridays from 12:00 pm to 2:00 pm for Friday prayers. Most shopping centers are open daily from 10 am to 10 pm, including Sundays. Private offices generally conduct business from 8 am to 5 pm on weekdays and from 8 am to 12 noon on Saturdays. Banks generally open from 9 am to 3 pm on weekdays, and from 9 am to 11 am on Saturdays. Some banks have branches open seven days a week until late. Most have ATMs and can exchange foreign currency. During Ramadan government work hours and other business hours may be shortened to facilitate personnel who are fasting.

Official Holidays

Date	Day	Holiday
Jan 1	Wednesday	New Year's Day
Jan 14	Friday	Prophet Muhammad's Birthday
Jan 31	Friday	Chinese New Year
Feb 23	Sunday	Brunei National Day
May 27	Tuesday	Israk Mi'raj
May 31	Saturday	Armed Forces Day
Jun 28	Saturday	1st Day of Ramadan*
Jul 15	Tuesday	His Majesty Sultan's Birthday
Jul 16	Wednesday	Nuzul Al-Quran*
Jul 28	Monday	Hari Raya Aidilfitri* (Marks the end of Ramadan)
Jul 29	Tuesday	Hari Raya Aidilfitri*
Jul 30	Wednesday	Hari Raya Aidilfitri*
Oct 5	Wednesday	Hari Raya Aidil Adha*
Oct 25	Saturday	Islamic New Year*
Dec 25	Thursday	Christmas Day

* Actual Holiday Subject to Sighting of the Moon

TEMPORARY ENTRY OF MATERIALS AND PERSONAL BELONGINGS

There is no sales tax in Brunei. Arriving passengers over 17 years old are eligible to import 60 ml of perfume and 250 ml of eau de toilette. Non-Muslims at least 17 years old may bring in up to two bottles of liquor or wine and 12 cans of beer for personal consumption, but these goods must be declared to customs upon entry.

A B$12 (USD9.60) airport departure tax must be paid upon departure.

WEB RESOURCES

Brunei Travel Information
http://travel.state.gov/travel/cis_pa_tw/cis/cis_1073.html
Brunei Employment and Immigration
http://www.bedb.com.bn/doing_guides_immigration.html

IMPORTANT CONTACTS

GOVERNMENT AGENCIES:

Attorney General's Chamber
http://www.agc.gov.bn

MINISTRY OF FOREIGN AFFAIRS AND TRADE
HTTP://WWW.MOFAT.GOV.BN

Trade Associations/Chambers of Commerce:
Chinese Chamber of Commerce & Industry
Tel: +673 223-5494
Fax: +673 223-5492
E-mail: cccbrunei2011@gmail.com

Brunei Darussalam International Chamber of Commerce & Industry
Tel: +673 223-6601
Fax: +673 222-8389
E-mail: shazalisulaiman@kpmg.com.sg

Indian Chamber of Commerce
Tel: +673 234-0974
Fax: +673 234-0976
E-mail: Nazmitex@yahoo.co.in

OPPORTUNITIES AND STRATEGIES IN HALAL MARKET: BRUNEI PERSPECTIVE[3]

OPPORTUNITIES IN THE HALAL INDUSTRY

Most of us are here because we have a broad awareness of the market opportunities in the halal industry. The brochure on this event has already highlighted in broad terms the population size of Muslims world wide (1.8 billion). In Asia over 1 billion are Muslims with South East Asia and Middle East having more than 400 million Muslims. ASEAN has around 200 million out of population of around 550 million. Fastest population growth rates are in India, China, Indonesia and Pakistan.

In terms of market value, in 2006 I have heard estimates that the global halal market for food and non – food products was worth approximately USD$2.1 trillion annually.

In the halal food sector, Kasehdia Consulting presented an estimate of US$ 580 billion as the annual value of the halal food industry with growth in halal food spending at 2% per annum

We also believe that the natural increase in the Muslim population and the associated increase in their food spending are 2 important drivers for growth in the halal industry.

However, we also believe that there are additional drivers that will further expand the halal industry. These are the improving incomes among the Muslim population, changing lifestyles and demographics as well as increasing awareness and understanding of halal. Those 3 factors would increase demand for better and pricier products in the food industry. Similarly, we also expect increase in various product sectors whereby Muslim consumers will be

[3] Dato Haji Mohd Hamid Haji Mohd Jaafar Permanent Secretary at the Ministry of Industry and Primary Resources, and Chairman of the Brunei Darussalam Halal Management Committee

demanding halal compliance. These would include personal care products, cosmetics and pharmaceuticals. Thus, we share the optimism of the business or economic opportunities that the Ummah in Asia and around the world can provide.

OPPORTUNITIES IN THE NON-MUSLIM POPULATION

Having mentioned that, we also believe that opportunities for halal compliant products and services are also bountiful. This is popularly called the "cross over market" for halal. This statement is guided by the belief in the principle that Halal is for all. Considering that there are around 6 billion people around the world, we can very well imagine the business opportunities that are open for halal compliant businesses.

Let me cite some statistics:

o On the global food retail business, according to USDA Economic Research Service, global food retail sales exceed US $2 trillion annually, with supermarkets/ hypermarkets accounting for 52% of the sales.

o In cosmetics, in 2004, Eurostat estimated that the market size of the European market had a retail sale price value of at least 65 billion euros.

o Another example is personal care products. Euromonitor reported that global sales of personal care product almost hit the US $100 billion mark in 2006.

o In pharmaceuticals, IMS Health, a world leading provider of market intelligence to the pharmaceutical and healthcare industries, announced that the global sale of pharmaceuticals in 2006 was valued at US $ 643 billion.

o The realization that business and economic opportunities in halal is not only in the food sector is also reflected in the inclusion of non-food items in the various exhibition highlighting the halal industry such as this one. Noting that the world population is growing at an average rate of 1.17%, the potential markets for Halal compliant products globally are very large indeed – and growing!

STRATEGIES IN THE HALAL INDUSTRY

It is no wonder therefore that many governments and big companies are actively embarking on various strategies so they can take a slice of halal industry pie to sustain their economies.

Some of the multinationals that are already halal compliant or are in the process of halal compliance would include Nestle and McDonalds, AlIslami.

As far as governments are concerned, in the halal food business, some of the most active governments are in South East Asia.

o Malaysia's strategy revolves around their desire to be the global Halal hub in the production and trade of Halal goods and services.

o The Philippines has a Halal Export Trade Development Program that would certainly include developing Mindanao as the production center of Halal products

o Singapore's is using Tasty Singapore brand, a world-class benchmark that captures the essence of Singaporean cuisine, processes and standards.

o Thailand is promoting itself as the "Kitchen of World" to showcase the success of Thailand's agricultural export. Part of that strategy is long term plan to penetrate the global halal market

o For Brunei, we have the Brunei Halal Branding Project as the main vehicle that will carry out our goals and aspirations in the global halal industry.

BRUNEI'S STRATEGY IN THE HALAL INDUSTRY

This brings me now to the subject of Brunei's perspective in the halal industry.

Ladies and Gentlemen, having mentioned that companies and governments are pursuing their respective strategies in taking advantage of the opportunities in the halal industry, let me say with confidence that those respective strategies have been formulated after careful consideration of their national objectives as well as their strengths and weaknesses.

For Brunei Darussalam, the reality is that, while our per capita GDP of around B$ 47,964 or USD 30,166[1] is one of the highest in the region, this may not be sustainable in the future. The

[1] [2] Average Exchange Rate 2006 US$ 1.00 = B$ 1.59, Brunei Darussalam Statistical Yearbook 2006 p. 178

underlying socio-economic structure for that wealth is based on one industry, i.e., the oil and gas industry, which is nonrenewable. Thus, one of our national goals is diversifying the economic base of the country sources of wealth.

• In this respect, the Ministry of Industry and Primary Resources is one of the government agencies that has been given the task to contribute towards achieving the vision of "A Diversified, Competitive and Sustainable Economy" for Brunei Darussalam. And in realizing that vision, we in MIPR have looked at the industry sectors under our jurisdiction which can become a sustainable source of new socio-economic growth. This search has led us to the conclusion that the halal industry is one industry that can sustain our future needs. We have also come to the conclusion that branding Brunei Halal would be a one of main strategies that would allow us to take a slice of this industry. What led us to this conclusion? Let me explain.

BRUNEI HALAL BRAND

Traditionally, halal is often associated with food. As Brunei's food production industry is not well developed, we import a substantial amount of food products. In fact almost 80% of our food requirements are imported. In 2006, our importation of food and live animals was valued at B$ 374.4 million (roughly US$ 235.47 million). That constituted around 14% of our total import value. One of our limitations therefore is that we don't have the production capacity that can compete with our neighbours.

However, since we import much of our food, relevant authorities must ensure that imported foods conform to strict Halal

requirements. That led to the development of Brunei's stringent Halal regulatory and certification system. Halal is therefore one of our strengths that could be used to support economic diversification objectives. Thus, there is therefore a dual nature of our participation in the halal industry. One is fulfilling a religious obligation of ensuring that Muslim's consume halal food and the second is to take advantage of the economic opportunities in this industry. So we decided to develop a Brunei Halal Initiative in late 2005.

The next question for us was -In what way will Brunei participate in this market. We know, that we could not be a significant and producer of halal food like our neighbours in the region. So we explored again for a niche where Brunei can be a significant player in the industry.

Bearing in mind that the halal industry is a highly complex and fragmented market, we understood that many companies were also faced with similar a similar question. While opportunities are indeed huge, the competition in the market place is also high. To penetrate and sustain markets, we need to differentiate

– not differentiating Halal only in the marketing and promotion of brand, ourselves from the competition.

There are of course several approaches to differentiating a company's products and services in the market. One of them is branding. We are well aware of the power of global brands in the food industry. We are familiar with Kellogg's, Heinz, Nestle, Danone and Kraft. Years of promotion and strict quality control have assured consumers that those brands provide guarantees

of quality, nutritious, "clean and healthy" food that is good value for money.

To have an idea on the power of branding, let me cite some statistics. According to Interbrand, the brand value of the Kellogg's in 2007 was US$ 9.3 billion while Heinz's brand value was US$ 6.4 billion. Compare this to the value of annual sales by the 2 companies. In 2006, the global sales of Kellogg's were estimated at US$ 11 billion. In 2007, Heinz 's sales globally was nearly US$ 9 billion. We can see that brand value of those companies is close to the value of their annual sales.

Inspired by those well known brands and believing that Halal has the highest potential for brand value and brand loyalty, we took the decision to launch a Brunei Halal Branding project in 2006 at the First Brunei International Halal Products Expo. Brunei is taking advantage of the power of branding as one of the strategies for economic diversification, but with a "Halal" twist. It revolves around a simple concept of establishing partnerships with interested companies and applying Brunei's Halal Certification system in the production and marketing of quality and safe halal compliant products and services in the international market. The Brunei Halal Branding project therefore embodies our goals and aspirations in the Halal industry to contribute towards fulfilling a collective "fardhu kifayah" on providing Halal foods and products to the growing world Muslim population as well as to "ensure the sustainability of Brunei's socio-economy long after oil and gas".

CURRENT PROGRESS IN THE BRUNEI

Ladies and Gentlemen

Since its launch in 2006, the Brunei team has made progress in realizing the goals and aspirations of the Brunei Halal Brand. It has further consolidated the support structure for halal food certification by enhancing coordination among the various government agencies involved in halal certification.

2007 was a busy year for the Brunei Halal Team

o At the 2nd Brunei International Halal Products Expo in August, we released the documents guiding the Brunei Halal Brand. These includes:

Brunei Darussalam Standard for Halal Food

Brunei Halal Brand guidelines

Brunei Certification Guidelines for Halal

  Guideline for Halal Certification

  Guideline for Audit and Compliance

  Guideline for Halal Compliance Auditor

• Guideline for Halal Surveillance Audit D Fatwa of State Mufti on Issues on Halal Products

  o His Majesty the Sultan personally launched the new Brunei Halal Accreditation Label which embodies the core idea and supporting values of Brunei Halal

  o To further attract investments in the development of Brunei Halal Branding, we earmarked a 263 hectare Agro Technology Park in Tungku alongside the highway to Jerudong. The area would be for joint Venture and FDI manufacturing industries as well as R & D activities and support service industries for developing Halal related industries such as a Halal port.

  o Final phase of negotiation for the establishment of a Brunei Halal Brand commercial hub that will act as the main vehicle to operate the brand marketing and promotion activities in a totally commercial way.

  o We have also undertaken preliminary work on preparation of the Brand logo and its protection

• For 2008, we have set our ambitious targets to move the project with significant outcomes in time for the 3rd Brunei International Halal Products Expo in August.

  o Our work on the establishment of the commercial hub should be finalized to meet the business requirements of companies interested in Brunei Halal Branding. In this regard, I am pleased to inform you that around 200 companies in Australia have indicated their preparedness in being associated with the Brunei Halal Brand. This includes over 160 food manufacturers and 40 companies involved in providing services to the food industry – packaging, storage, transport, and specialist advisory services (legal, financial, new product development, technical). We hope that the first accreditation of several Australian food companies will have been completed by February 2008.

o We also plan to launch the Brand logo internationally in the, with products in the new brand image being in the marketplace between the first half or 3rd quarter of 2008.

o We will continue to invest in our capacity to support the expected demand on the Brunei Halal Certification system and establish smart partnerships to strengthen the credibility of the Brunei Halal Brand as well as in safeguarding our brand and promoting it.

o Our objective is that within 5 years, the Brunei Halal Brand will be truly a major feature in the international Halal food market. Insya Allah!

CONCLUSION

Ladies and Gentlemen, in concluding my presentation, I'd like to share 2 points:

o First is state our approach in the Halal industry. Like many Islamic countries, our business strategies in the Brunei Halal Branding project are guided by the very principles of Islamic faith and income from the Brunei Halal initiative is only to ensure sustainability of Brunei's socio-economy in line with our policy to diversify our economy away from oil and gas.

o The second point is to highlight the benefits to companies in joining the Brunei Halal Branding initiative. We offer you a win-win and long term relationship that will complement your companies own goals for growing the business in the halal industry. We are confident that the project will help simplify your choice in seeking for a reliable partner in the Halal industry.

o In this regard, I like to extend His Majesty's invitation to foreign investors and I quote *"We have always welcomed foreign investment. We are ready to look at suggestions from would-be investors"*. That excerpt from His Majesty's Titah embodies our commitment in the Brunei Halal Branding.

o We assure you of quality and friendly service and we will grow with you in meeting the changing demands of the halal market.

Lastly, let me invite you to Brunei. Visit the Green Heart of Borneo and its hospitable people. You will appreciate why Brunei Halal Branding is a worthy partner in the growing global halal industry. For more information visit our booth and our website at http://www.bruneihalal.gov.bn

In closing, I thank the organizers for giving an opportunity to share Brunei's perspective in the taking advantage of the opportunities in the global halal industry.

Thank you and Good Afternoon

IMPORTANT REGULATIONS RELATED FOR BUSINESS, TRADE AND INVESTMENT ACTIVITIES

IMPORTANT LAWS AFFECTING BUSINESS AND INVESTMENTS

Criminal Conduct (Recovery of Proceeds) Order
International Banking Order 2000
International Business Companies Order 2000
International Limited Partnerships Order 2000
International Trusts Order 2000
International Insurance and Takaful Order 2000
Money Laundering Order
Mutual Fund Order 2001
Registered Agents and Trustees Licensing Order 2000
Securities Order 2001

As a sovereign nation of high repute, Brunei served notice at the outset that criminal abuses of its financial systems would not be tolerated. The country took these steps voluntarily, rather than under pressure. This reflects responsible economic and social attitudes. Similarly, participation in international regulatory groups has been, and is being, extended.

The first tranche of IFC legislation therefore included Money-Laundering and Criminal Conduct (Recovery of Proceeds) measures implemented to international standards. Strict Drug Trafficking legislation has been in place for some time. Moreover, meaningful and enforceable regulation of the Trust, Company Administration, Insurance and Banking industries was legislated for and established before these activities commenced.

It should be noted that the Money Laundering Order, the Criminal Conduct (Recovery of Proceeds) Order, the Mutual Funds Order and the Securities Order apply to regulate those areas both domestically and internationally.

BRUNEI TRUST LAW

Brunei has very comprehensive international trust legislation, which will appeal both to private clients as well as major corporations. For the private clients, provision is made for asset protection trusts as well as special trust regimes. Under this regime, it is not the beneficiary who enforces a trust but an independent Enforcer. This addresses certain tax and security issues.

For the major corporations, commercial purpose trusts may be created whereby it is not necessary to have an individual beneficiary. Such trusts are widely used for special purpose vehicles (SPV) and planning, varying from project finance to securitization and segregation. The legislation also provides a more modern definition of inquired charities. This enables charitable trusts to be established to protect the environment and historic buildings, for example.

Under the International Trust Order, 2000 ('ITO'), an IT must be in writing, settled by a non-resident of Brunei, declared in its terms to be an international trusts (on creation or migration to Brunei), and at least one trustee must be a licensed under RATLO or an authorised wholly-owned subsidiary of a licensee. Generally, only non-residents may be beneficiaries when an IT is first established. Purpose and Special trusts are provided for, whether charitable or non-charitable. At least one trustee must be licensed under The Registered Agents and Trustees Licensing Order, 2000 (RATLO) or an authorised wholly-owned subsidiary of a licensee. Generally, only non-residents may be beneficiaries when an IT is first established. The retention of certain powers (specified in the ITO) by the settlor will not invalidate an IT. Such powers are not, however, deemed to exist in the absence of specific provision in the Trust instrument.

There are wide powers of investment, with an ability for trustees to seek "proper advice" as defined. Having done so, a trustee will not be liable for acts taken pursuant to such advice. There are powers to appoint agents and to delegate. Trustees may charge, and similar provisions appear for enforcers and protectors. Powers of maintenance and advancement are wide, spendthrift and protective trusts are recognized.

Arrangements for appointment or change of trustees follow generally accepted lines. The Court is given wide powers to interpret, assist and amend. Hearings may be held in camera. Trustees may pay funds into Court for determination of matters arising in the course of administering the fund, and there is power to apply to the Court for an opinion, advice or a direction relating to trust assets.

Purpose Trusts are provided for, whether charitable or non-charitable. Without prejudice to the generality, a trust for the purpose of holding securities or other assets is by statute deemed a purpose trust. The purposes must be reasonable, practicable, not immoral nor contrary to public policy. The trust instrument must state that the trust is to be an authorized purpose trust at creation or on migration to Brunei. Provision must be made for the disposal of surplus assets (although no perpetuity period applies), and an enforcer is required. On completion or impossibility of achieving purposes, further trusts may be activated.

In Part IX of the ITO, a power is said to be held on trust if granted or reserved subject to any duty to exercise the power. A trust or power is subject to Part IX and is described as a special trust, if at the creation of the trust or when it first becomes subject to the law of Brunei Darussalam the settlor is non-resident and the trust instrument provides that that the trust is to be a special trust. The objects of a special trust or power may be persons or purposes or both, the person may be of any number, and the purposes may be of any number or kind, charitable or non-charitable. The hallmark of a special trust is that a beneficiary does not, as such, have standing to enforce the trust or any enforceable right to the trust property. The only persons who have standing to enforce a special trust are such persons as are appointed to be its enforcers:

- by the trust instrument; or
- under the provisions of the trust instrument; or
- by the Court.

An enforcer of a special trust has a duty to act responsibly with a view to enforcing the proper execution of the trust, and to consider responsibly at appropriate intervals whether and how to exercise his power and then to act accordingly. A trustee or another enforcer, or any person expressly authorized by the trust instrument, has standing to bring an action against an enforcer to compel him to perform his duties. An enforcer is entitled to necessary rights of access to documents and records. Generally a special trust is not void for uncertainty, and its terms may give to the trustee or any other person power to resolve any uncertainty as to its objects or mode of execution.

If such an uncertainty cannot be resolved as aforesaid, the Court may act to resolve the uncertainty, and insofar as the objects of the trust are uncertain and the general intent of the trust cannot be found from the admissible evidence as a manner of probability, may declare the trust void. If the execution of a special trust is or becomes in whole or in part:

- impossible or impracticable; or
- unlawful or contrary to publish policy; or

- obsolete in that, by reason of changed circumstances it fails to achieve the general intent of the special trust,

the trustee must, unless the trust is reformed pursuant to it own terms, apply to the Court to reform the trust cy-près.

As regards charitable trusts, the law has been modified to include, for example, benefits to the environment, fauna and flora, historic sites and similar objects which hitherto have fallen short of the legal definition of charity.

BRUNEI BANKING LAW

The International Banking Order 2000 ("IBO") governs the provision of international banking services to non-residents. While encompassing the traditional definition of banking by reference to taking of deposits, the IBO recognises that this is not the daily concern of a sophisticated International Bank.

Four classes of licence are provided for:

- a full international licence for the purpose of carrying on international banking business generally;
- an international investment banking licence for the purpose of carrying on international investment banking business;
- an international Islamic banking licence for the purpose of carrying on international Islamic banking business, granted in respect of full, investment or restricted activities.
- a restricted international banking licence for the purpose of carrying on international banking business subject to the restriction that the licensee may not offer, conduct or provide such business except to or for persons named or described in an undertaking embodied in the application for the licence.

"International banking business" includes the taking of deposits from the (non-resident) public, the granting of credits, the issue of credit cards and money collections and transmissions. But the definition is expanded to embrace foreign exchange transactions, the issue of guarantees, trade finance, development finance and sectoral credits, consumer credit, investment banking, Islamic banking business, broking and risk management services whether conducted by conventional practices or using Internet or other electronic technology and includes electronic banking .

"International investment banking business" includes:

- providing consultancy and advisory services relating to corporate and investment matters, industrial strategy and related questions, and advice and services relating to mergers and restructuring and acquisitions, or making and managing investments on behalf of any person;
- providing credit facilities including guarantees and commitments;
- participation in stock, or share issues and the provision of services relating thereto: or
- the arrangement and underwriting of debt and equity issues.

"International Islamic banking business" is banking business whose aims and operations do not involve any element which is not approved by the Islamic Religion. Provision for Syari'ah Law to over-ride a conflicting provision in the IBO is made, subject to good banking practice, and there is a requirement for the appointment of a Syari'ah Council. The restriction to local ownership which applies under the domestic Islamic Banking Act does not apply to the international regime.

Under section 4 of the Order, an institution desiring to carry on international conventional or Islamic banking business may apply for a license. "Institution" is defined in section 2 as a company incorporated or registered under the Companies Act, (Chapter 39), an international business company or a foreign international company (i.e. incorporated or registered respectively under the International Business Companies Order, 2000. The alternatives "incorporated" and "registered" in relation to the Companies Act are used to clarify that the company is either initially incorporated, or is a company incorporated outside Brunei, which establishes a place of business in Brunei and is registered with the (domestic) Registrar of Companies under section 299 of Part IX of the Companies Act. In the last-mentioned case, the Bank will need strictly to segregate its international business and the conduct and accounting thereof from the domestic operation. This is both a regulatory and a tax issue, the latter because section 25 of the Order exempts international banking conducted under the Order exempts international banking business conducted under the Order from taxation and revenue fillings with the tax authorities.

The IBO imposes strict standards of confidentiality on both the Authority and the banks and their officers. In line with what are becoming expected international standards, mutual assistance between designated supervisory authorities exercising similar powers to the Authority in other jurisdictions is permitted. This is, subject to continuing confidentiality and guarantees of reciprocal assistance.
In respect of banking supervisory actions, the Authority will require:

- to receive audited annual accounts;
- to conduct on-site inspection;
- to be given notice of significant charges in ownership and key personnel (which respectively attract consent procedures for Brunei headquartered banks); and
- to investigate and take action in appropriate cases of criminal or unlawful acts and when the circumstances of the bank justify intervention;

and is empowered to apply to the High Court for such assistance as may be necessary in appropriate cases to avert criminal or solvency/liquidity matters which are beyond the mutually-exercised corrective measures available to the bank and the Authority acting in concert.
Those who conduct activities included in the services also offered by banks will be exempted from the IBO provisions. But companies which conduct banking activities without any regulatory controls, consents or licences will not be permitted to do so in Brunei, except by means of full disclosure and Ministerial exemption in exceptional cases, on specified terms.
Brunei expects and looks to attract the presence of good quality institutions whose credentials are based on quality and activity rather than size alone.

BRUNEI INSURANCE LAW

Comprehensive and imaginative legislation, coupled with a flexible regime to suit sophisticated business and personal international insurance and insurance related activities are governed by the International Insurance and Takaful Order, 2002 ('IITO)'.

There are 7 types of licenses available, which include general insurance, life insurance, life and general insurance and captive insurance businesses and International Insurance Manager, International Underwriting Manager and International Insurance Broker. Applicants can be companies, including an established foreign or domestic insurance company, or licensed registered agent and trust company in Brunei acting as representative for the purpose of license application.
Special provision is made for Financial Unit-linked and Reinsurance (access to domestic market) insurers. All long term products are protected against creditors in the absence of fraud and the concepts of insurable interest and ability of a beneficiary to enforce a contract enjoy constructive modification.

International insurance business (i.e. non-domestic business, conducted with non-residents, with the exception of re-insurance) must be carried on by an IBC or a foreign international company

For additional analytical, business and investment opportunities information,
please contact Global Investment & Business Center, USA
at (703) 370-8082. Fax: (703) 370-8083. E-mail: ibpusa3@gmail.com
Global Business and Investment Info Databank - www.ibpus.com

incorporated under the International Business Companies Order, 2000 ("IBCO"), a company incorporated under the (domestic) Companies Act (Chapter 39) or a company registered under Part IX of the Companies Act (Chapter 39), which holds a valid licence under IITO

Further, no person (including a corporation) may carry on any business as an international insurance manager, international underwriting manager or international insurance broker unless he holds a licence relating to such business.

Every application must include a business plan for the first three years of operation; copies of the applicant's constituent documents, where applicable a copy of the applicant's audited annual accounts for the 3 consecutive years immediately preceding the application, and in the case of a takaful or re-takaful provider, the names of the Shari'ah Council duly appointed to advise that provider. The Authority may request further or other information or documents.
Licence applications for international insurance managers, underwriters and brokers must satisfy the Authority that the controllers, directors and chief executive officers of the applicant are fit and proper persons having knowledge of the insurance related activities proposed to be conducted and is able to maintain sufficient funds to cover its expenses in the proposed activities for the period covered by its business plan.

Prior written consent of the Authority is required to open an office or establish any subsidiary in Brunei Darussalam or elsewhere.

Services offered by a licensee are limited to those specified in the licence granted and may be provided only to other licensees under the Order. Services can not be offered relating to domestic insurance business, but a licensed international insurance broker may, notwithstanding any other written law, handle the re-insurance of domestic insurance business.

No taxes or duties of any description are levied, withheld or collected in respect of international insurance business of any licensee (includes insurer, managers, brokers, underwriters) of shares, and no filing or presentation of documents with or to any taxing or analogous authority in Brunei Darussalam is required. The tax/duty exemption may, at no extra charge, be evidenced by a certificate issued by the Minister, any such certificate to be valid for a period of 10 years from its date.

Dedicated Cell Companies ("DCC") are established pursuant to Part XIIA of IBCO, and are subject to the prior consent of the Authority, may be initially established or reconstituted as a DCC. A DCC is a single legal person and may establish one or more cells for the purpose of segregating and protecting dedicated assets. The assets are either dedicated assets or general assets, and separate records and protection of dedicated assets by way of segregation and identification must be maintained.
Creditors are restricted in their rights to the cell in respect of which they have made funds available or have a claim.

Criteria for License to Carry on International Insurance Business.
Subject to section 7 (discretion for Authority to require greater or permit a lesser amount), the working funds of an applicant shall meet requirements prescribed by the Minister by notice in the Gazette, and until so prescribed:

- where the applicant proposes to carry on long-term insurance business (other than linked long-term business only), shall be at least Brunei $500,000 or its equivalent in any foreign currency;
- where the applicant proposes to carry on only general insurance business, shall be at least $250,000 or its equivalent;

For additional analytical, business and investment opportunities information,
please contact Global Investment & Business Center, USA
at (703) 370-8082. Fax: (703) 370-8083. E-mail: ibpusa3@gmail.com
Global Business and Investment Info Databank - www.ibpus.com

- where the applicant proposes to carry on only re-insurance business, shall be at least $1,000,000 or its equivalent;
- where the applicant proposes to carry on both general and long-term insurance business shall be at least $750,000 or its equivalent currency;
- where the applicant proposes to carry on only international captive insurance business shall be at least $75,000 or its equivalent in any foreign currency or, if the applicant is a Dedicated Cell Company (under IBCO) having two or more cells, at least $75,000 or its equivalent in any foreign currency in respect of each cell;
- where the applicant proposes to carry on only linked long-term business, shall be at least $100,000 or its equivalent in any foreign currency plus such amount (if any) as the applicant may deem prudent having regard to that portion of any linked long-term business under which the benefits payable exceed benefits determined by reference to the linked investment.

Every applicant must satisfy the Authority:

- that it meets the prescribed requirements for working capital and that such specified working capital is certified held in a bank in Brunei Darussalam;
- its controllers, directors and chief executive officers must be approved;
- management with adequate knowledge and expertise must be established in Brunei Darussalam and at least one director must be a resident or a licensed international underwriting manager in Brunei Darussalam appointed.

The Authority will keep a Register of all licensees and such Register is to be open to public inspection.

Every licensee must appoint an approved auditor, and in the case of long-term business must also appoint an actuary.

Every international insurer shall keep the accounts and funds in respect of each type of international insurance business separate.

Every licensee shall submit audited annual balance sheet, profit and loss account, revenue account and, in respect of life insurance business, a report setting out the actuarial valuation of its assets and liabilities to the Authority.

For a foreign international company a certified copy of its latest audited annual balance sheet in respect of its entire operations both in and outside the Brunei Darussalam is also required.
IITO contains extensive protections for long-term insurance policy-holders.

BRUNEI MUTUAL FUND LAW

The Mutual Funds Order, 2001 ('MFO') applies to domestic and international funds and their promoters/managers/custodians. Provision is made for Public Funds, Private Funds and Professional Funds. Islamic Funds are provided for and are defined as funds which do not offend against the Religion of Islam. A Shari'ah Council must be appointed in respect of an Islamic fund. Mutual funds may be in the form of a body corporate, a unit trust, a limited partnership or other arrangement whereby participants (investors) may benefit from the pooling of funds, diversification and the spreading of risk. No bearer shares may be issued.

The MFO provides 'for the regulation of mutual funds in Brunei Darussalam, the supervision and licensing of such funds and of persons promoting and providing services in connection therewith and for other matters relating to mutual funds'.

For additional analytical, business and investment opportunities information,
please contact Global Investment & Business Center, USA
at (703) 370-8082. Fax: (703) 370-8083. E-mail: ibpusa3@gmail.com
Global Business and Investment Info Databank - www.ibpus.com

Provision is made for Public Funds, Private Funds and Professional Funds. Islamic Funds are specifically defined as funds which do not offend against the Religion of Islam.
Mutual Funds may be in the form of a body corporate, a unit trust, a limited partnership or other arrangement whereby participants (investors) may benefit from the pooling of funds, diversification and the spreading of risk. No bearer shares may be issued without the specific consent of the Minister.

No mutual fund may be established, domiciled, offered to the public, traded listed, managed or administered from within Brunei Darussalam unless it holds the appropriate licence or permission issued by the Authority.

Managers, administrators, custodians and trustees (together referred to as "operators") are required to be appropriately licensed or permitted. Trust companies licensed under the Registered Agents and Licensed Trustees Order, 2000 and appropriately licensed banks (domestic or international) are permitted operators.

Applications for licences are made to the Authority in the manner required, with full disclosure to the Authority of particulars of participants. There is a requirement for the appointment of an appropriate Syari'ah Council in the case of an Islamic fund.
A person cannot be both (i) a manager and (ii) a trustee or custodian of the same fund.
Provisional licensing is accommodated on terms permitted by the Authority, which may also impose conditions on the terms of licensing of both funds and operators.

INVESTMENT INCENTIVES ORDER

In exercise of the power conferred by subsection (3) of section 83 of the Constitution of Brunei Darussalam, His Majesty the Sultan and Yang Di-Pertuan hereby makes the following Order —

PART I PRELIMINARY

Citation, commencement and long title.

1. (1) This Order may be cited as the Investment Incentives Order, 2001 and shall commence on 1st. June, 2001.

(2) The long title of this Order is "An Order to make new provision for encouraging the establishment and development in Brunei Darussalam of industrial and other economic enterprises, for economic expansion and for incidental and related purposes".

Order to be construed as one with the Income Tax Act (Chapter 35).

2. This Order shall, unless otherwise expressly provided for in this Order, be construed as one with the Income Tax Act.

Interpretation.

3. In this Order, unless the context otherwise requires —

"approved foreign loan" means a loan which is certified under section 75 to be an approved foreign loan;

"approved product" means a product declared under section 30 to be an approved product;

"Collector" means the Collector of Income Tax appointed under the Income Tax Act (Chapter 35);

"company" means any company incorporated or registered in accordance with the provisions of any written law relating to companies;

"expanding enterprise" means any company which has been approved by the Minister and to which an expansion certificate has been issued under section 31;

"expansion certificate" means an expansion certificate issued under section 31;

"expansion day", in relation to an expanding enterprise, means the date specified in its expansion certificate under subsection (4) or (5) of section 31; "export enterprise" means any company which has been approved by the Minister and

to which an export certificate has been issued under section 40;

"export enterprise certificate" means an export enterprise certificate issued under section 40; "export produce" means a produce of agriculture, forestry and fisheries approved

under section 39 as export produce; "export product" means a product approved under section 39 as export product; "export year" means the year specified in the export enterprise certificate under

subsection (2) of section 40 or section 41; "foreign loan certificate" means a foreign loan certificate issued under section 75; "high-tech park" means an area declared by the Minister to be a high-tech park; "manufacture", in relation to a product, includes any process or method used in

making or developing the product;

"Minister" means the Minister charged with the responsibility for industrial development; "new trade or business" means the trade or business of a pioneer enterprise deemed

under section 8 to have been set up and commenced on the day following the end of its

tax relief period; "officer of customs" and "senior officer of customs" have the same meanings as in the Customs Act (Chapter 36);

"old trade or business" means the trade or business of a pioneer enterprise carried on by it during its tax relief period in accordance with section 8, and which either ceases within or is deemed, under that section, to cease at the end of that period;

"pioneer certificate" means a pioneer certificate issued under section 5;

"pioneer enterprise" means any company which has been approved by the Minister and to which a pioneer certificate has been issued under section 5; "pioneer industry" means an industry declared under section 4 to be a pioneer

industry; "pioneer product" means a product declared under section 4 to be a pioneer product;

For additional analytical, business and investment opportunities information,
please contact Global Investment & Business Center, USA
at (703) 370-8082. Fax: (703) 370-8083. E-mail: ibpusa3@gmail.com
Global Business and Investment Info Databank - www.ibpus.com

"production date", in relation to a pioneer enterprise, means the date specified in its pioneer certificate under subsection (3) or (4) of section 5;

"productive equipment" means machinery or plant which would normally qualify for deduction under sections 16, 17 and 18 of the Income Tax Act (Chapter 35);

"repealed Act" means the Investment Incentives Act (Chapter 97) repealed by this Order;

"tax" means income tax imposed by the Income Tax Act (Chapter 35);

PART II PIONEER INDUSTRIES

Power and procedure for declaring an industry and a product a pioneer industry and a pioneer product.

4. (1) Subject to subsection (2), the Minister may, if he considers it expedient in the public interest to do so, by order declare an industry, which is not being carried on in Brunei Darussalam on a scale adequate to the economic needs of Brunei Darussalam and for which in his opinion there are favourable prospects for development, to be a pioneer industry and any specific product of that industry to be a pioneer product.

(2) The Minister may revoke any order made under this section but any such revocation shall not affect the operation of any pioneer certificate issued to any pioneer enterprise before the revocation.

Application for and issue and amendment of pioneer certificate.

5. (1) Any company which is desirous of producing a pioneer product may make an application in writing to the Minister to be approved as a pioneer enterprise in such form and with such particulars as may be prescribed.

(2) Where the Minister is satisfied that it is expedient in the public interest to do so and, in particular, having regard to the production or anticipated production of the pioneer product from all sources of production in Brunei Darussalam, he may approve that company a pioneer enterprise and issue a pioneer certificate to the company, subject to such terms and conditions as he thinks fit.

(3) Every pioneer certificate issued under this section shall specify —

(a)
    the date on or before which it is expected that the pioneer enterprise will commence to produce in marketable quantities the product specified in the certificate; and

(b)
    the rate of production of that product which it is expected will be attained on or before that date,

and that date shall be deemed to be the production day of the pioneer enterprise for the purposes of this Order.

(4) The Minister may, in his discretion, upon the application of any pioneer enterprise, amend its pioneer certificate by substituting for the production day specified therein such earlier or later date

For additional analytical, business and investment opportunities information,
please contact Global Investment & Business Center, USA
at (703) 370-8082. Fax: (703) 370-8083. E-mail: ibpusa3@gmail.com
Global Business and Investment Info Databank - www.ibpus.com

as he thinks fit and thereupon the provisions of this Order shall have effect as if the date so substituted were the production day in relation to that pioneer enterprise.

Tax relief period of pioneer enterprise.

6. (1) The tax relief period of a pioneer enterprise shall commence on its production day and shall continue for a period of —

(a)

5 years, where its fixed capital expenditure is not less than $500,000 but is less than $2.5 million;

(b)

8 years, where its fixed capital expenditure is more than $2.5 million;

(c)

11 years, where it is located in a high tech park.

(2)

Where the tax relief period of a pioneer enterprise is 5 years and the Minister is satisfied that it has incurred by the end of the year following the end of that period fixed capital of not less than $2.5 million, the Minister may extend its tax relief period to 8 years from the production day.

(3)

In this section, "fixed capital expenditure" in relation to a pioneer enterprise, means capital expenditure incurred by the pioneer enterprise on its factory building (excluding land) or on plant, machinery or other apparatus used in Brunei Darussalam in connection with and for the purposes of the pioneer enterprise.

Further extension of tax relief period.

7. (1) The Minister may, subject to such terms and conditions as he may impose, extend the tax relief period of a pioneer enterprise (other than a pioneer enterprise that is located in a high-tech park) for such further period or periods as he may determine except that the tax relief period of the pioneer enterprise shall not in aggregate exceed 11 years.

(2) The Minister may, subject to such terms and conditions as he may impose, extend the tax relief period of a pioneer enterprise that is located in a high-tech park for such further period or periods not exceeding 5 years at any one time as he may determine except that the tax relief period of the pioneer enterprise shall not in aggregate exceed 20 years.

Provisions governing old and new trade or business.

8. For the purposes of the Income Tax Act (Chapter 35) and this Order —

(a)

the old trade or business of a pioneer enterprise shall be deemed to have permanently ceased at the end of its tax relief period;

(b)

the pioneer enterprise shall be deemed to have set up and commenced a new trade or business on the day immediately following the end of its tax relief period;

(c)

the pioneer enterprise shall make up accounts of its old trade or business for a period not exceeding one year, commencing on its production day, for successive periods of one year thereafter and for the period not exceeding one year ending at the date when its tax relief period ends; and

(d)

in making up the first accounts of its new trade or business the pioneer enterprise shall take as the opening figures for those accounts the closing figures in respect of its assets and liabilities as shown in its last accounts in respect of its tax relief period, and its next accounts of its new trade or business shall be made up by reference to the closing figures in such first accounts an any subsequent accounts shall be similarly made up by reference to the closing figures of the preceding accounts of its new trade or business.
Restrictions on trading before end of tax relief period.

9. (1) During its tax relief period, a pioneer enterprise shall not carry on any trade or business other than the trade or business relating to the relevant pioneer product, unless the Minister has given his permission in writing therefor.

(2)

Where the carrying on of a separate trade or business has been permitted under subsection (1), separate accounts shall be maintained in respect of that trade or business and in respect of the same accounting period.

(3)

Where the carrying on of such separate trade results in a loss in any accounting period, the loss shall be brought into the computation of the income of the pioneer enterprise for that period unless the Collector, having regard to all the circumstances of the case, is satisfied that the loss was not incurred for the purpose of obtaining a tax advantage.

(4)

Where the carrying on of such separate trade results in a profit in any accounting period, and the profit, computed in accordance with the provisions of the Income Tax Act as modified by this section, amounts to less than 5% on the full sum receivable from the sale of goods or the provision of services, the statutory income from that source shall be deemed to
be 5% (or such lower rate as the Minister may specify in any particular case) of the full sum so receivable and the income of the pioneer enterprise shall be abated accordingly.

(5)

Where in the opinion of the Collector the carrying on of such separate trade is subordinate and incidental to the carrying on of the trade or business relating to the relevant pioneer product, the income or loss arising from such activities shall be deemed to form part of the income or loss of the pioneer enterprise.

(6)

In this section, "relevant pioneer product" means the pioneer product specified in its pioneer certificate.
Power to give directions.

10. For the purposes of the Income Tax Act and this Order, the Collector may direct that —

(a)

any sums payable to a pioneer enterprise in any accounting period which, but for the provisions of this Order, might reasonably and properly have been expected to be payable, in the normal course of business, after the end of that period shall be treated —

(i)

as not having been payable in that period but as having been payable on such date, after that period as the Collector thinks fit; and

(ii)

where that date is after the end of the tax relief period of the pioneer enterprise, as having been so payable, on that date, as a sum payable in respect of its new trade or business;

(b)

any expense incurred by a pioneer enterprise within one year after the end of its tax relief period which, but for the provisions of this Order, might reasonable and properly have been expected to be incurred, in the normal course of business, during its tax relief period shall be treated as not having been incurred within that year but as having been incurred —

(i)

for the purposes of its old trade or business; and

(ii)

on such date, during its tax relief period, as the Collector thinks fit.
Ascertainment of income in respect of old trade or business.

11. (1) The income of a pioneer enterprise in respect of its old trade or business shall be ascertained in accordance with the provisions of the Income Tax Act after making such adjustments as may be necessary in consequence of any direction given under section 10.

(2)

In determining the income of a pioneer enterprise referred to in subsection (1), the allowances provided for in sections 13, 14, 15, 16, 17 and 18 of the Income Tax Act shall be taken into account.

(3)

Where the tax relief period of a pioneer enterprise referred to in subsection (1) expires during the basis period for any year of assessment, for the purpose of determining the income in respect of its old trade or business and its new trade or business for that year of assessment, there shall be deducted allowances provided for in sections 13, 14, 15, 16, 17 and 18 of the Income Tax Act; and for the purpose of computing such allowances —

(a)

the allowances for that year of assessment shall be computed as if the old trade or business of the pioneer enterprise had not been deemed to have permanently ceased at the end of the tax relief period; and

(b)

the allowances computed in accordance with paragraph (a) shall be apportioned between the old trade or business and the new trade or business of the pioneer enterprise in such manner as appears to the Collector to be reasonable in the circumstances.

(4)

Where in any year of assessment full effect cannot, by reason of an insufficiency of profits for that year of assessment, be given to the allowances mentioned in subsection (2), then the balance of the allowances shall be added to, and be deemed to form part of, the corresponding allowances, if any, for the next succeeding year of assessment, and, if no such corresponding allowances fall to be made for that year, shall be deemed to constitute the corresponding allowances for that year, and so on for subsequent years of assessment.
Application of Part X of Income Tax Act (Chapter 35).

12. Part X of the Income Tax Act (relating to returns of income) shall apply in all respects as if the income of a pioneer enterprise in respect of its old trade or business were chargeable to tax.

Collector to issue statement of income.

13. For each year of assessment, the Collector shall issue to the pioneer enterprise a statement showing the amount of income for that year of assessment, and Parts XI and XII of the Income Tax Act (relating to objections and appeals) and any regulations made thereunder shall apply with the necessary modifications, as if that statement were a notice of assessment given under those provisions.

Exemption from income tax.

14. (1) Subject to subsection (6) of section 15, where any statement issued under section 13 has become final and conclusive, the amount of the income shown by the statement shall not form part of the statutory income of the pioneer enterprise for any year of assessment and shall be exempt from tax.

(2) The Collector may, in his discretion and before such a statement has become final and conclusive, declare that a specified part of the amount of such income is not in dispute and such an undisputed amount of income is exempt from tax, pending such a statement becoming final and conclusive.

Certain dividends exempted from income tax.

15. (1) As soon as any amount of income of a pioneer enterprise has been exempt under section 14, that amount shall be credited to an account to be kept by the pioneer enterprise for the purposes of this section.

(2)

Where that account is in credit at the date on which any dividends are paid by the pioneer enterprise out of income which has been exempted, an amount equal to those dividends or to that credit, whichever is the less, shall be debited to the account.

(3)

So much of the amount of any dividends so debited to that account as are received by a shareholder of the pioneer enterprise shall, if the Collector is satisfied with the entries in the account, be exempt from tax in the hands of the shareholder.

(4)

Notwithstanding subsection (3), where a dividend is paid on any share of a preferential nature, it shall not be so exempt in the hands of the shareholder.

(5)

Any dividends debited to that account shall be treated as having been distributed to the shareholders of the pioneer enterprise or any particular class of those shareholders in the same proportions as the shareholders were entitled to payment to payment of the dividends giving rise to the debit.

(6)

The pioneer enterprise shall deliver to the Collector a copy of that account, made up to a date specified by him, whenever called upon to do so by notice in writing sent by him to its registered office, until such time as he is satisfied that there is no further need for maintaining the account.

(7)

Notwithstanding section 14 and subsections (1) to (6), where it appears to the Collector that —

(a)

any amount of exempted income of a pioneer enterprise; or

(b)

any dividend exempted in the hands of any shareholder, including any dividend paid by a holding company to which subsection (10) applies, ought not to have been exempted by reason of any direction made under section 10 or the revocation under section 114 of a pioneer certificate issued to the pioneer enterprise, the Collector may subject to section 62 of the Income Tax Act —

(i)

make such assessment or additional assessment upon the pioneer enterprise or any such shareholder as may appear to be necessary in order to counteract any profit obtained from any such amount; or

(ii)

direct the pioneer enterprise to debit its account, kept in accordance with subsection (1), with such amount as the circumstances require.

(8)

Parts XI and XII of the Income Tax Act (relating to objections and appeals) and any regulations made thereunder shall apply, with the necessary modifications, to any direction given under subsection (7) as if it were a notice of assessment given under those provisions.

(9)

Section 36 of the Income Tax Act shall not apply in respect of any dividend or part thereof which is debited to the account required to be kept for the purposes of this section.

(10)

Where an amount has been received by way of dividend from a pioneer enterprise by a shareholder and the amount is exempt from tax under this section, if that shareholder is a company (referred to in this section as the holding company) which holds, throughout its tax relief period, the beneficial interest in all the issued shares of the pioneer enterprise (or in not less than such proportion of those shares as the Minister may require at the time when the pioneer certificate is issued to that pioneer enterprise) any dividends paid by the holding company to its shareholders, to the extent that the Collector is satisfied that those dividends are paid out of that amount, shall be exempt from tax in the hands of those shareholders; and section 36 of the Income Tax Act shall not apply in respect of any dividend or part thereof so exempt.

(11)

Any holding company may, with the approval of the Minister and subject to such terms and conditions as he may impose, pay such exempt dividends to its shareholders even if it has not held the requisite shareholding in the pioneer enterprise for the whole of the tax relief period.

Carry forward of loss and allowance.

16. (1) Where a pioneer enterprise has, during its tax relief period, incurred a loss for any year, that loss shall be deducted as provided for in subsection (2) of section 30 of the Income Tax Act but only against the income of the pioneer enterprise as ascertained under section 11, except that the balance of any such loss which remains unabsorbed at the end of its tax relief period is available to the new trade or business in accordance with that Act.

(2) Notwithstanding paragraph *(a)* of section 8, the balance of any allowance as provided for in section 11 which remains unabsorbed at the end of the tax relief period of the pioneer enterprise is available to the new trade or business in accordance with the Income Tax Act.

PART III PIONEER SERVICE COMPANIES

Interpretation of this Part.

17. For the purposes of this Part, unless the context otherwise requires —

"commencement day", in relation to a pioneer service company, means the date specified under subsection (3) or (4) of section 18 in the certificate issued to that company under that section;

"pioneer service company" means a company which has been issued with a certificate under section 18;

"qualifying activity" means any of the following —

(a)
any engineering or technical services including laboratory, consultancy and research and development activities;

(b)
computer-based information and other computer related services;

(c)
the development or production of any industrial design;

(d)
services and activities which relate to the provision of leisure and recreation;

(e)
publishing services;

(f)
services which relate to the provision of education;

(g)
medical services;

(h)
services and activities which relate to agricultural technology;

(i)
services and activities which relate to the provision of warehousing facilities;

(j)
services which relate to the organisation or management of exhibitions and conferences;

(k)
financial services;

(l)
business consultancy, management and professional services;

(m)
venture capital fund activity;

(n)
operation or management of any mass rapid transit system;

(o)
services provided by an auction house;

(p)
maintaining and operating a private museum; and

(q)
such other services or activities as the Minister may prescribe.
Application for and issue and amendment of certificate for pioneer service company.

18. (1) Where a company is engaged in any qualifying activity, the company may apply in the prescribed form to the Minister for approval as a pioneer service company.

(2)
The Minister may, if he considers it expedient in the public interest to do so, approve the application and issue the company with a certificate subject to such terms and conditions as he thinks fit.

(3)

Every certificate issued under this section shall specify a date as the commencement day from which the company shall be entitled to tax relief under this Part.

(4)

The Minister may in his discretion, upon the application of the company, amend its certificate by substituting for the commencement day specified therein such earlier or later date as he thinks fit and thereupon the provisions of this Part shall have effect as if the date so substituted were the commencement day in relation to that certificate.

Tax relief period of pioneer service company.

19. The tax relief period of a pioneer service company, in relation to any qualifying activity specified in any certificate issued to that company under section 18, shall commence on the commencement day and shall continue for a period of 8 years or such longer period, not exceeding 11 years, as the Minister may determine.

Application of sections 8 to 16 to pioneer service company.

20. Sections 8 to 16 shall apply to a pioneer service company under this Part and for the purposes of such application —

(a) any reference to a pioneer enterprise shall be read as a reference to a pioneer service company;
(b) any reference to a pioneer product shall be read as a reference to a qualifying activity;
(c) any reference to the production day of a pioneer enterprise shall be read as a reference to the commencement day of a pioneer service company;
(d) any reference to a pioneer certificate shall be read as a reference to a certificate issued under section 18.

PART IV POST-PIONEER COMPANIES

Interpretation of this Part.

21. For the purposes of this Part, unless the context otherwise requires —

"commencement day", in relation to a post-pioneer company, means the date specified under subsection (3) of section 22 in the certificate issued to that company under that section; "pioneer company" means a company certified by a pioneer certificate to be a pioneer company under the repealed Act;

"post-pioneer company" means a company which has been issued with a certificate under subsection (2) of section 22;

"qualifying activity", in relation to a post-pioneer company, means its trade or business in respect of which tax relief had been granted under Part II, III or VII and any other trade or business approved by the Minister.

Application for and issue of certificate to post-pioneer company.

22. (1) Any company which is —

(a)

a pioneer company on or after 1st. May, 1975;

(b)

For additional analytical, business and investment opportunities information,
please contact Global Investment & Business Center, USA
at (703) 370-8082. Fax: (703) 370-8083. E-mail: ibpusa3@gmail.com
Global Business and Investment Info Databank - www.ibpus.com

(c)

a pioneer enterprise or a pioneer service company;

an export enterprise which had been a pioneer enterprise immediately before its tax relief period as an export enterprise,

may apply in the prescribed form to the Minister for approval as a post-pioneer company.

(2)

The Minister may, if he considers it expedient in the public interest to do so, approve the application and issue the company with a certificate subject to such terms and conditions as he may impose.

(3)

Every certificate issued to a post-pioneer company under this section shall specify —

(a)

a date as the commencement day from which the company shall be entitled to tax relief under this Part;

(b)

its qualifying activities; and

(c)

the concessionary rate of tax to be levied for the purposes of this Part.

(4)

The Minister may, in his discretion, upon an application of a post-pioneer company, amend its certificate by substituting for the commencement day specified therein such other date as he thinks fit and thereupon the provisions of this Part shall have effect as if that date were the commencement day in relation to that certificate.

(5)

Notwithstanding section 35 of the Income Tax Act, tax at such concessionary rate, not being less than 10% as the Minister may specify, shall be levied and paid for each year of assessment upon the income derived by a post-pioneer company during its tax relief period from its qualifying activities.

Tax relief period of post-pioneer company.

23. (1) The tax relief period of a post-pioneer company shall commence on its commencement day and shall continue for a period not exceeding 6 years as the Minister may determine.

(2) The Minister may, subject to such terms and conditions as he may impose, extend the tax relief period of a post-pioneer company for such further period or periods as he may determine except that the tax relief period of the company shall not in the aggregate exceed 11 years.

Ascertainment of income in respect of other trade or business.

24. (1) Where during its tax relief period a post-pioneer company carries on any trade or business other than its qualifying activities, separate accounts shall be maintained in respect of that other trade or business and in respect of the same accounting period and the income from that other trade or business shall be computed and assessed in accordance with the Income Tax Act with such adjustments as the Collector thinks reasonable and proper.

(2) Where in the opinion of the Collector the carrying on of such other trade or business is subordinate or incidental to the carrying on of the qualifying activities of the post-pioneer company, the income or losses arising from such other trade or business shall be deemed to form part of the income or loss of the post-pioneer company in respect of its qualifying activities.

Deduction of losses.

25. The Minister may, in relation to post-pioneer companies, by regulations provide for —

(a)

the manner in which expenses, capital allowances and donations allowable under the Income Tax Act are to be deducted; and

(b)

the deduction of capital allowances and of losses otherwise than in accordance with sections 20 and subsection (2) of section 30 of the Income Tax Act.
Certain dividends exempted from income tax.

26. (1) As soon as any amount of income of a post-pioneer company has been subject to tax at the concessionary rate under section 22, the net amount of the income after deduction of the tax shall be credited to a special account (referred to in this section as the account) to be kept by the post-pioneer company for the purposes of this section.

(2)

Where the account is in credit at the date on which any dividends are paid by the post-pioneer company out of the net amount of the income credited to that account, an amount equal to those dividends or to that credit, whichever is the less, shall be debited to the account.

(3)

So much of the amount of any dividends so debited to the account as are received by a shareholder of the post-pioneer company shall, if the Collector is satisfied with the entries in the account, be exempt from tax in the hands of the shareholder.

(4)

Notwithstanding subsection (3), where a dividend is paid on any share of a preferential nature, it shall not be so exempt in the hands of the shareholder.

(5)

Section 36 of the Income Tax Act shall not apply in respect of any dividends or part thereof which are debited to the account.

(6)

Where an amount of dividends debited to the account has been received by a shareholder, and that shareholder is a company (referred to in this section as the holding company) which holds, throughout its tax relief period, the beneficial interest in all the issued shares of the post-pioneer company (or in not less that such proportion of those shares as the Minister may require at the time when the post-pioneer certificate is issued to the post-pioneer company) any dividends paid by the holding company to its shareholders, to the extent that the Collector is satisfied that those dividends are paid out of such amount, shall be exempt from tax in the hands of those shareholders; and section 36 of the Income Tax Act shall not apply to any such dividends or part thereof so exempt.

(7)

Any holding company may, with the approval of the Minister and subject to such terms and conditions as he may impose, pay such exempt dividends to its shareholders even if it has not held the requisite shareholding in the post-pioneer company for the whole of the tax relief period.

(8)

The post-pioneer company shall deliver to the Collector a copy of the account made up to any date specified by him whenever called upon to do so by notice in writing sent by him to its registered office, until such time as he is satisfied that there is no further need for maintaining the account.

(9) Notwithstanding subsections (1) to (7), where it appears to the Collector that —

(a)

any income of a post-pioneer company which has been subject to tax at the concessionary rate under section 22; or

(b)

any dividend, including a dividend paid by a holding company under subsection (6), which has been exempted from tax in the hands of any shareholder,

ought not to have been so taxed or exempted for any year of assessment, the Collector may subject to section 62 of the Income Tax Act —

(i)

make such assessment or additional assessment upon the company or any such shareholder as may be necessary in order to make good any loss of tax; or

(ii)

direct the company to debit the account with such amount as the circumstances require.
Power to give directions.

27. For the purposes of the Income Tax Act and this Order, the Collector may direct that —

(a)

any sums payable to a post-pioneer company in the tax relief period which might reasonably and properly have been expected to be payable, in the normal course of business, after the end of that period shall be treated as not having been payable in that period but as having been payable on such date, after that period, as the Collector thinks fit; and

(b)

any expense incurred by a post-pioneer company within one year after the end of its tax relief period which might reasonably and properly have been expected to be incurred, in the normal course of business, during its tax relief period shall be treated as not having been incurred within that year but as having been incurred for the purposes of its qualifying activities and on such date, during its tax relief period, as the Collector thinks fit.
Ascertainment of income in respect of qualifying activities.

28. (1) The qualifying income of a post-pioneer company shall, subject to subsection (2) and section 29, be ascertained in accordance with the provisions of the Income Tax Act after making such adjustments as may be necessary in consequence of any direction given under section 27.

(2) In determining the qualifying income of the post-pioneer company for the basis period for any year of assessment —

(a)

the allowance provided for in sections 13, 14, 15, 16, 17 and 18 of the Income Tax Act shall be taken into account;

(b)

the allowances referred to in paragraph *(a)* for that year of assessment shall firstly be deducted against the qualifying income, and any unabsorbed
allowances shall be deducted against the other income of the company subject to tax at the rate of tax under section 35 of the Income Tax Act in accordance with section 29;

(c)

For additional analytical, business and investment opportunities information,
please contact Global Investment & Business Center, USA
at (703) 370-8082. Fax: (703) 370-8083. E-mail: ibpusa3@gmail.com
Global Business and Investment Info Databank - www.ibpus.com

the balance, if any, of the allowances after the deduction in paragraph *(b)* shall be available for deduction for any subsequent year of assessment in accordance with section 20 of the Income Tax Act and shall be made in the manner provided in paragraph *(b)*;

(d)

any loss incurred for that basis period shall be deducted in accordance with section 29 against the other income of the company subject to tax at the rate of tax under section 35 of the Income Tax Act; and

(e)

the balance, if any, of the losses after the deduction in paragraph *(d)* shall be available for deduction for any subsequent year of assessment in accordance with section 30 of the Income Tax Act firstly against the qualifying income, and any balance of the losses shall be deducted against the other income of the company subject to tax at the rate of tax under section 35 of the Income Tax Act in accordance with section 29.

Adjustment of capital allowances and losses.

29. (1) Where, for any year of assessment, there are any unabsorbed allowances or losses in respect of the qualifying income of a post pioneer company, and there is any chargeable normal income of the company, those unabsorbed allowances and losses shall be deducted against the chargeable normal income in accordance with the following provisions —

(a)

in the case where those unabsorbed allowances or losses do not exceed that chargeable normal income multiplied by the adjustment factor, that chargeable normal income shall be reduced by an amount arrived at by dividing those unabsorbed allowances or losses by the adjustment factor, and those unabsorbed allowances or losses shall be nil; and

(b)

in any other case, those unabsorbed allowances or losses shall be reduced by an amount arrived at by multiplying that chargeable normal income by the adjustment factor, and those unabsorbed allowances or losses so reduced shall be added to, and be deemed to form part of, the corresponding allowances or losses in respect of the qualifying income, for the next succeeding year of assessment in accordance with section 20 or 30 (as the case may be) of the Income Tax Act, and that chargeable normal income shall be nil.

(2)

Where, for any year of assessment, there are any unabsorbed allowances or losses in respect of the normal income of a post-pioneer company, and there is any chargeable qualifying income of the company, those unabsorbed allowances or losses shall be deducted against that qualifying income in accordance with the following provisions —

(a)

in the case where those unabsorbed allowances or losses do not exceed that chargeable qualifying income multiplied by the adjustment factor, that chargeable qualifying income shall be reduced by an amount arrived at by dividing those unabsorbed allowances or losses by the adjustment factor, and those unabsorbed allowances or losses shall be nil; and

(b)

in any other case, those unabsorbed allowances or losses shall be reduced by an amount arrived at by multiplying that chargeable qualifying income by the adjustment factor, and those unabsorbed allowances or losses so reduced shall be added to, and be deemed to form part of, the corresponding allowances or losses in respect of the normal income, for the next succeeding year of assessment in accordance with section 20 or 30 (as the case may be) of the Income Tax Act, and that chargeable qualifying income shall be nil.

(3)

Where a post pioneer company ceases to derive any qualifying income in the basis period for any year of assessment but derives normal income in that basis period, subsection (1) shall apply, with the necessary modifications, to any unabsorbed allowances or losses in respect of the qualifying income of the company for any year of assessment subsequent to that year of assessment.

(4)

Where a post pioneer company ceases to derive any normal income in the basis period for any year of assessment but derives qualifying income in that basis period, subsection (2) shall apply, with the necessary modifications, to any unabsorbed allowances or losses in respect of the normal income of the company for any year of assessment subsequent to that year of assessment.

(5)

Nothing in subsections (1) to (4) shall be construed as affecting the application of section 20 or 30 of the Income Tax Act unless otherwise provided in this section.

(6) In this section —

"adjustment factor", in relation to any year of assessment, means the factor ascertained in accordance with the formula

$$A , B$$

where A is the rate of tax under section 35 of the Income Tax Act for that year of assessment; and

B is the concessionary rate of tax for that year of assessment at which the qualifying income is subject to tax;

"allowances" means the allowances under section 13, 14, 16, 16A, 17, 18 or 20 including unabsorbed allowances which arose in any year of assessment prior to the year of assessment 2002;

"chargeable normal income" means normal income after deducting expenses, donations, allowances or losses allowable under the Income Tax Act against the normal income;

"chargeable qualifying income" means the qualifying income after deducting expenses, donations, allowances or losses allowable under the Income Tax Act against the qualifying income;

"losses" means losses which are deductible under section 30 of the Income Tax Act including unabsorbed losses incurred in respect of any year of assessment prior to the year of assessment 2002;

"normal income" means income subject to tax at the rate of tax under section 35 of the Income Tax Act;

"unabsorbed allowances or losses in respect of the qualifying income" means the balance of such allowances or losses after deducting expenses, donations, allowances or losses allowable under the Income Tax Act against the qualifying income;

"unabsorbed allowances or losses in respect of the normal income" means the balance of such allowances or losses after deducting expenses, donations, allowances or losses allowable under the Income Tax Act against the qualifying income;

"qualifying income" means the income of a post-pioneer company in respect of its qualifying activities.

PART V EXPANSION OF ESTABLISHED ENTERPRISES

Power and procedure for declaring an industry and a product an approved industry and an approved product.

30. (1) Subject to subsection (2), where the Minister is satisfied that the increased manufacture of the product of any industry would be of economic benefit to Brunei Darussalam, he may, if he considers it expedient in the public interest to do so, by order, declare that industry to be an approved industry and the product thereof to be an approved product for the purposes of this Part.

(2) The Minister may revoke any order made under this section but any such revocation shall not affect the operation of any expansion certificate issued to any expanding enterprise before the revocation.

Issue of expansion certificate and amendment thereof.

31. (1) Any company intending to incur new capital expenditure for the purpose of the manufacture or increased manufacture of an approved product may —

(a)
where the expenditure exceeds $1 million; or

(b)
where the expenditure is less than $1 million but exceeds $500,000, and will result in an increase of not less than 30% in value at the original cost of all the productive equipment of the company,

make an application in writing to the Minister to be approved as an expanding enterprise, in such form and with such particulars as may be prescribed.

(2)
Where the Minister is satisfied that it is expedient in the public interest to do so, he may approve that company as an expanding enterprise and issue an expansion certificate to the company, subject to such terms and conditions as he thinks fit.

(3)
In this Part, "new capital expenditure" means expenditure incurred by a company in the purchase of productive equipment which is intended to increase its production or profitability.

(4)
Any expenditure incurred in the purchase of productive equipment which is not new shall be deemed not to be new capital expenditure unless it is proved to the satisfaction of the Minister that —

(a)
the purchase of the productive equipment is economically justifiable; and

(b)
the purchase price represents a fair open market value of the productive equipment.

(5)

Every expansion certificate issued under this section shall specify the date on or before which the productive equipment shall be put into operation and that date shall be deemed to be the expansion day for the purpose of this Part.

(6)

The Minister may, in his discretion, upon the application of any expanding enterprise, amend its expansion certificate by substituting for the expansion day specified therein such earlier or later date as he thinks fit and thereupon the provisions of this Part shall have effect as if the date so substituted were the expansion day in relation to that expanding enterprise.

Tax relief period of expanding enterprise.

32. (1) The tax relief period of an expanding enterprise shall commence on its expansion day or if the expansion day falls within the tax relief period specified in any certificate previously issued to the enterprise under Part II or VII for the same or similar product, commence on the day immediately following the expiry of that tax relief period and shall —

(a)

where such expanding enterprise has incurred new capital expenditure not exceeding $1 million, continue for a period of 3 years; and

(b)

where such expanding enterprise has incurred new capital expenditure exceeding $1 million, continue for a period of 5 years.

(2) The Minister may, where he is satisfied that it is expedient in the public interest to do so and subject to such terms and conditions as he may impose, extend the tax relief period of an expanding enterprise for such further period or periods, not exceeding 3 years at any one time, as he may determine, except that the tax relief period of the expanding enterprise shall not in the aggregate exceed 15 years.

Application of section 10 to expanding enterprise.

33. Section 10 shall apply, with the necessary modifications, to an expanding enterprise as it applies to a pioneer enterprise.

Tax relief.

34. (1) Subject to the provisions of this Order, an expanding enterprise is entitled, during its tax relief period, to relief in the manner provided by this section.

(2)

The income of the expanding enterprise in respect of its trade or business to which its expansion certificate relates (referred to in this Part as the expansion income) shall be ascertained, for any accounting period during its tax relief period, in accordance with the provisions of the Income Tax Act and any regulations made under this Order.

(3)

In determining the income of the expanding enterprise, the allowances provided for in sections 13, 14, 15, 16, 17 and 18 of the Income Tax Act shall be taken into account.

(4)

Where an expanding enterprise carries on trading activities other than those to which its expansion certificate relates, the expansion income to be ascertained for the purposes of this section shall be determined in such manner as appears to the Collector to be reasonable in the circumstances.

(5)

Where in the opinion of the Collector the carrying on of such trading activities is subordinate or incidental to the carrying on of the trade or business to which its expansion certificate relates, the income or loss arising from such activities shall be deemed to form part of the expansion income of the expanding enterprise.

(6)

The expansion income so ascertained shall be compared with the average corresponding income (referred to in this section as the pre-relief income) of the expanding enterprise as determined in subsection (8) and relief shall be given to the following extent —

(a)

where the pre-relief income equals or exceeds the expansion income, no relief shall be given;

(b)

where the expansion income exceeds the pre-relief income, the amount of the excess shall not form part of the statutory income of the expanding enterprise for any year of assessment and shall be exempt from tax.

(7)

The amount of exempt income shall not, unless the Minister in his discretion otherwise decides, exceed the sum which bears the same proportion to the expansion income as the new capital expenditure on productive equipment bears to the total of such new capital expenditure and the value at original cost of the productive equipment owned or used by the expanding enterprise prior to its expansion.

(8)

For the purposes of subsection (6), the average corresponding income of an expanding enterprise, in relation to a certificate issued under section 31, shall be determined by taking one-third of the total of the corresponding income of the expanding enterprise for the 3 years immediately preceding the expansion day specified in that certificate.

(9)

Where an expanding enterprise has carried on the trade or business to which its certificate relates for less than 3 years immediately prior to its expansion day or where the expanding enterprise has no corresponding income for any of those 3 years, the Minister may specify such amount to be its average corresponding income as he thinks fit.

(10)

Where an expanding enterprise has been approved as a pioneer enterprise or as an export enterprise or as both, the total amount of income exempted under this section and Part II or VII shall not exceed 100% of the expansion income.
Exemption from income tax of dividends from expanding enterprise.

35. (1) As soon as any amount of expansion income has become exempt under section 34, that amount shall be credited to an account to be kept by the expanding enterprise for the purposes of this section.

(2)

Where that account is in credit at the date on which any dividends are paid by the expanding enterprise out of income which has been exempted, an amount equal to those dividends or to that credit, whichever is the less, shall be debited to the account.

(3)

So much of the amount of any dividends so debited to that account as are received by a shareholder of the expanding enterprise shall, if the Collector is satisfied with the entries in the account, be exempt from tax in the hands of the shareholder.

(4)

Notwithstanding subsection (3), where a dividend is paid on any share of a preferential nature, it shall not be so exempt in the hands of the shareholder.

(5)

Any dividends debited to that account shall be treated as having been distributed to the shareholders of the expanding enterprise or any particular class of those shareholders in the same proportions as the shareholders were entitled to payment of the dividends giving rise to the debit.

(6)

The expanding enterprise shall deliver to the Collector a copy of that account, made up to a date specified by him, whenever called upon to do so by notice in writing sent by him to its registered office, until such time as he is satisfied that there is no further need for maintaining the account.

(7)

Notwithstanding section 34 and subsections (1) to (6) where it appears to the Collector that —

(a)

any amount of exempted income of an expanding enterprise; or

(b)

any dividend exempted in the hands of any shareholder, including any dividend paid by a holding company to which subsection (10) applies,

ought not to have been exempted by reason of a direction under section 10 (as applied to this Part by section 33) or the revocation under section 114 of an expansion certificate issued to the expanding enterprise, the Collector may, subject to section 62 of the Income Tax Act —

(i)

make such assessment or additional assessment upon the expanding enterprise or any such shareholder as may appear to be necessary in order to counteract any profit obtained from any such amount; or

(ii)

direct the expanding enterprise to debit its account, kept in accordance with subsection (1), with such amount as the circumstances require.

(8)

Parts XI and XII of the Income Tax Act (relating to objections and appeals) and any regulations made thereunder shall apply, with the necessary modifications, to any direction given under subsection (7) as if it were a notice of assessment given under those provisions.

(9)

Section 36 of the Income Tax Act shall not apply in respect of any dividend or part thereof which is debited to the account required to be kept for the purposes of this section.

(10)

Where an amount has been received by way of dividend from an expanding enterprise by a shareholder and the amount is exempt from tax under this section, if that shareholder is a company (referred to in this section as the holding company) which holds, at the time any dividend is declared, the beneficial interest in all the issued shares of the expanding enterprise (or in not less than such proportion of those shares as the Minister may approve), any dividends paid by the holding company to its shareholders, to the extent that the Collector is satisfied that those dividends are paid out of that amount, shall be exempt from tax in the hands of those shareholders; and section 36 of the Income Tax Act shall not apply in respect of any dividend or part thereof so exempt.

PART VI EXPANDING SERVICE COMPANIES

Application for and issue and amendment of certificate for expanding service company.

36. (1) Where a company engaged in any qualifying activity as defined in section 17 intends to substantially increase the volume of that activity, it may make an application in writing to the Minister to be approved as an expanding service company.

(2)

Where the Minister is satisfied that it is expedient in the public interest to do so, he may approve that company as an expanding service company and issue a certificate to the company, subject to such terms and conditions as he thinks fit.

(3)

Every certificate issued under this section shall specify a date (not earlier than 1st. January, 2001) on or before which the expansion of the qualifying activity shall commence and that date shall be deemed to be the expansion day for the purpose of this Part.

Tax relief period of expanding service company.

37. (1) The tax relief period of an expanding service company shall —

(a)

commence on its expansion day; or

(b)

if the expansion day falls within the tax relief period specified in any certificate previously issued to the company for the same or similar qualifying activity under Part III, commence on the day immediately following the expiry of that tax relief period,

and shall continue for such period, not exceeding 11 years, as the Minister may, in his discretion, determine.

(2) The Minister may, where he is satisfied that it is expedient in the public interest to do so and subject to such terms and conditions as he may impose, extend the tax relief period of an expanding enterprise for such further period or periods, not exceeding 5 years at any one time, as he may determine, except that the tax relief period of the expanding enterprise shall not in the aggregate exceed 20 years.

Application of certain sections to expanding service company.

38. Subsection (6) of section 31 and sections 33 to 35 shall apply to an expanding service company under this Part and for the purposes of such application —

(a)

any reference to an expanding enterprise shall be read as a reference to an expanding service company;

(b)

any reference to an expansion certificate shall be read as a reference to a certificate issued under subsection (2) of section 36;

(c)

subsection (7) of section 34 shall not have effect.

PART VII PRODUCTION FOR EXPORT

Power to approve a product or produce as an export product or export produce.

39. The Minister may, if he considers it expedient in the public interest to do so, approve any product manufactured in Brunei Darussalam or any produce of agriculture, forestry or fisheries as an export product or export produce for the purposes of this Part.

Application for the issue of export enterprise certificate.

40. (1) The Minister may, on the application in the prescribed form of any company which is manufacturing or proposes to manufacture any export product or is engaged or proposes to engage in agriculture, forestry and fishery activities, either wholly or partly for export, approve the company as an export enterprise and issue to the company an export enterprise certificate subject to such terms and conditions as he thinks fit.

(2) Every export enterprise certificate issued under this section shall specify the accounting period in which it is expected that the export sales of the export product or export produce —

(a)
will be not less than 20% of the value of its total sales; and
(b)
will not be less than $20,000,

and that accounting period shall be deemed to be the export year of the export enterprise for the purposes of this Part.

(3) For the purposes of this Part —

"export sales" means export sales (f.o.b.) whether made directly by the export enterprise or through an agent or independent contractor;

"f.o.b." means free on board.

Amendment of export enterprise certificate.

41. The Minister may, in his discretion, upon the application of the export enterprise, amend its export enterprise certificate by substituting for the export year specified therein such other earlier or later accounting period as he thinks fit and thereupon the provisions of this Part shall have effect as if the accounting period so substituted were the export year in relation to that export enterprise.

Tax relief period.

42. (1) The tax relief period of an export enterprise shall —

(a)
not being a pioneer enterprise, commence from its export year and shall continue for a period of 8 years inclusive of the export year; or
(b)
being a pioneer enterprise, commence on the first day of its export year or, if the export year falls within the period of its old trade or business, on the date of the commencement

of its new trade or business, and shall continue for a period of 6 years and shall not in the aggregate exceed 11 years.

(2) Notwithstanding subsection (1), where an export enterprise has incurred or is intending to incur a fixed capital expenditure of —

(a)

not less than $50 million; or

(b)

not less than $500,000 but less than $50 million and —

(i)

more than 40% of the paid-up capital of the export enterprise is held by citizens and persons to whom a Resident Permit has been granted under regulations made under the Immigration Act (Chapter 17); and

(ii)

in the opinion of the Minister the export enterprise will promote or enhance the economic or technological development of Brunei Darussalam,

its tax relief period —

(A)

where the export enterprise is not a pioneer enterprise, shall commence from its export year and continue for a period of 15 years inclusive of the export year; or

(B)

where the export enterprise is a pioneer enterprise, shall commence from its export year or, if the export year falls within the period of its old trade or business, from the date of the commencement of its new trade or business, and continue for such period as together with its tax relief period as a pioneer enterprise will extend in the aggregate to 15 years.

(3)

The Minister may, where he is satisfied that it is expedient in the public interest to do so and subject to such terms and conditions as he may impose, extend the tax relief period of any export enterprise for such further period as he thinks fit.

(4)

In subsection (2), "fixed capital expenditure" means capital expenditure which has been or is intended to be incurred by the export enterprise, in connection with its export product, on its factory building (excluding land) in Brunei Darussalam, and on any new plant or new machinery used in Brunei Darussalam and, subject to the approval of the Minister, on any secondhand plant or secondhand machinery used in Brunei Darussalam.
Power to give directions.

43. Section 10 shall apply, with the necessary modifications, to an export enterprise as it applies to a pioneer enterprise.

Application of Part X of Income Tax Act.

44. (1) Part X of the Income Tax Act (relating to returns of income) shall apply in all respects as if the whole of the income of an export enterprise in respect of its export profits were chargeable to tax.

(2) The annual return of income shall be accompanied by a separate export statement showing the quantity and value at f.o.b. prices of its export product or export produce exported during the

For additional analytical, business and investment opportunities information,
please contact Global Investment & Business Center, USA
at (703) 370-8082. Fax: (703) 370-8083. E-mail: ibpusa3@gmail.com
Global Business and Investment Info Databank - www.ibpus.com

accounting period in respect of which the return is furnished, together with such further evidence as, in the opinion of the Collector, is necessary to verify the accuracy of the export statement.

Cognizance of export.

45. For the purposes of tax relief to an export enterprise, the Collector may take cognizance of the export of any export product or export produce when the export has been made in accordance with the provisions of the Customs Act (Chapter 36) or any regulations made thereunder, as the case may be, but if the Collector is satisfied that in the course of the export of the product or produce a breach of the provisions of this Order or any regulations made thereunder has been committed, he may refuse to take cognizance of the export of the product or produce and refuse a claim for tax relief in respect of the export.

Export to be in accordance with regulations and conditions.

46. No export product or export produce shall be exported by an export enterprise except in accordance with such regulations as are prescribed and under such conditions as may be approved by the Controller of Customs.

Computation of export profits.

47. (1) The income of an export enterprise in respect of its trade or business to which its export enterprise certificate relates shall be ascertained (after making any necessary adjustments in consequence of a direction under section 10, as applied to this Part by section 43) for any accounting period during its tax relief period in accordance with the provisions of the Income Tax Act, before taking into account the allowances provided for in sections 13, 14, 15, 16, 17 and 18 of that Act.

(2) The total export profits of an export enterprise shall be deemed to be that part of the income so ascertained which bears the same proportion to that income as the total value of the export sales (f.o.b.) of its export product or export produce whether made, directly or indirectly, by sale to an independent exporter (referred to in this Part as the export sales) bears to the total value of the sums receivable in respect of —

(a)
its domestic sales of manufactured products or produce at ex-factory prices;
(b)
its export sales (f.o.b.) of its export product and export produce;
(c)
its export sales (f.o.b.) of other products; and
(d)
all other sales and provisions of service,

(referred to in this Part as the total sales).

(3)
Where a company exports any products or produce to which its export enterprise certificate relates, the amount of its export profit arising from the export of those products or produce which will qualify for the relief provided by section 49 is the excess of that profit over a fixed sum to be determined in the following manner —
(a)

in the case of a company which has previously exported those products or produce, the average annual export profit of the company shall be ascertained in the manner provided by subsection (5); and

(b)

in the case of a company which has not prior to its application under section 38 exported those products or produce for 3 years immediately preceding its application, the fixed sum shall be such an amount as the Minister may determine having regard to the total sales of the company and the percentage of the total sales of other major export enterprises exporting like articles.

(4)

Where such a company is a pioneer enterprise, subsection (3) shall apply notwithstanding that the company was deemed to commence a new trade or business at the end of its tax relief period as a pioneer enterprise.

(5) For the purposes of this section —

(a)

"average annual export profit" means a sum equal to one-third of the total export profits of the company from the export of those products or produce ascertained in the manner provided by subsection (2) during the 3 years immediately preceding the date of its application under section 40; and

(b)

where a company has adopted an accounting period ending on a date other than 31st. December, the Collector may make such adjustment on a time

basis as appears to him to be reasonable in ascertaining the total export profits of that period.

Conditions for relief.

48. (1) The tax relief provided under this Part applies to an export enterprise during its tax relief period subject to the following conditions —

(a)

in respect of the first year of assessment, for which the export year forms the basis period, the export sales shall amount, in proportion, to not less than 20% of the total sales and, in value, to not less than $20,000 during that accounting period;

(b)

in respect of subsequent years of assessment, subject to the export sales having satisfied that minimum proportion and value in the export year or where a direction has been made by the Minister under subsection (2) in respect of that year, the export sales shall amount in value to not less than $20,000 during the relevant accounting period; and

(c)

where the minimum requirements as to proportion and value have not been satisfied in the export year, and no direction has been made by the Minister under subsection (2), the relief provided by this Part shall apply for the first time only in respect of a year of assessment where during the relevant accounting period the minimum requirements as to proportion and value have both been satisfied or where a direction to this effect has been made by the Minister under subsection (2), and thereafter shall continue to be available where during the relevant accounting period the minimum requirement as to value has been satisfied.

(2) Notwithstanding subsection (1), where, in its export year, the export sales of an export enterprise amount in value to $20,000 or more, but in proportion, to less than 20% of the total

sales, and the Minister is satisfied, on the representations of the enterprise that the failure to realise that proportion of the total sales was due to causes beyond the control of the enterprise, or having regard to the quantum of its output and sales other than export sales, it is reasonable and expedient in the public interest to do so, the Minister may direct that the relief provided under this Part shall apply in respect of the year of assessment corresponding to its export year or in respect of any subsequent year of assessment during its tax relief period.

Tax relief on export profits.

49. (1) Where an amount of the export profit of an export enterprise qualifies under sections 47 and 48 for the relief provided by this section (referred to in this section as the qualifying export profit), there shall be deducted from that amount such part of the allowances provided for in sections 13, 14, 15, 16, 17 and 18 of the Income Tax Act as may be attributable to the qualifying export profit; and the part of the allowances so attributable to the qualifying export profit shall be deemed to be such amount which bears the same proportion to the total allowances deductible by the export enterprise under sections 13, 14, 15, 16, 17 and 18 of the Income Tax Act as the amount of the qualifying export profit bears to the income of the export enterprise ascertained under subsection (1) of section 47.

(2)

For each year of assessment the Collector shall issue to the export enterprise a statement for that year of assessment showing the balance of the qualifying export profit after deduction of the allowances under subsection (1) and the provisions of Parts XI and XII of the Income Tax Act (relating to objections and appeals) and any regulations made thereunder shall apply, with the necessary modifications, as if such a statement were a notice of assessment given under those provisions.

(3)

Subject to subsection (7) of section 50, where any statement issued under subsection (2) has become final and conclusive, an amount equal to 100% of the balance of such qualifying export profit shall not form part of the statutory income of the export enterprise for that year of assessment and shall be exempt from tax.

Certain dividends exempted from income tax.

50. (1) As soon as any amount of export income has become exempt under section 49, that amount shall be credited to an account to be kept by the export enterprise for the purposes of this section.

(2)

Where that account is in credit at the date on which any dividends are paid by the export enterprise out of income which has been exempted, an amount equal to those dividends or to that credit, whichever is the less, shall be debited to the account.

(3)

So much of the amount of any dividends so debited to that account as are received by a shareholder of the export enterprise shall, if the Collector is satisfied with the entries in the account, be exempt from tax in the hands of the shareholder.

(4)

Notwithstanding subsection (3), where a dividend is paid on any share of a preferential nature, it shall not be so exempt in the hands of the shareholder.

(5)

Any dividends debited to that account shall be treated as having been distributed to the shareholders of the export enterprise or any particular class of the shareholders in the same proportions as the shareholders were entitled to payment of the dividends giving rise to the debit.

(6)

    The export enterprise shall deliver to the Collector a copy of that account, made up to a date specified by him, whenever called upon to do so by notice in writing sent by him to its registered office, until such time as he is satisfied that there is no further need for maintaining the account.

(7)

    Notwithstanding section 49 and subsections (1) to (6) where it appears to the Collector that —

(a)

    any amount of exempted income of an export enterprise; or

(b)

    any dividend exempted in the hands of any shareholder, including any dividend paid by a holding company to which subsection (10) applies,

ought not to have been exempted by reason of a direction under section 10, as applied to this Part by section 43, having been made with respect to the export enterprise, after any income of that enterprise has been exempted under the provisions of this Order or the revocation under section 114 of a certificate issued to the export enterprise, the Collector may, subject to section 62 of the Income Tax Act —

(i)

    make such assessment or additional assessment upon the export enterprise or any such shareholders as may appear to be necessary in order to counteract any profit obtained from any such amount which ought not to have been exempted; or

(ii)

    direct the export enterprise to debit its account, kept in accordance with subsection (1), with such amount as the circumstances require.

(8)

    Parts XI and XII of the Income Tax Act (relating to objections and appeals) and any regulations made thereunder shall apply, with the necessary modifications, to any direction given under subsection (7) as if it were a notice of assessment given under those provisions.

(9)

    Section 36 of the Income Tax Act shall not apply in respect of any dividend or part thereof which is debited to the account required to be kept for the purposes of this section.

(10)

    Where an amount has been received by way of dividend from an export enterprise by a shareholder and the amount is exempt from tax under subsections (1) to (9), if that shareholder is a company (referred to in this section as the holding company) which holds, at the time any dividend is declared, the beneficial interest in all the issued shares of the export enterprise (or in not less than such proportion of those shares as the Minister may approve), any dividends paid by the holding company to its shareholders, to the extent that the Collector is satisfied that those dividends are paid out of that amount, shall be exempt from tax in the hands of those shareholders; and section 36 of the Income Tax Act shall not apply in respect of any dividend or part thereof so exempt.
Power of entry into premises and taking of samples.

51. Any officer, authorised by the Collector or any senior officer of customs or any officer of customs authorised by a senior officer of customs for the purpose, shall at all times have access to any premises of an export enterprise or of an independent exporter of any export product or export produce or any place where any export product or export produce is stored, for the purpose of checking the production, storage and packing of the export product or export produce and all records and accounts thereof, and for such other purpose as may be deemed necessary, and may take samples of any goods therefrom.

No relanding of export product or export produce.

52. No export product or export produce shall, unless the Controller of Customs otherwise authorises, be relanded at any time in Brunei Darussalam after they have been exported.

Powers of search, seizure and arrest by officers of customs.

53. Notwithstanding any written law to the contrary, if there is reasonable cause to believe that an offence has been or is being committed under section 46 or 52 of this Order or any regulations made thereunder in relation to any export product or export produce, sections 90 and 91 and Part XII of the Customs Act (Chapter 36) (relating to search, seizure and arrest) shall apply, insofar as they are applicable, as if the export product or export produce were goods that were dutiable and uncustomed goods or goods liable to forfeiture under the Customs Act, and as if the offence had been or were being committed under that Act.

Offence under other laws deemed to be an offence under this Order.

54. Where an export product or export produce is the subject-matter of an offence committed under the Customs Act (Chapter 36), or any regulations made thereunder, and the Collector is satisfied that, if the offence had not been detected, the export enterprise concerned in the commission of such an offence would have been able to claim relief from tax to which it was not entitled, then such an offence shall be deemed to be an offence under this Order whether a claim for tax relief has been made or not and may be dealt with accordingly but so that no person shall be punished more than once for the same offence.

PART VIII EXPORT OF SERVICES

Interpretation of this Part.

55. For the purposes of this Part, unless the context otherwise requires —

"commencement day", in relation to an export service company or export service firm, means the date specified under subsection (3) of section 56 in the certificate issued to that company or firm under that section;

"export service company" means a company which has been issued with a certificate under subsection (2) of section 56;

"qualifying services" means any of the following services undertaken with respect to overseas projects for persons who are neither residents of nor permanent establishments in Brunei Darussalam —

(a)
technical services including construction, distribution, design and engineering services;
(b)
consultancy, management, supervisory or advisory services relating to any technical matter or to any trade or business;
(c)
fabrication of machinery and equipment and procurement of materials, components an equipment;
(d)

data processing, programming, computer software development, telecommunications and other computer services;

(e)

professional services including accounting, legal, medical and architectural services;

(f)

educational and training services; and

(g)

any other services as the Minister may prescribe.

Application for and issue of certificate to export service company.

56. (1) Where a company is engaged in any qualifying service, the company may apply in the prescribed form to the Minister for approval as an export service company.

(2)

The Minister may if he considers it expedient in the public interest to do so, approve the application and issue the company with a certificate, subject to such terms and conditions as he may impose.

(3)

Every certificate issued to an export service company under this section shall specify —

(a)

a date as the commencement day from which the company shall be entitled to tax relief under this Part;

(b)

its qualifying services; and

(c)

its base amount of income for the purpose of subsection (2) of section 59.

(4)

The Minister may, in his discretion, upon the application of an export service company, amend its certificate by substituting for the commencement day specified therein such earlier or later date as he thinks fit and thereupon the provisions of this Part shall have effect as if the date so substituted were the commencement day in relation to that certificate.

Tax relief period of export service company.

57. (1) The tax relief period of an export service company shall commence on its commencement day and shall continue for such period, not exceeding 11 years, as the Minister may, in his discretion, determine.

(2) The Minister may, where he is satisfied that it is expedient in the public interest to do so and subject to such terms and conditions as he may impose, extend the tax relief period of any export service company or firm for such further periods, not exceeding 3 years at any one time, as he may determine, except that the tax relief period of the export service company shall not in the aggregate exceed 20 years.

Application of certain sections to export service company.

58. (1) Section 10 shall apply, with the necessary modifications, to an export service company as it applies to a pioneer enterprise.

(2)

Section 50 shall apply, with the necessary modifications, to an export service company as it applies to an export enterprise.

(3)

Sections 68 and 69 shall apply, with the necessary modifications, to an export service company as they apply to an international trading company and for the purposes of such application, the reference in subsection (2) of section 68 to the export sales of qualifying manufactured goods, Brunei Darussalam domestic produce and qualifying commodities shall be read as a reference to the provision of qualifying services.

Ascertainment of income of export service company.

59. (1) The income of an export service company in respect of its qualifying services shall be ascertained (after making such adjustments as may be necessary in consequence of a direction under section 10 as made applicable by section 58) for any accounting period during its tax relief period in accordance with the Income Tax Act, and, in particular, the following provisions shall apply —

(a)

income from sources other than the qualifying services shall be excluded and separately assessed;

(b)

there shall be deducted in arriving at the income derived from the qualifying services —

(i)

all direct costs and expenses incurred in respect of the qualifying services;

(ii)

all indirect expenses which are reasonably and properly attributable to the qualifying services;

(c)

the allowances provided for in sections 13 to 18 of the Income Tax Act attributable to income derived from the qualifying services during the tax relief period shall be taken into account; and

(d)

for the purposes of subparagraph (ii) of paragraph *(b)* and paragraph *(c)*, the amounts attributable to the qualifying services shall be determined on such basis as the Collector thinks reasonable and proper.

(2) The amount of income ascertained under subsection (1) which will qualify for the relief under section 60 shall be the excess of the amount of the income ascertained under subsection (1) over a base amount of income to be determined by the Minister.

Controller to issue statement of income.

60. (1) For each year of assessment, the Collector shall issue to an export service company or firm a statement for that year of assessment showing the amount of income ascertained under subsection (2) of section 59 which will qualify for the relief provided by this section, and Parts XI and XII of the Income Tax Act (relating to objections and appeals) and any regulations made thereunder shall apply, with the necessary modifications, as if that statement were a notice of assessment given under those provisions.

(2) Subject to subsection (7) of section 50, where any statement issued under subsection (1) has become final and conclusive, 100% of the amount of the qualifying income referred to in subsection (1) shall not form part of the statutory income of the export service company or firm for the year of assessment to which the income relates and shall be exempt from tax.

Certification by auditor.

61. The Controller may require an auditor to certify the income derived by an export service company from its qualifying services and any direct costs and expenses incurred therefor.

Deduction of allowances and losses.

62. The Minister may by regulations provide, in relation to an export service company, for the deduction of —

(a)

any unabsorbed allowances provided for under sections 13 to 18 of the Income Tax Act attributable to income derived from qualifying services by it during its tax relief period otherwise than in accordance with section 20 of that Act; and

(b)

losses incurred by it during its tax relief period otherwise than in accordance with subsection (2) of section 30 of the Income Tax Act.

PART IX

INTERNATIONAL TRADE INCENTIVES

Interpretation of this Part.

63. For the purposes of this Part, unless the context otherwise requires —
"commencement day", in relation to an international trading company, means the date specified in the certificate issued to the company as the date from which that company shall be entitled to tax relief under this Part;

"export sales" means export sales free on board but shall exclude the cost of samples, gifts, test-market materials, trade exhibits and other promotional materials;

"international trading company" means a company which has been issued with a certificate under section 64;

"qualifying commodities" means any commodity in respect of which one or more certificates of origin or other documents have been issued by the Minister for the purpose of the export of such commodity;

"qualifying manufactured goods" means Brunei Darussalam manufactured goods in respect of which one or more certificates of origin or other documents indicating that the goods are manufactured in Brunei Darussalam have been issued by the Minister for the purpose of the export of such goods;

"relevant export sales" means the export sales of an international trading company in respect of qualifying manufactured goods and Brunei Darussalam domestic produce or in respect of qualifying commodities, as the case may be;

"Brunei Darussalam domestic produce" means prawns, fish (including aquarium fish), chicken, ornamental plants and orchids produced in Brunei Darussalam and such other domestic produce as may be approved by the Minister.

For additional analytical, business and investment opportunities information,
please contact Global Investment & Business Center, USA
at (703) 370-8082. Fax: (703) 370-8083. E-mail: ibpusa3@gmail.com
Global Business and Investment Info Databank - www.ibpus.com

International trading company.

64. (1) Where a company is engaged in —

(a)

international trade in qualifying manufactured goods or Brunei Darussalam domestic produce and the export sales of those goods or produce separately or in combination exceed or are expected to exceed $3 million per annum; or

(b)

entrepot trade in any qualifying commodities and the export sales of those qualifying commodities exceed or are expected to exceed $5 million per annum,

the company may apply in the prescribed form to the Minister for approval as an international trading company.

(2)

The Minister may, if he considers it expedient in the public interest to do so, approve the application and issue the company with a certificate subject to such terms and conditions as he thinks fit.

(3)

The Minister may issue separate certificates to an international trading company for the purposes of paragraphs *(a)* and *(b)* of subsection (1).

(4)

Every certificate issued under this section shall specify a date as the commencement day from which the company shall be entitled to tax relief under this Part.

(5)

The Minister may, in his discretion upon the application of an international trading company, amend its certificate by substituting for the commencement day specified therein such earlier or later date as he thinks fit and thereupon the provisions of this Part shall have effect as if the date so substituted were the commencement day in relation to that certificate.

(6)

A company shall furnish to the Minister at the time of application to be an international trading company a statement of all its associated companies and export agents and the activities they are engaged in and such other particulars as may be required; and where there is any change in the particulars, the company shall notify the Minister as soon as possible of the change.

Tax relief period of international trading company.

65. The tax relief period of an international trading company, in relation to any certificate issued to that company, shall commence on the commencement day and shall continue for a period of 8 years.

Power to give directions

66. For the purposes of the Income Tax Act and this Order, the Collector may direct that —

(a)

any sums payable to an international trading company in any accounting period which, but for the provisions of this Order might reasonably and properly have been expected to be payable, in the normal course of business, after the end of that period shall be treated as not having been payable in that period but as having been payable on such date, after that period, as the Collector thinks fit and, where that date is after the end of the tax relief period of the international trading company, as having been so payable on that date as a sum payable in respect of its post tax relief trade or business; and

(b)

any expenses incurred by an international trading company within one year after the end of its tax relief period which, but for the provisions of this Order might reasonably and properly have been expected to be incurred, in the normal course of business, during its tax relief period shall be treated as not having been incurred within that year but as having been incurred on such date, during its tax relief period, as the Collector thinks fit.
Application of Part X of Income Tax Act.

67. (1) Part X of the Income Tax Act (relating to returns of income) shall apply in all respects as if the whole of the income of an international trading company were chargeable to tax.

(2) The annual return of income shall be accompanied by such evidence as, in the opinion of the Collector, is necessary to verify the income derived from the export sales of qualifying manufactured goods, Brunei Darussalam domestic produce and qualifying commodities.

Ascertainment of income in respect of other trade or business.

68. Where during its tax relief period an international trading company carries on any trade or business which is distinct from the trade or business which includes its relevant export sales, separate accounts shall be maintained in respect of that distinct trade or business and in respect of the same accounting period, and the income from that distinct trade or business shall be computed and assessed in accordance with the provisions of the Income Tax Act with such adjustments as the Collector thinks reasonable and proper.

Computation of export income and exemption from tax.

69. (1) The total income of an international trading company, in respect of its trade or business which includes its relevant export sales, shall be ascertained (after making such adjustments as may be necessary in consequence of any direction given under section 66), for any accounting period during its tax relief period in accordance with the provisions of the Income Tax Act, and, in particular, the following provisions shall apply —

(a)

income from any commissions and other non-trading sources shall be excluded and separately assessed;

(b)

the allowances provided for in sections 13, 14, 15, 16, 17, and 18 (where applicable) of the Income Tax Act shall be taken into account, and where in any year of assessment full effect cannot, by reason of an insufficiency of profits for that year of assessment, be given to those allowances, section 20 of the Income Tax Act shall apply;

(c)

the amount of any unabsorbed allowances in respect of any year of assessment immediately preceding the tax relief period which would otherwise be available under section 20 of the Income Tax Act shall be taken into account;

(d)

section 30 of the Income Tax Act shall apply in respect of any loss incurred prior to or during its tax relief period;

(e)

any unabsorbed allowances granted under sections 13, 14, 16 and 17 of the Income Tax Act and losses incurred in respect of any distinct trade or business shall be brought into the computation;

(f)

any unabsorbed allowances granted under sections 13, 14, 16 and 17 of the Income Tax Act and losses incurred in respect of the trade or business referred to in this subsection shall, during the tax relief period, only be deducted against the income derived from that trade or business;

(g)

subject to sections 20 and 30 of the Income Tax Act, any allowances and losses which remain unabsorbed at the end of the tax relief period shall be available for deduction in its post tax relief period.

(2)

The amount of the export income of an international trading company which will qualify for the relief for any year of assessment shall be deemed to be such amount which bears to the total income ascertained under subsection (1) the same proportion as the excess of the total value of the relevant export sales over the relevant base export value bears to the total amount of the sums received or receivable in respect of its total sales; and subject to section 70, one-half of the amount of the export income which qualifies for the relief as ascertained in this subsection shall not form part of the chargeable income of the international trading company for that year of assessment and shall be exempt from tax.

(3) The relevant base export value referred to in subsection (2) shall be —

(a)

for the basis period for the first year of assessment within the tax relief period of an international trading company, a sum equal to one-third of the total value of the relevant export sales during the 3 years immediately preceding the date of its application to be an international trading company; and

(b)

for the basis period for any subsequent year of assessment within the tax relief period, a sum equal to one-third of the total value of the relevant export sales during the 3 qualifying years immediately preceding that basis period.

(4)

For the purposes of paragraph *(b)* of subsection (3), a "qualifying year" is a year in which the export sales —

(a)

in respect of qualifying manufactured goods or Brunei Darussalam domestic produce exceed $3 million; and

(b)

in respect of qualifying commodities exceed $5 million.

(5) Where an international trading company —

(a)

was engaged in the trading of qualifying manufactured goods, Brunei Darussalam domestic produce or qualifying commodities for less than 3 years immediately preceding its application under this Part;

(b)

during its tax relief period has acquired any sales in respect of qualifying manufactured goods, Brunei Darussalam domestic produce or qualifying commodities from any person or has acquired the beneficial interest, directly or indirectly, of any company engaged in similar trade or business; or

(c)

has less than 3 qualifying years for the purpose of determining its relevant base export value under paragraph *(b)* of subsection (3), the Minister may specify such other relevant base export value for one or more basis periods as he thinks fit having regard to the circumstances of the case.

Conditions for relief.

70. The tax relief provided under section 69 shall, for a year of assessment, apply only if an international trading company has complied with the conditions stipulated under this Part and such other conditions as may be specified in its certificate.

Certain dividends exempted from income tax.

71. (1) As soon as any amount of chargeable income of an international trading company has become exempt under section 69, that amount shall be credited to a tax exempt account to be kept by the company for the purposes of this Part.

(2)
Where a tax exempt account is in credit at the date on which any dividends are paid by a company, out of income which has been so exempted, an amount equal to those dividends or to that credit, whichever is the less, shall be debited to the account.

(3)
So much of the amount of any dividends so debited to the tax exempt account as is received by a shareholder of the company shall, if the Collector is satisfied with the entries in the account, be exempt from tax in the hands of the shareholder.

(4)
Notwithstanding subsection (3), where a dividend is paid on any share of a preferential nature, it shall not be exempt from tax in the hands of the shareholder.

(5)
Any dividends debited to the tax exempt account shall be treated as having been distributed to the shareholders of the company or any particular class of those shareholders in the same proportions as the shareholders were entitled to payment of the dividends giving rise to the debit.

(6)
The company shall deliver to the Collector a copy of the tax exempt account, made up to a date specified by him, whenever called upon to do so by notice in writing sent by him to its registered office, until such time as he is satisfied that there is no further need for maintaining the account.

(7)
Where an amount has been received by way of dividend from a company by a shareholder and the amount is exempt from tax under this Part, if that shareholder is a company, any dividends paid by that company to its shareholders, to the extent that the

Collector is satisfied that those dividends are paid out of that amount, shall be exempt from tax in the hands of those shareholders.

Recovery of tax exempted.

72. Notwithstanding any other provisions of this Part, where it appears to the Collector that —

(a)
any amount of exempted income of an international trading company; or

(b)
any dividend exempted in the hands of any shareholder,

ought not to have been exempted by reason of a direction made under section 66 or the revocation under section 114 of the certificate issued under section 64 to the company, the Collector may subject to section 62 of the Income Tax Act —

(i)

make such assessment or additional assessment upon the company or any such shareholder as may appear to be necessary in order to recover such tax as may have been exempted under this Part; or

(ii)

direct the company to debit its tax exempt account with such amount as the circumstance require.

Application of Parts XI and XII of Income Tax Act.

73. (1) Parts XI and XII of the Income Tax Act (relating to objection and appeals) and any regulations made thereunder shall apply, with the necessary modifications, to any direction given under section 72 as if it were a notice of assessment given under those provisions.

(2) Section 36 of the Income Tax Act shall not apply in respect of any dividend or part thereof which is exempted from tax under this Part.

Application of certain sections to international trading company.

74. Sections 45, 51, 52, 53 and 54 shall apply, with the necessary modifications, to an international trading company as they apply to an export enterprise and the reference to export product or export produce in those sections shall be read as a reference to qualifying manufactured goods, Brunei Darussalam domestic produce or qualifying commodities.

PART X FOREIGN LOANS FOR PRODUCTIVE EQUIPMENT

Application for and issue of approved foreign loan certificate.

75. (1) Where a company engaged in any industry is desirous of raising a loan of not less than $200,000 from a non-resident person (referred to in this Part as a foreign lender) by means of a financial agreement whereby credit facilities are granted for the purchase of productive equipment for the purposes of its trade or business, the company may apply to the Minister for a certificate certifying that foreign loan to be an approved foreign loan.

(2)

The Minister may, where he thinks it expedient to do so, consider an application for a foreign loan certificate in respect of a foreign loan of less than $200,000.

(3)

The application shall be in such form and with such particulars as may be prescribed, and shall be accompanied by a copy of the financial agreement.

(4)

Where the Minister is satisfied as to the *bona fides* of such an application and that it is expedient in the public interest to do so, he may issue a certificate certifying the loan specified in the application as an approved foreign loan.

(5)

Every certificate issued under subsection (4) shall be in such form and contain such particulars as may be prescribed, and shall be subject to such terms and conditions as the Minister thinks fit.

Restriction on disposal of specified productive equipment.

76. Any productive equipment purchased and financed from an approved foreign loan shall not be sold, transferred, or otherwise disposed of without the prior written permission of the Minister, unless the loan has been repaid in full.

Exemption of approved foreign loan interest from tax.

77. (1) Notwithstanding section 37 of the Income Tax Act, the Minister may, subject to subsection (2), if he is satisfied that it is expedient in the public interest to do so, by an endorsement to that effect on the approved foreign loan certificate, exempt from tax any interest on an approved foreign loan payable to a foreign lender.

(2)

Where a company has contravened section 76 or any conditions imposed by the Minister under subsection (4) of section 75, the amount which, but for subsection (1), would have been deductible by the company from the interest paid by it to the foreign lender under section 37 of the Income Tax Act shall be deemed to have been deducted from that interest and shall be a debt due from the company to the Government and be recoverable in the manner provided by section 76 of the Income Tax Act.

(3) No action shall be taken by the Collector to recover any debt under subsection (2)

without the prior sanction of the Minister.

Exemption of additional interest on approved foreign loan from tax.

78. (1) Subject to subsection (3), section 77 shall apply to any additional interest payable on an approved foreign loan by reason of any arrangement whereby the period within which the loan must be repaid in full has been extended.

(2)

The rate of interest payable in respect of any such extended period shall not, without the prior sanction of the Minister, be higher than the rate of interest specified in the certificate relating to the approved foreign loan.

(3)

Any company making any such arrangement shall give notice thereof in writing to the Minister within 30 days from the date on which the arrangement is made.

PART XI INVESTMENT ALLOWANCES

Interpretation of this Part.

79. (1) For the purposes of this Part, unless the context otherwise requires —

"approved project" means a project approved by the Minister under subsection

(2)

of section 80;
"construction operations" means —
(a)

construction, alteration, repair, extension or demolition of buildings and structures;
(b)

construction, alteration, repair, extension or demolition of any works forming, or to form, part of any land; or
(c)

any operations which form an integral part of, or are preparatory to, or are for renderings complete the operations described in paragraph *(a)* or *(b)* including site clearance, earth-moving excavation, laying of foundations, site restoration , landscaping and the provision of drains and of roadways and other access works;

"fixed capital expenditure" means capital expenditure to be incurred on an approved project by a company on factory building (excluding land) in Brunei Darussalam, on the acquisition of any know-how or patent rights, and on any new productive equipment (and, subject to the approval of the Minister, on any secondhand productive equipment) to be used in Brunei Darussalam, and the reference to factory building in this definition shall, in relation to a project under paragraph *(b)*, *(c)*, *(d)*, *(f)* or *(g)* of subsection (1) of section 80, include a building or structure specially designed and used for carrying out that project;

"investment day", in relation to a company, means the date specified in its certificate as the date from which the company shall qualify for the investment allowance;

"research and development" has the same meaning as in the Income Tax Act (Chapter 35).

(2) For the purposes of this Part, fixed capital expenditure shall not be deemed to be incurred by a company unless —

(a)

in the case of any factory building or productive equipment to be constructed or installed on site, the expenditure is attributable to payment against work done in the construction of the building or the construction or installation of the productive equipment;

(b)

in the case of any productive equipment, other than that to be constructed or installed on site, the company has received delivery of the equipment in Brunei Darussalam.
Capital expenditure investment allowance.

80. (1) Where a company proposes to carry out a project —

(a)

for the manufacture or increased manufacture of any product;

(b)

for the provision of specialised engineering or technical services;

(c)

for research and development;

(d)

for construction operation;

(e)

for the recycling of domestic and industrial waste;

(f)

in relation to any qualifying activity as defined in section 17;

(g)

for the promotion of the tourist industry (other than a hotel) in Brunei Darussalam,

the company may apply in the prescribed form to the Minister for the approval of an investment allowance in respect of the fixed capital expenditure for the project.

(2)

Where the Minister considers it expedient, having regard to the economic, technical and other merits of the project, he may approve the project and issue the company with a certificate which shall qualify the company for an investment allowance (as stipulated in the certificate) in respect of the fixed capital expenditure for the approved project subject to such terms and conditions as he thinks fit.

(3)

Every certificate issued under this section shall specify a date as the investment day from which the company shall be entitled to investment allowance under this Part.

(4)

The Minister may, in his discretion upon the application of a company amend its certificate by substituting for the investment day specified therein such earlier or later date as he thinks fit and thereupon the provisions of this Part shall have effect as if the date so substituted were the investment day in relation to that certificate.

Investment allowance.

81. (1) The investment allowance granted under section 80 shall be a specified percentage not exceeding 100% of the amount (which may be subject to a specified maximum) of fixed capital expenditure incurred on each item specified by the Minister under subsection (2) on an approved project if the fixed capital expenditure is incurred —

(a)

within such period (referred to in this Order as the qualifying period), not exceeding 5 years, commencing from the investment day as the Minister may determine; and

(b)

in the case of a project under paragraph (g) of subsection (1) of section 80, within such period (hereinafter referred to as the qualifying period), not exceeding 11 years, commencing from the investment day as the Minister may determine.

(2) The Minister —

(a)

shall specify the items of the fixed capital expenditure for the purposes of subsection (1); and

(b)

may specify the maximum amount of the investment allowance granted for the approved project.

(3) Where any question arises as to whether a particular item qualifies as one of the items under paragraph (a) of subsection (2), it shall be determined by the Minister whose decision shall be final.

(4) In subsection (1), "specified" means specified by the Minister.

Crediting of investment allowance.

82. (1) Where in the basis period for a year of assessment a company has incurred fixed capital expenditure, the company shall be given for that year of assessment an investment allowance in respect of such amount of the fixed capital expenditure as qualifies for the investment allowance under the terms and conditions of its certificate and in accordance with section 81.

(2) Where any investment allowance is given to a company for an approved project, the investment allowance shall be kept in an account to be called "investment allowance account" which shall be kept by the company for the purposes of this Part.

Prohibition to sell, lease out or dispose of assets.

83. (1) During its qualifying period or within 2 years after the end of its qualifying period, a company shall not, without the written approval of the Minister, sell, lease out or otherwise dispose of any assets in respect of which an investment allowance has been given.

(2)

Where during its qualifying period or within 2 years after the end of its qualifying period, a company has sold, leased out or otherwise disposed any asset in respect of which an investment allowance has been given, an amount equal to the aggregate of the investment allowance given in respect of that asset shall be recovered.

(3)

Where that account is insufficient to give full effect to the recovery, an assessment or additional assessment in respect of the amount unrecovered shall be made upon the company or any shareholder of the company and the tax exempt account, kept in accordance with section 71 (as made applicable by section 85), shall be debited accordingly.

(4)

Notwithstanding subsections (2) and (3), the Minister may waive wholly or partly the recovery of the investment allowance.

Exemption from income tax.

84. (1) Where for any year of assessment the investment allowance account of a company is in credit and the company has for that year of assessment any chargeable income —

(a)

an amount of the chargeable income, not exceeding the credit in the investment allowance account, shall be exempt from tax and the investment allowance account shall be debited with such amount; and

(b)

any remaining balance in the investment allowance account shall be carried forward to be used by the company in the first subsequent year of assessment when the company has chargeable income, and so on for subsequent year of assessment until the credit in the investment allowance account has been fully used.

(2) Any amount of chargeable income of a company debited from the investment allowance account shall be exempt from tax.

Certain dividends exempted from income tax.

85. Section 71 shall apply, with the necessary modifications, to a company which has been granted an investment allowance under this Part as it applies to an international trading company and the reference to section 69 in that section shall be read as a reference to section

84.

Recovery of tax exempted.

86. Notwithstanding any other provisions in this Part, where it appears to the Collector that —

(a)

any amount exempted income of a company; or

(b)

any dividend exempted in the hands of any shareholder,

ought not to have been exempted by reason of the revocation under section 114 of the certificate issued under section 80 to the company, the Collector may subject to section 62 of the Income Tax Act —

(i)

make such assessment or additional assessment upon the company or any such shareholder as may appear to be necessary in order to recover such tax as may have been exempted under this Part; or

(ii)

direct the company to debit its tax exempt account with such amount as the circumstances require.

Application of Parts XI and XII of Income Tax Act.

87. (1) Parts XI and XII of the Income Tax Act (relating to objections and appeals) and any regulations made thereunder shall apply, with the necessary modifications, to any direction given under section 86 as if it were a notice of assessment given under those provisions.

(2) Section 36 of the Income Tax Act shall not apply in respect of any dividend or part thereof which is exempted from tax under this Part.

PART XII WAREHOUSING AND SERVICING INCENTIVES

Interpretation of this Part.

88. For the purposes of this Part, unless the context otherwise requires —
"commencement day", in relation to a warehousing company or a servicing company, means the date specified in its certificate as the date from which that company shall be entitled to tax relief under this Part;

"earnings" means —

(a)

in relation to a warehousing company, the consideration received or receivable from the sales of goods (including the provisions of services connected with or related to such sales) or the commissions received or receivable therefrom; and

(b)

in relation to a service company, the consideration received or receivable from the provision of services;

"eligible goods or services", in relation to a warehousing company or a servicing company, means the eligible goods or services specified in the certificate issued to that company under subsection (3) of section 89;

"export earnings" means —

(a)

in relation to a warehousing company, the consideration received or receivable from export sales free on board of eligible goods (including the provision of services connected with or related to such sales) or the commissions received or receivable therefrom; and

(b)

in relation to a servicing company, the consideration received or receivable from the provision of eligible services to persons outside Brunei Darussalam who are not resident in Brunei Darussalam.

"fixed capital expenditure" means capital expenditure to be incurred on any building (excluding land) and on any new productive equipment (and, subject to the approval of the Minister, on any secondhand productive equipment) to be used in Brunei Darussalam;

"servicing company" means a company which has been approved as a servicing company under section 89;

"warehousing company" means a company which has been approved as a warehousing company under section 89.

Approved warehousing company or servicing company.

89. (1) Any company intending to incur fixed capital expenditure of not less than $2 million for —

(a)

the establishment or improvement of warehousing facilities wholly or mainly for the storage and distribution of manufacture goods to be sold and
exported by the company, with or without processing or the provision of related services; or
(b)

the purpose of providing technical or engineering services (or such other services as the Minister may, by notification in the *Gazette*, specify) wholly or mainly to persons not resident in Brunei Darussalam,

may apply in the prescribed form to the Minister for approval as a warehousing company or a servicing company.

(2)

Where the Minister considers it expedient in the public interest to do so, he may approve the application and issue a certificate to the company subject to such terms and conditions as he thinks fit.
(3) Every certificate issued under this section shall specify —
(a)

a date as the commencement day from which the company shall be entitled to tax relief under this Part; and
(b)

the eligible goods or services for the purpose of tax relief under this Part.
(4)

The Minister may, in his discretion, upon the application of a warehousing company or a servicing company, amend its certificate by substituting for the commencement day specified therein such earlier or later date as he thinks fit and thereupon the provisions of this Part shall have effect as if the date so substituted were the commencement day in relation to that certificate.
Tax relief period of warehousing company or servicing company.

90. (1) The tax relief period of a warehousing company or a servicing company shall commence on its commencement day and shall continue for such period, not exceeding 11 years, as the Minister may, in his discretion, determine.

(2) The Minister may, where he is satisfied that it is expedient in the public interest to do so and subject to such terms and conditions as he may impose, extend the tax relief period of any warehousing company or servicing company for such further period or periods, not exceeding 3 years at any one time, as he may determine, except that the tax relief period of the warehousing company or servicing company shall not in the aggregate exceed 20 years.

Prohibition of acquisition without approval.

91. (1) During its tax relief period, a warehousing company shall not acquire any sales and a servicing company shall not acquire any services from any other person in connection with its trade or business without the written approval of the Minister.

(2) Where the Minister permits a warehousing company or a servicing company to acquire such sales or services, he may vary the base export earnings as determined under subsection (3) of section 94 and impose such terms and conditions as he thinks fit.

Application of certain sections to warehousing company or servicing company.

92. (1) Sections 66 and 68 shall apply, with the necessary modifications, to a warehousing company or a servicing company as they apply to an international trading company, and the reference in section 68 to relevant export sales shall be read as a reference to export of eligible goods or provision of eligible services.

(2) Sections 45, 46, 51, 52, 53 and 54 shall apply, with the necessary modifications, to a warehousing company as they apply to an export enterprise and the reference to export product or export produce in those sections shall be read as a reference to eligible goods.

Application of Part X of Income Tax Act.

93. (1) Part X of the Income Tax Act (relating to returns of income) shall apply in all respects as if the whole of the income of a warehousing company or a servicing company were chargeable to tax.

(2) The annual return of income shall be accompanied by such evidence as, in the opinion of the Collector, is necessary to verify the income derived by a warehousing company or a servicing company.

Computation of export earnings and exemption from tax.

94. (1) The total income of a warehousing company or a servicing company in respect of its trade or business which includes its export of eligible goods or provision of eligible services shall be ascertained (after making such adjustments as may be necessary in consequence of any direction given under section 66 as made applicable by section 92), for any accounting period during its tax relief period in accordance with the provisions of the Income Tax Act, and, in particular, the following provisions shall apply —

(a)
    income from other non-trading sources shall be excluded and separately assessed;

(b)
    the allowances provided for in sections 13, 14, 15, 16, 17 and 18 (where applicable) of the Income Tax Act shall be taken into account notwithstanding that no claim for those allowances has been made, and where in any year of assessment full effect cannot, by

reason of an insufficiency of profits for that year of assessment, be given to those allowances, section 20 of the Income Tax Act shall apply;

(c)

the amount of any unabsorbed allowances in respect of any year of assessment immediately preceding the tax relief period which would otherwise be available under section 20 of the Income Tax Act shall be taken into account;

(d)

section 30 of the Income Tax Act shall apply in respect of any loss incurred prior to or during its tax relief period;

(e)

any unabsorbed allowances granted under sections 13, 14, 16, 17 and 18 of the Income Tax Act and losses incurred in respect of any distinct trade or business shall be brought into the computation;

(f)

any unabsorbed allowances granted under sections 13, 14, 16, 17 and 18 of the Income Tax Act and losses incurred in respect of the trade or business referred to in this subsection shall, during the tax relief period, only be deducted against the income derived from that trade or business; and

(g)

subject to sections 20 and 30 of the Income Tax Act, any allowances and losses which remain unabsorbed at the end of the tax relief period shall be available for deduction in its post tax relief period.

(2)

The amount of the export income of a warehousing company or a servicing company which will qualify for the relief for any year of assessment shall be deemed to be such amount which bears to the total income ascertained under subsection (1) the same proportion as the excess of the total amount of the export earnings of that company over its base export earnings bears to the total amount of its earnings; and one-half of the amount of the export income which qualifies for the relief as ascertained in this subsection shall not form part of the chargeable income of the company for the year of assessment and shall be exempt from tax.

(3)

The base export earnings referred to in subsection (2) shall be where a warehousing company or a servicing company has been carrying on its trade or business —

(a)

for 3 or more years immediately preceding the date of its application under this Part, an amount equal to one-third of the export earnings for the 3 years immediately preceding the date of its application under this Part; and

(b)

for less than 3 years immediately preceding the date of its application under this Part, such amount as the Minister may specify having regard to the export earnings of other warehousing companies or servicing companies, as the case may be.

Certain dividends exempted from income tax.

95. Section 71 shall apply, with the necessary modifications, to a warehousing company or a servicing company as it applies to an international trading company and the reference to section 69 in subsection (1) of section 71 shall be read as a reference to section 94.

Recovery of tax exempted.

96. Notwithstanding any other provisions of this Part, where it appears to the Collector that —

(a)

any amount of exempted income of a warehousing company or a servicing company; or

(b)

any dividend exempted in the hand of any shareholder,

ought not to have been exempted by reason of a direction made under section 66 (as made applicable by section 92) or the revocation under section 114 of the certificate issued under section 89 to the warehousing company or the servicing company, the Collector may subject to section 62 of the Income Tax Act —

(i)

make such assessment or additional assessment upon the company or any such shareholder as may appear to be necessary in order to recover such tax as may have been exempted under this Part; or

(ii)

direct the company to debit its tax exempt account with such amount as the circumstances may require.

Application of Parts XI and XII of Income Tax Act.

97. (1) Parts XI and XII of the Income Tax Act (relating to objections and appeals) and any regulations made thereunder shall apply, with the necessary modifications, to any direction given under section 96 as if it were a notice of assessment given under those provisions.

(2) Section 36 of the Income Tax Act shall not apply in respect of any dividend or part thereof which is exempted from tax under this Part.

PART XIII INVESTMENTS IN NEW TECHNOLOGY COMPANIES

Interpretation of this Part.

98. For the purposes of this Part, unless the context otherwise requires —

"eligible holding company", in relation to a technology company, means a company incorporated in Brunei Darussalam —

(a)

which is resident in Brunei Darussalam;

(b)

which holds shares in the technology company; and

(c)

in respect of which not less than 30% of the paid-up capital is beneficially owned by citizens or persons to whom a Resident Permit has been granted under regulations made under the Immigration Act (Chapter 17) throughout the whole of the qualifying period of the technology company, unless the Minister otherwise decides;

"qualifying period", in relation to a technology company, means a period of 3 years from the day it commences, for the purposes of the Income Tax Act (Chapter 35), to carry on its relevant trade or business;

"relevant trade or business", in relation to a technology company, means the trade or business to which the certificate, issued to the company under subsection (2) of section 99, relates;

"technology company" means a company approved as a technology company under subsection (2) of section 99.

Application for and issue of certificate to technology company.

99. (1) Any company incorporated in Brunei Darussalam which is desirous of using in Brunei Darussalam a new technology in relation to a product, process or service may make an application in the prescribed form to the Minister to be approved as a technology company.

(2)

Where the Minister is satisfied that the technology, if introduced in Brunei Darussalam, would promote or enhance the economic or technological development in Brunei Darussalam, he may approve the company as a technology company and issue a certificate to that company subject to such conditions as he thinks fit.

(3)

Every certificate issued under this section shall specify a percentage, not exceeding 30%, of such amount of the paid-up capital of the technology company as is held by any eligible holding company for the purpose of determining the deduction under section 100.

Deductions allowable to eligible holding company.

100. (1) Where a technology company has incurred an overall loss in respect of its relevant trade or business at the end of its qualifying period, it may, within 6 years from that date, by notice in writing to the Collector elect for the overall loss (less any amount which has been deducted up to the date of the notice) and the amount of any unabsorbed capital allowances (less any amount which has been deducted up to the date of the notice) to be made available to an eligible holding company as a deduction against the statutory income of the eligible holding company.

(2)

The deduction to be made available to an eligible holding company under subsection (1) shall be an amount to be ascertained by multiplying the overall loss (less any amount which has been deducted up to the date of the notice) or the unabsorbed capital allowances (less any amount which has been deducted up to the date of the notice), as the case may be, by the percentage of the paid-up capital of the technology company held by that eligible holding company throughout the whole of the qualifying period of the technology company.

(3)

The deduction shall not in the aggregate exceed such percentage as may be specified in the certificate issued to the technology company under section 99 of the paid-up capital of the technology company held by the eligible holding company (excluding any shares acquired from other shareholders of the technology company) as at the end of such qualifying period.

(4)

Notwithstanding subsections (2) and (3), where the percentage of the paid-up capital of the technology company held by an eligible holding company is increased at any time during the qualifying period of the technology company, the Minister may, upon the application by the eligible holding company, if he considers it just and reasonable to do so, increase the amount of the deduction available under subsection (2) up to 50% of the paid-up capital of the technology company held by the eligible holding company as at the end of such qualifying period.

(5)

Where any deduction is made available to an eligible holding company in accordance with this section, any overall loss or unabsorbed capital allowances to the extent of the deductions so made available shall cease to be deductible by the technology company under section 20 or 30 of the Income Tax Act (Chapter 35), and those sections shall apply to the eligible holding company in respect of the deduction made available as if the eligible holding company was carrying on the trade or business in respect of which the overall loss or the unabsorbed capital allowances were made.

(6)

The overall loss or unabsorbed capital allowances made available to an eligible holding company under this section shall first be deducted against the statutory income of the eligible holding company for the year of assessment immediately following the year in which the notice given under subsection (1).

(7) In this section —

"overall loss", in relation to a technology company, means the amount by which the total of the losses exceed the total of the statutory income arising from its relevant trade or business for the whole of its qualifying period ascertained in accordance with the provisions of the Income Tax Act and subject to such regulations as may be prescribed under this Order;

"unabsorbed capital allowances", in relation to a technology company, means the balance of any allowance provided for in sections 13, 14, 15, 16, 17 and 18 of the Income Tax Act which remain unabsorbed at the end of the qualifying period of the company in respect of capital expenditure incurred for the purpose of its relevant trade or business before the end of the qualifying period.

(8) For the purposes of the Income Tax Act and this Part, the Collector may direct that —

(a)

any sums payable to a technology company before or after its qualifying period which, but for the provisions of this Part, might reasonably and properly have been expected to be payable to the technology company, in the normal course of business, during its qualifying period shall be treated as having been payable on such date within the qualifying period, as the Collector thinks fit; and

(b)

any expense incurred by a technology company during its qualifying period which, but for the provisions of this Part, might reasonably and properly have been expected to be incurred, in the normal course of business, before or after the qualifying period shall be treated as not having been incurred within the qualifying period but as having been incurred on such date before or after that qualifying period, as the Collector thinks fit.
Prohibition of other trade or business.

101. (1) During its qualifying period, a technology company shall not, without the written approval of the Minister, carry on any trade or business other than its relevant trade or business.

(2) Where the carrying on of a separate trade or business has been approved under subsection (1), separate accounts shall be maintained in respect of that trade or business.

Recovery of tax.

102. Notwithstanding anything in this Part, where it appears to the Collector that any deduction under section 100 ought not to have been given to an eligible holding company by reason of any direction under subsection (8) of section 100 or the revocation under section 114 of a certificate issued to a technology company, the Collector may, subject to section 62 of the Income Tax Act, make such assessment or additional assessment upon the eligible holding company or any of its shareholders as may be necessary in order to recover any tax which should have been payable by the eligible holding company.

PART XIV OVERSEAS INVESTMENT AND VENTURE CAPITAL INCENTIVES

Interpretation of this Part.

103. For the purposes of this Part, unless the context otherwise requires —

"eligible holding company", in relation to a venture company, a technology investment company or an overseas investment company, means a company incorporated in Brunei Darussalam —

(a)
    which is resident in Brunei Darussalam;

(b)
    which has invested not less than 60% of its shareholders' fund in Brunei Darussalam;

(c)
    which holds not less than 30% of the shares in the venture company, the technology investment company or the overseas investment company; and

(d)
    in respect of which not less than 30% of the paid-up capital is beneficially owned by citizens or person to whom a Resident Permit has been granted under regulations made under the Immigration Act (Chapter 17) throughout the period during which it holds shares in the venture company, the technology investment company or the overseas investment company, unless the Minister otherwise decides;

"overseas investment company" means a company approved as an overseas investment company under subsection (4) of section 105;

"technology investment company" means a company approved as a technology investment company under subsection (2) of section 105;

"venture company" means a company approved as a venture company under subsection (2) of section 104;

"shareholders' fund" means the aggregate amount of a company's paid up capital (in respect of preference shares and ordinary shares and not including any amount in respect of bonus shares to the extent they were issued out of capital reserves created by revaluation of fixed assets), reserves (other than any capital reserve which was created by revaluation of fixed assets and provisions for depreciation, renewals or replacements and diminution in value of assets), balance of share premium account (not including any amount credited therein at the instance of issuing bonus shares at premium out of capital reserve created by revaluation of fixed assets), and balance of profit and loss appropriation account.

Application for and issue of certificate to venture company.

104. (1) Any company incorporated in Brunei Darussalam which is desirous of developing or using in Brunei Darussalam a new technology in relation to a product, process or service may make an application in the prescribed form to the Minister to be approved as a venture company.

(2) Where the Minister is satisfied that the technology, if introduced in Brunei Darussalam, would promote or enhance the economic or technological development of Brunei Darussalam, he may approve the company as a venture company and issue a certificate to the company subject to such terms and conditions as he may impose.

For additional analytical, business and investment opportunities information,
please contact Global Investment & Business Center, USA
at (703) 370-8082. Fax: (703) 370-8083. E-mail: ibpusa3@gmail.com
Global Business and Investment Info Databank - www.ibpus.com

Application for and issue of certificate to technology investment company or overseas investment company.

105. (1) Any company, incorporated and resident in Brunei Darussalam, desirous of investing in an overseas company which is developing or using a new technology in relation to a product, process or service may make an application in the prescribed form to the Minister to be approved as a technology investment company.

(2)

Where the Minister is satisfied in respect of any application under subsection (1) that the technology, if introduced in Brunei Darussalam would promote or enhance the economic or technological development of Brunei Darussalam, he may approve the company as a technology investment company and issue a certificate to the company subject to such terms and conditions as he may impose.

(3)

Any company, incorporated and resident in Brunei Darussalam, desirous of investing in an overseas company for the purpose of acquiring for use in Brunei Darussalam any technology from the overseas company or for the purpose of gaining access to any overseas market for its eligible holding company or any subsidiary thereof, may make an application in the prescribed form to the Minister to be approved as an overseas investment company.

(4)

Where the Minister is satisfied in respect of any application under subsection (3) that the technology acquired, if introduced in Brunei Darussalam or the access which would be gained to any overseas market, would promote or enhance the technological or economic development of Brunei Darussalam, he may approve the company as an overseas investment company and issue a certificate to the company subject to such terms and conditions as he may impose.

Deduction of losses allowable to eligible holding company.

106. (1) Where any eligible holding company has incurred any loss arising from —

(a)

the sale of shares held by it in a venture company; or

(b)

the liquidation of a venture company,

the loss shall be allowed as a deduction against the statutory income of the company in accordance with subsection 2 of section 30 of the Income Tax Act as if the loss were incurred from a trade or business carried on by it.

(2) Where any eligible holding company has incurred any loss arising from —

(a)

the sale of shares held by it in a technology investment company or an overseas investment company; or

(b)

the liquidation of a technology investment company or an overseas investment company,

the loss shall be allowed as a deduction against its statutory income in accordance with subsection (2) of section 30 of the Income Tax Act as if the loss were incurred from a trade or business carried on by it.

For additional analytical, business and investment opportunities information,
please contact Global Investment & Business Center, USA
at (703) 370-8082. Fax: (703) 370-8083. E-mail: ibpusa3@gmail.com
Global Business and Investment Info Databank - www.ibpus.com

(3)

Notwithstanding subsections (1) and (2), no deduction shall be allowed in respect of any loss referred to in those subsection if —

(a)

the shares in respect of which the loss was incurred were held by an eligible holding company in a venture company, or by an eligible holding company in a technology investment company or in an overseas investment company, for a period of less than 3 years from the date of issue of the shares, unless the loss was incurred as a result of the liquidation of the venture company, technology investment company or overseas investment company; or

(b)

the sale of shares or liquidation occurred after 8 years from the date of approval under this Part of the venture company, technology investment company or overseas investment company.

(4)

For the purposes of subsections (1) and (2), the loss shall be the excess of the purchase price of the shares —

(a)

over the proceeds from the sale; and where the open market value at the date of the sale (or the value of net asset backing as determined by the Collector in the case of a company not quoted on any stock exchange) of the shares is greater than the sale proceeds, that value shall be deemed to be the proceeds from the sale; or

(b)

over the proceeds from the liquidation,

as the case may be.

Prohibition of other trade or business.

107. (1) A venture company shall not, without the written approval of the Minister, carry on any trade or business other than the trade or business to which its certificate relates.

(2) A technology investment company and an overseas investment company shall not carry on any trade or business.

Recovery of tax.

108. Notwithstanding anything in this Part, where it appears to the Collector that any deduction under section 106 ought not to have been given to an eligible holding company by reason of the revocation under section 114 of a certificate issued to a venture company, a technology investment company or an overseas investment company, the Collector may, subject to section 62 of the Income Tax Act, make such assessment or additional assessment upon the eligible holding company (or any of its shareholders) as may be necessary in order to recover any tax which should have been payable by the eligible holding company (or any of its shareholders).

PART XV RELIEF FROM IMPORT DUTIES

Exemption from import duties.

109. (1) Notwithstanding the provision of section 11 of the Customs Act (Chapter 36) or any written laws or regulations in force, the Minister may, subject to such terms and conditions as he thinks fit, exempt a pioneer enterprise or an export enterprise from the payment of the whole or any part of any customs duty which may be payable on any machinery, equipment, component parts and accessories including prefabricated factory or building structures to be installed as necessary part of parts of the factory:

Provided that similar machinery, equipment, component parts, accessories or building structures of approximately equal price and equal quality are not being produced or available within Brunei Darussalam.

Restriction on disposal.

110. No machinery, equipment, component parts and accessories imported under section 109 shall be sold, transferred, mortgaged or otherwise disposed of or used for other purposes than those specified or allowed by the Minister without the written approval of the Minister.

Duty to be paid if disposed.

111. (1) Any machinery, equipment, component parts and accessories imported under section 109 which are sold, transferred, mortgaged or otherwise disposed of under section 110 shall be subject to payment of customs duty imposed under the Customs Act (Chapter 36).

(2) For the purpose of determining the duty imposed under subsection (1), all machinery, equipment, component parts and accessories shall be assessed and valued by the Controller of Customs and duties shall be payable on the assessed value.

Exemption from import duties on raw material.

112. Notwithstanding the provision of section 11 of the Customs Act or any written laws or regulations in force, a pioneer enterprise and an export enterprise shall be exempt from the payment of import duties on raw materials imported for use in the pioneer enterprise to be used in the production of a pioneer product specified in the pioneer certificate:

Provided that such raw materials are not available or produced within Brunei Darussalam.

PART XVI MISCELLANEOUS PROVISIONS

Prohibition of publication of application and certificate.

113. (1) The contents of any application made by, or of any certificate issued to, any company under any of the provisions of this Order shall not, except at the instance of the company, be published.

(2) The Minister may cause to be published by notification in the *Gazette* the name of any company to which any such certificate has been issued or whose certificate has been revoked, and the industry and product or produce to which the certificate relates.

Revocation of certificate.

114. (1) Where the Minister is satisfied that any company to which a certificate has been issued under the provisions of this Order has contravened or has failed to comply with any of the provisions of this Order or any regulations made thereunder, or of any terms or conditions imposed on the certificate, he may, by notice in writing, require the company within 30 days from the date of service of the notice to show cause why the certificate should not be revoked; and if the Minister is satisfied that, having regard to all the circumstances of the case it is expedient to do so, he may revoke the certificate.

(2) Where a certificate is revoked under subsection (1), the Minister shall specify the date, which may be the date of the certificate, from which its revocation shall be operative and the provisions of this Order shall cease to have effect in relation to the certificate from that date.

Provisions of Income Tax Act (Chapter 35) not affected.

115. Except as otherwise provided, nothing in this Order shall exempt any company to which a certificate has been issued under the provisions of this Order from making any return to the Collector or from complying with the provisions of the Income Tax Act in any respect so as to establish the liability to tax, if any, of the company.

Offences and penalties.

116. (1) Any person who contravenes or fails to comply with section 46 or 52 or any regulations made under this Order shall be guilty of an offence and shall be liable on conviction to a fine not exceeding $10,000, to imprisonment for a term not exceeding 2 years or both.

(2) Any person who —

(a)

obstructs or hinders any senior officer of customs or officer of customs acting in the discharge of his duty under this Order or any regulations made thereunder; or

(b)

fails to produce to a senior officer of customs or officer of customs any invoices, bills of lading, certificates of origin or of analysis or any other documents relating to the export of any export product or export produce which the officer may require, shall be guilty of an offence and shall be liable on conviction to a fine not exceeding $5,000, to imprisonment for a term not exceeding 12 months or both.

(3)

Any person required by a senior officer of customs or officer of customs to give information on any subject into which it is the officer's duty to inquire and which it is in the person's power to give, who refuses to give such information or furnishes as true information that which he knows or has reason to believe is false shall be guilty of an offence and shall be liable on conviction to a fine not exceeding $5,000, or imprisonment for a term not exceeding 12 months or both.

(4)

When any such information is proved to be untrue or incorrect, in whole or in part, it is no defence to allege that the information, or any part thereof, was furnished inadvertently, without criminal intent or fraudulent intent, or was misinterpreted or not fully interpreted by an interpreter provided by the informant.

(5)

Nothing in subsection (3) shall oblige a person to furnish any information which would have a tendency to expose him to a criminal charge or to a penalty or forfeiture.

Attempts or abetments.

117. Any person who attempts to commit any offence punishable under section 46, 52 or 116 or any regulations made under this Order or abets the commission of any such offence shall be liable to the punishment provided for that offence.

Conduct of prosecution.

118. Any prosecution in respect of an offence under section 46, 52 or 116 or any regulations made under this Order may be conducted by an officer authorised by the Controller of Customs.

Composition of offences.

119. (1) Any officer authorised by the Collector or any senior officer of customs may compound any offence which is prescribed to be a compoundable offence by accepting from the person reasonably suspected of having committed the offence a sum not exceeding $1,000.

(2) On payment of that sum, the person reasonably suspected of having committed an offence, if in custody, shall be discharged, any property seized shall be released and no further proceedings shall be taken against that person or property.

Offences by companies and by employees and agents.

120. (1) Where an offence under section 46, 52 or 116 or any regulations made under this Order has been committed by a company, any person who at the time of the commission of the offence was a director, secretary or other similar officer of the company, or was purporting to act in such capacity shall be deemed to be guilty of that offence unless he proves that the offence was committed without his consent or connivance and that he exercised all such diligence to prevent the commission of the offence as he ought to have exercised, having regard to the nature of his functions in that capacity and to all the circumstances.

(2) Where any person would be liable under section 46, 52 or 116 to any punishment, penalty or forfeiture for any act, omission, neglect or default, he shall be liable to the same punishment, penalty or forfeiture for every such act, omission, neglect or default of any employee or agent, or of the employee of an agent, provided that the act, omission, neglect or default was committed by the employee in the course of his employment or by the agent when acting on behalf of that person or by the employee of the agent when acting in the course of his employment in such circumstance that had the act, omission, neglect or default been committed by the agent his principal would have been liable under this section.

Action of officers no offence.

121. Nothing done by an officer of the Government in the course of his duties shall be deemed to be offence under this Order.

Regulations.

122. (1) The Minister, with the approval of His Majesty the Sultan and Yang Di-Pertuan, may make such regulations as may be necessary or expedient for the purpose of carrying out the provisions of this Order.

(2)
 Without prejudice to the generality of subsection (1), the Minister may make regulations for or with respect to all or any of the following matters —

(a)
 any matters required by this Order to be prescribed;

(b)
 the procedure relating to applications for and the issue of certificates under this Order;

(c)

the terms and conditions to be imposed on any certificate issued under this Order; and

(d)

the furnishing of such information, including progress and sales reports and statements of accounts, as may be required for the purposes of this Order.

(3)

The Minister may in writing authorise any person or authority to prescribe such forms as are required to be or may be prescribed under this Order.

Repeal of Chapter 97, saving and transitional.

123. (1) The Investment Incentives Act is repealed.

(2) Anything done under the Investment Incentives Act (repealed by this Order) shall, upon the commencement of this Order, continue to be of full force and effect until other provisions has been made therefor under this Order.

Made this 28th. day of Safar, 1422 Hijriah corresponding to the 22nd. day of May, 2001 at Our Istana Nurul Iman, Bandar Seri Begawan, Brunei Darussalam.

BRUNEI INVESTMENT AGENCY (CHAPTER 137)

An Act to establish a body corporate to be called the Brunei Investment Agency the principal objects of which shall be the holding and management of the General Reserve Fund of the Government and all external assets of the Government, to provide the Government with money management services and to carry out such other objects as His Majesty the Sultan and Yang Di-Pertuan may specify.

Commencement: 1st July 1983

PART I PRELIMINARY

Citation.

1. This Act may be cited as the Brunei Investment Agency Act.

Interpretation.

2. In this Act, unless the context otherwise requires —

"Agency" means the Brunei Investment Agency establishedunder section 3 of this Act;

"bank" means a bank licensed under the Banking Act (Chapter 95); or the Islamic Banking Act (Chapter 168);

[S 43/92]

"board" means the board of directors of the Agency;

"director" means a director appointed under subsection (2) ofsection 5 of this Act and the chairman of the board and the deputy chairman;

"General Reserve Fund of the Government and all external assets of theGovernment" means the moneys as defined in Article 7(3) of theConstitution (Financial Procedure) Order (Const. III);

[S 20/85]

"managing director" means a director appointed undersubsection (1) of section 7 of this Act;

"Minister of Finance" in respect of the period prior to 1st January 1984 means the Menteri Besar and in respect of the period after 1st January 1984 where the context permits includes the Deputy Minister of Finance.

PART II ESTABLISHMENT AND ADMINISTRATION OF THE AGENCY

Establishment of the Agency.

3. (1) There shall be established an Agency to be called the "Brunei Investment Agency" which shall be a body corporate and shall have perpetual succession and may sue and be sued in its own name.

(2) The Agency shall have a common seal and such seal may, from time totime, be broken, changed, altered and made anew as to the Agency seems fit, and,until a seal is provided under this section, a stamp bearing the inscription"The Brunei Investment Agency" may be used as the common seal.

(3) All deeds, documents and other instruments requiring the seal of theAgency shall be sealed with the common seal of the Agency by the authority ofthe Agency in the presence of the managing director and of some other persons duly authorised by the Agency to act in that behalf and shall be signed by the managing director and by such duly authorised person, and such signing shall besufficient evidence that the common seal of the Agency has been duly andproperly affixed and that the said seal is the lawful common seal of theAgency.

(4) The Agency may by resolution or otherwise appoint an officer of theAgency or any other agent either generally or in a particular case to execute orsign on behalf of the Agency any agreement or other instrument not under seal inrelation to any matter coming within the powers of the Agency.

Principal objects.

4. The principal objects of the Agency shall be —

(a) to hold and manage in Brunei Darussalam and overseas the GeneralReserve Fund of the Government and all external assets of the Government;

(b) to provide the Government with money management servicesin respect of such sums as the Government may from time to time remit and inrespect of interest, dividend and any other payments or corporate actionsarising from the investment of such sums;

(ba) to take all steps and incur any expenditure that may be required in order to recover or protect assets and property that are or may be, or are or may be derived (directly or indirectly and in whole or in part) from, the property of the Government or the Agency and to hold, manage and deal with the same on such terms as the Agency (acting in its own name or by the use of subsidiaries or agents) in its absolute discretion shall see fit;

[S 22/99]

(c) to carry out such other objects as His Majesty the Sultan and YangDi-Pertuan may by Order published in the Government *Gazette* specify.

Board of directors.

5. (1) There shall be a board of directors of the Agency which shallbe responsible for the policy and general administration of the affairsand business of the Agency.

(2) The board shall consist of a Chairman and such number of otherdirectors as His Majesty may appoint.

(3) The board may with the approval of His Majesty invite any person as itthinks fit to attend a meeting of the board for the purpose of giving advice tothe board on any matter.

Appointment of directors.

6. (1) The directors so appointed —

(a) shall not act as delegates on the board from any commercial,financial, agricultural, industrial or other interests with which they may beconnected;

(b) shall hold office for a term not exceeding 3 years and shall beeligible for reappointment;

(c) may be paid by the Agency out of the funds of the Agency such remuneration and allowances as may be determined by His Majesty.

(2) The provisions of paragraph *(b)* of subsection (1) of thissection does not apply to a director who is appointed managing director undersection 7 of this Act.

Appointment of managing director.

7. (1) His Majesty shall appoint one of the directors appointedunder section 5 of this Act to be the managing director.

[S 7/87]

(2) The managing director shall be engaged on such terms andconditions of service as His Majesty may decide.

(3) The managing director shall be entrusted with the day-to-dayadministration of the Agency, and may, subject to this Act, make decisions andexercise all powers and do all acts which may be exercised or done by theAgency.

(4) The managing director shall be answerable to the board for his acts anddecisions.

(5) In the event of the absence or inability to act of the managingdirector, His Majesty may appoint a director to discharge his duties during theperiod of such absence or inability.

Disqualification of directors.

8. His Majesty may terminate the appointment of any director appointedunder subsection (1) of section 5 of this Act if he —

(a) resigns his office;

(b) becomes of unsound mind or incapable of carrying out hisduties;

(c) becomes bankrupt or suspends payment to or compounds with hiscreditors;

(d) is convicted of an offence involving dishonesty or fraud ormoral turpitude;

(e) is guilty of serious misconduct in relation to his duties;

(f) is absent, without leave, from 3 consecutive meetings of theboard; or

(g) fails to comply with his obligations under section 11 of this Act.

Vacancies in the office of director.

9. If any director dies or resigns or otherwise vacates his officebefore the expiry of the term for which he has been appointed another person maybe appointed by His Majesty for the unexpired period of the term of office ofthe director in whose place he is appointed.

Meeting and decisions of the board.

10. (1) The Chairman of the board shall summon meetings as often asmay be required but not less frequently than once in 3 months.

[S 7/87]

(2) At every meeting of the board a quorum shall consist of 3directors, and decisions shall be adopted by a simple majority of the votes ofthe directors present and voting except that in the case of an equality of votesthe Chairman shall have a casting vote.

Director's interest in contract to be made known.

11. (1) A director who is directly or indirectly interested in acontract or investment made or disposed of, or proposed to be made or disposedof, by the Agency shall disclose the nature of his interest at the first meetingof the board at which he is present after the relevant facts have come to his knowledge.

(2) A disclosure under subsection (1) of this section shall berecorded in the minutes of the board and, after the disclosure, the director—

(a) shall not take part in any deliberation or decision of the boardwith respect to that contract; and

(b) shall be disregarded for the purpose of constituting aquorum of the board for any such deliberation or decision.

(3) No act or proceeding of the board shall be questioned by any person whois not a member of the board on the ground that a director has contravened theprovisions of this section.

Preservation of secrecy.

12. (1) Except for the purpose of the performance of his duties orthe exercise of his functions or when lawfully required to do so by any court orunder the provisions of any written law, no director, officer or employee of theAgency shall disclose to any person any information relating to the affairs of the Agency or any person which he has acquired in the performance ofhis duties or the exercise of his functions.

(2) Any person who contravenes the provisions of subsection (1) of thissection shall be guilty of an offence under this Act and shall be liable onconviction to imprisonment for 3 years and to a fine of $5,000.

Remuneration not to be related to profits.

13. No salary, fee, wage or other remuneration shall be computed byreference to the results of any money management services undertaken by or onbehalf of the Agency pursuant to this Act.

Public servants.

14. (1) The directors, including the managing director, and theofficers and employees of the Agency of every description shall be deemed to bepublic servants within the meaning of the Penal Code (Chapter 22).

(2) The officers and employees of the Agency shall be deemed to hold office in the Public Service for the purposes of the Pensions Act (Chapter 38) and shall be eligible for the allowances, pensions and gratuities provided thereunder.

PART III PROVISIONS RELATING TO STAFF, TRANSFER OF FUNCTIONS, EMPLOYEES AND ASSETSETC.

List of posts and appointment of employees.

15. (1) The Agency may from time to time approve a list of posts (excluding the directors) which it thinks necessary for the purposes of this Act and may add to or amend this list.

(2) Subject to the provisions of this section —

(a) appointments and promotions to all posts shall be made by theAgency; and

(b) the termination of appointment, dismissal and disciplinarycontrol of the employees of the Agency shall be vested in the Agency.

(3) In the discharge of its functions under subsection (2) of this sectionthe Agency shall, if directed by His Majesty, in any particular case orgenerally, consult with the Public Service Commission before exercising any ofits powers under subsection (2).

(4) Notwithstanding the provisions of this section, the Agency may appointpersons temporarily for a period not exceeding one year to posts in the list ofposts for the time being in force.

(5) The Agency may, with the approval of His Majesty, make rules, notinconsistent with the provisions of this Act or of any other written law, for the appointment, promotion, disciplinary control and terms andconditions of service of all persons employed by the Agency.

(6) Without prejudice to the generality of subsection (5) of thissection, the Agency shall prescribe the rates of remuneration payable to personsemployed by the Agency and no person so employed shall be paid otherwise than inaccordance with such rates.

Transfer of assets and liabilities to the Agency.

16. (1) Upon the coming into operation of this Act such movable property, assets, rights, interests and privileges as constitute any part of the General Reserve Fund, together with any debts, liabilities or obligations connected therewith or appertaining thereto shall be deemed to have been transferred to and vested in the Agency without the requirement of any further action.

(2) The Minister of Finance shall have power to do all acts or things thathe considers necessary or expedient to give effect to the provisions ofsubsection (1) of this section.

(3) If the question arises as to whether —

(a) any of the functions, duties and powers; or

(b) any movable property, assets, rights, interests, privileges,debts, liabilities and obligations, have been transferred to or vested in the Agency under subsection (1) of thissection, a certificate executed by the Minister of Finance shall be conclusiveevidence of such transfer or vesting.

PART IV POWERS, DUTIES AND FUNCTIONS OF THE AGENCY

Powers, duties and functions of the Agency.

17. (1) The Agency may, for the purpose of carrying out theprovisions of this Act, exercise and discharge the following powers, duties and functions, that is to say, it may —

(a) open and operate securities and cash clearing accounts and placedeposits on such terms as it may decide;

(b) purchase, acquire by exchange or other means, hold, sell orotherwise dispose of various types of investment assets as shall be specificallyauthorised by this Act or by His Majesty on the recommendations of theBoard;

(c) borrow money, establish credits and give guarantees in anycurrency inside and outside Brunei Darussalam on such terms and conditions as itmay deem fit;

(d) open and operate accounts with central banks outside Brunei Darussalam;

(e) purchase, acquire or develop, inside or outsideBrunei Darussalam facilities for accounting for and reporting on the assets andliabilities of the General Reserve Fund and any other assets or liabilitiesvested in the Agency;

(f) enter into contracts with third parties inside or outside Brunei Darussalam for the purpose set forth in section 20 of this Act;

(g) underwrite loans and securities in which it may invest;

(h) undertake the issue and management of loans publiclyissued by the Government or by any public authority;

(i) pay the expenses of the Agency, including specifically anypayments contemplated by sections 6(1) *(c)* , 7(2), 15(6) and 20 *(b)* of this Act out of the assets transferred to and vested in the Agency pursuantto section 16(1) of this Act; and

(j) do generally all such things as may be commonly done by investmentmanagers and are not inconsistent with the exercise of its powers or thedischarge of its duties under this Act.

(2) After the coming into operation of this Act, there shall be vested inthe Agency such other functions, duties and powers as His Majesty may, from timeto time, by notification in the Government *Gazette* , specify.

Investment of funds.

18. Investments which the Agency may hold, as provided inparagraph

(b) of subsection (1) of section 17 of this Act shall include—

(a) gold coin or bullion and other precious metals;

(b) real property and interests therein;

(c) notes, coin, bank balances and money at call in such country orcountries as may be approved by the board;

(d) Treasury bills of such government or governments as may beapproved by the board;

(e) securities of, or guaranteed by, such government orgovernments or international financial institutions as may beapproved by the board;

(f) such other classes of investments assets as may beauthorised by the board from time to time and set forth in a written investmentguideline to the Agency; and

(g) such other specific investments not otherwise authorisedhereunder as may be authorised by His Majesty on therecommendation of the board.

Agency as a financial agent of the Government and manager of its externalassets.

19. (1) The Agency shall act as a financial agent of theGovernment.

(2) Whenever the Agency receives and disburses Government moneys itshall keep account thereof.

(3) The Agency may act generally as representative for theGovernment on such terms and conditions as may be agreed between the Agency andthe Government, where the Agency can do so appropriately and consistently withthe provisions of this Act and with its duties and functions.

Representatives.

20. In the exercise of its powers and the performance of its functionsunder this Act the Agency may —

(a) establish offices and representatives at such places outside Brunei Darussalam as it thinks fit;

(b) arrange or contract with and authorise a person or persons,which may be individuals or corporate entities, to act as agent orrepresentative of the Agency outside Brunei Darussalam, including the performance of investment management, legal, auditing and measurement ofinvestment performance activities on behalf of the Agency, and in conjunctionwith the performance of such activities such agents or representatives may bepaid fees for services rendered and may be reinbursed by the Agency forout-of-pocket expenses.

PART V MISCELLANEOUS

Agency's financial year.

21. The financial year of the Agency shall begin on the 1st day of January and end on the 31st day of December of each year except that for the year 1983 the financial year shall begin on the date of the establishment of the Agency and shall end on the 31st day of December 1983.

Audit.

22. The accounts of the Agency shall be audited by the Auditor Generalor by such independent auditors as His Majesty may appoint.

Preparation and publication of annual account and annual report.

[S 24/98]

23. The Agency shall within 6 months from the close of its financialyear submit to His Majesty the Sultan and Yang Di-Pertuan of Brunei Darussalamin Council —

(a) a copy of the annual accounts; and

(b) a report by the Board on the working of the Agencythroughout the year.

Power to appoint attorney.

24. The Agency may, by instrument under its common seal, appoint aperson (whether in Brunei Darussalam or in a place outside Brunei Darussalam) to be its attorney, and the person so appointed may,subject to the instrument, do any act or execute any power or function which heis authorised by the instrument to do or execute.

Validity of act and transactions of Agency.

25. The validity of an act or transaction of the Agency shall not becalled in question in any court on the ground that any provision of this Act hasnot been complied with.

Guarantee by Government.

26. The Government shall be responsible for the payment of all moneysdue by the Agency but nothing in this section authorises a creditor or otherperson claiming against the Agency to sue the Government in respect of hisclaim.

Fiat of Attorney General.

27. No prosecution in respect of any offence under this Act shall beinstituted without the consent in writing of the Attorney General.

Jurisdiction.

28. Notwithstanding the provisions of any other written law, a Courtof a Magistrate has jurisdiction to try all offences under this Act and toimpose the full penalty prescribed therefor.

[S 7/87]

Power of Agency to make regulations.

29. The Agency may, with the approval of His Majesty, make regulationsfor the better carrying out of the objects and purposes of this Act.

Preliminary acts and expenses.

30. Notwithstanding the provisions of section 1 of this Act theMinister of Finance may at any time before the date of the coming into operationof Part II of this Act do all such acts and incur all such expenses as he mayconsider necessary in connection with the establishment of the Agency; and uponthat date all such acts and expenses shall be deemed to have been done andincurred by the board.

PART VI TRANSITIONAL

Transitional provisions.

31. Any legal proceeding or cause of action pending or existing immediately before the commencement of this Act by or against the Government in respect of any functions or assets which under and by virtue of this Act are transferred to, or vested in, the Agency, may be continued and enforced by or against the Agency as it might have been by or against the Government, as the case may be, had this Act not come into operation.

IMPORTANT EXPORT-IMPORT REGULATIONS

Examination is carried out after the declaration of goods has been accepted and duties have been collected.

Goods for examination must be produced by the importer or the importer's agent at prescribed places during the normal working hours. If an importer or the importer's agent request his/her goods to examined outsite the normal working hours, he/she has to pay overtime fees to Customs.

- Examination is carried out in the presence of the importer or the importer's agent. He/she will be responsible for opening, weighting, sorting and marking of goods and all other necessary operations as directed by the Customs Officer.
- Examination is carried out to the satisfaction of the Customs Officer. He/she may, as his/her duty requires, take samples of any goods or cause such goods to be detained.

LICENCE OR PERMIT

Licence or Permit is a verification or approval given/issued by the relevant Government Department/Agency responsible for the commodities before importation or exportation.

Application of licence/permit

Written application or completed form (subject to the requirement of the Department/Agency) must be submitted to the Government/Agency responsible for such prohibited and controlled commodities.

Additional requirement

There are some prohibited or controlled commodities that require A.P (Approval Permit) issued by the RCED other than the license/permit issued by the relevant Government Agency before being imported or exported.

Types of commodities and issuing Government Department/Agency

Types of Commodities	Government/Agency	Hotlines/email
Religious Publications/ Prints, Films, CD, LD VCD, DVD, Cassette, Recital of Al-Quran, Hadith, Religious books, Talisman commodities (such as textiles/clothing /etc.), bearing dubious Chop/photo	Royal Brunei Police Force	-+673-2459500 -info@police.gov.bn
	Islamic Dakwah Center	-+673-2382525 -info@pusat-dakwah.gov.bn
	Internal Security Department	-+673-2223225 -info@internal-security.gov.bn

Halal, Fresh, Cold And Frozen Meat	Halal Import Permit Issuing Board	-+673-2382525 -info@religious-affairs.gov.bn
	Health Services Department	-+673-2381640 -info@moh.gov.bn
	Agriculture Department	-+673-2380144 -info@agriculture.gov.bn
	Royal Customs and Excise department	-+673-2382333 -info@customs.gov.bn
Firearms, Explosives, Fire Crackers, Dangerous Weapons, Scrap Metal	Royal Brunei Police Force	-+673-2459500 -info@agriculture.gov.bn
Plants, Crops, Live Animals, Vegetables, Fruits, Eggs	Agriculture Department	-+673-2380144 -info@police.gov.bn
Fishes, Prawns, Shells, Water Organisms and Fishing equipments etc	Fisheries Department	-+673-2382068 -info@fisheries.gov.bn
Poison, chemicals and radioactive materials. Medicines, Herbal, Health Foods, Soft Drinks and Snacks.	Ministry of Health (Refer to the Food Quality Control Section. Health Services Department) (Refer to Medical Enforcement Section, Pharmaceutical Services Department	-+673-2381640 -info@moh.gov.bn
Radio Transmitter and Receiver and Communications Equipment such as Telephone, Fax	Info-Communication Technology Industry (AiTi)	-+673-2333780 -aiti@brunet.bn

For additional analytical, business and investment opportunities information, please contact Global Investment & Business Center, USA at (703) 370-8082. Fax: (703) 370-8083. E-mail: ibpusa3@gmail.com Global Business and Investment Info Databank - www.ibpus.com

Machines, Walkie-
Talkie, etc.

Used Vehicles such as Cars, Motorcycles, Mini Buses, Pickups, Trucks, Trailers and non-motor vehicles such as Bicycles	Land Transport Department Royal Customs and Excise Department	-+673-2451979 -info@land-transport.gov.bn -+673-2382333 -info@customs.gov.bn
Timber and products thereof	Forestry Department	-+673-2381013 -info@forestry.gov.bn
Badges, Banners, Souvenirs comprising of Government Flags and emblems, Royals Regalias, Government flags and crests	Adat Istiadat Department	-+673-2244545 -info@adat-istiadat.gov.bn
Historical Antiques made 2244545 or found in Brunei	Museums Department	-+673- -info@museums.gov.bn
Mineral water and Building Construction Materials such as cements	Ministry of Industry and Primary Resources	-+673-2382822 -info@mipr.gov.bn
Rice, Sugar and Salt	Information Technology and State Store Department	-+673-2382822 -info@itss.gov.bn
Broadcasting Equipments such as Parabola, Decorder, etc.	Prime Minister's Office	-+673-2242780 -info@jpm.gov.bn

CUSTOM IMPORT DUTY (CUSTOM TAXES)

According to Section 9 Part B of Customs Import Duties Order 1973, passengers aged 17 and above arriving to this country are allowed to bring in their personal effect not exceeding the given concession as follows:-

Personally used goods (not new)

- Perfume - 60 milliliters
- Scented Water - 250 grams
- Cigarettes - 200 sticks or Tobacco - 250 grams
- Alcoholic beverages
  For non-muslim passengers over 17 years of age may be allowed to bring in not more than:-
  ▶ 2 bottles of liquor (approximately 2 liters)
  ▶ 12 cans of beer @ 330ml

- The importer may only import alcoholic liquor not less than 48 hours since the last importation.

- The alcoholic liquor shall be for importer's personal used and not to be given, transferred or sold to another person.

- The alcoholic liquor shall be stored and consumed at the place of residence of importer.

- The owner should declare liquor to Customs Officers in charge.

- Liquor form can be obtained from any Customs Control Posts or Customs Branches of Passenger Ships.

IMPORT AND EXPORT PROCEDURES OF GOODS UNDER CEPT SCHEME.   DOCUMENT PROCEDURE

Type of declaration

- For import - Customs Import Declaration.
- For export - Customs Export Declaration.

Processing and approval
Traders are required to submit their application to the Customs at the point of importation or exportation.

Requirement for issuing CEPT form
- Manufactures must first apply to the Ministry of Foreign Affairs and Trade (MoFAT).
- Application must be complied with rules of origin of the CEPT Scheme.
- With the approved CEPT Form D, the manufacturers or exporters may apply for the Customs Export Declarations.

Customs Export Declarations

For additional analytical, business and investment opportunities information,
please contact Global Investment & Business Center, USA
at (703) 370-8082. Fax: (703) 370-8083. E-mail: ibpusa3@gmail.com
Global Business and Investment Info Databank - www.ibpus.com

The CEPT Form D comprises of 4 copies. The original and triplicate are given to the importer for submission to the Customs authority at the importing country. The duplicate copy is retained by MoFAT and the quadruplicate is retained by the manufacturer or exporter.

Import Procedure

The importer shall produce the cargoes together with Customs Import Declaration, CEPT Form D, invoice, packing list, bill of landing/airway bill and other relevent supporting document to the Customs at the entry point for verification and examination.

- Dutiable goods imported to Brunei Darussalam are subject to Customs Import Duties Order 2007. ASEAN Common Effective Preferential Tariff (CEPT) could be given to importer based on qualification given by Ministry of Foreign Affairs and Trade (MoFAT). Most import duties are imposed based on Ad Valorem rate and only some taxes are based on specific rate. Ad Valorem is the percentage, for example, 20% of the price of good, while specific rate is calculated by the amount of weight or quantity such as $60 per kg or $220 per tonne. Determination of classification of imported goods whether dutiable or not are based on Customs Import Duties Order 2007. Since 1973 Brunei did not impose duties on exported goods. It is intended to promote local enterpreneurship.

CUSTOMS IMPORT DUTY GUIDE

Every person arriving in Negara Brunei Darussalam shall declare all dutiable goods in his possession, either on his person OR in any baggages OR in any vehicles to the proper officer of customs for examination.
If failed to do so, such goods shall be deemed to be uncustomed goods and imprisonment OR fine can be imposed.

Dutiable Goods
All goods subject to payment of customs duty and on such duty has not yet been paid.
According to paragraph 3(3) of customs import duties order 2007 where the total amount of import duty:

- Is less than $1 no import duty shall be charged.
- Exceed $1 and includes a fraction of $ 1, the fraction shall be treated as a complete dollar.
Importer of Dutiable Goods shall:
- Declare his/her goods.
- Produce documents such as invoice, bill and etc.
- Produce customs dutiable import declaration form no 5/C-16. (If necessary)

List of some Dutiable Goods and rate of Customs Import Duty

DUTIABLE GOODS	RATE OF CUSTOMS IMPORT DUTY
Coffee (not roasted)	11 cents/ 1 kg
Coffee (roasted)	22 cents/ 1 kg
Tea	22 cents/ 1 kg
Instant coffee/tea (Extract, essences and concentrates)/ coffee mate	5%
Grease	11 cents/ 1 kg
Lubricants	44 cents/ 1 kg
Carpet and other textile floor covering	5%
Mat and matting	10%
Wood and articles of wood	20%
Footware, slippers and the like	5%
Headgear and parts thereof	10%
Cosmetic, perfumes, toilet waters, soap, hair shampoo and other washing preparations	5%
Other preparations for use on the hair	30%
Electrical goods	5% OR 20%
Auto parts	20%
Articles of apparel and clothing accessories, of leather OR of composition leather	10%
Jewellery including imitation jewellery	5%
Clocks and watches and parts thereof	5%
Musical instruments	10%

EXPORT-IMPORT PROCEDURES

Goods To Be Imported & Export

All goods may be imported or exported except for restricted, prohibited and controlled goods under Section 31 of the Customs order, 2006.

Customs Declaration

Every imported & exported goods should be declared to the RCED by a declaration form except for the following goods:
- Passenger hand baggage's or personal effect on arrival.
- Goods arriving by post except for dutiable goods.

Declaration should give full and true account of the number of packages, cases description of goods, value, weight, measure or quantity and country of origin of the goods.

Customs Declaration Form must be submitted in triplicate and attached together with the following supporting documents :
- Invoice or purchase bill.
- Freight and Insurance Payment Slips.
- Delivery Order or Air Waybill.
- Packing List.

Other than the above documents, importer should also provide other documents related to the

imported goods required by Customs coinciding with the declaration of goods such as:
- Certificate of Origin.
- Certificate of Analysis.
- A.P (Approval Permit) of the RCED.
- Import license issued by the relevant Government Department/Agencies.
- Verification Certificate of a recognized foreign agency.
- Other relevant documents.
- Personal qualified to declare.

The owners:

- The owners or importers or exporters are qualified to declare the imported/exported goods to RCED.

Representatives:

- The owner may authorize the agents or forwarders as their representatives in declaration.

Conditions of qualification of importer and exporter:

- Trader or Agent ID registrations;
- Every company or agents/forwarder must be registered with the RCED.
- Individual registration is not compulsory however customers (traders) are advised to make use of the services of Customs agents (forwarders).

Registration of Company:

- Application form available at the Customer Services Unit of RCED Headquaters, Jalan Menteri Besar.
- The application will be entered into the computer system of RCED, i.e Computer Control and Information System (CCIS).

Documents for Registration:

- A copy of the company's registration certificate.

- A copy of smart identity card.

CHAPTER 196 ELECTRONIC TRANSACTIONS ACT

AN ACT TO MAKE PROVISION FOR THE SECURITY AND USE OF ELECTRONIC TRANSACTIONS AND FOR CONNECTED PURPOSES

Commencement (except Part X): 1st May 2001 [S 40/01]

PART I PRELIMINARY

CITATION.

1. (1) This Act may be cited as the Electronic Transactions Act.

(2) The Minister may, with the approval of His Majesty the Sultan and Yang Di-Pertuan, by notification in the *Gazette*, appoint different dates for the commencement of different provisions of this Act and for different purposes of the same provision.

INTERPRETATION.

2. In this Act, unless the context otherwise requires —

"asymmetric cryptosystem" means a system capable of generating a secure key pair, consisting of a private key for creating a digital signature, and a public key to verify the digital signature;

"certification authority" means a person who or an organisation that issues a certificate;

"certification practice statement" means a statement issued by a certification authority to specify the practices that the certification authority employs in issuing certificates;

"Controller" means the Controller of Certification Authorities appointed under section 41(1) and includes a Deputy or an Assistant Controller of Certification Authorities appointed under section 41(2);

"correspond", in relation to private or public keys, means to belong to the same key pair;

"data message" means information generated, sent, received or stored by electronic, optical or similar means, including, but not limited to, electronic data interchange (EDI), electronic mail, telegram, telex or telecopy;

"digital signature" means an electronic signature consisting of a transformation of an electronic record using an asymmetric cryptosystem and a hash function such that a person having the initial untransformed electronic record and the signer's public key can accurately determine —

(a)
whether the transformation was created using the private key that corresponds to the signer's public key; and

(b)
whether the initial electronic record has been altered since the transformation was made;

"electronic record" means a record generated, communicated, received or stored by electronic, magnetic, optical or other means in an information system or for transmission from one information system to another;

"electronic signature" means any letters, characters, numbers or other symbols in digital form attached to or logically associated with an electronic record, and executed or adopted with the intention of authenticating or approving the electronic record;

"hash function" means an algorithm mapping or translating one sequence of bits into another, generally smaller, set (the hash result) such that —

(a)
a record yields the same hash result every time the algorithm is executed using the same record as input;

(b)

it is computationally infeasible that a record can be derived or reconstituted from the hash result produced by the algorithm; and

(c)

it is computationally infeasible that 2 records can be found that produce the same hash result using the algorithm;

"information" includes data, text, images, sound, codes, computer programs, software and databases;

"information system" means a system for generating, sending, receiving, storing or otherwise processing data messages;

"key pair", in an asymmetric cryptosystem, means a private key and its mathematically related public key, having the property that the public key can verify a digital signature that the private key creates;

"licensed certification authority" means a certification authority licensed by the Controller pursuant to regulations made under section 42;

"Minister" means the Minister of Finance;

"operational period of a certificate" begins on the date and time the certificate is issued by a certification authority (or on any later date and time stated in the certificate), and ends on the date and time it expires as stated in the certificate or when it is earlier revoked or suspended;

"private key" means the key of a key pair used to create a digital signature;

"public key" means the key of a key pair used to verify a digital signature;

"record" means information that is inscribed, stored or otherwise fixed on a tangible medium or that is stored in an electronic or other medium and is retrievable in perceivable form;

"repository" means a system for storing and retrieving certificates or other information relevant to certificates;

"revoke a certificate" means to permanently end the operational period of a certificate from a specified time;

"rule of law" includes a written law;

"security procedure" means a procedure for the purpose of —

(a)

verifying that an electronic record is that of a specific person; or

B.L.R.O. 4/2008

(b)

detecting error or alteration in the communication, content or storage of an electronic record since a specific point in time,

which may require the use of algorithms or codes, identifying words or numbers, encryption, answerback or acknowledgement procedures, or similar security devices;

"signed" or "signature" includes any symbol executed or adopted, or any methodology or procedure employed or adopted, by a person with the intention of authenticating a record, including electronic or digital methods;

"subscriber" means a person who is the subject named or identified in a certificate issued to him and who holds a private key that corresponds to a public key listed in that certificate;

"suspend a certificate" means to temporarily suspend the operational period of a certificate from a specified time;

"transaction" includes a transaction of a non-commercial nature;

"trustworthy system" means computer hardware, software and procedures that —

(a) are reasonably secure from intrusion and misuse;

(b) provide a reasonable level of availability, reliability and correct operation;

(c) are reasonably suited to performing their intended functions; and

(d) adhere to generally accepted security procedures;

"valid certificate" means a certificate that a certification authority has issued and which the subscriber listed in it has accepted,

"verify a digital signature", in relation to a given digital signature, record and public key, means to determine accurately —

(a) that the digital signature was created using the private key corresponding to the public key listed in the certificate; and

(b) the record has not been altered since its digital signature was created.

PURPOSES AND CONSTRUCTION.

3. (1) This Act shall be construed consistently with what is commercially reasonable under the circumstances and to give effect to the following purposes —

(a) to facilitate electronic communications by means of reliable electronic records;

(b) to facilitate electronic commerce, eliminate barriers to electronic commerce resulting from uncertainties over writing and signature requirements, and to promote the development of the legal and business infrastructure necessary to implement secure electronic commerce;

(c) to facilitate electronic filing of documents with government agencies and statutory corporations, and to promote efficient delivery of government services by means of reliable electronic records;

(d)

to minimise the incidence of forged electronic records, intentional and unintentional alteration of records, and fraud in electronic commerce and other electronic transactions;

(e)

to help to establish uniformity of rules, regulations and standards regarding the authentication and integrity of electronic records; and

(f)

to promote public confidence in the integrity and reliability of electronic records and electronic commerce, and to foster the development of electronic commerce through the use of electronic signatures to lend authenticity and integrity to correspondence in any electronic medium.

(2)

In the interpretation of this Act, regard is to be had to its international origin and the need to promote uniformity in its application and the observance of good faith.

(3)

Questions concerning matters governed by this Act which are not expressly settled in it are to be settled in conformity with the general principles on which this Act is based.

APPLICATION.

4. (1) Parts II or IV shall not apply to any rule of law requiring writing or signatures in any of the following matters —

(a)

the creation of any legal instrument or document under any written law relating to Islamic law;

(b)

the creation or execution of a will under any written law relating wills;

(c) negotiable instruments;

(d)

the creation, performance or enforcement of an indenture, declaration of trust or power of attorney with the exception of constructive and resulting trusts;

(e)

any contract for the sale or other disposition of immovable property, or any interest in such property;

(f)

the conveyance of immovable property or the transfer of any interest in such property;

(g) documents of title relating to immovable property.

(2) The Minister may, with the approval of His Majesty the Sultan and Yang Di-Pertuan, by order in the *Gazette* modify the provisions of subsection (1) by adding, deleting or amending any class of transactions or matters mentioned therein.

VARIATION BY AGREEMENT.

5. As between parties involved in generating, sending, receiving, storing or otherwise processing electronic records, any provision of Parts II or IV may be varied by agreement.

PART II ELECTRONIC RECORDS AND SIGNATURES GENERALLY

LEGAL RECOGNITION OF ELECTRONIC RECORDS.

6. For the avoidance of doubt, it is hereby declared that information shall not be denied legal effect, validity or enforceability solely on the ground that it is in the form of an electronic record.

REQUIREMENT FOR WRITING.

7. Where any rule of law requires information to be written in writing to be presented in writing or provides for certain consequences if it is not, an electronic record satisfies that rule of law if the information contained therein is accessible so as to be usable for subsequent reference.

ELECTRONIC SIGNATURES.

8. (1) Where any rule of law requires a signature, or provides for certain consequences if a document is not signed, an electronic signature satisfies that rule of law.

(2) An electronic signature may be proved in any manner, including by showing that a procedure existed by which it is necessary for a party, in order to proceed further with a transaction, to have executed a symbol or security procedure for the purpose of verifying that an electronic record is that of such party.

RETENTION OF ELECTRONIC RECORDS.

9. (1) Where any rule of law requires that certain documents, records or information be retained, that requirement is satisfied by retaining them in the form of electronic records if the following conditions are satisfied —

(a)
   the information contained therein remains accessible so as to be usable for subsequent reference;

(b)
   the electronic record is retained in the format in which it was originally generated, sent or received, or in a format which can be demonstrated to represent accurately the information originally generated, sent or received;

B.L.R.O. 4/2008

(c)
   such information, if any, as enables the identification of the origin and destination of an electronic record and the date and time when it was sent or received, is retained; and

(d)
   the consent of the department or ministry of the Government, organ of State, or the statutory corporation which has supervision over the requirement for the retention of such records has been obtained.

(2)
   An obligation to retain documents, records or information in accordance with subsection (1)(c) shall not extend to any information necessarily and automatically generated solely for the purpose of enabling a record to be sent or received.

(3) A person may satisfy the requirement referred to in subsection
(1)
   by using the services of any other person, if the conditions in subsections (1)(a) to (d) are complied with.

(4)
   Nothing in this section shall —

(a)
   apply to any rule of law which expressly provides for the retention of documents, records or information in the form of electronic records;

(b)
preclude any department or ministry of the Government, organ of State or a statutory corporation from specifying additional requirements for the retention of electronic records that are subject to the jurisdiction of such department, ministry, organ of State or statutory corporation.

PART III LIABILITY OF NETWORK SERVICE PROVIDERS

LIABILITY OF NETWORK SERVICE PROVIDERS.

10. (1) A network service provider shall not be subject to any civil or criminal liability under any rule of law in respect of third-party material in the form of electronic records to which he merely provides access if such liability is founded on —

(a) the making, publication, dissemination or distribution of such materials or any statement made in such material; or
(b) the infringement of any rights subsisting in or in relation to such material.

(2) Nothing in this section shall affect —

(a) any obligation founded on contract;
(b) the obligation of a network service provider as such under a licensing or other regulatory regime established under any written law; or
(c) any obligation imposed under any written law or by a court to remove, block or deny access to any material.

(3)
   For the purposes of this section —

"providing access", in relation to third-party material, means the provision of the necessary technical means by which third-party material may be accessed and includes the automatic and temporary storage of the third-party material for the purpose of providing access;

"third-party", in relation to a network service provider, means a person over whom the provider has no effective control.

PART IV ELECTRONIC CONTRACTS

FORMATION AND VALIDITY.

11. (1) For the avoidance of doubt, it is hereby declared that in the context of the formation of contracts, unless otherwise agreed by the parties, an offer and the acceptance of an offer may be expressed by means of electronic records.

(2) Where an electronic record is used in the formation of a contract, that contract shall not be denied validity or enforceability on the sole ground that an electronic record was used for that purpose.

EFFECTIVENESS BETWEEN PARTIES.

For additional analytical, business and investment opportunities information,
please contact Global Investment & Business Center, USA
at (703) 370-8082. Fax: (703) 370-8083. E-mail: ibpusa3@gmail.com
Global Business and Investment Info Databank - www.ibpus.com

12. As between the originator and the addressee of an electronic record, a declaration of intent or other statement shall not be denied legal effect, validity or enforceability solely on the ground that it is in the form of an electronic record.

ATTRIBUTION.

13. (1) An electronic record is that of the originator if it was sent by the originator himself.

(2) As between the originator and the addressee, an electronic record is deemed to be that of the originator if it was sent —
(a) by a person who had the authority to act on behalf of the originator in respect of that electronic record; or
(b) by an information system programmed by or on behalf of the originator to operate automatically.

(3)
As between the originator and the addressee, an addressee is entitled to regard an electronic record as being that of the originator and to act on that assumption if —
(a) in order to ascertain whether the electronic record was that of the originator, the addressee properly applied a procedure previously agreed to by the originator for that purpose; or
(b) the data message as received by the addressee resulted from the actions of a person whose relationship with the originator or with any agent of the originator enabled that person to gain access to a method used by the originator to identify electronic records as its own.

(4) Subsection (3) shall not apply —

(a) from the time when the addressee has both received notice from the originator that the electronic record is not that of the originator and had reasonable time to act accordingly;
(b) in a case within subsection (3)*(b)*, at any time when the addressee knew or ought to have known, had it exercised reasonable care or used any agreed procedure, that the electronic record was not that of the originator; or
(c) if in all the circumstances of the case, it is unconscionable for the addressee to regard the electronic record as that of the originator or to act on that assumption.

(5)
Where an electronic record is that of the originator or is deemed to be that of the originator, or the addressee is entitled to act on that assumption, then, as between the originator and the addressee, the addressee is entitled to regard the electronic record received as being what the originator intended to send, and to act on that assumption.
(6)
The addressee is not so entitled when the addressee knew or should have known, had the addressee exercised reasonable care or used any agreed procedure, that the transmission resulted in any error in the electronic record as received.
(7)
The addressee is entitled to regard each electronic record received as a separate electronic record and to act on that assumption, except to the extent that the addressee duplicates another electronic record and the addressee knew or should have known, had the addressee exercised reasonable care or used any agreed procedure, that the electronic record was a duplicate.
(8)
Nothing in this section shall affect the law of agency or the law on the formation of contracts.

ACKNOWLEDGEMENT OF RECEIPT.

14. (1) Subsections (2), (3) and (4) shall apply where, on or before sending an electronic record, or by means of that electronic record, the originator has requested or has agreed with the addressee that receipt of the electronic record be acknowledged.

(2)

Where the originator has not agreed with the addressee that the acknowledgement be given in a particular form or by a particular method, an acknowledgement may be given by —

(a)

any communication by the addressee, automated or otherwise; or

(b)

any conduct of the addressee, sufficient to indicate to the originator that the electronic record has been received.

(3)

Where the originator has stated that the electronic record is conditional on receipt of the acknowledgement, the electronic record shall be treated as though it had never been sent, until the acknowledgement is received.

(4)

Where the originator has not stated that the electronic record is conditional on receipt of the acknowledgement, and the acknowledgement has not been received by the originator within the time, specified or agreed or, if no time has been specified or agreed within a reasonable time, the originator —

(a)

may give notice to the addressee stating that no acknowledgement has been received and specifying a reasonable time by which the acknowledgement must be received; and

(b)

if the acknowledgement is not received within the time specified in paragraph (a), may, upon notice to the addressee, treat the electronic record as though it has never been sent, or exercise any other rights it may have.

(5)

Where the originator receives the addressee's acknowledgement of receipt, it is presumed, unless evidence to the contrary is adduced, that the related electronic record was received by the addressee, but that presumption does not imply that the content of the electronic record corresponds to the content of the record received.

(6)

Where the received acknowledgement states that the related electronic record meets technical requirements, either agreed upon or set forth in applicable standards, it is presumed, unless evidence to the contrary is adduced, that those requirements have been met.

(7)

Except in so far as it relates to the sending or receipt of the electronic record, this Part is not intended to deal with the legal consequences that may flow either from that electronic record or from the acknowledgement of its receipt.

TIME AND PLACE OF DISPATCH AND RECEIPT.

15. (1) Unless otherwise agreed to between the originator and the addressee, the dispatch of an electronic record occurs when it enters an information system outside the control of the originator or the person who sent the electronic record on behalf of the originator.

(2)

Unless otherwise agreed between the originator and the addressee, the time of receipt of an electronic record is determined as follows —

(a)

if the addressee has designated an information system for the purpose of receiving electronic records, receipt occurs —

(i)

at the time when the electronic record enters the designated information system; or

(ii)

if the electronic record is sent to an information system of the addressee that is not the designated information system, at the time when the electronic record is retrieved by the addressee;

(b)

if the addressee has not designated such an information system, receipt occurs when the electronic record enters an information system of the addressee.

(3)

Subsection (2) shall apply notwithstanding that the place where the information system is located may be different from the place where the electronic record is deemed to be received under subsection (4).

(4)

Unless otherwise agreed between the originator and the addressee, an electronic record is deemed to be dispatched at the place where the originator has its place of business, and is deemed to be received at the place where the addressee has its place of business.

(5)

For the purposes of this section —

(a)

if the originator or the addressee has more than one place of business, the place of business is that which has the closest relationship to the underlying transaction or, where there is no underlying transaction, the principal place of business;

(b)

if the originator or the addressee does not have a place of business, reference is to be made to the usual place of residence; and

(c)

"usual place of residence" in relation to a body corporate, means the place where it is incorporated or otherwise legally constituted.

(6)

This section shall not apply to such circumstances as the Minister may by regulations prescribe.

PART V SECURE ELECTRONIC RECORDS AND SIGNATURES

SECURE ELECTRONIC RECORD.

16. (1) If a prescribed security procedure or a commercially reasonable security procedure agreed to by the parties involved has been properly applied to an electronic record to verify that the electronic record has not been altered since a specified point in time, such record shall be treated as a secure electronic record from such specified point in time to the time of verification.

(2) For the purposes of this section and of section 17, whether a security procedure is commercially reasonable shall be determined having regard to the purposes of the procedure and the commercial circumstances at the time the procedure was used, including —

(a) the nature of the transaction;
(b) the sophistication of the parties;
(c) the volume of similar transactions engaged in by either or all parties;
(d) the availability of alternatives offered to but rejected by any party;

(e) the cost of alternative procedures; and
(f) the procedures in general use for similar types of transactions.

SECURE ELECTRONIC SIGNATURE.

17. If, through the application of a prescribed security procedure or a commercially reasonable security procedure agreed to by the parties involved, it can be verified that all electronic signature was, at the time it was made —

(a) unique to the person using it;
(b) capable of identifying such person;
(c) created in a manner or using a means under the sole control of the person using it; and
(d) linked to the electronic record to which it relates in a manner such that if the record was changed the electronic signature would be invalidated, such signature shall be treated as a secure electronic signature.

PRESUMPTIONS RELATING TO SECURE ELECTRONIC RECORDS AND SIGNATURES.

18. (1) In any proceedings involving a secure electronic record, it shall be presumed, unless evidence to the contrary is adduced, that the secure electronic record has not been altered since the specific point in time to which the secure status relates.

(2)
> In any proceedings involving a secure electronic signature, it shall be presumed, unless evidence to the contrary is adduced, that —

(a) the secure electronic signature is the signature of the person with whom it correlates; and
(b) the secure electronic signature was affixed by that person with the intention of signing or approving the electronic record.

(3) In the absence of a secure electronic record or a secure electronic signature, nothing in this Part shall create any presumption relating to the authenticity and integrity of the electronic record or an electronic signature.

(4) For the purposes of this section —

"secure electronic record" means an electronic record treated as a secure electronic record by virtue of sections 16 or 19;

"secure electronic signature" means an electronic signature treated as a secure electronic signature by virtue of sections 17 or

PART VI EFFECT OF DIGITAL SIGNATURES

SECURE ELECTRONIC RECORD WITH DIGITAL SIGNATURE.

19. The portion of an electronic record that is signed with a digital signature shall be treated as a secure electronic record if the digital signature is a secure electronic signature by virtue of section 20.

SECURE DIGITAL SIGNATURE.

20. When any portion of an electronic record is signed with a digital signature, the digital signature shall be treated as a secure electronic signature with respect to such portion of the record if —

(a)
the digital signature was created during the operational period of a valid certificate and is verified by reference to the public key listed in such certificate; and

(b)
the certificate is considered trustworthy, in that it is an accurate binding of a public key to a person's identity because —

(i)
the certificate was issued by a licensed certification authority operating in compliance with the regulations made under section 42;

(ii)
the certificate was issued by a certification authority outside Brunei Darussalam recognised for this purpose by the Controller pursuant to requirements made under section 43;

(iii) the certificate was issued by a department or ministry of the Government, an organ of State or a statutory body or corporation approved by the Minister to act as a certification authority on such conditions as he may by regulations impose or specify; or

(iv) the parties have expressly agreed between themselves (sender and recipient) to use digital signatures as a security procedure, and the digital signature was properly verified by reference to the sender's public key.

PRESUMPTIONS REGARDING CERTIFICATES.

21. It shall be presumed, unless evidence to the contrary is adduced, that the information listed in a certificate issued by a licensed certification authority is correct, except for information identified as subscriber information which has not been verified, if the certificate was accepted by the subscriber.

UNRELIABLE DIGITAL SIGNATURES.

22. Unless otherwise provided by any rule of law or by contract, a person relying on a digitally signed electronic record assumes the risk that the digital signature is invalid as a signature or authentication of the signed electronic record, if reliance on the digital signature is not reasonable under the circumstances having regard to the following factors —

(a) facts which the person relying on the digitally signed electronic record knows or has notice of, including all facts listed in the certificate or incorporated in it by reference;
(b) the value or importance of the digitally signed record, if known;
(c) the course of dealing between the person relying on the digitally signed electronic record and the subscriber and any available indicia of reliability or unreliability apart from the digital signature; and
(d)
usage of trade, particularly trade conducted by trustworthy systems or other electronic means.

PART VII GENERAL DUTIES RELATING TO DIGITAL SIGNATURES

RELIANCE ON CERTIFICATES FORSEEABLE.

- 269 -

---

23. It is foreseeable that persons relying on a digital signature will also rely on a valid certificate containing the public key by which the digital signature can be verified.

PREREQUISITES TO PUBLICATION OF CERTIFICATE.

24. No person shall publish a certificate or otherwise make it available to a person known by that first-mentioned person to be in a position to rely on the certificate or on a digital signature that is verifiable with reference to a public key listed in the certificate, if that first-mentioned person knows that —

(a)
   the certification authority listed in the certificate has not issued it;
(b) the subscriber listed in the certificate has not accepted it; or
(c)
   the certificate has been revoked or suspended, unless such publication is for the purpose of verifying a digital signature created prior to such suspension or revocation.

PUBLICATION FOR FRAUDULENT PURPOSE.

25. Any person who knowingly creates, publishes or otherwise makes available a certificate for any fraudulent or unlawful purpose shall be guilty of an offence and be liable on conviction to a fine not exceeding $20,000, imprisonment for a term not exceeding 2 years or both.

FALSE OR UNAUTHORISED REQUEST.

26. Any person who knowingly misrepresents to a certification authority his identity or authorisation for the purpose of requesting for a certificate or for suspension or revocation of a certificate shall be guilty of an offence and be liable on conviction to a fine not exceeding $10,000, imprisonment for a term not exceeding 6 months or both.

PART VIII DUTIES OF CERTIFICATION AUTHORITIES

TRUSTWORTHY SYSTEM.

27. A certification authority must utilise trustworthy systems in performing its services.

DISCLOSURE.

28. (1) A certification authority shall disclose —

(a) its certificate that contains the public key corresponding to the private key used by that certification authority to digitally sign another certificate (referred to in this section as a certification authority certificate);
(b) any relevant certification practice statement;
(c)
   notice of the revocation or suspension of its certification authority certificate; and
(d) any other fact that materially and adversely affects either the reliability of a certificate that the authority has issued or the authority's ability to perform its services.

(2) In the event of an occurrence that materially and adversely affects a certification authority's trustworthy system or its certification authority certificate, the certification authority shall —

(a) use reasonable efforts to notify any person who is known to be or foreseeably will be affected by that occurrence; or

(b) act in accordance with procedures governing such an occurrence specified in its certification practice statement.

ISSUING OF CERTIFICATE.

29. (1) A certification authority may issue a certificate to a prospective subscriber only after the certification authority —

(a) has received a request for issuance from the prospective subscriber; and

(b) has —

(i) if it has a certification practice statement, complied with all of the practices and procedures set forth in such certification practice statement including procedures regarding identification of the perspective subscriber; or

B.L.R.O. 4/2008

(ii) in the absence of a certification practice statement, complied with the conditions in subsection (2).

(2) In the absence of a certification practice statement, the certification authority shall confirm by itself or through an authorised agent that —

(a) the prospective subscriber is the person to be listed in the certificate to be issued;

(b) if the prospective subscriber is acting through one or more agents, the subscriber authorised the agent to have custody of the subscriber's private key and to request issuance of a certificate listing the corresponding public key;

(c) the information in the certificate to be issued is accurate;

(d) the prospective subscriber rightfully holds the private key corresponding to the public key to be listed in the certificate;

(e) the prospective subscriber holds a private key capable of creating a digital signature; and

(f) the public key to be listed in the certificate can be used to verify a digital signature affixed by the private key held by the prospective subscriber.

REPRESENTATIONS UPON ISSUANCE OF CERTIFICATE.

30. (1) By issuing a certificate, a certification authority represents, to any person who reasonably relies on the certificate or a digital signature verifiable by the public key listed in the certificate, that the certification authority has issued the certificate in accordance with any applicable certification practice statement incorporated by reference in the certificate, or of which the relying person has notice.

(2)

In the absence of such certification practice statement, the certification authority represents that it has confirmed that —

(a) the certification authority has complied with all applicable requirements of this Act in issuing the certificate, and if the certification authority has published the certificate or otherwise made it available to such relying person, that the subscriber listed in the certificate has accepted it;

(b) the subscriber identified in the certificate holds the private key corresponding to the public key listed in the certificate;

(c) the subscriber's public key and private key constitute a functioning key pair;

(d) all information in the certificate is accurate, unless the certification authority has stated in the certificate or incorporated by reference in the certificate a statement that the accuracy of specified information is not confirmed; and

(e) that the certification authority has no knowledge of any material fact which if it had been included in the certificate would adversely affect the reliability of the representations in paragraphs (a) to (d).

(3) Where there is an applicable certification practice statement which has been incorporated by reference in the certificate, or of which the relying person has notice, subsection (2) shall apply to the extent that the representations are not inconsistent with the certification practice statement.

SUSPENSION OF CERTIFICATE.

31. Unless the certification authority and the subscriber agree otherwise, the certification authority that issued a certificate shall suspend the certificate as soon as possible after receiving a request by a person whom the certification authority believes to be —

(a) the subscriber named in the certificate;
(b) a person duly authorised to act for that subscriber; or

(c) a person acting on behalf of that subscriber, who is unavailable.

REVOCATION OF CERTIFICATE.

32. A certification authority shall revoke a certificate that is issued after —

(a) receiving a request for revocation by the subscriber named in the certificate; and, confirming that the person requesting revocation is the subscriber or is an agent of the subscriber with authority to request the revocation;
 (b) receiving a certified copy of the subscriber's death certificate, or upon confirming by other evidence that the subscriber is dead; or
(c) upon presentation of documents effecting a dissolution of the subscriber, or upon confirming by other evidence that the subscriber has been dissolved or has ceased to exist.

REVOCATION WITHOUT SUBSCRIBER'S CONSENT.

33. (1) A certification authority shall revoke a certificate, regardless of whether the subscriber listed in the certificate consents, if the certification authority confirms that —

(a) a material fact represented in the certificate is false;

(b) a requirement for issuance of the certificate was not satisfied;
(c) the certification authority's private key or trustworthy system was compromised in a manner materially affecting the certificate's reliability;
(d) an individual subscriber is dead; or
(e) a subscriber has been dissolved, wound-up or otherwise ceased to exist.

(2) Upon effecting such a revocation, other than under subsections (1)(a) or (e), the certification authority shall immediately notify the subscriber named in the revoked certificate.

NOTICE OF SUSPENSION.

34. (1) Immediately upon suspension of a certificate by a certification authority, the certification authority shall publish a signed notice of the suspension in the repository specified in the certificate for publication of notice of suspension.

(2) Where one or more repositories are specified, the certification authority shall publish signed notices of the suspension in all such repositories.

NOTICE OF REVOCATION.

35. (1) Immediately upon revocation of a certificate by a certification authority, the certification authority shall publish a signed notice of the revocation in the repository specified in the certificate for publication of notice of revocation.

(2) Where one or more repositories are specified, the certification authority shall publish signed notices of the revocation in all such repositories.

PART IX DUTIES OF SUBSCRIBERS

GENERATING KEY PAIR.

36. (1) If the subscriber generates the key pair whose public key is to be listed in a certificate issued by a certification authority and accepted by the subscriber, the subscriber shall generate that key pair using a trustworthy system.

(2) This section shall not apply to a subscriber who generates the key pair using a system approved by the certification authority.

OBTAINING CERTIFICATE.

37. All material representations made by the subscriber to a certification authority for purposes of obtaining a certificate, including all information known to the subscriber and represented in the certificate, shall be accurate and complete to the best of the subscriber's knowledge and belief, regardless of whether such representation are confirmed by the certification authority.

ACCEPTANCE OF CERTIFICATE.

38. (1) A subscriber shall be deemed to have accepted a certificate if he —

(a) publishes or authorises the publication of a certificate —

(i) to one or more persons; or
(ii) in a repository; or

(b) otherwise demonstrates approval of a certificate while knowing or having notice of its contents.

(2) By accepting a certificate issued by himself or a certification authority, the subscriber listed in the certificate certifies to all who reasonably rely on the information contained in the certificate that —

(a) the subscriber rightfully holds the private key corresponding to the public key listed in the certificate;

(b) all representations made by the subscriber to the certification authority and material to the information listed in the certificate are true; and

(c) all information in the certificate that is within the knowledge of the subscriber is true.

CONTROL OF PRIVATE KEY.

39. (1) By accepting a certificate issued by a certification authority, the subscriber identified in the certificate assumes a duty to exercise reasonable care to retain control of the private key corresponding to the public key listed in such certificate and prevent its disclosure to a person not authorised to create the subscriber's digital signature.

(2) Such duty shall continue during the operational period of the certificate and during any period of suspension of the certificate.

INITIATING SUSPENSION OR REVOCATION.

40. A subscriber who has accepted a certificate shall as soon as possible request the issuing certification authority to suspend or revoke the certificate if the private key corresponding to the public key listed in the certificate has been compromised.

PART X REGULATION OF CERTIFICATION AUTHORITIES

APPOINTMENT OF CONTROLLER AND OTHER OFFICERS.

41. (1) The Minister shall be the Controller of Certification Authorities for the purposes of this Act.

(2)
The Minister may appoint such number of Deputy and Assistant Controllers of Certification Authorities and officers as he considers necessary to exercise and perform all or any of the powers and duties of the Controller under this Act or any regulations made thereunder.

(3)
The Controller, the Deputy and Assistant Controllers and officers appointed under subsection (2) shall exercise, discharge and perform the powers, duties and functions conferred on the Controller under this Act or any regulations made thereunder, subject to such directions as may be issued by the Minister.

(4)
The Controller shall maintain a publicly accessible database containing a certification authority disclosure record for each licensed certification authority which shall contain all the particulars required under the regulations made under this Act.

(5)
In the application of the provisions of this Act to certificates issued by the Controller and digital signatures verified by reference to those certificates, the Controller shall be deemed to be a licensed certification authority.

REGULATION OF CERTIFICATION AUTHORITIES.

42. (1) The Minister may, with the approval of His Majesty the Sultan and Yang Di-Pertuan, make regulations for the regulation and licensing of certification authorities and to define when a digital signature qualifies as a secure electronic signature.

(2) Without prejudice to the generality of subsection (1), the Minister may make regulations for or with respect to —

(a)

applications for licences or renewal of licences of certification authorities and their authorised representatives and matters incidental thereto;

(b)

the activities of certification authorities including the manner, method and place of soliciting business, the conduct of such solicitation and the prohibition of such solicitation from members of the public by certification authorities which are not licensed;

(c) the standards to be maintained by certification authorities;

(d)

prescribing the appropriate standards with respect to the qualifications, experience and training of applicants for any licence or their employees;

(e)

prescribing the conditions for the conduct of business by a certification authority;

(f)

providing for the content and distribution of written, printed or visual material and advertisements that may be distributed or used by a person in respect of a digital certificate or key;

(g)

prescribing the form and content of a digital certificate or key;

(h)

prescribing the particulars to be recorded in, or in respect of, accounts kept by certification authorities;

(i)

providing for the appointment and remuneration of an auditor appointed under the regulations and for the costs of an audit carried out under the regulations;

(j)

providing for the establishment and regulation of any electronic system by a certification authority, whether by itself or in conjunction with other certification authorities, and for the imposition and variation of such requirements, conditions or restrictions as the Controller may think fit;

(k)

the manner in which a holder of a licence conducts its dealings with its customers, conflicts of interest involving the holder of a licence and its customers, and the duties of a holder of a licence to its customers with respect to digital certificates;

(l)

prescribing any forms for the purposes of the regulations; and

(m)

prescribing fees to be paid in respect of any matter or thing required for the purposes of this Act and the regulations.

(3) Regulations made under this section may provide that a contravention of a specified provisions shall be an offence and may provide for penalties for a fine not exceeding $50,000, imprisonment for a term not exceeding one year or both.

RECOGNITION OF FOREIGN CERTIFICATION AUTHORITIES.

43. The Minister may, by order published in the *Gazette,* recognise certification authorities outside Brunei Darussalam that satisfy the prescribed requirements for any of the following purposes —

(a) the recommended reliance limit, if any, specified in a certificate issued by the certification authority;

(b) the presumption referred to in sections 20*(b)*(ii) and 21.

RECOMMENDED RELIANCE LIMIT.

44. (1) A licensed certification authority shall, in issuing a certificate to a subscriber, specify a recommended reliance limit in the certificate.

(2) The licensed certification authority may specify different limits in different certificates as it considers fit.

LIABILITY LIMITS FOR LICENSED CERTIFICATION AUTHORITIES.

45. Unless a licensed certification authority waives the application of this section, a licensed certification authority —

(a)

shall not be liable for any loss caused by reliance on a false or forged digital signature of a subscriber if, with respect to the false or forged digital signature, the licensed certification authority complied with the requirements of this Act;

(b)

shall not be liable in excess of the amount specified in the certificate as its recommended reliance limit for either —

(i) a loss caused by reliance on a misrepresentation in the certificate of any fact that the licensed certification authority is required to confirm; or

ii) failure to comply with sections 29 and 30 in issuing the certificate.

REGULATION OF REPOSITORIES.

46. The Minister may, with the approval of His Majesty the Sultan and Yang Di-Pertuan, make regulations for the purpose of ensuring the quality of repositories and the services they provide, including provisions for the standards, licensing or accreditation of repositories.

PART XI GOVERNMENT USE OF ELECTRONIC RECORDS AND SIGNATURES

ACCEPTANCE OF ELECTRONIC FILING AND ISSUE OF DOCUMENTS.

47. (1) Any department or ministry of the Government, organ of State or statutory body that, pursuant to any written law —

(a) accepts the filing of documents, or requires that documents be created or retained;

(b)

issues any permit, licence or approval; or

(c) provides for the method and manner of payment,

may, notwithstanding anything to the contrary in such written law —

(i) accept the filing of such documents, or the creation or retention of such documents in the form of electronic records;
(ii) issue such permit, licence or approval in the form of electronic records; or

(iii) make such payment in electronic form.

(2) In any case where a department or ministry of the Government, organ of State or statutory body decides to perform any of the functions in subsections (1)(i), (ii) or (iii), it may specify —
(a) the manner and format in which such electronic records shall be filed, created, retained or issued;
(b) where such electronic records have to be signed, the type of electronic signature required including, if applicable, a requirement that the sender use a digital signature or other secure electronic signature;
(c) the manner and format in which such signature shall be affixed to the electronic record, and the identity of or criteria that shall be met by any certification authority used by the person filing the document;
(d) control processes and procedures as appropriate to ensure adequate integrity, security and confidentiality of electronic records or payments; and
(e) any other required attributes for electronic records or payments that are currently specified for corresponding paper documents.
(3)
Nothing in this Act shall by itself compel any department or ministry of the Government, organ of State or statutory body to accept or issue any document in the form of electronic records.

PART XII GENERAL

OBLIGATION OF CONFIDENTIALITY.

48. (1) Except for the purposes of this Act or for any prosecution for an offence under any written law or pursuant to any order of court, no person who has, pursuant to any powers conferred under this Part, obtained access to any electronic record, book, register, correspondence, information, document or other material shall disclose such electronic record, book, register, correspondence, information, document or other material to any other person.

(2) Any person who contravenes subsection (1) shall be guilty of an offence and be liable on conviction to a fine not exceeding $10,000, imprisonment for a term not exceeding one year or both.

OFFENCES BY BODIES CORPORATE.

49. Where an offence under this Act or any regulations made thereunder committed by a body corporate is proved to have committed with the consent or connivance of, or to be attributable to any act or default on the part of, any director, manager, secretary or other similar officer of that body corporate, or of any person purporting to act in any such capacity, he, as well as the body corporate, shall also be guilty of that offence and be liable to be proceeded against and punished accordingly.

AUTHORISED OFFICERS OR EMPLOYEES.

50. (1) The Controller may in writing authorise any officer or employee to exercise any of the powers of the Controller under this Part.

(2)

Any such officer or employee shall be deemed to be a public servant for the purposes of the Penal Code (Chapter 22).

(3)

In exercising any of the powers of enforcement under this Act, an authorised officer or employee shall on demand produce to the person against whom he is acting the authority issued to him by the Controller.

CONTROLLER MAY GIVE DIRECTIONS FOR COMPLIANCE.

51. (1) The Controller may by notice in writing direct a certification authority or any officer or employee thereof to take such measures or stop carrying on such activities as are specified in the notice if they are necessary to ensure compliance with the provisions of this Act or any regulations made thereunder.

(2) Any person who fails to comply with any direction specified in a notice issued under subsection (1) shall be guilty of an offence and be liable on conviction to a fine not exceeding $50,000, imprisonment for a term not exceeding one year or both.

POWER TO INVESTIGATE.

52. (1) The Controller or an authorised officer or employee may investigate the activities of a certification authority in relation to its compliance with this Act and any regulations made thereunder.

(2) For the purposes of subsection (1), the Controller may in writing issue an order to a certification authority to further its investigation or to secure compliance with this Act or any regulations made thereunder.

ACCESS TO COMPUTERS AND DATA.

53. (1) The Controller or an authorised officer or employee shall —

(a) be entitled at any time to —
(i) have access to and inspect and check the operation of any computer system and any associated apparatus or material which he has reasonable cause to suspect is or has been in use in connection with any offence under this Act;
(ii) use or caused to be used any such computer system to search any data contained in or available to such computer system; or
(b) be entitled to require —
(i) the person by whom or on whose behalf the Controller or authorised officer has reasonable cause to suspect the computer is or has been so used; or
(ii) any person having charge of, or otherwise concerned with the operation of, the computer, apparatus or material, to provide him with such reasonable technical and other assistance as he may require for the purposes of paragraph (a).

(2) Any person who obstructs the lawful exercise of the powers under subsection (1)(a) or who fails to comply with a request under subsection (1)(b) is guilty of an offence and liable on conviction to a fine not exceeding $20,000, imprisonment for a term not exceeding one year or both.

OBSTRUCTION OF AUTHORISED OFFICER OR EMPLOYEE.

54. Any person who obstructs, impedes, assaults or interferes with the Controller or any authorised officer or employee in the performance of his functions under this Act shall be guilty of an offence.

PRODUCTION OF DOCUMENTS, DATA ETC.

55. The Controller or an authorised officer or employee shall, for the purposes of the execution of this Act, have power to do all or any of the following —

(a) require the production of records, accounts, data and documents kept by a licensed certification authority and to inspect, examine and copy any of them;
(b) require the production of any identification document from any person in relation to any offence under this Act or any regulations made thereunder;
(c) make such inquiry as may be necessary to ascertain whether the provisions of this Act or any regulations made thereunder have been complied with.

GENERAL PENALTIES.

56. Any person guilty of an offence under this Act or any regulations made thereunder for which no penalty is expressly provided shall be liable on conviction to a fine not exceeding $20,000, imprisonment for a term not exceeding 6 months or both.

SANCTION OF PUBLIC PROSECUTOR.

57. No prosecution in respect of any offence under this Act or any regulations made thereunder shall be instituted except by or with the sanction of the Public Prosecutor.

JURISDICTION OF COURTS.

58. A Court of a Magistrate shall have jurisdiction to hear and determine all offences under this Act and any regulations made thereunder and, notwithstanding anything to the contrary in any other written law, shall have power to impose the full penalty or punishment in respect of any such offence.

COMPOSITION OF OFFENCES.

59. (1) The Controller may, in his discretion, compound any offence under this Act or any regulations made thereunder which is prescribed as being an offence which may be compounded by collecting from any person reasonably suspected of having committed that offence a sum not exceeding $5,000.

(2) The Minister may, with the approval of His Majesty the Sultan and Yang Di-Pertuan, make regulations prescribing the offences which may be compounded under this Act.

POWER TO EXEMPT.

60. Notwithstanding anything contained in this Act or in any other written law, the Minister may exempt, subject to such terms and conditions as he thinks fit, any person or classes of person from all or any of the provisions of this Act or any regulations made thereunder.

REGULATIONS.

61. (1) The Minister may, with the approval of His Majesty the Sultan and Yang Di-Pertuan, make regulations to prescribe anything which is required to be prescribed under this Act and generally for the carrying out of the provisions of this Act.

(2) Any regulations made under this Act may make different provision for different cases or classes of case and for different purposes of the same provision.

TRAVEL TO BRUNEI

US STATE DEPARTMENT SUGGESTIONS

COUNTRY DESCRIPTION: Brunei (known formally as the State of Brunei Darussalam) is a small Islamic Sultanate on the north coast of the island of Borneo. The capital, Bandar Seri Begawan, is the only major city. Tourist facilities are good, and generally available.

ENTRY REQUIREMENTS: For information about entry requirements, travelers may consult the Consular Section of the Embassy of the State of Brunei Darussalam, Suite 300, 2600 Virginia Ave., N.W. Washington, D.C. 20037; tel. (202) 342-0159.

MEDICAL FACILITIES: Adequate public and private hospitals and medical services are available in Brunei. Medical care clinics do not require deposits usually, but insist upon payment in full at time of treatment, and may require proof of ability to pay prior to treating or discharging a foreigner. U.S. medical insurance is not always valid outside the United States, and may not be accepted by health providers in Brunei. Travelers may wish to check with their health insurance providers regarding whether their U.S. policy applies overseas. The Medicare/ Medicaid program does not provide payment of medical services outside the United States. Supplemental medical insurance with specific overseas coverage, including provision for medical evacuation may be useful. Travel agents or insurance providers often have information about such programs. Useful information on medical emergencies abroad is provided in the Department of State, Bureau of Consular Affairs' brochure *Medical Information for Americans Traveling Abroad*, available via our home page and autofax service. For additional health information, the international travelers hotline of the Centers for Disease Control and Prevention may be reached at 1-877-FYI-TRIP (1-877-394-8747), via the CDC autofax service at 1-888-CDC-FAXX (1-888-232-3299), or via the CDC home page on the Internet: http://www.cdc.gov.

INFORMATION ON CRIME: The crime rate in Brunei is low, and violent crime is rare. The loss or theft abroad of a U.S. passport should be reported immediately to the local police and to the U.S. Embassy. Useful information on guarding valuables and protecting personal security while traveling abroad is provided in the Department of State pamphlet, *A Safe Trip Abroad*. It is available from the Superintendent of Documents, U.S. Government Printing Office, Washington, D.C. 20402 or via the Internet at http://www.access.gpo.gov /su_docs.

CRIMINAL PENALTIES: While in a foreign country, a U.S. citizen is subject to that country's laws and regulations, which sometimes differ significantly from those in the United States and do not afford the protections available to the individual under U.S. law. Penalties for breaking the law can be more severe than in the United States for similar offenses. Persons violating the law, even unknowingly, may be expelled, arrested or imprisoned. The trafficking in and the illegal importation of controlled drugs are very serious offenses in Brunei. Brunei has a mandatory death penalty for many narcotics offenses. Under the current law, possession of heroin and morphine derivatives of more than 15 grams, and cannabis of more than 20 grams, carries the death sentence. Possession of lesser amounts carries a minimum twenty-year jail term and caning.

AVIATION OVERSIGHT: The U.S. Federal Aviation Administration (FAA) has assessed the Government of Brunei's Civil Aviation Authority as Category 1 - in compliance with international aviation safety standards for oversight of Brunei's air carrier operations. For further information, travelers may contact the Department of Transportation within the U.S. at 1-800-322-7873, or visit the FAA's Internet website at http://www.faa.gov/avr/iasa/index.htm. The U.S. Department of Defense (DOD) separately assesses some foreign air carriers for suitability as official providers of air services. For information regarding the DOD policy on specific carriers, travelers may contact DOD at 618-256-4801.

ROAD SAFETY: Roads are generally good and most vehicles are new and well-maintained. However, vehicular accidents are now one of the leading causes of death in Brunei. Possibly due to excessive speed, tropical torrential rains, or driver carelessness, Brunei suffers a very high traffic accident rate.

CUSTOMS INFORMATION: More detailed information concerning regulations and procedures governing items that may be brought into Brunei is available from the Embassy of the State of Brunei Darussalam in the United States.

Registration/Embassy Location: U.S. citizens living in or visiting Brunei are encouraged to register in person or via telephone with the U.S. Embassy in Bandar Seri Begawan and to obtain updated information on travel and security within the country. The U.S Embassy is located on the third floor, Teck Guan Plaza, Jalan Sultan, in the capital city of Bandar Seri Begawan. The mailing address is American Embassy PSC 470 (BSB), FPO AP, 96534; the telephone number is (673)(2) 229-670; the fax number is (673) (2) 225-293.

Brunei-Muara

On her state visit to Brunei in September of 1998, Her Majesty Queen Elizabeth II of Britain made a tour of the Kampung Ayer in the capital a part of her busy itinerary. Made up of numerous communities, and home to some 30,000 people, the Kampung Ayer ("Villages on Water") is certainly the most well-known of all attractions in the country.

Kampung Ayer has been around for a very long time. When Antonio Pigafetta visited the country in the mid-16th century; Kampung Ayer was already a well-established, "home to some 25,000 families," according to Pigafetta. It was the hub for governance, business and social life in Brunei at that time.

The Kampung Ayer of today retains many of its old-world features described by Pigafetta. Only now, its daily well being is overlooked by the chiefs of the many villages in the area. The Kampung has almost all the amenities available in other communities, such as schools, shops and mosques. The houses there are usually well equipped with the latest in modern technology.

For as low as $1, boatmen will ferry passengers along the breadth and length of the Brunei river.

River cruises aboard ferryboats can start at both ends of the Brunei river, one at the Muara side, at the Queen Elizabeth jetty (named after the reigning British queen after her first Brunei visit in 1972), and others at the various river boat taxi stations in the heart of town.

The journey from the other end of the river starts at Kota Batu, the 16th century capital. The upstream journey during the 10 miles per hour cruise passes an ancient landmark, the tomb of Brunei's fifth ruler, Sultan Bolkiah, the Singing Captain, under whose reign Brunei was a dominant power in the 15th century.

On one bank of the Brunei river is a newer relic, a British warship used dur-ing World War II, sheltered from the elements.

The ferry moves on to Kampong Ayer, the Venice of the East. During the 18th century, here lived the fisher-men, blacksmiths, kris (native sword) makers, brass artisans, nipa palm mat makers, pearl and oyster collectors, traders and goldsmiths.

A new Kampong Ayer has risen, settlements of concrete houses with glass windowpanes, and connected by cement bridges instead of the rickety, wooden catwalks.

Overlooking the old Kampong Ayer is the House of Twelve Roofs (Bum-bungan Dua Belas), built in 1906 and formerly the official home of the British resident. In the Kota Batu area on Jalan Residency is the Arts and Handicrafts Centre, where traditional arts and crafts have been revived.

But Kampung Ayer is only one of the many charms of Brunei that intrigue visitors to the country.

The Sultan Omar Ali Saifuddien Mosque in the heart of Bandar Seri Begawan continues to attract visitors fascinated by its majestic presence, and its role in the spiritual development of the Muslim citizens of the country. The mosque is practically synonymous with Brunei in general, and with the capital in particular.

Situated very close to the mosque is the public library with its attractive mural depicting Brunei's lifestyles in the 60s. The mural was done by one of Brunei's foremost artist, Pg Dato Hj Asmalee, formerly the director of Welfare, Youth and Sports, but now the country's ambassador to a neighbour-ing country.

Another landmark of the capital is the Yayasan Sultan Hj Hassanal Bolkiah commercial complex, across the road from the Sultan Omar Ah Saifuddien mosque. The newly estab-lished complex is the prime shopping centre in Brunei - four storeys of some of the premier big-name retailers in the region! There're outlets bran-dishing branded clothing, fast food, video games, books and many more. There's a supermarket in the Yayasan's west wing, and a food court on the east.

The Royal Regalia Building is a new addition to the attractions found in the capital. Within easy walking distance of all the hotels in the capital centre, the Royal Regalia Building houses artifacts used in royal cere-monies in the country. Foremost among the displays are the Royal Chariot, the gold and silver ceremonial armoury and the jewel-encrusted crowns used in coronation ceremonies.

Entrance is free, and visitors are expected to take off their shoes before entering. Opening hours are from 8.30am to 5.00pm daily except for Fridays, the Building opens from 9.00am until II.30am, and in the afternoon, from 2.30pm till 5.00pm.

Located next to the Royal Regalia Building is the Brunei History Centre. Drop by the centre and learn all about the genealogy and history of the sultans of Brunei, and members of the royal family. There is an exhibition area open to the public from 7.45 am to 12.I5pm, and I.30pm to 4.3Opm daily except for Fridays.

Across the road from the Brunei Hotel, is what is known throughout Borneo as the 'tamu.' A 'tamu' is a congregation of vendors selling farm produce and general items. If you are lucky, you can find valuable bargains among the potpourri of metalware and handicraft hawked by some peddlers.

The main Chinese temple in the country lies within sight of the 'tamu.' Its elaborately designed roof and loud red color of its outer walls make the temple stand out from among the more staid schemes of nearby buildings.

For additional analytical, business and investment opportunities information, please contact Global Investment & Business Center, USA at (703) 370-8082. Fax: (703) 370-8083. E-mail: ibpusa3@gmail.com
Global Business and Investment Info Databank - www.ibpus.com

A visit during one of the many festivals that is observed at this sanctum of Taoist beliefs would be a celebration of colors, spectacle and smell. Another place of worship that should not be missed by visitors to Brunei is the Church of St Andrew's. The church, possibly the oldest in Brunei, is designed like an English country parish, complete with bells in the let fry. It lies within walking distance of the Royal Regalia Building.

If you are staying in a hotel or Bandar Seri Begawan, why not pay the nightly foodstalls a visit? The stalls are located at a site in front of Sheraton Hotel, and serve a wide variety of hawker fare cheap! A dollar worth of the fried noodles is enough to fill you up.

Check out the local burgers. They're as delicious as those you'll find in established fast food outlets. Or try out 'Roti John'-the Malay version of the Big Mac. Ask for 'goreng pisang' (banana fritters), 'begedil' (potato balls), or 'popiah' (meat rolls), in your jaunts to the sweetmeat stalls.

Outside the capital center, a worthwhile place to visit is the Jame' Asr Hassanil Bolkiah Mosque in Kiarong, about six kilometers away. This is a beautiful sanctuary for communication with God, a personal bequest from His Majesty the Sultan of Brunei himself for the people of the country.

More than just a place of worship, the Jame' Asr is also a center for learning. Classes teaching Islamic religious principles and practices are held there regularly, as do religious lectures. And every Friday morning, the lobbies of its vast edifice are filled with children studying the Quran.

A visit to the mosque is usually part of the itinerary of package tours to Brunei, but if not, visitors can make the necessary arrangement with local tour operators. Visitors wishing to come inside the mosque need to report to the officers on duty, at the security counter on the ground floor.

Further on, you will find the Jerudong Park Playground. Situated some 20 kms to the west of the capital, JP as it is popularly called, is a must-go place for visitors to the country. It has been described as "Brunei's first high-tech wonderland for people of all ages."

There are many amusement rides at the Jerudong Park Playground to cater to everyone's need.

For those who like to live life on the edge, you would be pleased to know that JP has THREE (that's right, three) roller coasters, each with different degrees of thrills (or insanity factors if you want).

'Pusing Lagi' takes riders up a crest almost six storeys high, and then takes them down a steep incline, before twisting and turning at breakneck speed, so much so you will regret the 'Roti John' you just had.

'Boomerang' is for people who would rather go for diabolical twists and turns, while 'Pony Express' is a ride for those newly-initiated to roller-coasters.

Other popular rides include the 'Condor', a very fast merry-go-round that takes you up some five stores high, the 'Aladdin' (a mechanical 'flying carpet'), 'Flashdance' (no dancing experience required), and the wildly swinging 'Pirate Ship'.

There is also a bumper car arena, only for children and youngsters though, a video arcade and tracks for skateboarding and carting. For those who prefer something more sedate, also available are a 'Merry-Go-Round', certainly the most beautiful this side of London, and the 'Simulator Tour' (virtual reality rides into the fantastic and the exotic). Try the up-tower rides, where you are taken up a tower 15 stores high, and given a superb view of the park, and the surrounding area.

Situated next to the playground is the 20-acre Jerudong Park Gardens, which is well-known for its concert class auditorium. This was where Michael Jackson had his performances some years back, drawing a record 60,000 people to a colorful extravaganza the first time he performed.

Whitney Houston was another megastar who has had performed here, as well as Stevie ("I Just Called To Say I Love You) Wonder and the wonderful Seal ("Kissed By A Rose").

And if all that running and riding gives you an appetite, there's good food to be found in the eating area next to the parking lot. Almost anything you could crave for is available, ranging from the local hawker spreads to international fast food fare. If you're not doing anything on a Friday morning or late afternoon, take the no.55 purple bus to the end of its line at Jerudong Beach. Jerudong Beach on Fridays, especially around 9.00-10.00am, is a hive of activity as fishermen start landing their catch and customers rush to avail themselves of the freshest fish possible. The people you'll get to meet there are among the friendliest in the country, easy with the smile and always ready for the idle chatter.

But the place is more than just an informal fish market. Local fruits hang prominently from many of the stalls, and food stalls sell take-outs to cater to hungry visitors. Swim in the calm, waveless waters of the man-made cove, or try your luck fishing, if that is what you want to do. Just go around people watching.

And if you need to go back to town, just board the purple bus to make the return journey.

The Bukit Shabbandar Forest Park is just the place to put those hiking legs to use. About ten minutes drive from the Jerudong Park Playground, the park is hectares upon hectares of greenery, dissected by tracks and paths for hiking, jogging and biking. While hiking, you can partake the wonders of the local forests - the rich diversity of its plant life, the exquisite charms and colors of the insects and reptiles that live within, and the symphony in the singing of the birds. Bukit Shahbandar Forest Park is just one of the 11 forest reserves in the country. To the east of Bandar Seri Begawan, about 6 kms into the Kota Batu area, visitors will find the Brunei Museum exhibits artifacts that archive the history of Negara Brunei Darussalam, both ancient and the relatively recent.

Well made cannons and kettles with their dragon motifs and elaborate patterns recall the glory days of the country -when Brunei was an important political and mercantile power in the region with territories that stretched that stretched all the way from Luzon Island in the Philippines to the whole western Borneo island.

There are exhibits which depict the traditional lifestyles of the various communities in the country, plus displays on the local flora and fauna. The exhibit by the local petroleum company Brunei Shell, illustrates the history on the discovery of oil in the country, and the commodity's significant role in economy of Brunei.

The Museum is open every day except Mondays from 9.00am till 5.00pm. On Fridays however, there is a scheduled prayer break from 11.30am until 2.30pm.

And situated downhill of the Brunei Museum is the Malay Technology Museum, which, as its name implies, houses the technological tools utilised by the Malays in ancient times.

A government booklet describes it as offering the "the visitor an intriguing insight into the lifestyle of the people of Brunei in by-gone eras". The Technology Museum is open daily, except

Tuesdays, from 9.00 am till 5.00 pm. with a 3-hour midday prayer break on Fridays. Entrance is free.

There is an "Asean Square" in Persiaran Damuan which is located on a stretch between Jalan Tutong and the bank of the Brunei River about 4.5km from the capital. The "Asean Square" has on permanent display the work of a chosen sculptor themed Harmony in Diversity from each of the Asean member countries.

HOLIDAYS

Brunei Darussalam's vision is to promote the country as a unique tourist destination and gateway to tourism excellence in South East Asia. The objectives are to create international awareness of Brunei Darussalam as a holiday destination; to maximize earings of foreign exchange and make tourism as one of the main contributor to GDP. In addition, it will create employment opportunities.

The country offers a wide variety of attractive places to be visited and experienced. The rainforest and National Parks are rich in flora and fauna. Its most magnificent mosques, water village (traditional and historic houses on stilts), rich culture and Jerudong Theme Park are among the uniqueness of Brunei Darussalam.

The government is now actively promoting tourism as an important part of its economic diversification. It would like to see a target of 1 million-visitor arrival by the year 2000. From January to August 1999, the statistic recorded 405,532 visitors visited Brunei Darussalam.

National Day Celebration

The nation celebrates this joyous occasion on the 23rd of February and the people usually prepare themselves two months beforehand. Schoolchildren, private sector representatives and civil servants work hand-in-hand rehearsing their part in flash card displays and other colourful crowd formations. In addition mass prayers and reading of Surah Yaasin are held at mosques throughout the country.

Fasting Month (Ramadhan)

Ramadhan is a holy month for all Muslims. This marks the beginning of the period of fasting - abstinence from food, drink and other material comforts from dawn to dusk. During this month, religious activities are held at mosques and *suraus* throughout the country

Hari Raya Aidilfitri

Hari Raya is a time for celebration after the end of the fasting month of Ramadhan. In the early part of the first day, prayers are held at every mosque in the country. Families get together to seek forgiveness from the elders and loved ones. You will see Bruneians decked-out in their traditional garb visiting relatives and friends.

Special festive dishes are made especially for Hari Raya including satay (beef, chicken or mutton kebabs), ketupat or lontong (rice cakes in coconut or banana leaves), rendang (spicy marinated beef) and other tantalizing cuisines. In these auspicious occassion Istana Nurul Iman was open to the public as well as to visitors for 3 days. This provides the nation and other visitors the opportunity to meet His Majesty and other members of the Royal Family, in order to wish them a Selamat Hari Raya Aidilfitri.

Royal Brunei Armed Forces Day

31st of May marks the commemoration of the Royal Brunei Armed Forces formation day. The occassion is celebrated with military parades, artillery displays, parachuting and exhibitions.

Hari Raya Aidiladha

This is also known as Hari Raya Korban. Sacrifices of goats and cows are practiced to commemorate the Islamic historical event of Prophet Ibrahim S.A.W. The meat is then distributed among relatives, friends and the less fortunates.

His Majesty the Sultan's Birthday

This is one of the most important events in the national calendar with activities and festivities taking place nationwide. Celebrated on 15th July, this event begins with mass prayer throughout the country. On this occassion, His Majesty the Sultan delivers a 'titah' or royal address followed by investiture ceremony held at the Istana Nurul Iman. The event is also marked with gatherings at the four districts where His Majesty meets and gets together with his subjects.

Birthday of the Prophet Muhammad

In Brunei Darussalam, this occasion is known as the Mauludin Nabi S.A.W. Muslims throughout the country honour this event. Readings from the Holy Koran - the Muslim Holy Book, and an address on Islam from officials of the Ministry of Religious Affairs marks the beginning of this auspicious occasion. His Majesty the Sultan also gives a royal address and with other members of the Royal family, leads a procession on foot through the main streets of Bandar Seri Begawan. Religious functions, lectures and other activities are also held to celebrate this important occasion nationwide.

Chinese New Year

Celebrated by the Chinese community, this festival lasts for two weeks. It begins with a reunion dinner on the eve of the Lunar New Year to encourage closer rapport between family members. For the next two week, families visit one another bringing with them oranges to symbolize longevity and good fortune. Traditional cookies and food are aplenty during this festivity. Unmarried young people and children will receive 'angpow' or little red packets with money inside, a symbolic gesture of good luck, wealth and health.

Christmas Day

Throughout the world, 25th of December marks Christmas day, a significant day for all Christians. Christmas is nevertheless a joyous and colourful celebration enjoyed by Christians throughout the country.

Teachers' Day

Teachers' Day is celebrated on every 23rd September in recognition of the good deeds of the teachers to the community, religion and the country. It is celebrated in commemoration of the birthday of the late Sultan Haji Omar 'Ali Saifuddien Saadul Khairi Waddien, the 28th Sultan of Brunei for his contribution in the field of education including religious education. On this occassion, three awards are given away namely, Meritorious Teacher's Award, Outstanding Teacher's Award and *"Guru Tua"* Award.

Public Service Day

The date 29th September is observed as the Public Service Day with the objective to uphold the aspiration of the Government of His Majesty the Sultan and Yang Di-Pertuan of Brunei Darussalam towards creating an efficient, clean, sincere and honest public service. The Public Service Day commemorates the promulgation of the first written Constitution in Brunei Darussalam. The Public Service Day is celebrated with the presentation of the meritorious service award to Ministries and Government Departments.

PUBLIC HOLIDAYS

1 January	New Year's Day
8 January	* Hari Raya Aidilfitri
5 February	Chinese New Year
23 February	National Day
16 Mac	* Hari Raya Aidiladha
6 April	Muslim Holy Month of Hijiriah
31 May	Royal Brunei Armed Forces Day
15 Jun	The Birthday of Prophet Muhammad S.A.W.
15 July	The Birthday of His Majesty Sultan Haji Hassanal Bolkiah Mu'izzaddin Waddaulah, Sultan and Yang Di-Pertuan of Brunei Darussalam
25 October	* Israk Mikraj
27 November	* First Day of Ramadhan (Muslim fasting month)
13 December	Anniversary of The Revelation of the Quran
25 December	Christmas
27 December	* Hari Raya Aidilfitri

BUSINESS CUSTOMS

Customs & Traditions:	Brunei Darussalam possess a long heritage of traditions and customs, behavioural traits and forms of address. Muslims observe religious rites and rituals, which is woven into the lifestyle of Bruneian Malays. Breach of Malay conduct can be liable to prosecution in Islamic courts.
Social Protocol for non-Muslims:	It is customary for Bruneians to eat with their fingers rather than use forks and spoons. Always use the right hand when eating. It is polite to accept even just a little food and drink when offered. When refusing anything that is being offered, it is polite to touch the plate lightly with the right hand . As the left hand is considered unclean, one should use one's right hand to give and receive things. Bruneians sit on the floor, especially when there's a fairly large gathering of people. It is considered feminine to sit on the floor with a woman's legs tucked to one side, and equally polite for men to sit with folded legs crossed at the ankles. It's rude for anyone to sit on the floor with the legs stretched out in front, especially if someone is sitting in front. It is considered impolite to eat or drink while walking about in public except at

picnics or fairs.

During the Islamic fasting (Puasa) month, Muslims do not take any food from sunrise to sundown. It would be inconsiderate to eat and drink in their presence during this period.

It is not customary for Muslims to shake hands with members of the opposite sex. Public display of affection such as kissing and hugging are seen to be in bad taste. Casual physical contact with the opposite sex will make Muslims feel uncomfortable.

In the relationship between sexes, Islam enforces strict legislation. If a non-Muslim is found in the company of a Muslim of the opposite sex in a secluded place rather than where there are a lot of people, he/she could be persecuted.

If you are found committing 'khalwat' that is seen in a compromising position with a person of the opposite sex who is a Muslim, you could be deported.

When walking in front of people, especially the elderly and those senior in rank or position, it is a gesture of courtesy and respect for one to bend down slightly, as if one is bowing, except this time side way to the person or persons in front of whom one is passing. One of the arms should be positioned straight downwards along the side of the body.

Leaning on a table with someone seated on it especially if he/she is an official or colleague in an office is considered rude.

Resting one's feet on the table or chair is seen as overbearing. So is sitting on the table while speaking to another person who is seated behind it. To touch or pat someone, including children, on the head is regarded as extremely disrespectful.

The polite way of beckoning at someone is by using all four fingers of the right hand with the palm down and motioning them towards yourself. It is considered extremely impolite to beckon at someone with the index finger.

SUPPLEMENTS

STRATEGIC GOVERNMENT CONTACT IN BRUNEY

Prime Minister's Office
E-Mail: PRO@jpm.gov.bn
Telephone: 673 - 2 - 229988
Fax: 673 - 2 - 241717
Telex: BU2727
Address:
Prime Minister's Office
Istana Nurul Iman
Bandar Seri Begawan BA1000

Audit Department
Prime Minister's Office
Jalan Menteri Besar
Bandar Seri Begawan BB 39 10
Brunei Darussalam
Telephone: (02) 380576
Facsimile: (02) 380679
E-mail: jabaudbd@brunet.bn

Information Department
Prime Minister's Office
Berakas Old Airport
Bandar Seri Begawan
BB 3510
Brunei Darussalam.
E-mail:- pelita@brunet.bn
Fax: 673 2 381004
Tel: 673 2 380527

Narcotics Control Bureau
Prime Minister's Office
Jalan Tungku Gadong
Bandar Seri Begawan BE 2110
Tel No: 02-448877 / 422479 / 422480 /
422481
Fax No: 02-422477
E-mail: ncb@brunet.bn

One-Stop Agency
The Ministry of Industry and Primary Resources
Bandar Seri Begawan 1220
Brunei Darussalam

Telefax: (02) 244811
Telex: MIPRS BU 2111
Cable: MIPRS BRUNEI

Head Policy and Administration Division
Ministry of Industry and Primary Resources
Jalan Menteri Besar, Bandar Seri Begawan 1220
Brunei Darussalam
Tel: (02) 382822

Secretary of Public Service Commission
Old Airport
Bandar Seri Begawan BB 3510
Tel No: 02-381961
E-mail: bplspa@brunet.bn

Semaun Holdings Sdn Bhd
Unit 2.02, Block D, 2nd Floor
Yayasan Sultan Haji Hassanal Bolkiah
Complex
Jalan Pretty
Bandar Seri Begawan BS8711
Brunei Darussalam
E-mail address: semaun@brunet.bn

Department of Agriculture
Ministry of Industry & Primary Resources
BB3510
Brunei Darussalam
Telephone: + 673 2 380144
Fax: + 673 2 382226
Telex: PERT BU 2456

Land Transport Department
KM 6, Jalan Gadong,
Beribi BE1110,
Brunei Darussalam.
Tel : (673-2) 451979
Fax : (673-2) 424775
Email : latis@brunet.bn

FOREIGN MISSIONS

AUSTRALIA

Australian High Commission
(His Excellency Mr. Neal Patrick Davis -
High Commissioner)

4th flr Teck Guan Plaza, Jln Sultan
Bandar Seri Begawan BS8811
Brunei Darussalam
or
P.O. Box 2990
Bandar Seri Begawan, BS8675
Brunei Darussalam
Tel: 673 2 229435/6
Fax: 673 2 221652

AUSTRIA

Austrian Consulate General
No. 5 Taman Jubli, Spg 75,
Jalan Subok,
Bandar Seri Begawan BD2717
Brunei Darussalam
or
P.O. Box 1303,
Bandar Seri Begawan, BS8672
Brunei Darussalam
Tel : 673 2 261083
Email: austroko@brunet.bn

BANGLADESH

High Commission of People's Republic of Bangladesh
(His Excellency Mr. Muhammad Mumtaz Hussain - High Commissioner)
AAR Villa, House No. 5,
Simpang 308, Jalan Lambak Kanan,
Berakas, BB1714
Brunei Darussalam
Tel: 673 2 394716
Fax: 673 2 394715

BELGIUM

Consulate of Belgium
2nd Floor, 146 Jln Pemancha
Bandar Seri Begawan BS8711
Brunei Darussalam
or
P.O.Box 65,
Bandar Seri Begawan, BS8670
Brunei Darussalam
Tel: 673 2 222298
Fax: 673 2 220895

BRITAIN

British High Commission
(His Excellency Mr. Stuart Laing - High Commissioner)
Unit 2.01, Block D of Yayasan Sultan Hassanal Bolkiah
Bandar Seri Begawan BS8711
Brunei Darussalam
or
P.O.Box 2197
Bandar Seri Begawan, BS8674
Brunei Darussalam
Tel: 673 2 222231
Fax: 673 2 226001

CAMBODIA

Royal Embassy of Cambodia
(His Highness Prince Sisowath Phandaravong - Ambassador)
No. 8, Simpang 845
Kampong Tasek Meradun, Jalan Tutong,
BF1520
Brunei Darussalam
Tel: 673 2 650046
Fax: 673 2 650646

CANADA

High Commission of Canada
(His Excellency Mr. Neil Reeder - High Commissioner)
Suite 51 - 52, Britannia House, Jalan Cator
Bandar Seri Begawan, BS8811
Brunei Darussalam
Tel: 673 2 220043
Fax: 673 2 220040

CHINA

Embassy of People's Republic of China
(His Excellency Mr. Wang Jianli - Ambassador)
No. 1, 3 & 5, Simpang 462
Kampong Sungai Hanching,
Jln Muara, BC2115
Brunei Darussalam
or
P.O.Box 121
M.P.C, Berakas BB3577
Brunei Darussalam
Tel: 673 2 339609
Fax: 673 2 339612

DENMARK

Consulate of Denmark
Unit 6, Bangunan Hj Tahir,
Spg 103, Jln Gadong
Bandar Seri Begawan
Brunei Darussalam
or
P.O.Box 140
Bandar Seri Begawan, BS8670
Brunei Darussalam
Tel: 673 2 422050, 427525, 447559
Fax: 673 2 427526

FINLAND

Consulate of Finland
Bee Seng Shipping Company
No.7 1st Floor Sufri Complex
KM 2, Jalan Tutong
Bandar Seri Begawan, BA2111
Brunei Darussalam
or
P.O.Box 1777
Bandar Seri Begawan, BS8673
Brunei Darusslaam
Tel: 673 2 243847
Fax: 673 2 224495

FRANCE

Embassy of the Republic of France
(His Excelleny Mr. Jean Pierre Lafosse -
Ambassador)
#306-310 Kompleks Jln Sultan,
3rd Floor, 51-55 Jln Sultan
Bandar Seri Begawan BS8811
Brunei Darussalam
or
P.O.Box 3027
Bandar Seri Begawan, BS8675
Brunei Darussalam
Tel: 673 2 220960 / 1
Fax: 673 2 243373

GERMANY

Embassy of the Federal Republic of Germany
(His Excellency Klaus-Peter Brandes -
Ambassador)
6th flr, Wisma Raya Building
Lot 49-50, Jln Sultan

Bandar Seri Begawan, BS8811
Brunei Darussalam
or
P.O.Box 3050
Bandar Seri Begawan, BS8675
Brunei Darussalam
Tel: 673 2 225547 / 74
Fax: 673 2 225583

INDIA

High Commission of India
(His Excellency Mr. Dinesh K. Jain - High
Commissioner)
Lot 14034, Spg 337,
Kampong Manggis, Jln Muara, BC3515
Brunei Darussalam
Tel: 673 2 339947 / 339751
Fax: 673 2 339783
Email: hicomind@brunet.bn

INDONESIA

Embassy of the Republic of Indonesia
(His Excellency Mr. Rahardjo Djojonegoro -
Ambassador)
Lot 4498, Spg 528
Sungai Hanching Baru, Jln Muara, BC3013
Brunei Darussalam
or
P.O.Box 3013
Bandar Seri Begawan, BS8675
Brunei Darussalam
Tel: 673 2 330180 / 445
Fax: 673 2 330646

IRAN

Embassy of the Islamic Republic of Iran
No. 2, Lot 14570, Spg 13
Kampong Serusop, Jalan Berakas, BB2313
Brunei Darussalam
Tel: 673 2 330021 / 29
Fax: 673 2 331744

JAPAN

Embassy of Japan
(His Excellency Mr. Hajime Tsujimoto -
Ambassador)
No 1 & 3, Jalan Jawatan Dalam
Kampong Mabohai
Bandar Seri Begawan, BA1111

For additional analytical, business and investment opportunities information,
please contact Global Investment & Business Center, USA
at (703) 370-8082. Fax: (703) 370-8083. E-mail: ibpusa3@gmail.com
Global Business and Investment Info Databank - www.ibpus.com

Brunei Darussalam
or
P.O.Box 3001
Bandar Seri Begawan, BS8675
Brunei Darussalam
Tel: 673 2 229265 / 229592, 237112 - 5
Fax: 673 2 229481

KOREA

Embassy of the Republic of Korea
(His Excellency Kim Ho-tae - Ambassador)
No.9, Lot 21652
Kg Beribi, Jln Gadong, BE1118
Brunei Darussalam
Tel: 673 2 650471 / 300, 652190
Fax: 673 2 650299

LAOS

Embassy of the Lao People's Democratic Republic
(His Excellency Mr. Ammone Singhavong - Ambassador)
Lot. No. 19824, House No. 11
Simpang 480, Jalan Kebangsaan Lama
Off Jalan Muara, BC4115
Brunei Darussalam
or
P.O.Box 2826
Bandar Seri Begawan, BS8675
Brunei Darussalam
Tel: 673 2 345666
Fax: 673 2 345888

MALAYSIA

Malaysian High Commission
(His Excellency Wan Yusof Embong - High Commissioner)
No.27 & 29, Simpang 396-39
Kampong Sungai Akar
Jalan Kebangsaan, BC4115
Brunei Darussalam
or
P.O.Box 2826
Bandar Seri Begawan, BS8675
Brunei Darussalam
Tel: 673 2 345652
Fax: 673 2 345654

MYANMAR

Embassy of the Union of Myanmar
(His Excellency U Than Tun - Ambassador)
No. 14, Lot 2185 / 46292
Simpang 212, Kampong Rimba, Gadong
BE3119
Brunei Darussalam
Tel: 673 2 450506 / 7
Fax: 673 2 451008

NETHERLANDS

Netherlands Consulate
c/o Brunei Shell Petroleum Co. Sdn Bhd
Seria KB3534
Brunei Darussalam
Tel: 673 3 372005, 373045

NEW ZEALAND

New Zealand Consulate
36A Seri Lambak Complex,
Jalan Berakas, BB1714
Brunei Darussalam
or
P.O.Box 2720
Bandar Seri Begawan, BS8675
Brunei Darusslam
Tel: 673 2 331612, 331010
Fax: 673 2 331612

NORWAY

Royal Norwegian Consulate
Unit No. 407A - 410A
4th Floor, Wisma Jaya
Jalan Pemancha
Bandar Seri Begawan, BS8811
Brunei Darussalam
Tel: 673 2 239091 / 2 / 3 / 4
Fax: 673 2 239095/6

OMAN

Embassy of the Sultanate of Oman
(His Excellency Mr. Ahmad Moh,d Masoud Al-Riyami - Ambassador)
No.35 Simpang 100,
Jalan Tungku Link
Kampong Pengkalan, Gadong BE3719
Brunei Darussalam
or
P.O.Box 2875
Bandar Seri Begawan, BS8675

For additional analytical, business and investment opportunities information,
please contact Global Investment & Business Center, USA
at (703) 370-8082. Fax: (703) 370-8083. E-mail: ibpusa3@gmail.com
Global Business and Investment Info Databank - www.ibpus.com

Brunei Darussalam
Tel: 673 2 446953 / 4 / 7 / 8
Fax: 673 2 449646

PAKISTAN

Pakistan High Commission
(His Excellency Major General (Rtd) Irshad
Ullah Tarar - High Commission)
No.5 Kampong Sungai Akar
Jalan Kebangsaan, BC4115
Brunei Darussalam
Tel: 673 2 6334989, 339797
Fax: 673 2 334990

PHILIPPINES

Embassy of the Republic of Philippines
His Excellency Mr. Enrique A. Zaldivar -
Ambassador)
Rm 1 & 2, 4th & 5th floor
Badiah Building, Mile 1 1/2 Jln Tutong
Brunei Darussalam, BA2111
or
P.O.Box 3025
Bandar Seri Begawan, BS8675
Brunei Darussalam
Tel: 673 2 241465 / 6
Fax: 673 2 237707

SAUDI ARABIA

Royal Embassy of Kingdom of Saudi Arabia
No. 1, Simpang 570
Kampong Salar
Jalan Muara, BU1429
Brunei Darusslam
Tel: 673 2 792821 / 2 / 3
Fax: 673 2 792826 / 7

SINGAPORE

Singapore High Commission
(His Excellency Tee Tua Ba - High
Commissioner)
No. 8, Simpang, 74,
Jalan Subok, BD1717
Brunei Darussalam
or
P.O.Box 2159
Bandar Seri Begawan, BS8674
Brunei Darussalam

Tel: 673 2 227583 / 4 / 5
Fax: 673 2 220957

SWEDEN

Consulate of Sweden
Blk A, Unit 1, 2nd Floor
Abdul Razak Plaza,
Jalan Gadong,
Bandar Seri Begawan, BE3919
Brunei Darussalam
Tel: 673 2 448423, 444326
Fax: 673 2 448419

THAILAND

Royal Thai Embassy
(His Excellency Thinakorn Kanasuta -
Ambassador
No. 2, Simpang 682,
Kampong Bunut, Jalan Tutong, BF1320
Brunei Darussalam
Tel: 673 2 653108 / 9
Fax: 673 2 262752

UNITED STATE OF AMERICA

Embassy of the United States of America
3rd Flr, Teck Guan Plaza,
Jalan Sultan
Bandar Seri Begawan BS8811
Brunei Darussalam
Tel: 673 2 229670
Fax: (02) 225293

VIETNAM

Embassy of the Socialist Republic of Vietnam
(His Excellency Tran Tien Vinh -
Ambassador)
No. 10, Simpang 485
Kampong Sungai Hanching
Jalan Muara,BC2115
Brunei Darussalam
Tel: 673 2 343167 / 8
Fax: 673 2 343169

BRUNEI'S MISSIONS IN ASEAN, CHINA, JAPAN AND KOREA

For additional analytical, business and investment opportunities information,
please contact Global Investment & Business Center, USA
at (703) 370-8082. Fax: (703) 370-8083. E-mail: ibpusa3@gmail.com
Global Business and Investment Info Databank - www.ibpus.com

CAMBODIA
Embassy of Brunei Darussalam
No : 237, Pasteur St. 51
Sangkat Boeung Keng Kang I
Khan Chamkar Mon
Phnom Penh
Kingdom of Cambodia
Tel : (855) 23211 457 & 23211 458
Fax: (855) 23211 456
E-Mail : Brunei@bigpond.com.kh

CHINA
Embassy of Brunei Darussalam
No. 3 Villa, Qijiayuan Diplomatic Compound
Chaoyang District
Beijing 100600
People's Republic of China 1000600
Tel : 86 (10) 6532 4093 - 6
Fax : 86 (10) 6532 4097
E-Mail : bdb@public.bta.net.cn

INDONESIA
Embassy of Brunei Darussalam
Wisma GKBI
 (Gabungan Koperasi Batik Indonesia)
Suite 1901, Jl. Jend. Sudirman No. 28
Jakarta 10210
Indonesia
Tel : 62 (21) 574 1437 - 39 / 574 1470 - 72
Fax : 62 (21) 574 1463

JAPAN
Embassy of Brunei Darussalam
5-2 Kitashinagawa 6-Chome
Shinagawa-ku
Tokyo 141
Japan
Tel : 81 (3) 3447 7997 / 9260
Fax : 81 (3) 344 79260

REPUBLIC OF KOREA
Embassy of Brunei Darussalam
7th Floor, Kwanghwamoon Building
211, Sejong-ro, Chongro-Ku
Seoul
Republic of Korea.
Tel : 82 (2) 399 3707 / 3708
Fax : 82 (2) 399 3709
E-Mail : kbrunei@chollian.net

LAOS
Embassy of Brunei Darussalam
No. 333 Unit 25 Ban Phonxay

Xaysettha District
Lanexang Avenue
Vientiane
Laos People's Democratic Republic
Tel : (856) 2141 6114 / 2141 4169
Fax : (856) 2141 6115
E-Mail : kbnbd@laonet.net

MALAYSIA
High Commission of Brunei Darussalam
Tingkat 8 Wisma Sin Heap Lee (SHL)
Jalan Tun Razak
50400 Kuala Lumpur
Malaysia.
Tel : 60 (3) 261 2828
Fax : 60 (3) 263 1302
E-Mail : Sjtnbdkl@tm.net.my

THE UNIION OF MYANMAR
Embassy of Brunei Darussalam
No : 51 Golden Valley
Bahan Township
Yangon
The Union of Myanmar.
Tel: 95 (1) 510 422
Fax: 95 (1) 512 854

PHILIPPINES
Embassy of Brunei Darussalam
11th Floor BPI Building
Ayala Avenue, Corner Paseo De Roxas
Makati City, Metro Manila
Philippines
Tel : 63 (2) 816 2836 - 8
Fax : 63 (2) 816 2876
E-Mail : kbnbdmnl@skynet.net

SINGAPORE
High Commission of Brunei Darussalam
325 Tanglin Road
Singapore 247955
Tel : (65) 733 9055
Fax : (65) 737 5275
E-Mail : comstbs@singnet.com.sg

THAILAND
Embassy of Brunei Darussalam
No. 132 Sukhumvit 23 Road
Watana District
Bangkok 10110
Thailand
Tel : 66 (2) 204 1476 - 9
Fax : 66 (2) 204 1486

For additional analytical, business and investment opportunities information,
please contact Global Investment & Business Center, USA
at (703) 370-8082. Fax: (703) 370-8083. E-mail: ibpusa3@gmail.com
Global Business and Investment Info Databank - www.ibpus.com

VIETNAM
Embassy of Brunei Darussalam
No. 4 Thien Quang Street
Hai Ba Trung District
Hanoi

Vietnam
Tel : (84) 4 826 4816 / 4817 / 4818
Fax : (84) 4 822 2092
E-Mail : bruemviet@hotmail.com

FOOD AND RESTAURANTS

Brunei restaurants, including western style fast food centres, cater to a wide range of tastes and palates.
Visitors can also sample authentic local food offered at the tamu night market in the capital.
The market, along the Kianggeh river, is actually open from early morning. It takes on a special atmosphere at night when crowds throng its alleys to shop and eat at the lowest prices in town.
Tropical fruits like watermelon, papaya, mango and banana are also available.
Locals are fond of the Malay-style satay, bits of beef or chicken in a stick, cooked over low fire and dipped in a tangy peanut sauce.

Brunei's first Chinese halal restaurant is Emperor's Court, owned by Royal Brunei Catering, which caters to Cantonese and Western tastebuds.

A list of restaurants in the capital and Seria-Kuala Belait areas follows:
Bandar Seri Begawan
Aumrin Restaurant, 1 Bangunan Hasbullah, 4 Jalan Gadong
Airport Restaurant, Brunei International Airport
Coffee Tree, Unit 3, top floor ,Mabohai Shopping Complex
Emperor's Court, 1st Floor, Wisma Haji Mohd Taha, Jalan Gadong
Excellent Taste, G5 Gadong Properties Centre, Jalan Gadong
Express Fast Food, 22/23 Jalan Sultan
Ghawar Restaurant, 3 Ground Floor Bang Hasbullah 4
Jade Garden Chinese Restaurant, Riverview Inn, Km 1 Jalan Gadong
Jolibee Family Restaurant, Utama Bowling Centre, Km 11/2 Jalan Tutong
Kentucky Fried Chicken (B) Sdn Bhd, G15-G16 Plaza Athirah
Lucky Restaurant, Umi Kalthum Building, Jalan Tutong
McDonald's Restaurant, 10-12 Block H, Abdul Razak Complex, Simpang 137, Gadong
Phongmun Restaurant, Nos. 56-60, 2nd Floor Teck Guan Plaza
Pizza Hut, Block J, Unit 2 & 3 Abdul Razak Complex
Pondok Sari Wangi, 12 Blk A, Abdul Razak Complex, Jalan Gadong
Popular Restaurant, 5, Ground floor, PAP Hajjah Norain Building
QR Restaurant, Blk C, Abdul Razak Complex, Jalan Gadong
Rainbow Restaurant, 110 Jalan Batu Bersurat, Gadong
Rasa Sayang Restaurant, 607 Bangunan Guru-Guru Melayu
Rose Garden Restaurant, 8 Blk C, Abdul Razak Complex, Jalan Gadong
Season's Restaurant, Gadong Centrepoint
SD Cafe, 6-7 Bangunan Hj Othman, Simpang 105, Jalan Gadong
Seri Kamayan Restaurant, 4 & 5 Bangunan Hj Tahir ,Simpang 103, Jalan Gadong
Seri Maradum Baru, Block C6, Abdul Razak Complex
Sugar Bun Fast Food, Lot 16397 Mabohai Complex, Jalan Kebangsaan
Schezuan's Dynasty Restaurant, Gadong Centrepoint
Swensen's Ice Cream and Fine Food Restaurant, 17-18 Ground Floor Bagunan Halimatul Sa'adiah, Gadong
Tenaga Restaurant, 6 1st Floor Bangunan Hasbollah 4
The Stadium Restaurant, Stadium Negara Hassanal Bolkiah
Tropicana Seafood Restaurant, Block 1 Ground Floor, Pang's Building,Muara
Kuala Belait/Seria
Belait Restaurant, Jalan Bunga Raya

Buccaneer Steak House, Lot 94 Jalan McKerron
Cottage Restaurant, 38 Jalan Pretty
Jolene Restaurant, 83,1st Jalan Bunga Raya
New China Restaurant, 39/40 3rd Floor, Ang's Building, Jalan Sultan Omar Ali, Seria
New Cheng Wah Restaurant, 14 Jalan Sultan Omar Ali, Seria
Orchid Room, B5, 1st Floor, Jalan Bunga Raya
Red Wing Restaurant, 12 Jalan Sultan Omar Ali, Seria
Tasty Cake Shop/Pretty Inn, 26 Jalan Sultan Omar Ali, Seria
Tasconi's Pizza, Simpang 19, Jalan Sungai Pandan

WHERE TO SHOP

For many travellers one of the pleasures of visiting another country is finding something of interest and value for one's self, family or friends. There are many shops in Brunei offering a wide variety of goods at competitive prices. These range from modern department stores to small market stalls where bargaining is still commonly practised.

Modern department stores are found in the major towns of Bandar Seri Begawan, Tutong, Kuala Belait and Seria. In addition to these departmental stores there is a wide variety of old-fashioned shophouses as well as more modern air-conditioned shops.

Most items ranging from the latest electronic goods and imported luxury goods to common household items and groceries can be conveniently found in these shops.

Traditional items that reflect the culture of Brunei like the brass cannon, kris and kain songket, better known as "jong sarat" are excellent souvenirs to bring home from a visit to the country. These can be purchased at the Arts and Handicrafts Centre which is located off Kota Batu, and also at the airport.

Before leaving Brunei make sure you stop by the Duty Free shops at the airport. These offer a wide range of luxury goods, garments, jewellery, writing instruments, perfumes, handicrafts, Brunei souvenirs, books and chocolates at very reasonable prices.

SHOPPING CENTRES

Hua Ho Department Store, Jln Gadong, Bandar Seri Begawan

Kota Mutiara Department Store, Bangunan Darussalam, Bandar Seri Begawan

Lai Lai Department Store, Mile 1 Jln Tutong, Bandar Seri Begawan

Millimewah Department Store (BSB), Bangunan Darussalam, Bandar Seri Begawan

Millimewah Department Store (Tutong),Tutong

Millimewah Department Store (Seria), Seria

Princess Inn Department Store, Mile 1 Jln Tutong , Bandar Seri Begawan

Tiong Hin Superstore,Jln Muara, Bandar Seri Begawan

For additional analytical, business and investment opportunities information, please contact Global Investment & Business Center, USA at (703) 370-8082. Fax: (703) 370-8083. E-mail: ibpusa3@gmail.com
Global Business and Investment Info Databank - www.ibpus.com

Megamart,Jln Gadong, Bandar Seri Begawan

Wisma Jaya Complex, Jln Pemancha, Bandar Seri Begawan

First Emporium & Supermarket, Mohammad Yussof Complex, Jln Kubah Makam DiRaja, Bandar Seri Begawan

Seria Plaza, Seria

Seaview Department Store, Jln Maulana, Kuala Belait

TRAVEL AGENTS

BANDAR SERI BEGAWAN

Antara Travel & Tours Sdn Bhd 02-448805/808
Anthony Tours & Travel Sdn Bhd 02-228668
Borneo Leisure Travel Sdn Bhd 02-223420
Brunei Travel Services Sdn Bhd 02-236006
Century Travel Centre Sdn Bhd 02-227296
Churiah Travel Service 02-224422
Darat Dan Laut 02-426321
Freme Travel Services Sdn Bhd 02-234277
Halim Tours & Travel Sdn Bhd 02-226688
Intan Travel & Trading Agencies 02-427340
Jasra Harrisons (B) Sdn Bhd 02-236675
JB Travel & Insurance Agencies 02-239132
JJ Tour Service (B) Sdn Bhd 02-224761
Ken Travel & Trading Sdn Bhd 02-223127
Mahasiswa Travel Service 02-243452
Oriental Travel Services 02-226464
Overseas Travel Services Sdn Bhd 02-445322
Sarawak Travel Service Sdn Bhd 02-223361
Seri Islamic Tours & Travel Sdn Bhd 02-243341
Straits Central Agencies (B) Sdn Bhd 02-229356
Sunshine Borneo Tours & Travel Sdn Bhd 02-441791
SMAS 02-234741
Travel Centre (B) Sdn Bhd 02-229601
Travel Trade Agencies Sdn Bhd 02-229601/228439
Tai Wah Travel Service Sdn Bhd 02-224015
Tenega Travel Agency Sdn Bhd 02-422974
Titian Travel & Tours Sdn Bhd 02-448742
Twelve Roofs / Perusahaan Hj. Asmakhan 02-340395
Wing On Travel & Trading Agencies 02-220536
Zizen Travel Agency Sdn Bhd 02-236991
Zura Travel Service Sdn Bhd 02-234738

KUALA BELAIT

Freme Travel Services Sdn Bhd 03-335025
Jasra Harrisons Sdn Bhd 03-335391
JJ Tour Service Sdn Bhd 03-334069
Limbang Travel Service Sdn Bhd 03-335275
Overseas Travel Service Sdn Bhd 03-222090
Southern Cross Travel Agencies Sdn Bhd 03-334642

For additional analytical, business and investment opportunities information, please contact Global Investment & Business Center, USA at (703) 370-8082. Fax: (703) 370-8083. E-mail: ibpusa3@gmail.com Global Business and Investment Info Databank - www.ibpus.com

Straits Central Agencies Sdn Bhd 03-334589
Usaha Royako Travel Agency 03-334768

SELECTED COMPANIES

- Advance Computer Supplier and Services
- AJYAD Publishing
- Akitek SAA Home Page
- Amalgamated Electronic Sdn. Bhd.
- Anthony Tours & Travel Agency
- Baharuddin & Associates Consulting Engineers
- Beseller Sdn Bhd Homepage
- BIT Computer Services
- BruDirect Business Centre
- Brunei Hotel
- Brupost
- CfBT Homepage
- Compunet Computer & Office Systems
- Dalplus Technologies, Brunei
- DN Private Investigation and Security Consultant
- DP Happy Video House
- Elite Computer Systems Sdn. Bhd.
- Fabrica Interior Furnishing Co
- Glamour Homepage
- HSBC
- HSE Engineering Sdn. Bhd.
- Indah Sejahtera Development & Services
- Insurans Islam Taib
- Interhouse Marketing Sdn. Bhd.
- International School Brunei
- IP and Company
- ISS Thomas Cowan Sdn. Bhd.
- Jerudong Park Medical Centre
- Kristal
- L & M Prestressing Sdn. Bhd.
- Megamas Training Company Sdn. Bhd.
- Mekar General Enterprise Homepage
- Micronet Computer School
- National Insurance Company Berhad
- Paotools Supplies & Services Co.
- Petar Perunding Sdn. Bhd.
- Petrel Jaya Sdn Bhd
- Phongmun Restaurant Homepage
- Poh Lee Trading Company
- Q-Carrier
- Sabli Group of Companies - Brunei Darussalam
- Scanmark Design Sdn Bhd
- SDS System (B) Sdn. Bhd.
- SEAMEO VOCTECH Homepage
- Singapore Airlines
- Sistem Komputer Alif Sdn Bhd

- SPCastro And Associates Sdn Bhd
- Sunshine Borneo Tour & Travel Sdn.Bhd.
- Survey Service Consultants
- Syabas Publishers
- Syarikat Suraya Insan
- Syarikat Intellisense Technology
- Tabung Amanah Islam Brunei
- Tang Sung Lee Sdn. Bhd.
- The Lodge Resort (In Brunei)
- Trinkets Enterprise
- Twelve Roofs / Perusahaan Hj. Asmakhan
- Unicraft Enterprises
- Utama Komunikasi

BASIC TITLES ON BRUNEI
IMPORTANT!
All publications are updated annually!
Please contact IBP, Inc. at ibpusa3@gmail.com for the latest ISBNs and additional information

TITLE
Brunei A "Spy" Guide - Strategic Information and Developments
Brunei A Spy" Guide"
Brunei Air Force Handbook
Brunei Air Force Handbook
Brunei Business and Investment Opportunities Yearbook
Brunei Business and Investment Opportunities Yearbook
Brunei Business and Investment Opportunities Yearbook Volume 1 Strategic Information and Opportunities
Brunei Business and Investment Opportunities Yearbook Volume 2 Leading Export-Import, Business, Investment Opportunities and Projects
Brunei Business Intelligence Report - Practical Information, Opportunities, Contacts
Brunei Business Intelligence Report - Practical Information, Opportunities, Contacts
Brunei Business Law Handbook - Strategic Information and Basic Laws
Brunei Business Law Handbook - Strategic Information and Basic Laws
Brunei Business Law Handbook - Strategic Information and Basic Laws
Brunei Business Law Handbook - Strategic Information and Basic Laws
Brunei Business Law Handbook Volume 1 Srategic Information and Basic Laws
Brunei Business Success Guide - Basic Practical Information and Contacts
Brunei Company Laws and Regulations Handbook
Brunei Constitution and Citizenship Laws Handbook - Strategic Information and Basic Laws
Brunei Country Study Guide - Strategic Information and Developments
Brunei Country Study Guide - Strategic Information and Developments
Brunei Country Study Guide - Strategic Information and Developments Volume 1 Strategic Information and Developments
Brunei Criminal Laws, Regulations and Procedures Handbook - Strategic Information, Regulations, Procedures

TITLE
Brunei Customs, Export-Import Regulations, Incentives and Procedures Handbook - Strategic, Practical Information, Regulations
Brunei Customs, Trade Regulations and Procedures Handbook
Brunei Customs, Trade Regulations and Procedures Handbook
Brunei Darussalam Investment, Trade Strategy and Agreements Handbook - Strategic Information and Basic Agreements
Brunei Diplomatic Handbook - Strategic Information and Developments
Brunei Diplomatic Handbook - Strategic Information and Developments
Brunei Ecology & Nature Protection Handbook
Brunei Ecology & Nature Protection Handbook
Brunei Ecology & Nature Protection Laws and Regulation Handbook
Brunei Electoral, Political Parties Laws and Regulations Handbook - Strategic Information, Regulations, Procedures
Brunei Energy Policy, Laws and Regulation Handbook
Brunei Energy Policy, Laws and Regulations Handbook
Brunei Energy Policy, Laws and Regulations Handbook
Brunei Energy Policy, Laws and Regulations Handbook - Strategic Information, Policy, Regulations
Brunei Export-Import Trade and Business Directory
Brunei Export-Import Trade and Business Directory
Brunei Foreign Policy and Government Guide
Brunei Foreign Policy and Government Guide
Brunei Immigration Laws and Regulations Handbook - Strategic Information and Basic Laws
Brunei Industrial and Business Directory
Brunei Industrial and Business Directory
Brunei Investment and Business Guide - Strategic and Practical Information
Brunei Investment and Business Guide - Strategic and Practical Information
Brunei Investment and Business Guide - Strategic and Practical Information
Brunei Investment and Business Guide - Strategic and Practical Information
Brunei Investment and Business Guide Volume 2 Business, Investment Opportunities and Incentives
Brunei Investment and Business Profile - Basic Information and Contacts for Succesful investment and Business Activity
Brunei Investment and Trade Laws and Regulations Handbook
Brunei Labor Laws and Regulations Handbook - Strategic Information and Basic Laws
Brunei Land Ownership and Agriculture Laws Handbook
Brunei Mineral & Mining Sector Investment and Business Guide - Strategic and Practical Information
Brunei Mineral & Mining Sector Investment and Business Guide - Strategic and Practical Information
Brunei Mineral, Mining Sector Investment and Business Guide - Strategic Information and Regulations
Brunei Mining Laws and Regulations Handbook
Brunei Oil & Gas Sector Business & Investment Opportunities Yearbook
Brunei Oil & Gas Sector Business & Investment Opportunities Yearbook
Brunei Oil and Gas Exploration Laws and Regulation Handbook

For additional analytical, business and investment opportunities information, please contact Global Investment & Business Center, USA at (703) 370-8082. Fax: (703) 370-8083. E-mail: ibpusa3@gmail.com Global Business and Investment Info Databank - www.ibpus.com

TITLE
Brunei Recent Economic and Political Developments Yearbook
Brunei Recent Economic and Political Developments Yearbook
Brunei Recent Economic and Political Developments Yearbook
Brunei Starting Business (Incorporating) in....Guide
Brunei Sultan Haji Hassanal Bolkiah Mu'izzaddin Waddaulah Handbook
Brunei Sultan Haji Hassanal Bolkiah Mu'izzaddin Waddaulah Handbook
Brunei Tax Guide
Brunei Tax Guide
Brunei Tax Guide Volume 1 Strategic Information and Basic Regulations
Brunei Taxation Laws and Regulations Handbook
Brunei Telecommunication Industry Business Opportunities Handbook
Brunei Telecommunication Industry Business Opportunities Handbook
Brunei: Doing Business and Investing in ... Guide Volume 1 Strategic, Practical Information, Regulations, Contacts
Brunei: How to Invest, Start and Run Profitable Business in Brunei Guide - Practical Information, Opportunities, Contacts

For additional analytical, business and investment opportunities information, please contact Global Investment & Business Center, USA at (703) 370-8082. Fax: (703) 370-8083. E-mail: ibpusa3@gmail.com Global Business and Investment Info Databank - www.ibpus.com

INTERNATIONAL BUSINESS PUBLICATIONS, USA

ibpusa@comcast.net. http://www.ibpus.com

WORLD ISLAMIC BUSINESS LIBRARY
Price: $149.95 Each

Islamic Banking and Financial Law Handbook
Islamic Banking Law Handbook
Islamic Business Organization Law Handbook
Islamic Commerce and Trade Law Handbook
Islamic Company Law Handbook
Islamic Constitutional and Administrative Law Handbook
Islamic Copyright Law Handbook
Islamic Customs Law and Regulations Handbook
Islamic Design Law Handbook
Islamic Development Bank Group Handbook
Islamic Economic & Business Laws and Regulations Handbook
Islamic Environmental Law Handbook
Islamic Financial and Banking System Handbook vol 1
Islamic Financial and Banking System Handbook Vol. 2
Islamic Financial Institutions (Banks and Financial Companies) Handbook
Islamic Foreign Investment and Privatization Law Handbook
Islamic Free Trade & Economic Zones Law and Regulations Handbook
Islamic International Law and Jihad (War(Law Handbook
Islamic Labor Law Handbook
Islamic Legal System (Sharia) Handbook Vol. 1 Basic Laws and Regulations
Islamic Legal System (Sharia) Handbook Vol. 2 Laws and Regulations in
Selected Countries
Islamic Mining Law Handbook
Islamic Patent & Trademark Law Handbook
Islamic Taxation Law Handbook
Islamic Trade & Export-Import Laws and Regulations Handbook

For additional analytical, business and investment opportunities information,
please contact Global Investment & Business Center, USA
at (202) 546-2103. Fax: (202) 546-3275. E-mail: rusric@erols.com

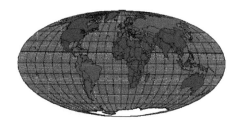

WORLD BUSINESS SUCCESS GUIDES LIBRARY

EVERYTHING YOU NEED FOR SUCCESFUL BUSINESS WORLDWIDE

World Business Information Catalog, USA: http://www.ibpus.com

Email: ibpusa@comcast.net.

Price: $99.95 Each

TITLE
Abkhazia (Republic of Abkhazia) Business Success Guide - Basic Practical Information and Contacts
Afghanistan Business Success Guide - Basic Practical Information and Contacts
Aland Business Success Guide - Basic Practical Information and Contacts
Albania Business Success Guide - Basic Practical Information and Contacts
Algeria Business Success Guide - Basic Practical Information and Contacts
Andorra Business Success Guide - Basic Practical Information and Contacts
Angola Business Success Guide - Basic Practical Information and Contacts
Anguilla Business Success Guide - Basic Practical Information and Contacts
Antigua and Barbuda Business Success Guide - Basic Practical Information and Contacts
Antilles (Netherlands) Business Success Guide - Basic Practical Information and Contacts
Argentina Business Success Guide - Basic Practical Information and Contacts
Armenia Business Success Guide - Basic Practical Information and Contacts
Aruba Business Success Guide - Basic Practical Information and Contacts
Australia Business Success Guide - Basic Practical Information and Contacts
Austria Business Success Guide - Basic Practical Information and Contacts
Azerbaijan Business Success Guide - Basic Practical Information and Contacts
Bahamas Business Success Guide - Basic Practical Information and Contacts
Bahrain Business Success Guide - Basic Practical Information and Contacts
Bangladesh Business Success Guide - Basic Practical Information and Contacts
Barbados Business Success Guide - Basic Practical Information and Contacts
Belarus Business Success Guide - Basic Practical Information and Contacts
Belgium Business Success Guide - Basic Practical Information and Contacts
Belize Business Success Guide - Basic Practical Information and Contacts
Benin Business Success Guide - Basic Practical Information and Contacts
Bermuda Business Success Guide - Basic Practical Information and Contacts
Bhutan Business Success Guide - Basic Practical Information and Contacts
Bolivia Business Success Guide - Basic Practical Information and Contacts
Bosnia and Herzegovina Business Success Guide - Basic Practical Information and Contacts
Botswana Business Success Guide - Basic Practical Information and Contacts
Brazil Business Success Guide - Basic Practical Information and Contacts
Brunei Business Success Guide - Basic Practical Information and Contacts
Bulgaria Business Success Guide - Basic Practical Information and Contacts
Burkina Faso Business Success Guide - Basic Practical Information and Contacts
Burundi Business Success Guide - Basic Practical Information and Contacts
Cambodia Business Success Guide - Basic Practical Information and Contacts
Cameroon Business Success Guide - Basic Practical Information and Contacts

For additional analytical, business and investment opportunities information,
Please contact Global Investment & Business Center, USA
at (202) 546-2103. Fax: (202) 546-3275. E-mail: ibpusa3@gmail.com

TITLE
Canada Business Success Guide - Basic Practical Information and Contacts
Cape Verde Business Success Guide - Basic Practical Information and Contacts
Cayman Islands Business Success Guide - Basic Practical Information and Contacts
Central African Republic Business Success Guide - Basic Practical Information and Contacts
Chad Business Success Guide - Basic Practical Information and Contacts
Chile Business Success Guide - Basic Practical Information and Contacts
China Business Success Guide - Basic Practical Information and Contacts
Colombia Business Success Guide - Basic Practical Information and Contacts
Comoros Business Success Guide - Basic Practical Information and Contacts
Congo Business Success Guide - Basic Practical Information and Contacts
Congo, Democratic Republic Business Success Guide - Basic Practical Information and Contacts
Cook Islands Business Success Guide - Basic Practical Information and Contacts
Costa Rica Business Success Guide - Basic Practical Information and Contacts
Cote d'Ivoire Business Success Guide - Basic Practical Information and Contacts
Croatia Business Success Guide - Basic Practical Information and Contacts
Cuba Business Success Guide - Basic Practical Information and Contacts
Cyprus Business Success Guide - Basic Practical Information and Contacts
Czech Republic Business Success Guide - Basic Practical Information and Contacts
Denmark Business Success Guide - Basic Practical Information and Contacts
Djibouti Business Success Guide - Basic Practical Information and Contacts
Dominica Business Success Guide - Basic Practical Information and Contacts
Dominican Republic Business Success Guide - Basic Practical Information and Contacts
Ecuador Business Success Guide - Basic Practical Information and Contacts
Egypt Business Success Guide - Basic Practical Information and Contacts
El Salvador Business Success Guide - Basic Practical Information and Contacts
Equatorial Guinea Business Success Guide - Basic Practical Information and Contacts
Eritrea Business Success Guide - Basic Practical Information and Contacts
Estonia Business Success Guide - Basic Practical Information and Contacts
Ethiopia Business Success Guide - Basic Practical Information and Contacts
Falkland Islands Business Success Guide - Basic Practical Information and Contacts
Faroes Islands Business Success Guide - Basic Practical Information and Contacts
Fiji Business Success Guide - Basic Practical Information and Contacts
Finland Business Success Guide - Basic Practical Information and Contacts
France Business Success Guide - Basic Practical Information and Contacts
Gabon Business Success Guide - Basic Practical Information and Contacts
Gambia Business Success Guide - Basic Practical Information and Contacts
Georgia Business Success Guide - Basic Practical Information and Contacts
Germany Business Success Guide - Basic Practical Information and Contacts
Ghana Business Success Guide - Basic Practical Information and Contacts
Gibraltar Business Success Guide - Basic Practical Information and Contacts
Greece Business Success Guide - Basic Practical Information and Contacts
Greenland Business Success Guide - Basic Practical Information and Contacts
Grenada Business Success Guide - Basic Practical Information and Contacts
Guam Business Success Guide - Basic Practical Information and Contacts
Guatemala Business Success Guide - Basic Practical Information and Contacts
Guernsey Business Success Guide - Basic Practical Information and Contacts

For additional analytical, business and investment opportunities information,
Please contact Global Investment & Business Center, USA
at (202) 546-2103. Fax: (202) 546-3275. E-mail: ibpusa3@gmail.com

TITLE
Guinea Business Success Guide - Basic Practical Information and Contacts
Guinea-Bissau Business Success Guide - Basic Practical Information and Contacts
Guyana Business Success Guide - Basic Practical Information and Contacts
Haiti Business Success Guide - Basic Practical Information and Contacts
Honduras Business Success Guide - Basic Practical Information and Contacts
Hungary Business Success Guide - Basic Practical Information and Contacts
Iceland Business Success Guide - Basic Practical Information and Contacts
India Business Success Guide - Basic Practical Information and Contacts
Indonesia Business Success Guide - Basic Practical Information and Contacts
Iran Business Success Guide - Basic Practical Information and Contacts
Iraq Business Success Guide - Basic Practical Information and Contacts
Ireland Business Success Guide - Basic Practical Information and Contacts
Israel Business Success Guide - Basic Practical Information and Contacts
Italy Business Success Guide - Basic Practical Information and Contacts
Jamaica Business Success Guide - Basic Practical Information and Contacts
Japan Business Success Guide - Basic Practical Information and Contacts
Jersey Business Success Guide - Basic Practical Information and Contacts
Jordan Business Success Guide - Basic Practical Information and Contacts
Kazakhstan Business Success Guide - Basic Practical Information and Contacts
Kenya Business Success Guide - Basic Practical Information and Contacts
Kiribati Business Success Guide - Basic Practical Information and Contacts
Korea, North Business Success Guide - Basic Practical Information and Contacts
Korea, South Business Success Guide - Basic Practical Information and Contacts
Kosovo Business Success Guide - Basic Practical Information and Contacts
Kurdistan Business Success Guide - Basic Practical Information and Contacts
Kuwait Business Success Guide - Basic Practical Information and Contacts
Kyrgyzstan Business Success Guide - Basic Practical Information and Contacts
Laos Business Success Guide - Basic Practical Information and Contacts
Latvia Business Success Guide - Basic Practical Information and Contacts
Lebanon Business Success Guide - Basic Practical Information and Contacts
Lesotho Business Success Guide - Basic Practical Information and Contacts
Liberia Business Success Guide - Basic Practical Information and Contacts
Libya Business Success Guide - Basic Practical Information and Contacts
Liechtenstein Business Success Guide - Basic Practical Information and Contacts
Lithuania Business Success Guide - Basic Practical Information and Contacts
Luxembourg Business Success Guide - Basic Practical Information and Contacts
Macao Business Success Guide - Basic Practical Information and Contacts
Macedonia Business Success Guide - Basic Practical Information and Contacts
Madagascar Business Success Guide - Basic Practical Information and Contacts
Madeira Business Success Guide - Basic Practical Information and Contacts
Malawi Business Success Guide - Basic Practical Information and Contacts
Malaysia Business Success Guide - Basic Practical Information and Contacts
Maldives Business Success Guide - Basic Practical Information and Contacts
Mali Business Success Guide - Basic Practical Information and Contacts
Malta Business Success Guide - Basic Practical Information and Contacts
Man Business Success Guide - Basic Practical Information and Contacts

For additional analytical, business and investment opportunities information,
Please contact Global Investment & Business Center, USA
at (202) 546-2103. Fax: (202) 546-3275. E-mail: ibpusa3@gmail.com

TITLE
Marshall Islands Business Success Guide - Basic Practical Information and Contacts
Mauritania Business Success Guide - Basic Practical Information and Contacts
Mauritius Business Success Guide - Basic Practical Information and Contacts
Mayotte Business Success Guide - Basic Practical Information and Contacts
Mexico Business Success Guide - Basic Practical Information and Contacts
Micronesia Business Success Guide - Basic Practical Information and Contacts
Moldova Business Success Guide - Basic Practical Information and Contacts
Monaco Business Success Guide - Basic Practical Information and Contacts
Mongolia Business Success Guide - Basic Practical Information and Contacts
Montserrat Business Success Guide - Basic Practical Information and Contacts
Montenegro Business Success Guide - Basic Practical Information and Contacts
Morocco Business Success Guide - Basic Practical Information and Contacts
Mozambique Business Success Guide - Basic Practical Information and Contacts
Myanmar Business Success Guide - Basic Practical Information and Contacts
Nagorno-Karabakh Republic Business Success Guide - Basic Practical Information and Contacts
Namibia Business Success Guide - Basic Practical Information and Contacts
Nauru Business Success Guide - Basic Practical Information and Contacts
Nepal Business Success Guide - Basic Practical Information and Contacts
Netherlands Business Success Guide - Basic Practical Information and Contacts
New Caledonia Business Success Guide - Basic Practical Information and Contacts
New Zealand Business Success Guide - Basic Practical Information and Contacts
Nicaragua Business Success Guide - Basic Practical Information and Contacts
Niger Business Success Guide - Basic Practical Information and Contacts
Nigeria Business Success Guide - Basic Practical Information and Contacts
Niue Business Success Guide - Basic Practical Information and Contacts
Northern Cyprus (Turkish Republic of Northern Cyprus) Business Success Guide - Basic Practical Information and Contacts
Northern Mariana Islands Business Success Guide - Basic Practical Information and Contacts
Norway Business Success Guide - Basic Practical Information and Contacts
Oman Business Success Guide - Basic Practical Information and Contacts
Pakistan Business Success Guide - Basic Practical Information and Contacts
Palau Business Success Guide - Basic Practical Information and Contacts
Palestine (West Bank & Gaza) Business Success Guide - Basic Practical Information and Contacts
Panama Business Success Guide - Basic Practical Information and Contacts
Papua New Guinea Business Success Guide - Basic Practical Information and Contacts
Paraguay Business Success Guide - Basic Practical Information and Contacts
Peru Business Success Guide - Basic Practical Information and Contacts
Philippines Business Success Guide - Basic Practical Information and Contacts
Pitcairn Islands Business Success Guide - Basic Practical Information and Contacts
Poland Business Success Guide - Basic Practical Information and Contacts
Polynesia French Business Success Guide - Basic Practical Information and Contacts
Portugal Business Success Guide - Basic Practical Information and Contacts
Qatar Business Success Guide - Basic Practical Information and Contacts
Romania Business Success Guide - Basic Practical Information and Contacts
Russia Business Success Guide - Basic Practical Information and Contacts
Rwanda Business Success Guide - Basic Practical Information and Contacts

For additional analytical, business and investment opportunities information,
Please contact Global Investment & Business Center, USA
at (202) 546-2103. Fax: (202) 546-3275. E-mail: ibpusa3@gmail.com

TITLE
Sahrawi Arab Democratic Republic Volume 1 Strategic Information and Developments
Saint Kitts and Nevis Business Success Guide - Basic Practical Information and Contacts
Saint Lucia Business Success Guide - Basic Practical Information and Contacts
Saint Vincent and The Grenadines Business Success Guide - Basic Practical Information and Contacts
Samoa (American) A Business Success Guide - Basic Practical Information and Contacts
Samoa (Western) Business Success Guide - Basic Practical Information and Contacts
San Marino Business Success Guide - Basic Practical Information and Contacts
Sao Tome and Principe Business Success Guide - Basic Practical Information and Contacts
Saudi Arabia Business Success Guide - Basic Practical Information and Contacts
Scotland Business Success Guide - Basic Practical Information and Contacts
Senegal Business Success Guide - Basic Practical Information and Contacts
Serbia Business Success Guide - Basic Practical Information and Contacts
Seychelles Business Success Guide - Basic Practical Information and Contacts
Sierra Leone Business Success Guide - Basic Practical Information and Contacts
Singapore Business Success Guide - Basic Practical Information and Contacts
Slovakia Business Success Guide - Basic Practical Information and Contacts
Slovenia Business Success Guide - Basic Practical Information and Contacts
Solomon Islands Business Success Guide - Basic Practical Information and Contacts
Somalia Business Success Guide - Basic Practical Information and Contacts
South Africa Business Success Guide - Basic Practical Information and Contacts
Spain Business Success Guide - Basic Practical Information and Contacts
Sri Lanka Business Success Guide - Basic Practical Information and Contacts
St. Helena Business Success Guide - Basic Practical Information and Contacts
St. Pierre & Miquelon Business Success Guide - Basic Practical Information and Contacts
Sudan (Republic of the Sudan) Business Success Guide - Basic Practical Information and Contacts
Sudan South Business Success Guide - Basic Practical Information and Contacts
Suriname Business Success Guide - Basic Practical Information and Contacts
Swaziland Business Success Guide - Basic Practical Information and Contacts
Sweden Business Success Guide - Basic Practical Information and Contacts
Switzerland Business Success Guide - Basic Practical Information and Contacts
Syria Business Success Guide - Basic Practical Information and Contacts
Taiwan Business Success Guide - Basic Practical Information and Contacts
Tajikistan Business Success Guide - Basic Practical Information and Contacts
Tanzania Business Success Guide - Basic Practical Information and Contacts
Thailand Business Success Guide - Basic Practical Information and Contacts
Timor Leste (Democratic Republic of Timor-Leste) Business Success Guide - Basic Practical Information and Contacts
Togo Business Success Guide - Basic Practical Information and Contacts
Tonga Business Success Guide - Basic Practical Information and Contacts
Trinidad and Tobago Business Success Guide - Basic Practical Information and Contacts
Tunisia Business Success Guide - Basic Practical Information and Contacts
Turkey Business Success Guide - Basic Practical Information and Contacts
Turkmenistan Business Success Guide - Basic Practical Information and Contacts
Turks & Caicos Business Success Guide - Basic Practical Information and Contacts
Tuvalu Business Success Guide - Basic Practical Information and Contacts
Uganda Business Success Guide - Basic Practical Information and Contacts

For additional analytical, business and investment opportunities information,
Please contact Global Investment & Business Center, USA
at (202) 546-2103. Fax: (202) 546-3275. E-mail: ibpusa3@gmail.com

TITLE
Ukraine Business Success Guide - Basic Practical Information and Contacts
United Arab Emirates Business Success Guide - Basic Practical Information and Contacts
United Kingdom Business Success Guide - Basic Practical Information and Contacts
United States Business Success Guide - Basic Practical Information and Contacts
Uruguay Business Success Guide - Basic Practical Information and Contacts
Uzbekistan Business Success Guide - Basic Practical Information and Contacts
Vanuatu Business Success Guide - Basic Practical Information and Contacts
Vatican City (Holy See) Business Success Guide - Basic Practical Information and Contacts
Venezuela Business Success Guide - Basic Practical Information and Contacts
Vietnam Business Success Guide - Basic Practical Information and Contacts
Virgin Islands, British Business Success Guide - Basic Practical Information and Contacts
Wake Atoll Business Success Guide - Basic Practical Information and Contacts
Wallis & Futuna Business Success Guide - Basic Practical Information and Contacts
Western Sahara Business Success Guide - Basic Practical Information and Contacts
Yemen Business Success Guide - Basic Practical Information and Contacts
Zambia Business Success Guide - Basic Practical Information and Contacts
Zimbabwe Business Success Guide - Basic Practical Information and Contacts

For additional analytical, business and investment opportunities information,
Please contact Global Investment & Business Center, USA
at (202) 546-2103. Fax: (202) 546-3275. E-mail: ibpusa3@gmail.com